T0261454

Python for Algorithmic Trading
From Idea to Cloud Deployment

Yves Hilpisch

Beijing · Boston · Farnham · Sebastopol · Tokyo

Python for Algorithmic Trading

by Yves Hilpisch

Copyright © 2021 Yves Hilpisch. All rights reserved.

Published by O'Reilly Media, Inc., 1005 Gravenstein Highway North, Sebastopol, CA 95472.

O'Reilly books may be purchased for educational, business, or sales promotional use. Online editions are also available for most titles (*http://oreilly.com*). For more information, contact our corporate/institutional sales department: 800-998-9938 or *corporate@oreilly.com*.

Acquisitions Editor: Michelle Smith
Development Editor: Michele Cronin
Production Editor: Daniel Elfanbaum
Copyeditor: Piper Editorial LLC
Proofreader: nSight, Inc.

Indexer: WordCo Indexing Services, Inc.
Interior Designer: David Futato
Cover Designer: Jose Marzan
Illustrator: Kate Dullea

November 2020:   First Edition

Revision History for the First Edition
2020-11-11:   First Release

See *http://oreilly.com/catalog/errata.csp?isbn=9781492053354* for release details.

The O'Reilly logo is a registered trademark of O'Reilly Media, Inc. *Python for Algorithmic Trading*, the cover image, and related trade dress are trademarks of O'Reilly Media, Inc.

The views expressed in this work are those of the author, and do not represent the publisher's views. While the publisher and the author have used good faith efforts to ensure that the information and instructions contained in this work are accurate, the publisher and the author disclaim all responsibility for errors or omissions, including without limitation responsibility for damages resulting from the use of or reliance on this work. Use of the information and instructions contained in this work is at your own risk. If any code samples or other technology this work contains or describes is subject to open source licenses or the intellectual property rights of others, it is your responsibility to ensure that your use thereof complies with such licenses and/or rights. This book is not intended as financial advice. Please consult a qualified professional if you require financial advice.

978-1-492-05335-4

[LSI]

Table of Contents

Preface

Dataism says that the universe consists of data flows, and the value of any phenomenon or entity is determined by its contribution to data processing....Dataism thereby collapses the barrier between animals [humans] and machines, and expects electronic algorithms to eventually decipher and outperform biochemical algorithms.[1]

—Yuval Noah Harari

Finding the right algorithm to automatically and successfully trade in financial markets is the holy grail in finance. Not too long ago, algorithmic trading was only available and possible for institutional players with deep pockets and lots of assets under management. Recent developments in the areas of open source, open data, cloud compute, and cloud storage, as well as online trading platforms, have leveled the playing field for smaller institutions and individual traders, making it possible to get started in this fascinating discipline while equipped only with a typical notebook or desktop computer and a reliable internet connection.

Nowadays, Python and its ecosystem of powerful packages is the technology platform of choice for algorithmic trading. Among other things, Python allows you to do *efficient data analytics* (with pandas (*http://pandas.pydata.org*), for example), to apply *machine learning* to stock market prediction (with scikit-learn (*http://scikit-learn.org*), for example), or even to make use of Google's *deep learning* technology with TensorFlow (*http://tensorflow.org*).

This is a book about Python *for* algorithmic trading, primarily in the context of *alpha generating strategies* (see Chapter 1). Such a book at the intersection of two vast and exciting fields can hardly cover all topics of relevance. However, it can cover a range of important meta topics in depth.

---

1 Harari, Yuval Noah. 2015. *Homo Deus: A Brief History of Tomorrow.* London: Harvill Secker.

These topics include:

Financial data
> Financial data is at the core of every algorithmic trading project. Python and packages like `NumPy` and `pandas` do a great job of handling and working with structured financial data of any kind (end-of-day, intraday, high frequency).

Backtesting
> There should be no automated algorithmic trading without a rigorous testing of the trading strategy to be deployed. The book covers, among other things, trading strategies based on simple moving averages, momentum, mean-reversion, and machine/deep-learning based prediction.

Real-time data
> Algorithmic trading requires dealing with real-time data, online algorithms based on it, and visualization in real time. The book provides an introduction to socket programming with `ZeroMQ` and streaming visualization.

Online platforms
> No trading can take place without a trading platform. The book covers two popular electronic trading platforms: Oanda (*http://oanda.com*) and FXCM (*http://fxcm.com*).

Automation
> The beauty, as well as some major challenges, in algorithmic trading results from the automation of the trading operation. The book shows how to deploy Python in the cloud and how to set up an environment appropriate for automated algorithmic trading.

The book offers a unique learning experience with the following features and benefits:

Coverage of relevant topics
> This is the only book covering such a breadth and depth with regard to relevant topics in Python for algorithmic trading (see the following).

Self-contained code base
> The book is accompanied by a Git repository with all codes in a self-contained, executable form. The repository is available on the Quant Platform (*http://py4at.pqp.io*).

Real trading as the goal
> The coverage of two different online trading platforms puts the reader in the position to start both paper and live trading efficiently. To this end, the book equips the reader with relevant, practical, and valuable background knowledge.

Do-it-yourself and self-paced approach
>   Since the material and the code are self-contained and only rely on standard
>   Python packages, the reader has full knowledge of and full control over what is
>   going on, how to use the code examples, how to change them, and so on. There is
>   no need to rely on third-party platforms, for instance, to do the backtesting or to
>   connect to the trading platforms. With this book, the reader can do all this on
>   their own at a convenient pace and has every single line of code to do so.

User forum
>   Although the reader should be able to follow along seamlessly, the author and
>   The Python Quants are there to help. The reader can post questions and com-
>   ments in the user forum on the Quant Platform (*http://py4at.pqp.io*) at any time
>   (accounts are free).

Online/video training (paid subscription)
>   The Python Quants offer comprehensive online training programs (*https://
>   oreil.ly/Qy90w*) that make use of the contents presented in the book and that add
>   additional content, covering important topics such as financial data science, arti-
>   ficial intelligence in finance, Python for Excel and databases, and additional
>   Python tools and skills.

Contents and Structure

Here's a quick overview of the topics and contents presented in each chapter.

Chapter 1, Python and Algorithmic Trading
>   The first chapter is an introduction to the topic of algorithmic trading—that is,
>   the automated trading of financial instruments based on computer algorithms. It
>   discusses fundamental notions in this context and also addresses, among other
>   things, what the expected prerequisites for reading the book are.

Chapter 2, Python Infrastructure
>   This chapter lays the technical foundations for all subsequent chapters in that it
>   shows how to set up a proper Python environment. This chapter mainly uses
>   conda as a package and environment manager. It illustrates Python deployment
>   via Docker (*http://docker.com*) containers and in the cloud.

Chapter 3, Working with Financial Data
>   Financial time series data is central to every algorithmic trading project. This
>   chapter shows you how to retrieve financial data from different public data and
>   proprietary data sources. It also demonstrates how to store financial time series
>   data efficiently with Python.

Chapter 4, Mastering Vectorized Backtesting

Vectorization is a powerful approach in numerical computation in general and for financial analytics in particular. This chapter introduces vectorization with NumPy and pandas and applies that approach to the backtesting of SMA-based, momentum, and mean-reversion strategies.

Chapter 5, Predicting Market Movements with Machine Learning

This chapter is dedicated to generating market predictions by the use of machine learning and deep learning approaches. By mainly relying on past return observations as features, approaches are presented for predicting tomorrow's market direction by using such Python packages as Keras (*https://keras.io*) in combination with TensorFlow (*https://oreil.ly/B44Fb*) and scikit-learn (*http://scikit-learn.org*).

Chapter 6, Building Classes for Event-Based Backtesting

While vectorized backtesting has advantages when it comes to conciseness of code and performance, it's limited with regard to the representation of certain market features of trading strategies. On the other hand, event-based backtesting, technically implemented by the use of object oriented programming, allows for a rather granular and more realistic modeling of such features. This chapter presents and explains in detail a base class as well as two classes for the backtesting of long-only and long-short trading strategies.

Chapter 7, Working with Real-Time Data and Sockets

Needing to cope with real-time or streaming data is a reality even for the ambitious individual algorithmic trader. The tool of choice is socket programming, for which this chapter introduces ZeroMQ (*http://zeromq.org*) as a lightweight and scalable technology. The chapter also illustrates how to make use of Plotly (*http://plot.ly*) to create nice looking, interactive streaming plots.

Chapter 8, CFD Trading with Oanda

Oanda (*http://oanda.com*) is a foreign exchange (forex, FX) and Contracts for Difference (CFD) trading platform offering a broad set of tradable instruments, such as those based on foreign exchange pairs, stock indices, commodities, or rates instruments (benchmark bonds). This chapter provides guidance on how to implement automated algorithmic trading strategies with Oanda, making use of the Python wrapper package tpqoa (*http://github.com/yhilpisch/tpqoa*).

Chapter 9, FX Trading with FXCM

FXCM (*http://fxcm.co.uk*) is another forex and CFD trading platform that has recently released a modern RESTful API for algorithmic trading. Available instruments span multiple asset classes, such as forex, stock indices, or commodities. A Python wrapper package that makes algorithmic trading based on Python code rather convenient and efficient is available (*http://fxcmpy.tpq.io*).

Chapter 10, Automating Trading Operations

> This chapter deals with capital management, risk analysis and management, as well as with typical tasks in the technical automation of algorithmic trading operations. It covers, for instance, the Kelly criterion for capital allocation and leverage in detail.

Appendix

> The appendix provides a concise introduction to the most important Python, NumPy, and pandas topics in the context of the material presented in the main chapters. It represents a starting point from which one can add to one's own Python knowledge over time.

Figure P-1 shows the layers related to algorithmic trading that the chapters cover from the bottom to the top. It necessarily starts with the Python infrastructure (Chapter 2), and adds financial data (Chapter 3), strategy, and vectorized backtesting code (Chapters 4 and 5). Until that point, data sets are used and manipulated as a whole. Event-based backtesting for the first time introduces the idea that data in the real world arrives incrementally (Chapter 6). It is the bridge that leads to the connecting code layer that covers socket communication and real-time data handling (Chapter 7). On top of that, trading platforms and their APIs are required to be able to place orders (Chapters 8 and 9). Finally, important aspects of automation and deployment are covered (Chapter 10). In that sense, the main chapters of the book relate to the layers as seen in Figure P-1, which provide a natural sequence for the topics to be covered.

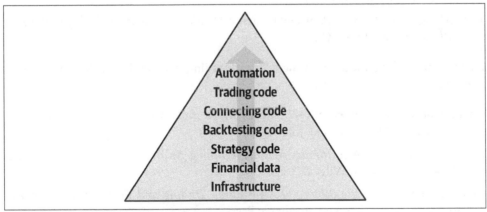

Figure P-1. The layers of Python for algorithmic trading

Who This Book Is For

This book is for students, academics, and practitioners alike who want to apply Python in the fascinating field of algorithmic trading. The book assumes that the reader has, at least on a fundamental level, background knowledge in both Python programming and in financial trading. For reference and review, the Appendix introduces important Python, NumPy, matplotlib, and pandas topics. The following are good references to get a sound understanding of the Python topics important for this book. Most readers will benefit from having at least access to Hilpisch (2018) for reference. With regard to the machine and deep learning approaches applied to algorithmic trading, Hilpisch (2020) provides a wealth of background information and a larger number of specific examples. Background information about Python as applied to finance, financial data science, and artificial intelligence can be found in the following books:

Hilpisch, Yves. 2018. *Python for Finance: Mastering Data-Driven Finance*. 2nd ed. Sebastopol: O'Reilly.

————. 2020. *Artificial Intelligence in Finance: A Python-Based Guide*. Sebastopol: O'Reilly.

McKinney, Wes. 2017. *Python for Data Analysis: Data Wrangling with Pandas, NumPy, and IPython*. 2nd ed. Sebastopol: O'Reilly.

Ramalho, Luciano. 2021. *Fluent Python: Clear, Concise, and Effective Programming*. 2nd ed. Sebastopol: O'Reilly.

VanderPlas, Jake. 2016. *Python Data Science Handbook: Essential Tools for Working with Data*. Sebastopol: O'Reilly.

Background information about algorithmic trading can be found, for instance, in these books:

Chan, Ernest. 2009. *Quantitative Trading: How to Build Your Own Algorithmic Trading Business*. Hoboken et al: John Wiley & Sons.

Chan, Ernest. 2013. *Algorithmic Trading: Winning Strategies and Their Rationale*. Hoboken et al: John Wiley & Sons.

Kissel, Robert. 2013. *The Science of Algorithmic Trading and Portfolio Management*. Amsterdam et al: Elsevier/Academic Press.

Narang, Rishi. 2013. *Inside the Black Box: A Simple Guide to Quantitative and High Frequency Trading*. Hoboken et al: John Wiley & Sons.

Enjoy your journey through the algorithmic trading world with Python and get in touch by emailing *py4at@tpq.io* if you have questions or comments.

Conventions Used in This Book

The following typographical conventions are used in this book:

Italic
> Indicates new terms, URLs, email addresses, filenames, and file extensions.

`Constant width`
> Used for program listings, as well as within paragraphs, to refer to program elements such as variable or function names, databases, data types, environment variables, statements, and keywords.

`Constant width bold`
> Shows commands or other text that should be typed literally by the user.

`Constant width italic`
> Shows text that should be replaced with user-supplied values or by values determined by context.

> This element signifies a tip or suggestion.

> This element signifies a general note.

> This element indicates a warning or caution.

Using Code Examples

You can access and execute the code that accompanies the book on the Quant Platform at *https://py4at.pqp.io*, for which only a free registration is required.

If you have a technical question or a problem using the code examples, please email *bookquestions@oreilly.com*.

This book is here to help you get your job done. In general, if example code is offered with this book, you may use it in your programs and documentation. You do not need to contact us for permission unless you're reproducing a significant portion of the code. For example, writing a program that uses several chunks of code from this book does not require permission. Selling or distributing examples from O'Reilly books does require permission. Answering a question by citing this book and quoting example code does not require permission. Incorporating a significant amount of example code from this book into your product's documentation does require permission.

We appreciate, but generally do not require, attribution. An attribution usually includes the title, author, publisher, and ISBN. For example, this book may be attributed as: "*Python for Algorithmic Trading* by Yves Hilpisch (O'Reilly). Copyright 2021 Yves Hilpisch, 978-1-492-05335-4."

If you feel your use of code examples falls outside fair use or the permission given above, feel free to contact us at *permissions@oreilly.com*.

O'Reilly Online Learning

 For more than 40 years, *O'Reilly Media* has provided technology and business training, knowledge, and insight to help companies succeed.

Our unique network of experts and innovators share their knowledge and expertise through books, articles, and our online learning platform. O'Reilly's online learning platform gives you on-demand access to live training courses, in-depth learning paths, interactive coding environments, and a vast collection of text and video from O'Reilly and 200+ other publishers. For more information, visit *http://oreilly.com*.

How to Contact Us

Please address comments and questions concerning this book to the publisher:

O'Reilly Media, Inc.
1005 Gravenstein Highway North
Sebastopol, CA 95472
800-998-9938 (in the United States or Canada)
707-829-0515 (international or local)
707-829-0104 (fax)

We have a web page for this book, where we list errata, examples, and any additional information. You can access this page at *https://oreil.ly/py4at*.

Email *bookquestions@oreilly.com* to comment or ask technical questions about this book.

For news and information about our books and courses, visit *http://oreilly.com*.

Find us on Facebook: *http://facebook.com/oreilly*

Follow us on Twitter: *http://twitter.com/oreillymedia*

Watch us on YouTube: *http://youtube.com/oreillymedia*

Acknowledgments

I want to thank the technical reviewers—Hugh Brown, McKlayne Marshall, Ramanathan Ramakrishnamoorthy, and Prem Jebaseelan—who provided helpful comments that led to many improvements of the book's content.

As usual, a special thank you goes to Michael Schwed, who supports me in all technical matters, simple and highly complex, with his broad and in-depth technology know-how.

Delegates of the Certificate Programs in Python for Computational Finance and Algorithmic Trading also helped improve this book. Their ongoing feedback has enabled me to weed out errors and mistakes and refine the code and notebooks used in our online training classes and now, finally, in this book.

I would also like to thank the whole team at O'Reilly Media—especially Michelle Smith, Michele Cronin, Victoria DeRose, and Danny Elfanbaum—for making it all happen and helping me refine the book in so many ways.

Of course, all remaining errors are mine alone.

Furthermore, I would also like to thank the team at Refinitiv—in particular, Jason Ramchandani—for providing ongoing support and access to financial data. The major data files used throughout the book and made available to the readers were received in one way or another from Refinitiv's data APIs.

To my family with love. I dedicate this book to my father Adolf whose support for me and our family now spans almost five decades.

## CHAPTER 1

Python and Algorithmic Trading

At Goldman [Sachs] the number of people engaged in trading shares has fallen from a peak of 600 in 2000 to just two today.[1]
—*The Economist*

This chapter provides background information for, and an overview of, the topics covered in this book. Although Python for algorithmic trading is a niche at the intersection of Python programming and finance, it is a fast-growing one that touches on such diverse topics as Python deployment, interactive financial analytics, machine and deep learning, object-oriented programming, socket communication, visualization of streaming data, and trading platforms.

For a quick refresher on important Python topics, read the Appendix first.

Python for Finance

The Python programming language originated in 1991 with the first release by Guido van Rossum of a version labeled 0.9.0. In 1994, version 1.0 followed. However, it took almost two decades for Python to establish itself as a major programming language and technology platform in the financial industry. Of course, there were early adopters, mainly hedge funds, but widespread adoption probably started only around 2011.

One major obstacle to the adoption of Python in the financial industry has been the fact that the default Python version, called CPython, is an interpreted, high-level language. Numerical algorithms in general and financial algorithms in particular are quite often implemented based on (nested) loop structures. While compiled, low-level languages like C or C++ are really fast at executing such loops, Python, which

---

1 "Too Squid to Fail." *The Economist*, 29. October 2016.

relies on interpretation instead of compilation, is generally quite slow at doing so. As a consequence, pure Python proved too slow for many real-world financial applications, such as option pricing or risk management.

Python Versus Pseudo-Code

Although Python was never specifically targeted towards the scientific and financial communities, many people from these fields nevertheless liked the beauty and conciseness of its syntax. Not too long ago, it was generally considered good tradition to explain a (financial) algorithm and at the same time present some pseudo-code as an intermediate step towards its proper technological implementation. Many felt that, with Python, the pseudo-code step would not be necessary anymore. And they were proven mostly correct.

Consider, for instance, the Euler discretization of the geometric Brownian motion, as in Equation 1-1.

Equation 1-1. Euler discretization of geometric Brownian motion

$$S_T = S_0 \exp\left(\left(r - 0.5\sigma^2\right)T + \sigma z\sqrt{T}\right)$$

For decades, the LaTeX markup language and compiler have been the gold standard for authoring scientific documents containing mathematical formulae. In many ways, Latex syntax is similar to or already like pseudo-code when, for example, laying out equations, as in Equation 1-1. In this particular case, the Latex version looks like this:

```
S_T = S_0 \exp((r - 0.5 \sigma^2) T + \sigma z \sqrt{T})
```

In Python, this translates to executable code, given respective variable definitions, that is also really close to the financial formula as well as to the Latex representation:

```
S_T = S_0 * exp((r - 0.5 * sigma ** 2) * T + sigma * z * sqrt(T))
```

However, the speed issue remains. Such a difference equation, as a numerical approximation of the respective stochastic differential equation, is generally used to price derivatives by Monte Carlo simulation or to do risk analysis and management based on simulation.[2] These tasks in turn can require millions of simulations that need to be finished in due time, often in almost real-time or at least near-time. Python, as an interpreted high-level programming language, was never designed to be fast enough to tackle such computationally demanding tasks.

---

2 For details, see Hilpisch (2018, ch. 12).

NumPy and Vectorization

In 2006, version 1.0 of the NumPy Python package (*http://numpy.org*) was released by Travis Oliphant. NumPy stands for *numerical Python*, suggesting that it targets scenarios that are numerically demanding. The base Python interpreter tries to be as general as possible in many areas, which often leads to quite a bit of overhead at run-time.[3] NumPy, on the other hand, uses specialization as its major approach to avoid overhead and to be as good and as fast as possible in certain application scenarios.

The major class of NumPy is the regular array object, called ndarray object for *n-dimensional array*. It is immutable, which means that it cannot be changed in size, and can only accommodate a single data type, called dtype. This specialization allows for the implementation of concise and fast code. One central approach in this context is *vectorization*. Basically, this approach avoids looping on the Python level and delegates the looping to specialized NumPy code, generally implemented in C and therefore rather fast.

Consider the simulation of 1,000,000 end of period values S_T according to Equation 1-1 with pure Python. The major part of the following code is a for loop with 1,000,000 iterations:

```
In [1]: %%time
        import random
        from math import exp, sqrt

        S0 = 100   ❶
        r = 0.05   ❷
        T = 1.0    ❸
        sigma = 0.2   ❹

        values = []   ❺

        for _ in range(1000000):   ❻
            ST = S0 * exp((r - 0.5 * sigma ** 2) * T +
                          sigma * random.gauss(0, 1) * sqrt(T))   ❼
            values.append(ST)   ❽
        CPU times: user 1.13 s, sys: 21.7 ms, total: 1.15 s
        Wall time: 1.15 s
```

❶ The initial index level.

❷ The constant short rate.

---

[3] For example, list objects are not only mutable, which means that they can be changed in size, but they can also contain almost any other kind of Python object, like int, float, tuple objects or list objects themselves.

❸   The time horizon in year fractions.

❹   The constant volatility factor.

❺   An empty `list` object to collect simulated values.

❻   The main `for` loop.

❼   The simulation of a *single* end-of-period value.

❽   Appends the simulated value to the `list` object.

With NumPy, you can avoid looping on the Python level completely by the use of vectorization. The code is much more concise, more readable, and faster by a factor of about eight:

```
In [2]: %%time
        import numpy as np

        S0 = 100
        r = 0.05
        T = 1.0
        sigma = 0.2

        ST = S0 * np.exp((r - 0.5 * sigma ** 2) * T +
                          sigma * np.random.standard_normal(1000000) *
                          np.sqrt(T))  ❶
        CPU times: user 375 ms, sys: 82.6 ms, total: 458 ms
        Wall time: 160 ms
```

❶   This single line of NumPy code simulates all the values and stores them in an `ndarray` object.

 Vectorization is a powerful concept for writing concise, easy-to-read, and easy-to-maintain code in finance and algorithmic trading. With NumPy, vectorized code does not only make code more concise, but it also can speed up code execution considerably (by a factor of about eight in the Monte Carlo simulation, for example).

It's safe to say that NumPy has significantly contributed to the success of Python in science and finance. Many other popular Python packages from the so-called *scientific Python stack* build on NumPy as an efficient, performing data structure to store and handle numerical data. In fact, NumPy is an outgrowth of the SciPy package project, which provides a wealth of functionality frequently needed in science. The SciPy project recognized the need for a more powerful numerical data structure and consolidated older projects like Numeric and NumArray in this area into a new, unifying one in the form of NumPy.

In algorithmic trading, a Monte Carlo simulation might not be the most important use case for a programming language. However, if you enter the algorithmic trading space, the management of larger, or even big, financial time series data sets is a very important use case. Just think of the backtesting of (intraday) trading strategies or the processing of tick data streams during trading hours. This is where the pandas data analysis package (*http://pandas.pydata.org*) comes into play.

pandas and the DataFrame Class

Development of pandas began in 2008 by Wes McKinney, who back then was working at AQR Capital Management, a big hedge fund operating out of Greenwich, Connecticut. As with for any other hedge fund, working with time series data is of paramount importance for AQR Capital Management, but back then Python did not provide any kind of appealing support for this type of data. Wes's idea was to create a package that mimics the capabilities of the R statistical language (*http://r-project.org*) in this area. This is reflected, for example, in naming the major class DataFrame, whose counterpart in R is called data.frame. Not being considered close enough to the core business of money management, AQR Capital Management open sourced the pandas project in 2009, which marks the beginning of a major success story in open source–based data and financial analytics.

Partly due to pandas, Python has become a major force in data and financial analytics. Many people who adopt Python, coming from diverse other languages, cite pandas as a major reason for their decision. In combination with open data sources like Quandl (*http://quandl.com*), pandas even allows students to do sophisticated financial analytics with the lowest barriers of entry ever: a regular notebook computer with an internet connection suffices.

Assume an algorithmic trader is interested in trading Bitcoin, the cryptocurrency with the largest market capitalization. A first step might be to retrieve data about the historical exchange rate in USD. Using Quandl data and pandas, such a task is accomplished in less than a minute. Figure 1-1 shows the plot that results from the following Python code, which is (omitting some plotting style related parameterizations) only four lines. Although pandas is not explicitly imported, the Quandl Python wrapper package by default returns a DataFrame object that is then used to add a simple moving average (SMA) of 100 days, as well as to visualize the raw data alongside the SMA:

```
In [3]: %matplotlib inline
        from pylab import mpl, plt   ❶
        plt.style.use('seaborn')   ❶
        mpl.rcParams['savefig.dpi'] = 300   ❶
```

```
        mpl.rcParams['font.family'] = 'serif'  ❶

In [4]: import configparser  ❷
        c = configparser.ConfigParser()  ❷
        c.read('../pyalgo.cfg')  ❷
Out[4]: ['../pyalgo.cfg']

In [5]: import quandl as q  ❸
        q.ApiConfig.api_key = c['quandl']['api_key']  ❸
        d = q.get('BCHAIN/MKPRU')  ❹
        d['SMA'] = d['Value'].rolling(100).mean()  ❺
        d.loc['2013-1-1':].plot(title='BTC/USD exchange rate',
                                figsize=(10, 6));  ❻
```

❶ Imports and configures the plotting package.

❷ Imports the `configparser` module and reads credentials.

❸ Imports the Quandl Python wrapper package and provides the API key.

❹ Retrieves daily data for the Bitcoin exchange rate and returns a pandas `Data Frame` object with a single column.

❺ Calculates the SMA for 100 days in vectorized fashion.

❻ Selects data from the 1st of January 2013 on and plots it.

Obviously, `NumPy` and `pandas` measurably contribute to the success of Python in finance. However, the Python ecosystem has much more to offer in the form of additional Python packages that solve rather fundamental problems and sometimes specialized ones. This book will make use of packages for data retrieval and storage (for example, `PyTables`, `TsTables`, `SQLite`) and for machine and deep learning (for example, `scikit-learn`, `TensorFlow`), to name just two categories. Along the way, we will also implement classes and modules that will make any algorithmic trading project more efficient. However, the main packages used throughout will be `NumPy` and `pandas`.

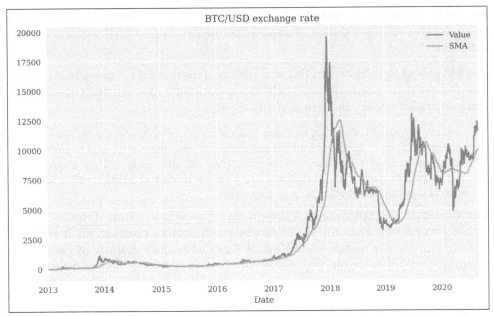

Figure 1-1. Historical Bitcoin exchange rate in USD from the beginning of 2013 until mid-2020

While NumPy provides the basic data structure to store numerical data and work with it, pandas brings powerful time series management capabilities to the table. It also does a great job of wrapping functionality from other packages into an easy-to-use API. The Bitcoin example just described shows that a single method call on a DataFrame object is enough to generate a plot with two financial time series visualized. Like NumPy, pandas allows for rather concise, vectorized code that is also generally executed quite fast due to heavy use of compiled code under the hood.

Algorithmic Trading

The term *algorithmic trading* is neither uniquely nor universally defined. On a rather basic level, it refers to the trading of financial instruments based on some formal algorithm. An *algorithm* is a set of operations (mathematical, technical) to be conducted in a certain sequence to achieve a certain goal. For example, there are mathematical algorithms to solve a Rubik's Cube.[4] Such an algorithm can solve the problem at hand via a step-by-step procedure, often perfectly. Another example is algorithms for

---

4 See The Mathematics of the Rubik's Cube (*https://oreil.ly/16pIA*) or Algorithms for Solving Rubik's Cube. (*https://oreil.ly/XM0ZP*)

finding the root(s) of an equation if it (they) exist(s) at all. In that sense, the objective of a mathematical algorithm is often well specified and an optimal solution is often expected.

But what about the objective of financial trading algorithms? This question is not that easy to answer in general. It might help to step back for a moment and consider general motives for trading. In Dorn et al. (2008) write:

> Trading in financial markets is an important economic activity. Trades are necessary to get into and out of the market, to put unneeded cash into the market, and to convert back into cash when the money is wanted. They are also needed to move money around within the market, to exchange one asset for another, to manage risk, and to exploit information about future price movements.

The view expressed here is more technical than economic in nature, focusing mainly on the process itself and only partly on why people initiate trades in the first place. For our purposes, a nonexhaustive list of financial trading motives of people and financial institutions managing money of their own or for others includes the following:

Beta trading
Earning market risk premia by investing in, for instance, exchange traded funds (ETFs) that replicate the performance of the S&P 500.

Alpha generation
Earning risk premia independent of the market by, for example, selling short stocks listed in the S&P 500 or ETFs on the S&P 500.

Static hedging
Hedging against market risks by buying, for example, out-of-the-money put options on the S&P 500.

Dynamic hedging
Hedging against market risks affecting options on the S&P 500 by, for example, dynamically trading futures on the S&P 500 and appropriate cash, money market, or rate instruments.

Asset-liability management
Trading S&P 500 stocks and ETFs to be able to cover liabilities resulting from, for example, writing life insurance policies.

Market making
Providing, for example, liquidity to options on the S&P 500 by buying and selling options at different bid and ask prices.

All these types of trades can be implemented by a discretionary approach, with human traders making decisions mainly on their own, as well as based on algorithms supporting the human trader or even replacing them completely in the decision-making process. In this context, computerization of financial trading of course plays an important role. While in the beginning of financial trading, floor trading with a large group of people shouting at each other ("open outcry") was the only way of executing trades, computerization and the advent of the internet and web technologies have revolutionized trading in the financial industry. The quotation at the beginning of this chapter illustrates this impressively in terms of the number of people actively engaged in trading shares at Goldman Sachs in 2000 and in 2016. It is a trend that was foreseen 25 years ago, as Solomon and Corso (1991) point out:

> Computers have revolutionized the trading of securities and the stock market is currently in the midst of a dynamic transformation. It is clear that the market of the future will not resemble the markets of the past.
>
> Technology has made it possible for information regarding stock prices to be sent all over the world in seconds. Presently, computers route orders and execute small trades directly from the brokerage firm's terminal to the exchange. Computers now link together various stock exchanges, a practice which is helping to create a single global market for the trading of securities. The continuing improvements in technology will make it possible to execute trades globally by electronic trading systems.

Interestingly, one of the oldest and most widely used algorithms is found in dynamic hedging of options. Already with the publication of the seminal papers about the pricing of European options by Black and Scholes (1973) and Merton (1973), the algorithm, called *delta hedging*, was made available long before computerized and electronic trading even started. Delta hedging as a trading algorithm shows how to hedge away all market risks in a simplified, perfect, continuous model world. In the real world, with transaction costs, discrete trading, imperfectly liquid markets, and other frictions ("imperfections"), the algorithm has proven, somewhat surprisingly maybe, its usefulness and robustness, as well. It might not allow one to perfectly hedge away market risks affecting options, but it is useful in getting close to the ideal and is therefore still used on a large scale in the financial industry.[5]

This book focuses on algorithmic trading in the context of *alpha generating strategies*. Although there are more sophisticated definitions for alpha, for the purposes of this book, alpha is seen as the difference between a trading strategy's return over some period of time and the return of the benchmark (single stock, index, cryptocurrency, etc.). For example, if the S&P 500 returns 10% in 2018 and an algorithmic strategy returns 12%, then alpha is +2% points. If the strategy returns 7%, then alpha is -3% points. In general, such numbers are not adjusted for risk, and other risk characteristics, such as maximal drawdown (period), are usually considered to be of second order importance, if at all.

---

5 See Hilpisch (2015) for a detailed analysis of delta hedging strategies for European and American options using Python.

This book focuses on alpha-generating strategies, or strategies that try to generate positive returns (above a benchmark) independent of the market's performance. Alpha is defined in this book (in the simplest way) as the excess return of a strategy over the benchmark financial instrument's performance.

There are other areas where trading-related algorithms play an important role. One is the *high frequency trading* (HFT) space, where speed is typically the discipline in which players compete.[6] The motives for HFT are diverse, but market making and alpha generation probably play a prominent role. Another one is *trade execution*, where algorithms are deployed to optimally execute certain nonstandard trades. Motives in this area might include the execution (at best possible prices) of large orders or the execution of an order with as little market and price impact as possible. A more subtle motive might be to disguise an order by executing it on a number of different exchanges.

An important question remains to be addressed: is there any advantage to using algorithms for trading instead of human research, experience, and discretion? This question can hardly be answered in any generality. For sure, there are human traders and portfolio managers who have earned, on average, more than their benchmark for investors over longer periods of time. The paramount example in this regard is Warren Buffett. On the other hand, statistical analyses show that the majority of active portfolio managers rarely beat relevant benchmarks consistently. Referring to the year 2015, Adam Shell writes:

> Last year, for example, when the Standard & Poor's 500-stock index posted a paltry total return of 1.4% with dividends included, 66% of "actively managed" large-company stock funds posted smaller returns than the index…The longer-term outlook is just as gloomy, with 84% of large-cap funds generating lower returns than the S&P 500 in the latest five year period and 82% falling shy in the past 10 years, the study found.[7]

In an empirical study published in December 2016, Harvey et al. write:

> We analyze and contrast the performance of discretionary and systematic hedge funds. Systematic funds use strategies that are rules-based, with little or no daily intervention by humans….We find that, for the period 1996-2014, systematic equity managers underperform their discretionary counterparts in terms of unadjusted (raw) returns, but that after adjusting for exposures to well-known risk factors, the risk-adjusted performance is similar. In the case of macro, systematic funds outperform discretionary funds, both on an unadjusted and risk-adjusted basis.

---

6 See the book by Lewis (2015) for a non-technical introduction to HFT.

7 Source: "66% of Fund Managers Can't Match S&P Results." *USA Today*, March 14, 2016.

Table 1-0 reproduces the major quantitative findings of the study by Harvey et al. (2016).[8] In the table, *factors* include traditional ones (equity, bonds, etc.), dynamic ones (value, momentum, etc.), and volatility (buying at-the-money puts and calls). The *adjusted return appraisal ratio* divides alpha by the adjusted return volatility. For more details and background, see the original study.

The study's results illustrate that systematic ("algorithmic") macro hedge funds perform best as a category, both in unadjusted and risk-adjusted terms. They generate an annualized alpha of 4.85% points over the period studied. These are hedge funds implementing strategies that are typically global, are cross-asset, and often involve political and macroeconomic elements. Systematic equity hedge funds only beat their discretionary counterparts on the basis of the adjusted return appraisal ratio (0.35 versus 0.25).

	Systematic macro	Discretionary macro	Systematic equity	Discretionary equity
Return average	5.01%	2.86%	2.88%	4.09%
Return attributed to factors	0.15%	1.28%	1.77%	2.86%
Adj. return average (alpha)	4.85%	1.57%	1.11%	1.22%
Adj. return volatility	0.93%	5.10%	3.18%	4.79%
Adj. return appraisal ratio	0.44	0.31	0.35	0.25

Compared to the S&P 500, hedge fund performance overall was quite meager for the year 2017. While the S&P 500 index returned 21.8%, hedge funds only returned 8.5% to investors (see this article (*https://oreil.ly/N59Hf*) in *Investopedia*). This illustrates how hard it is, even with multimillion dollar budgets for research and technology, to generate alpha.

Python for Algorithmic Trading

Python is used in many corners of the financial industry but has become particularly popular in the algorithmic trading space. There are a few good reasons for this:

Data analytics capabilities
> A major requirement for every algorithmic trading project is the ability to manage and process financial data efficiently. Python, in combination with packages like NumPy and pandas, makes life easier in this regard for every algorithmic trader than most other programming languages do.

---

8 Annualized performance (above the short-term interest rate) and risk measures for hedge fund categories comprising a total of 9,000 hedge funds over the period from June 1996 to December 2014.

Handling of modern APIs

Modern online trading platforms like the ones from FXCM (*http://fxcm.co.uk*) and Oanda (*http://oanda.com*) offer RESTful application programming interfaces (APIs) and socket (streaming) APIs to access historical and live data. Python is in general well suited to efficiently interact with such APIs.

Dedicated packages

In addition to the standard data analytics packages, there are multiple packages available that are dedicated to the algorithmic trading space, such as `PyAlgoTrade` (*https://oreil.ly/IpIt1*) and `Zipline` (*https://oreil.ly/2cSKR*) for the backtesting of trading strategies and `Pyfolio` (*https://oreil.ly/KT7V8*) for performing portfolio and risk analysis.

Vendor sponsored packages

More and more vendors in the space release open source Python packages to facilitate access to their offerings. Among them are online trading platforms like Oanda, as well as the leading data providers like Bloomberg (*https://oreil.ly/oSxei*) and Refinitiv (*https://oreil.ly/1SNBN*).

Dedicated platforms

Quantopian (*http://quantopian.com*), for example, offers a standardized backtesting environment as a Web-based platform where the language of choice is Python and where people can exchange ideas with like-minded others via different social network features. From its founding until 2020, Quantopian has attracted more than 300,000 users.

Buy- and sell-side adoption

More and more institutional players have adopted Python to streamline development efforts in their trading departments. This, in turn, requires more and more staff proficient in Python, which makes learning Python a worthwhile investment.

Education, training, and books

Prerequisites for the widespread adoption of a technology or programming language are academic and professional education and training programs in combination with specialized books and other resources. The Python ecosystem has seen a tremendous growth in such offerings recently, educating and training more and more people in the use of Python for finance. This can be expected to reinforce the trend of Python adoption in the algorithmic trading space.

In summary, it is rather safe to say that Python plays an important role in algorithmic trading already and seems to have strong momentum to become even more important in the future. It is therefore a good choice for anyone trying to enter the space, be it as an ambitious "retail" trader or as a professional employed by a leading financial institution engaged in systematic trading.

Focus and Prerequisites

The focus of this book is on Python as a programming language for algorithmic trading. The book assumes that the reader already has some experience with Python and popular Python packages used for data analytics. Good introductory books are, for example, Hilpisch (2018), McKinney (2017), and VanderPlas (2016), which all can be consulted to build a solid foundation in Python for data analysis and finance. The reader is also expected to have some experience with typical tools used for interactive analytics with Python, such as IPython, to which VanderPlas (2016) also provides an introduction.

This book presents and explains Python code that is applied to the topics at hand, like backtesting trading strategies or working with streaming data. It cannot provide a thorough introduction to all packages used in different places. It tries, however, to highlight those capabilities of the packages that are central to the exposition (such as vectorization with NumPy).

The book also cannot provide a thorough introduction and overview of all financial and operational aspects relevant for algorithmic trading. The approach instead focuses on the use of Python to build the necessary infrastructure for automated algorithmic trading systems. Of course, the majority of examples used are taken from the algorithmic trading space. However, when dealing with, say, momentum or mean-reversion strategies, they are more or less simply used without providing (statistical) verification or an in-depth discussion of their intricacies. Whenever it seems appropriate, references are given that point the reader to sources that address issues left open during the exposition.

All in all, this book is written for readers who have some experience with both Python and (algorithmic) trading. For such a reader, the book is a practical guide to the creation of automated trading systems using Python and additional packages.

 This book uses a number of Python programming approaches (for example, object oriented programming) and packages (for example, scikit-learn) that cannot be explained in detail. The focus is on applying these approaches and packages to different steps in an algorithmic trading process. It is therefore recommended that those who do not yet have enough Python (for finance) experience additionally consult more introductory Python texts.

Trading Strategies

Throughout this book, four different algorithmic trading strategies are used as examples. They are introduced briefly in the following sections and in some more detail in Chapter 4. All these trading strategies can be classified as mainly *alpha seeking strategies*, since their main objective is to generate positive, above-market returns independent of the market direction. Canonical examples throughout the book, when it comes to financial instruments traded, are a *stock index*, a *single stock*, or a *cryptocurrency* (denominated in a fiat currency). The book does not cover strategies involving multiple financial instruments at the same time (pair trading strategies, strategies based on baskets, etc.). It also covers only strategies whose trading signals are derived from structured, financial time series data and not, for instance, from unstructured data sources like news or social media feeds. This keeps the discussions and the Python implementations concise and easier to understand, in line with the approach (discussed earlier) of focusing on Python for algorithmic trading.[9]

The remainder of this chapter gives a quick overview of the four trading strategies used in this book.

Simple Moving Averages

The first type of trading strategy relies on simple moving averages (SMAs) to generate trading signals and market positionings. These trading strategies have been popularized by so-called technical analysts or chartists. The basic idea is that a shorter-term SMA being higher in value than a longer term SMA signals a long market position and the opposite scenario signals a neutral or short market position.

Momentum

The basic idea behind momentum strategies is that a financial instrument is assumed to perform in accordance with its recent performance for some additional time. For example, when a stock index has seen a negative return on average over the last five days, it is assumed that its performance will be negative tomorrow, as well.

Mean Reversion

In mean-reversion strategies, a financial instrument is assumed to revert to some mean or trend level if it is currently far enough away from such a level. For example, assume that a stock trades 10 USD under its 200 days SMA level of 100. It is then expected that the stock price will return to its SMA level sometime soon.

---

9 See the book by Kissel (2013) for an overview of topics related to algorithmic trading, the book by Chan (2013) for an in-depth discussion of momentum and mean-reversion strategies, or the book by Narang (2013) for a coverage of quantitative and HFT trading in general.

Machine and Deep Learning

With machine and deep learning algorithms, one generally takes a more black box approach to predicting market movements. For simplicity and reproducibility, the examples in this book mainly rely on historical return observations as features to train machine and deep learning algorithms to predict stock market movements.

 This book does not introduce algorithmic trading in a systematic fashion. Since the focus lies on applying Python in this fascinating field, readers not familiar with algorithmic trading should consult dedicated resources on the topic, some of which are cited in this chapter and the chapters that follow. But be aware of the fact that the algorithmic trading world in general is secretive and that almost everyone who is successful is naturally reluctant to share their secrets in order to protect their sources of success (that is, their alpha).

Conclusions

Python is already a force in finance in general and is on its way to becoming a major force in algorithmic trading. There are a number of good reasons to use Python for algorithmic trading, among them the powerful ecosystem of packages that allows for efficient data analysis or the handling of modern APIs. There are also a number of good reasons to learn Python for algorithmic trading, chief among them the fact that some of the biggest buy- and sell-side institutions make heavy use of Python in their trading operations and constantly look for seasoned Python professionals.

This book focuses on applying Python to the different disciplines in algorithmic trading, like backtesting trading strategies or interacting with online trading platforms. It cannot replace a thorough introduction to Python itself nor to trading in general. However, it systematically combines these two fascinating worlds to provide a valuable source for the generation of alpha in today's competitive financial and cryptocurrency markets.

References and Further Resources

Books and papers cited in this chapter:

Black, Fischer, and Myron Scholes. 1973. "The Pricing of Options and Corporate Liabilities." *Journal of Political Economy* 81 (3): 638-659.

Chan, Ernest. 2013. *Algorithmic Trading: Winning Strategies and Their Rationale.* Hoboken et al: John Wiley & Sons.

Dorn, Anne, Daniel Dorn, and Paul Sengmueller. 2008. "Why Do People Trade?" *Journal of Applied Finance* (Fall/Winter): 37-50.

Harvey, Campbell, Sandy Rattray, Andrew Sinclair, and Otto Van Hemert. 2016. "Man vs. Machine: Comparing Discretionary and Systematic Hedge Fund Performance." *The Journal of Portfolio Management* White Paper, Man Group.

Hilpisch, Yves. 2015. *Derivatives Analytics with Python: Data Analysis, Models, Simulation, Calibration and Hedging.* Wiley Finance. Resources under *http://dawp.tpq.io.*

———. 2018. *Python for Finance: Mastering Data-Driven Finance.* 2nd ed. Sebastopol: O'Reilly. Resources under *https://py4fi.pqp.io.*

———. 2020. *Artificial Intelligence in Finance: A Python-Based Guide.* Sebastopol: O'Reilly. Resources under *https://aiif.pqp.io.*

Kissel, Robert. 2013. *The Science of Algorithmic Trading and Portfolio Management.* Amsterdam et al: Elsevier/Academic Press.

Lewis, Michael. 2015. *Flash Boys: Cracking the Money Code.* New York, London: W.W. Norton & Company.

McKinney, Wes. 2017. *Python for Data Analysis: Data Wrangling with Pandas, NumPy, and IPython.* 2nd ed. Sebastopol: O'Reilly.

Merton, Robert. 1973. "Theory of Rational Option Pricing." *Bell Journal of Economics and Management Science* 4: 141-183.

Narang, Rishi. 2013. *Inside the Black Box: A Simple Guide to Quantitative and High Frequency Trading.* Hoboken et al: John Wiley & Sons.

Solomon, Lewis, and Louise Corso. 1991. "The Impact of Technology on the Trading of Securities: The Emerging Global Market and the Implications for Regulation." *The John Marshall Law Review* 24 (2): 299-338.

VanderPlas, Jake. 2016. *Python Data Science Handbook: Essential Tools for Working with Data.* Sebastopol: O'Reilly.

## CHAPTER 2

Python Infrastructure

In building a house, there is the problem of the selection of wood.
It is essential that the carpenter's aim be to carry equipment that will cut well and, when he has time, to sharpen that equipment.

—Miyamoto Musashi (*The Book of Five Rings*)

For someone new to Python, Python deployment might seem all but straightforward. The same holds true for the wealth of libraries and packages that can be installed optionally. First of all, there is not only one Python. Python comes in many different flavors, like CPython, Jython, IronPython, or PyPy. Then there is still the divide between Python 2.7 and the 3.x world. This chapter focuses on *CPython*, the most popular version of the Python programming language, and on version 3.8.

Even when focusing on CPython 3.8 (henceforth just "Python"), deployment is made difficult due to a number of reasons:

- The interpreter (a standard CPython installation) only comes with the so called *standard library* (e.g. covering typical mathematical functions).

- Optional Python packages need to be installed separately, and there are hundreds of them.

- Compiling ("building") such non-standard packages on your own can be tricky due to dependencies and operating system–specific requirements.

- Taking care of such dependencies and of version consistency over time (maintenance) is often tedious and time consuming.

- Updates and upgrades for certain packages might cause the need for recompiling a multitude of other packages.

- Changing or replacing one package might cause trouble in (many) other places.

- Migrating from one Python version to another one at some later point might amplify all the preceding issues.

Fortunately, there are tools and strategies available that help with the Python deployment issue. This chapter covers the following types of technologies that help with Python deployment:

Package manager

Package managers like `pip` (*https://oreil.ly/5vKCa*) or `conda` (*https://oreil.ly/uTZRn*) help with the installing, updating, and removing of Python packages. They also help with version consistency of different packages.

Virtual environment manager

A virtual environment manager like `virtualenv` (*https://oreil.ly/xMnlC*) or `conda` allows one to manage multiple Python installations in parallel (for example, to have both a Python 2.7 and 3.8 installation on a single machine or to test the most recent development version of a fancy Python package without risk).[1]

Container

Docker (*http://docker.com*) containers represent complete file systems containing all pieces of a system needed to run a certain software, such as code, runtime, or system tools. For example, you can run a Ubuntu 20.04 operating system with a Python 3.8 installation and the respective Python codes in a Docker container hosted on a machine running Mac OS or Windows 10. Such a containerized environment can then also be deployed later in the cloud without any major changes.

Cloud instance

Deploying Python code for financial applications generally requires high availability, security, and performance. These requirements can typically be met only by the use of professional compute and storage infrastructure that is nowadays available at attractive conditions in the form of fairly small to really large and powerful cloud instances. One benefit of a cloud instance (virtual server) compared to a dedicated server rented longer term is that users generally get charged only for the hours of actual usage. Another advantage is that such cloud instances are available literally in a minute or two if needed, which helps with agile development and scalability.

---

1 A recent project called `pipenv` combines the capabilities of the package manager `pip` with those of the virual environment manager `virtualenv`. See *https://github.com/pypa/pipenv*.

The structure of this chapter is as follows. "Conda as a Package Manager" on page 19 introduces conda as a package manager for Python. "Conda as a Virtual Environment Manager" on page 27 focuses on conda capabilities for virtual environment management. "Using Docker Containers" on page 30 gives a brief overview of Docker as a containerization technology and focuses on the building of a Ubuntu-based container with Python 3.8 installation. "Using Cloud Instances" on page 36 shows how to deploy Python and Jupyter Lab (*https://oreil.ly/4LqUS*), a powerful, browser-based tool suite for Python development and deployment in the cloud.

The goal of this chapter is to have a proper Python installation with the most important tools, as well as numerical, data analysis, and visualization packages, available on a professional infrastructure. This combination then serves as the backbone for implementing and deploying the Python codes in later chapters, be it interactive financial analytics code or code in the form of scripts and modules.

Conda as a Package Manager

Although conda can be installed alone, an efficient way of doing it is via *Miniconda,* a minimal Python distribution that includes conda as a package and virtual environment manager.

Installing Miniconda

You can download the different versions of Miniconda on the Miniconda page (*https://oreil.ly/-Z_6H*). In what follows, the Python 3.8 64-bit version is assumed, which is available for Linux, Windows, and Mac OS. The main example in this subsection is a session in an Ubuntu-based Docker container, which downloads the Linux 64-bit installer via wget and then installs Miniconda. The code as shown should work (with maybe minor modifications) on any other Linux-based or Mac OS–based machine, as well:[2]

```
$ docker run -ti -h pyalgo -p 11111:11111 ubuntu:latest /bin/bash

root@pyalgo:/# apt-get update; apt-get upgrade -y
...
root@pyalgo:/# apt-get install -y gcc wget
...
root@pyalgo:/# cd root
root@pyalgo:~# wget \
> https://repo.anaconda.com/miniconda/Miniconda3-latest-Linux-x86_64.sh \
> -O miniconda.sh
```

---

2 On Windows, you can also run the exact same commands in a Docker container (see *https://oreil.ly/GndRR*). Working on Windows directly requires some adjustments. See, for example, the book by Matthias and Kane (2018) for further details on Docker usage.

```
...
HTTP request sent, awaiting response... 200 OK
Length: 93052469 (89M) [application/x-sh]
Saving to: 'miniconda.sh'

miniconda.sh           100%[============>]  88.74M  1.60MB/s    in 2m 15s

2020-08-25 11:01:54 (3.08 MB/s) - 'miniconda.sh' saved [93052469/93052469]

root@pyalgo:~# bash miniconda.sh

Welcome to Miniconda3 py38_4.8.3

In order to continue the installation process, please review the license
agreement.
Please, press ENTER to continue
>>>
```

Simply pressing the ENTER key starts the installation process. After reviewing the
license agreement, approve the terms by answering yes:

```
...
Last updated February 25, 2020

Do you accept the license terms? [yes|no]
[no] >>> yes

Miniconda3 will now be installed into this location:
/root/miniconda3

  - Press ENTER to confirm the location
  - Press CTRL-C to abort the installation
  - Or specify a different location below

[/root/miniconda3] >>>
PREFIX=/root/miniconda3
Unpacking payload ...
Collecting package metadata (current_repodata.json): done
Solving environment: done

## Package Plan ##

  environment location: /root/miniconda3
...
  python              pkgs/main/linux-64::python-3.8.3-hcff3b4d_0
...
Preparing transaction: done
Executing transaction: done
installation finished.
```

After you have agreed to the licensing terms and have confirmed the install location, you should allow Miniconda to prepend the new Miniconda install location to the PATH environment variable by answering yes once again:

```
Do you wish the installer to initialize Miniconda3
by running conda init? [yes|no]
[no] >>> yes
...
no change        /root/miniconda3/etc/profile.d/conda.csh
modified         /root/.bashrc

==> For changes to take effect, close and re-open your current shell. <==

If you'd prefer that conda's base environment not be activated on startup,
    set the auto_activate_base parameter to false:

conda config --set auto_activate_base false

Thank you for installing Miniconda3!
root@pyalgo:~#
```

After that, you might want to update conda since the Miniconda installer is in general not as regularly updated as conda itself:

```
root@pyalgo:~# export PATH="/root/miniconda3/bin/:$PATH"
root@pyalgo:~# conda update -y conda
...
root@pyalgo:~# echo ". /root/miniconda3/etc/profile.d/conda.sh" >> ~/.bashrc
root@pyalgo:~# bash
(base) root@pyalgo:~#
```

After this rather simple installation procedure, there are now both a basic Python installation and conda available. The basic Python installation comes already with some nice batteries included, like the SQLite3 (*https://sqlite.org*) database engine. You might try out whether you can start Python in a *new shell instance* or after *appending the relevant path* to the respective environment variable (as done in the preceding example):

```
(base) root@pyalgo:~# python
Python 3.8.3 (default, May 19 2020, 18:47:26)
[GCC 7.3.0] :: Anaconda, Inc. on linux
Type "help", "copyright", "credits" or "license" for more information.
>>> print('Hello Python for Algorithmic Trading World.')
Hello Python for Algorithmic Trading World.
>>> exit()
(base) root@pyalgo:~#
```

Basic Operations with Conda

conda can be used to efficiently handle, among other things, the installation, updating, and removal of Python packages. The following list provides an overview of the major functions:

Installing Python x.x
```
conda install python=x.x
```

Updating Python
```
conda update python
```

Installing a package
```
conda install $PACKAGE_NAME
```

Updating a package
```
conda update $PACKAGE_NAME
```

Removing a package
```
conda remove $PACKAGE_NAME
```

Updating conda itself
```
conda update conda
```

Searching for packages
```
conda search $SEARCH_TERM
```

Listing installed packages
```
conda list
```

Given these capabilities, installing, for example, NumPy (as one of the most important packages of the so-called *scientific stack*) is a single command only. When the installation takes place on a machine with an Intel processor, the procedure automatically installs the Intel Math Kernel Library mkl (*https://oreil.ly/Tca2C*), which speeds up numerical operations not only for NumPy on Intel machines but also for a few other scientific Python packages:[3]

```
(base) root@pyalgo:~# conda install numpy
Collecting package metadata (current_repodata.json): done
Solving environment: done

## Package Plan ##

  environment location: /root/miniconda3
```

---

3 Installing the meta package nomkl, such as in conda install numpy nomkl, avoids the automatic installation and usage of mkl and related other packages.

```
    added / updated specs:
      - numpy


The following packages will be downloaded:

    package                    |              build
    ---------------------------|-----------------
    blas-1.0                   |              mkl           6 KB
    intel-openmp-2020.1        |              217         780 KB
    mkl-2020.1                 |              217       129.0 MB
    mkl-service-2.3.0          |     py38he904b0f_0         62 KB
    mkl_fft-1.1.0              |     py38h23d657b_0        150 KB
    mkl_random-1.1.1           |     py38h0573a6f_0        341 KB
    numpy-1.19.1               |     py38hbc911f0_0         21 KB
    numpy-base-1.19.1          |     py38hfa32c7d_0        4.2 MB
    ------------------------------------------------------------
                                           Total:       134.5 MB

The following NEW packages will be INSTALLED:

    blas              pkgs/main/linux-64::blas-1.0-mkl
    intel-openmp      pkgs/main/linux-64::intel-openmp-2020.1-217
    mkl               pkgs/main/linux-64::mkl-2020.1-217
    mkl-service       pkgs/main/linux-64::mkl-service-2.3.0-py38he904b0f_0
    mkl_fft           pkgs/main/linux-64::mkl_fft-1.1.0-py38h23d657b_0
    mkl_random        pkgs/main/linux-64::mkl_random-1.1.1-py38h0573a6f_0
    numpy             pkgs/main/linux-64::numpy-1.19.1-py38hbc911f0_0
    numpy-base        pkgs/main/linux-64::numpy-base-1.19.1-py38hfa32c7d_0


Proceed ([y]/n)? y


Downloading and Extracting Packages
numpy-base-1.19.1    | 4.2 MB   | ############################# | 100%
blas-1.0             | 6 KB     | ############################# | 100%
mkl_fft-1.1.0        | 150 KB   | ############################# | 100%
mkl-service-2.3.0    | 62 KB    | ############################# | 100%
numpy-1.19.1         | 21 KB    | ############################# | 100%
mkl-2020.1           | 129.0 MB | ############################# | 100%
mkl_random-1.1.1     | 341 KB   | ############################# | 100%
intel-openmp-2020.1  | 780 KB   | ############################# | 100%
Preparing transaction: done
Verifying transaction: done
Executing transaction: done
(base) root@pyalgo:~#
```

Multiple packages can also be installed at once. The -y flag indicates that all (potential) questions shall be answered with yes:

```
(base) root@pyalgo:~# conda install -y ipython matplotlib pandas \
> pytables scikit-learn scipy
...
Collecting package metadata (current_repodata.json): done
Solving environment: done

## Package Plan ##

  environment location: /root/miniconda3

  added / updated specs:
    - ipython
    - matplotlib
    - pandas
    - pytables
    - scikit-learn
    - scipy


The following packages will be downloaded:

    package                    |             build
    ---------------------------|-----------------
    backcall-0.2.0             |            py_0          15 KB
    ...
    zstd-1.4.5                 |       h9ceee32_0         619 KB
    ------------------------------------------------------------
                                       Total:         144.9 MB

The following NEW packages will be INSTALLED:

  backcall           pkgs/main/noarch::backcall-0.2.0-py_0
  blosc              pkgs/main/linux-64::blosc-1.20.0-hd408876_0
  ...
  zstd               pkgs/main/linux-64::zstd-1.4.5-h9ceee32_0


Downloading and Extracting Packages
glib-2.65.0          | 2.9 MB    | ############################ | 100%
...
snappy-1.1.8         | 40 KB     | ############################ | 100%
Preparing transaction: done
Verifying transaction: done
Executing transaction: done
(base) root@pyalgo:~#
```

After the resulting installation procedure, some of the most important libraries for financial analytics are available in addition to the standard ones:

IPython (http://ipython.org)
An improved interactive Python shell

matplotlib (http://matplotlib.org)
The standard plotting library for Python

NumPy (http://numpy.org)
Efficient handling of numerical arrays

pandas (http://pandas.pydata.org)
Management of tabular data, like financial time series data

PyTables (http://pytables.org)
A Python wrapper for the HDF5 (*http://hdfgroup.org*) library

scikit-learn (http://scikit-learn.org)
A package for machine learning and related tasks

SciPy (http://scipy.org)
A collection of scientific classes and functions

This provides a basic tool set for data analysis in general and financial analytics in particular. The next example uses IPython and draws a set of pseudo-random numbers with NumPy:

```
(base) root@pyalgo:~# ipython
Python 3.8.3 (default, May 19 2020, 18:47:26)
Type 'copyright', 'credits' or 'license' for more information
IPython 7.16.1 -- An enhanced Interactive Python. Type '?' for help.

In [1]: import numpy as np

In [2]: np.random.seed(100)

In [3]: np.random.standard_normal((5, 4))
Out[3]:
array([[-1.74976547,  0.3426804 ,  1.1530358 , -0.25243604],
       [ 0.98132079,  0.51421884,  0.22117967, -1.07004333],
       [-0.18949583,  0.25500144, -0.45802699,  0.43516349],
       [-0.58359505,  0.81684707,  0.67272081, -0.10441114],
       [-0.53128038,  1.02973269, -0.43813562, -1.11831825]])

In [4]: exit
(base) root@pyalgo:~#
```

Executing `conda list` shows which packages are installed:

```
(base) root@pyalgo:~# conda list
# packages in environment at /root/miniconda3:
#
# Name                    Version                   Build  Channel
_libgcc_mutex             0.1                        main
backcall                  0.2.0                      py_0
blas                      1.0                         mkl
blosc                     1.20.0                 hd408876_0
...
zlib                      1.2.11                 h7b6447c_3
zstd                      1.4.5                  h9ceee32_0
(base) root@pyalgo:~#
```

In case a package is not needed anymore, it is efficiently removed with `conda remove`:

```
(base) root@pyalgo:~# conda remove matplotlib
Collecting package metadata (repodata.json): done
Solving environment: done

## Package Plan ##

  environment location: /root/miniconda3

  removed specs:
    - matplotlib


The following packages will be REMOVED:

The following packages will be REMOVED:

  cycler-0.10.0-py38_0
  ...
  tornado-6.0.4-py38h7b6447c_1


Proceed ([y]/n)? y

Preparing transaction: done
Verifying transaction: done
Executing transaction: done
(base) root@pyalgo:~#
```

`conda` as a package manager is already quite useful. However, its full power only becomes evident when adding virtual environment management to the mix.

conda as a package manager makes installing, updating, and removing Python packages a pleasant experience. There is no need to take care of building and compiling packages on your own, which can be tricky sometimes given the list of dependencies a package specifies and given the specifics to be considered on different operating systems.

Conda as a Virtual Environment Manager

Having installed Miniconda with conda included provides a default Python installation depending on what version of Miniconda has been chosen. The virtual environment management capabilities of conda allow one, for example, to add to a Python 3.8 default installation a completely separated installation of Python 2.7.x. To this end, conda offers the following functionality:

Creating a virtual environment
```
conda create --name $ENVIRONMENT_NAME
```

Activating an environment
```
conda activate $ENVIRONMENT_NAME
```

Deactivating an environment
```
conda deactivate $ENVIRONMENT_NAME
```

Removing an environment
```
conda env remove --name $ENVIRONMENT_NAME
```

Exporting to an environment file
```
conda env export > $FILE_NAME
```

Creating an environment from a file
```
conda env create -f $FILE_NAME
```

Listing all environments
```
conda info --envs
```

As a simple illustration, the example code that follows creates an environment called py27, installs IPython, and executes a line of Python 2.7.x code. Although the support for Python 2.7 has ended, the example illustrates how legacy Python 2.7 code can easily be executed and tested:

```
(base) root@pyalgo:~# conda create --name py27 python=2.7
Collecting package metadata (current_repodata.json): done
Solving environment: failed with repodata from current_repodata.json,
will retry with next repodata source.
Collecting package metadata (repodata.json): done
Solving environment: done
```

```
## Package Plan ##

  environment location: /root/miniconda3/envs/py27

  added / updated specs:
    - python=2.7


The following packages will be downloaded:

    package                    |             build
    ---------------------------|-----------------
    certifi-2019.11.28         |          py27_0         153 KB
    pip-19.3.1                 |          py27_0         1.7 MB
    python-2.7.18              |       h15b4118_1         9.9 MB
    setuptools-44.0.0          |          py27_0         512 KB
    wheel-0.33.6               |          py27_0          42 KB
    ------------------------------------------------------------
                                          Total:        12.2 MB

The following NEW packages will be INSTALLED:

  _libgcc_mutex      pkgs/main/linux-64::_libgcc_mutex-0.1-main
  ca-certificates    pkgs/main/linux-64::ca-certificates-2020.6.24-0
  ...
  zlib               pkgs/main/linux-64::zlib-1.2.11-h7b6447c_3


Proceed ([y]/n)? y


Downloading and Extracting Packages
certifi-2019.11.28   | 153 KB    | ############################## | 100%
python-2.7.18        | 9.9 MB    | ############################## | 100%
pip-19.3.1           | 1.7 MB    | ############################## | 100%
setuptools-44.0.0    | 512 KB    | ############################## | 100%
wheel-0.33.6         | 42 KB     | ############################## | 100%
Preparing transaction: done
Verifying transaction: done
Executing transaction: done
#
# To activate this environment, use
#
#     $ conda activate py27
#
# To deactivate an active environment, use
#
#     $ conda deactivate

(base) root@pyalgo:~#
```

Notice how the prompt changes to include (py27) after the environment is activated:

```
(base) root@pyalgo:~# conda activate py27
(py27) root@pyalgo:~# pip install ipython
DEPRECATION: Python 2.7 will reach the end of its life on January 1st, 2020.
...
Executing transaction: done
(py27) root@pyalgo:~#
```

Finally, this allows one to use IPython with Python 2.7 syntax:

```
(py27) root@pyalgo:~# ipython
Python 2.7.18 |Anaconda, Inc.| (default, Apr 23 2020, 22:42:48)
Type "copyright", "credits" or "license" for more information.

IPython 5.10.0 -- An enhanced Interactive Python.
?          -> Introduction and overview of IPython's features.
%quickref -> Quick reference.
help       -> Python's own help system.
object?    -> Details about 'object', use 'object??' for extra details.

In [1]: print "Hello Python for Algorithmic Trading World."
Hello Python for Algorithmic Trading World.

In [2]: exit
(py27) root@pyalgo:~#
```

As this example demonstrates, conda as a virtual environment manager allows one to install different Python versions alongside each other. It also allows one to install different versions of certain packages. The default Python installation is not influenced by such a procedure, nor are other environments that might exist on the same machine. All available environments can be shown via conda info --envs:

```
(py27) root@pyalgo:~# conda env list
# conda environments:
#
base                     /root/miniconda3
py27                 *   /root/miniconda3/envs/py27

(py27) root@pyalgo:~#
```

Sometimes it is necessary to share environment information with others or to use environment information on multiple machines, for instance. To this end, one can export the installed packages list to a file with conda env export. However, this only works properly by default for the same operating system since the build versions are specified in the resulting yaml file. However, they can be deleted to only specify the package version via the --no-builds flag:

```
(py27) root@pyalgo:~# conda deactivate
(base) root@pyalgo:~# conda env export --no-builds > base.yml
(base) root@pyalgo:~# cat base.yml
name: base
```

```
channels:
  - defaults
dependencies:
  - _libgcc_mutex=0.1
  - backcall=0.2.0
  - blas=1.0
  - blosc=1.20.0
  ...
  - zlib=1.2.11
  - zstd=1.4.5
prefix: /root/miniconda3
(base) root@pyalgo:~#
```

Often, virtual environments, which are technically not that much more than a certain (sub-)folder structure, are created to do some quick tests.[4] In such a case, an environment is easily removed (after deactivation) via conda env remove:

```
(base) root@pyalgo:~# conda env remove -n py27

Remove all packages in environment /root/miniconda3/envs/py27:

(base) root@pyalgo:~#
```

This concludes the overview of conda as a virtual environment manager.

conda not only helps with managing packages, but it is also a virtual environment manager for Python. It simplifies the creation of different Python environments, allowing one to have multiple versions of Python and optional packages available on the same machine without them influencing each other in any way. conda also allows one to export environment information to easily replicate it on multiple machines or to share it with others.

Using Docker Containers

Docker containers have taken the IT world by storm (see Docker (*http://docker.com*)). Although the technology is still relatively young, it has established itself as one of the benchmarks for the efficient development and deployment of almost any kind of software application.

For our purposes, it suffices to think of a Docker container as a separated ("containerized") file system that includes an operating system (for example, Ubuntu 20.04 LTS for server), a (Python) runtime, additional system and development tools, and

---

4 In the official documentation, you will find the following explanation: "Python *Virtual Environments* allow Python packages to be installed in an isolated location for a particular application, rather than being installed globally." See the Creating Virtual Environments page (*https://oreil.ly/5Jgjc*).

further (Python) libraries and packages as needed. Such a Docker container might run on a local machine with Windows 10 Professional 64 Bit or on a cloud instance with a Linux operating system, for instance.

This section goes into the exciting details of Docker containers. It is a concise illustration of what the Docker technology can do in the context of Python deployment.[5]

Docker Images and Containers

Before moving on to the illustration, two fundamental terms need to be distinguished when talking about Docker. The first is a *Docker image*, which can be compared to a Python class. The second is a *Docker container*, which can be compared to an instance of the respective Python class.

On a more technical level, you will find the following definition for a *Docker image* in the Docker glossary (*https://oreil.ly/NNUiB*):

> Docker images are the basis of containers. An image is an ordered collection of root filesystem changes and the corresponding execution parameters for use within a container runtime. An image typically contains a union of layered filesystems stacked on top of each other. An image does not have state and it never changes.

Similarly, you will find the following definition for a *Docker container* in the Docker glossary (*https://oreil.ly/NNUiB*), which makes the analogy to Python classes and instances of such classes transparent:

> A container is a runtime instance of a Docker image.
>
> A Docker container consists of
>
> - A Docker image
> - An execution environment
> - A standard set of instructions
>
> The concept is borrowed from Shipping Containers, which define a standard to ship goods globally. Docker defines a standard to ship software.

Depending on the operating system, the installation of Docker is somewhat different. That is why this section does not go into the respective details. More information and further links are found on the Get Docker page (*https://oreil.ly/hGgxs*).

Building a Ubuntu and Python Docker Image

This sub-section illustrates the building of a Docker image based on the latest version of Ubuntu that includes Miniconda, as well as a few important Python packages. In

---

5 See Matthias and Kane (2018) for a comprehensive introduction to the Docker technology.

addition, it does some Linux housekeeping by updating the Linux packages index, upgrading packages if required and installing certain additional system tools. To this end, two scripts are needed. One is a Bash script doing all the work on the Linux level.[6] The other is a so-called *Dockerfile*, which controls the building procedure for the image itself.

The Bash script in Example 2-1, which does the installing, consists of three major parts. The first part handles the Linux housekeeping. The second part installs Miniconda, while the third part installs optional Python packages. There are also more detailed comments inline:

Example 2-1. Script installing Python and optional packages

```bash
#!/bin/bash
#
# Script to Install
# Linux System Tools and
# Basic Python Components
#
# Python for Algorithmic Trading
# (c) Dr. Yves J. Hilpisch
# The Python Quants GmbH
#
# GENERAL LINUX
apt-get update  # updates the package index cache
apt-get upgrade -y  # updates packages
# installs system tools
apt-get install -y bzip2 gcc git  # system tools
apt-get install -y htop screen vim wget  # system tools
apt-get upgrade -y bash  # upgrades bash if necessary
apt-get clean  # cleans up the package index cache

# INSTALL MINICONDA
# downloads Miniconda
wget https://repo.anaconda.com/miniconda/Miniconda3-latest-Linux-x86_64.sh -O \
  Miniconda.sh
bash Miniconda.sh -b  # installs it
rm -rf Miniconda.sh  # removes the installer
export PATH="/root/miniconda3/bin:$PATH"  # prepends the new path

# INSTALL PYTHON LIBRARIES
conda install -y pandas  # installs pandas
conda install -y ipython  # installs IPython shell

# CUSTOMIZATION
```

---

6 Consult the book by Robbins (2016) for a concise introduction to and a quick overview of Bash scripting. Also see see GNU Bash (*https://oreil.ly/SGHn1*).

```
cd /root/
wget http://hilpisch.com/.vimrc  # Vim configuration
```

The `Dockerfile` in Example 2-2 uses the `Bash` script in Example 2-1 to build a new Docker image. It also has its major parts commented inline:

Example 2-2. Dockerfile to build the image

```
#
# Building a Docker Image with
# the Latest Ubuntu Version and
# Basic Python Install
#
# Python for Algorithmic Trading
# (c) Dr. Yves J. Hilpisch
# The Python Quants GmbH
#

# latest Ubuntu version
FROM ubuntu:latest

# information about maintainer
MAINTAINER yves

# add the bash script
ADD install.sh /
# change rights for the script
RUN chmod u+x /install.sh
# run the bash script
RUN /install.sh
# prepend the new path
ENV PATH /root/miniconda3/bin:$PATH

# execute IPython when container is run
CMD ["ipython"]
```

If these two files are in a single folder and Docker is installed, then the building of the new Docker image is straightforward. Here, the tag `pyalgo:basic` is used for the image. This tag is needed to reference the image, for example, when running a container based on it:

```
(base) pro:Docker yves$ docker build -t pyalgo:basic .
Sending build context to Docker daemon  4.096kB
Step 1/7 : FROM ubuntu:latest
 ---> 4e2eef94cd6b
Step 2/7 : MAINTAINER yves
 ---> Running in 859db5550d82
Removing intermediate container 859db5550d82
 ---> 40adf11b689f
Step 3/7 : ADD install.sh /
 ---> 34cd9dc267e0
```

```
Step 4/7 : RUN chmod u+x /install.sh
 ---> Running in 08ce2f46541b
Removing intermediate container 08ce2f46541b
 ---> 88c0adc82cb0
Step 5/7 : RUN /install.sh
 ---> Running in 112e70510c5b
...
Removing intermediate container 112e70510c5b
 ---> 314dc8ec5b48
Step 6/7 : ENV PATH /root/miniconda3/bin:$PATH
 ---> Running in 82497aea20bd
Removing intermediate container 82497aea20bd
 ---> 5364f494f4b4
Step 7/7 : CMD ["ipython"]
 ---> Running in ff434d5a3c1b
Removing intermediate container ff434d5a3c1b
 ---> a0bb86daf9ad
Successfully built a0bb86daf9ad
Successfully tagged pyalgo:basic
(base) pro:Docker yves$
```

Existing Docker images can be listed via docker images. The new image should be on top of the list:

```
(base) pro:Docker yves$ docker images
REPOSITORY          TAG             IMAGE ID            CREATED            SIZE
pyalgo              basic           a0bb86daf9ad        2 minutes ago      1.79GB
ubuntu              latest          4e2eef94cd6b        5 days ago         73.9MB
(base) pro:Docker yves$
```

Having built the pyalgo:basic image successfully allows one to run a respective Docker container with docker run. The parameter combination -ti is needed for interactive processes running within a Docker container, like a shell process of IPython (see the Docker Run Reference page (*https://oreil.ly/s0_hn*)):

```
(base) pro:Docker yves$ docker run -ti pyalgo:basic
Python 3.8.3 (default, May 19 2020, 18:47:26)
Type 'copyright', 'credits' or 'license' for more information
IPython 7.16.1 -- An enhanced Interactive Python. Type '?' for help.

In [1]: import numpy as np

In [2]: np.random.seed(100)

In [3]: a = np.random.standard_normal((5, 3))

In [4]: import pandas as pd

In [5]: df = pd.DataFrame(a, columns=['a', 'b', 'c'])

In [6]: df
Out[6]:
```

```
          a         b          c
0 -1.749765  0.342680  1.153036
1 -0.252436  0.981321  0.514219
2  0.221180 -1.070043 -0.189496
3  0.255001 -0.458027  0.435163
4 -0.583595  0.816847  0.672721
```

Exiting IPython will exit the container as well, since it is the only application running within the container. However, you can detach from a container via the following:

```
Ctrl+p --> Ctrl+q
```

After having detached from the container, the docker ps command shows the running container (and maybe other currently running containers):

```
(base) pro:Docker yves$ docker ps
CONTAINER ID   IMAGE          COMMAND     CREATED           ...   NAMES
e93c4cbd8ea8   pyalgo:basic   "ipython"   About a minute ago      jolly_rubin
(base) pro:Docker yves$
```

Attaching to the Docker container is accomplished by docker attach $CONTAINER_ID. Notice that a few letters of the CONTAINER ID are enough:

```
(base) pro:Docker yves$ docker attach e93c
In [7]: df.info()
<class 'pandas.core.frame.DataFrame'>
RangeIndex: 5 entries, 0 to 4
Data columns (total 3 columns):
 #   Column  Non-Null Count  Dtype
---  ------  --------------  -----
 0   a       5 non-null      float64
 1   b       5 non-null      float64
 2   c       5 non-null      float64
dtypes: float64(3)
memory usage: 248.0 bytes
```

The exit command terminates IPython and therewith stops the Docker container, as well. It can be removed by docker rm:

```
In [8]: exit
(base) pro:Docker yves$ docker rm e93c
e93c
(base) pro:Docker yves$
```

Similarly, the Docker image pyalgo:basic can be removed via docker rmi if not needed any longer. While containers are relatively lightweight, single images might consume quite a bit of storage. In the case of the pyalgo:basic image, the size is close to 2 GB. That is why you might want to regularly clean up the list of Docker images:

```
(base) pro:Docker yves$ docker rmi a0bb86
Untagged: pyalgo:basic
Deleted: sha256:a0bb86daf9adfd0ddf65312ce6c1b068100448152f2ced5d0b9b5adef5788d88
```

```
...
Deleted: sha256:40adf11b689fc778297c36d4b232c59fedda8c631b4271672cc86f505710502d
(base) pro:Docker yves$
```

Of course, there is much more to say about Docker containers and their benefits in certain application scenarios. For the purposes of this book, they provide a modern approach to deploying Python, to doing Python development in a completely separated (containerized) environment, and to shipping codes for algorithmic trading.

 If you are not yet using Docker containers, you should consider starting to use them. They provide a number of benefits when it comes to Python deployment and development efforts, not only when working locally but also in particular when working with remote cloud instances and servers deploying code for algorithmic trading.

Using Cloud Instances

This section shows how to set up a full-fledged Python infrastructure on a DigitalOcean (*http://digitalocean.com*) cloud instance. There are many other cloud providers out there, among them Amazon Web Services (*http://aws.amazon.com*) (AWS) as the leading provider. However, DigitalOcean is well known for its simplicity and relatively low rates for smaller cloud instances, which it calls *Droplet*. The smallest Droplet, which is generally sufficient for exploration and development purposes, only costs 5 USD per month or 0.007 USD per hour. Usage is charged by the hour so that one can (for example) easily spin up a Droplet for two hours, destroy it, and get charged just 0.014 USD.[7]

The goal of this section is to set up a Droplet on DigitalOcean that has a Python 3.8 installation plus typically needed packages (such as NumPy and pandas) in combination with a password-protected and Secure Sockets Layer (SSL)-encrypted Jupyter Lab (*http://jupyter.org*) server installation.[8] As a web-based tool suite, Jupyter Lab provides several tools that can be used via a regular browser:

Jupyter Notebook
> This is one of the most popular (if not *the* most popular) browser-based, interactive development environment that features a selection of different language kernels like Python, R, and Julia.

---

7 For those who do not have an account with a cloud provider yet, on *http://bit.ly/do_sign_up*, new users get a starting credit of 10 USD for DigitalOcean.

8 Technically, Jupyter Lab is an extension of Jupyter Notebook. Both expressions are, however, sometimes used interchangeably.

Python console

This is an `IPython`-based console that has a graphical user interface different from the look and feel of the standard, terminal-based implementation.

Terminal

This is a system shell implementation accessible via the browser that allows not only for all typical system administration tasks, but also for usage of helpful tools such as `Vim` (*http://vim.org/download*) for code editing or `git` (*https://git-scm.com/*) for version control.

Editor

Another major tool is a browser-based text file editor with syntax highlighting for many different programming languages and file types, as well as typical text/code editing capabilities.

File manager

`Jupyter Lab` also provides a full-fledged file manager that allows for typical file operations, such as uploading, downloading, and renaming.

Having `Jupyter Lab` installed on a Droplet allows one to do Python development and deployment via the browser, circumventing the need to log in to the cloud instance via Secure Shell (SSH) access.

To accomplish the goal of this section, several scripts are needed:

Server setup script

This script orchestrates all steps necessary, such as copying other files to the Droplet and running them on the Droplet.

Python and `Jupyter` *installation script*

This script installs Python, additional packages, `Jupyter Lab`, and starts the `Jupyter Lab` server.

Jupyter Notebook configuration file

This file is for the configuration of the `Jupyter Lab` server, for example, with regard to password protection.

RSA public and private key files

These two files are needed for the SSL encryption of the communication with the `Jupyter Lab` server.

The following section works backwards through this list of files since although the setup script is executed first, the other files need to have been created beforehand.

RSA Public and Private Keys

In order to accomplish a secure connection to the Jupyter Lab server via an arbitrary browser, an SSL certificate consisting of RSA public and private keys (see RSA Wikipedia page (*https://oreil.ly/8UG1K*)) is needed. In general, one would expect that such a certificate comes from a so-called Certificate Authority (CA). For the purposes of this book, however, a self-generated certificate is "good enough."[9] A popular tool to generate RSA key pairs is OpenSSL (*http://openssl.org*). The brief interactive session to follow generates a certificate appropriate for use with a Jupyter Lab server (see the Jupyter Notebook docs (*https://oreil.ly/YxxaF*)):

```
(base) pro:cloud yves$ openssl req -x509 -nodes -days 365 -newkey rsa:2048 \
> -keyout mykey.key -out mycert.pem
Generating a RSA private key
.......+++++
.....+++++
+++++
writing new private key to 'mykey.key'
-----
You are about to be asked to enter information that will be incorporated
into your certificate request.
What you are about to enter is what is called a Distinguished Name or a DN.
There are quite a few fields but you can leave some blank.
For some fields there will be a default value,
If you enter '.', the field will be left blank.
-----
Country Name (2 letter code) [AU]:DE
State or Province Name (full name) [Some-State]:Saarland
Locality Name (e.g., city) []:Voelklingen
Organization Name (eg, company) [Internet Widgits Pty Ltd]:TPQ GmbH
Organizational Unit Name (e.g., section) []:Algorithmic Trading
Common Name (e.g., server FQDN or YOUR name) []:Jupyter Lab
Email Address []:pyalgo@tpq.io
(base) pro:cloud yves$
```

The two files mykey.key and mycert.pem need to be copied to the Droplet and need to be referenced by the Jupyter Notebook configuration file. This file is presented next.

Jupyter Notebook Configuration File

A public Jupyter Lab server can be deployed securely, as explained in the Jupyter Notebook docs (*https://oreil.ly/YxxaF*). Among others things, Jupyter Lab shall be password protected. To this end, there is a password hash code-generating function

---

9 With such a self-generated certificate, you might need to add a security exception when prompted by the browser. On Mac OS you might even explicitly register the certificate as trustworthy.

called `passwd()` available in the `notebook.auth` sub-package. The following code generates a password hash code with `jupyter` being the password itself:

```
In [1]: from notebook.auth import passwd

In [2]: passwd('jupyter')
Out[2]: 'sha1:da3a3dfc0445:052235bb76e56450b38d27e41a85a136c3bf9cd7'

In [3]: exit
```

This hash code needs to be placed in the `Jupyter Notebook` configuration file as presented in Example 2-3. The configuration file assumes that the RSA key files have been copied on the Droplet to the `/root/.jupyter/` folder.

Example 2-3. Jupyter Notebook configuration file

```
#
# Jupyter Notebook Configuration File
#
# Python for Algorithmic Trading
# (c) Dr. Yves J. Hilpisch
# The Python Quants GmbH
#
# SSL ENCRYPTION
# replace the following file names (and files used) by your choice/files
c.NotebookApp.certfile = u'/root/.jupyter/mycert.pem'
c.NotebookApp.keyfile = u'/root/.jupyter/mykey.key'

# IP ADDRESS AND PORT
# set ip to '*' to bind on all IP addresses of the cloud instance
c.NotebookApp.ip = '0.0.0.0'
# it is a good idea to set a known, fixed default port for server access
c.NotebookApp.port = 8888

# PASSWORD PROTECTION
# here: 'jupyter' as password
# replace the hash code with the one for your password
c.NotebookApp.password = \
        'sha1:da3a3dfc0445:052235bb76e56450b38d27e41a85a136c3bf9cd7'

# NO BROWSER OPTION
# prevent Jupyter from trying to open a browser
c.NotebookApp.open_browser = False

# ROOT ACCESS
# allow Jupyter to run from root user
c.NotebookApp.allow_root = True
```

The next step is to make sure that Python and `Jupyter Lab` get installed on the Droplet.

Deploying Jupyter Lab in the cloud leads to a number of security issues since it is a full-fledged development environment accessible via a web browser. It is therefore of paramount importance to use the security measures that a Jupyter Lab server provides by default, like password protection and SSL encryption. But this is just the beginning, and further security measures might be advised depending on what exactly is done on the cloud instance.

Installation Script for Python and Jupyter Lab

The bash script to install Python and Jupyter Lab is similar to the one presented in section "Using Docker Containers" on page 30 to install Python via Miniconda in a Docker container. However, the script in Example 2-4 needs to start the Jupyter Lab server, as well. All major parts and lines of code are commented inline.

Example 2-4. Bash script to install Python and to run the Jupyter Notebook server

```
#!/bin/bash
#
# Script to Install
# Linux System Tools and Basic Python Components
# as well as to
# Start Jupyter Lab Server
#
# Python for Algorithmic Trading
# (c) Dr. Yves J. Hilpisch
# The Python Quants GmbH
#
# GENERAL LINUX
apt-get update  # updates the package index cache
apt-get upgrade -y  # updates packages
# install system tools
apt-get install -y build-essential git  # system tools
apt-get install -y screen htop vim wget  # system tools
apt-get upgrade -y bash  # upgrades bash if necessary
apt-get clean  # cleans up the package index cache

# INSTALLING MINICONDA
wget https://repo.anaconda.com/miniconda/Miniconda3-latest-Linux-x86_64.sh \
             -O Miniconda.sh
bash Miniconda.sh -b  # installs Miniconda
rm -rf Miniconda.sh  # removes the installer
# prepends the new path for current session
export PATH="/root/miniconda3/bin:$PATH"
# prepends the new path in the shell configuration
cat >> ~/.profile <<EOF
export PATH="/root/miniconda3/bin:$PATH"
EOF
```

```
# INSTALLING PYTHON LIBRARIES
conda install -y jupyter  # interactive data analytics in the browser
conda install -y jupyterlab  # Jupyter Lab environment
conda install -y numpy  #  numerical computing package
conda install -y pytables  # wrapper for HDF5 binary storage
conda install -y pandas  #  data analysis package
conda install -y scipy  #  scientific computations package
conda install -y matplotlib  # standard plotting library
conda install -y seaborn  # statistical plotting library
conda install -y quandl  # wrapper for Quandl data API
conda install -y scikit-learn  # machine learning library
conda install -y openpyxl  # package for Excel interaction
conda install -y xlrd xlwt  # packages for Excel interaction
conda install -y pyyaml  # package to manage yaml files

pip install --upgrade pip  # upgrading the package manager
pip install q  # logging and debugging
pip install plotly  # interactive D3.js plots
pip install cufflinks  # combining plotly with pandas
pip install tensorflow  # deep learning library
pip install keras  # deep learning library
pip install eikon  # Python wrapper for the Refinitiv Eikon Data API
# Python wrapper for Oanda API
pip install git+git://github.com/yhilpisch/tpqoa

# COPYING FILES AND CREATING DIRECTORIES
mkdir -p /root/.jupyter/custom
wget http://hilpisch.com/custom.css
mv custom.css /root/.jupyter/custom
mv /root/jupyter_notebook_config.py /root/.jupyter/
mv /root/mycert.pem /root/.jupyter
mv /root/mykey.key /root/.jupyter
mkdir /root/notebook
cd /root/notebook

# STARTING JUPYTER LAB
jupyter lab &
```

This script needs to be copied to the Droplet and needs to be started by the orchestration script, as described in the next sub-section.

Script to Orchestrate the Droplet Set Up

The second bash script, which sets up the Droplet, is the shortest one (see Example 2-5). It mainly copies all the other files to the Droplet for which the respective IP address is expected as a parameter. In the final line, it starts the `install.sh` bash script, which in turn does the installation itself and starts the `Jupyter Lab` server.

Example 2-5. Bash script to set up the Droplet

```bash
#!/bin/bash
#
# Setting up a DigitalOcean Droplet
# with Basic Python Stack
# and Jupyter Notebook
#
# Python for Algorithmic Trading
# (c) Dr Yves J Hilpisch
# The Python Quants GmbH
#

# IP ADDRESS FROM PARAMETER
MASTER_IP=$1

# COPYING THE FILES
scp install.sh root@${MASTER_IP}:
scp mycert.pem mykey.key jupyter_notebook_config.py root@${MASTER_IP}:

# EXECUTING THE INSTALLATION SCRIPT
ssh root@${MASTER_IP} bash /root/install.sh
```

Everything now is together to give the set up code a try. On DigitalOcean, create a new Droplet with options similar to these:

Operating system
Ubuntu 20.04 LTS x64 (the newest version available at the time of this writing)

Size
Two core, 2GB, 60GB SSD (standard Droplet)

Data center region
Frankfurt (since your author lives in Germany)

SSH key
Add a (new) SSH key for password-less login[10]

Droplet name
Prespecified name or something like `pyalgo`

Finally, clicking on the `Create` button initiates the Droplet creation process, which generally takes about one minute. The major outcome for proceeding with the set-up procedure is the IP address, which might be, for instance, 134.122.74.144 when you

---

10 If you need assistance, visit either How To Use SSH Keys with DigitalOcean Droplets (*https://oreil.ly/Tggw7*) or How To Use SSH Keys with PuTTY on DigitalOcean Droplets (Windows users) (*https://oreil.ly/-jTif*).

have chosen Frankfurt as your data center location. Setting up the Droplet now is as easy as what follows:

```
(base) pro:cloud yves$ bash setup.sh 134.122.74.144
```

The resulting process, however, might take a couple of minutes. It is finished when there is a message from the `Jupyter Lab` server saying something like the following:

```
[I 12:02:50.190 LabApp] Serving notebooks from local directory: /root/notebook
[I 12:02:50.190 LabApp] Jupyter Notebook 6.1.1 is running at:
[I 12:02:50.190 LabApp] https://pyalgo:8888/
```

In any current browser, visiting the following address accesses the running `Jupyter Notebook` server (note the `https` protocol):

```
https://134.122.74.144:8888
```

After maybe adding a security exception, the `Jupyter Notebook` login screen prompting for a password (in our case `jupyter`) should appear. Everything is now ready to start Python development in the browser via `Jupyter Lab`, via the `IPython`-based console, and via a terminal window or the text file editor. Other file management capabilities like file upload, deletion of files, or creation of folders are also available.

Cloud instances, like those from DigitalOcean, and `Jupyter Lab` (powered by the `Jupyter Notebook` server) are a powerful combination for the Python developer and algorithmic trading practitioner to work on and to make use of professional compute and storage infrastructure. Professional cloud and data center providers make sure that your (virtual) machines are physically secure and highly available. Using cloud instances also keeps the exploration and development phase at rather low costs since usage is generally charged by the hour without the need to enter long term agreements.

Conclusions

Python is the programming language and technology platform of choice not only for this book but also for almost every leading financial institution. However, Python deployment can be tricky at best and sometimes even tedious and nerve-wracking. Fortunately, technologies are available today—almost all of which are younger than ten years—that help with the deployment issue. The open source software `conda` helps with both Python package and virtual environment management. Docker containers go even further in that complete file systems and runtime environments can be easily created in a technically shielded "sandbox," or the *container*. Going even one step further, cloud providers like DigitalOcean offer compute and storage capacity in professionally managed and secured data centers within minutes and billed by the hour. This in combination with a Python 3.8 installation and a secure `Jupyter Note book/Lab` server installation provides a professional environment for Python development and deployment in the context of Python for algorithmic trading projects.

References and Further Resources

For *Python package management*, consult the following resources:

- `pip` package manager page (*https://pypi.python.org/pypi/pip*)
- `conda` package manager page (*http://conda.pydata.org*)
- official Installing Packages page (*https://packaging.python.org/installing*)

For *virtual environment management*, consult these resources:

- `virtualenv` environment manager page (*https://pypi.python.org/pypi/virtualenv*)
- `conda` Managing Environments page (*http://conda.pydata.org/docs/using/envs.html*)
- `pipenv` package and environment manager (*https://github.com/pypa/pipenv*)

Information about *Docker containers* can found, among other places, at the Docker home page (*http://docker.com*), as well as in the following:

- Matthias, Karl, and Sean Kane. 2018. *Docker: Up and Running.* 2nd ed. Sebastopol: O'Reilly.

Robbins (2016) provides a concise introduction to and overview of the `Bash` *scripting language*:

- Robbins, Arnold. 2016. *Bash Pocket Reference.* 2nd ed. Sebastopol: O'Reilly.

How to *run a public Jupyter Notebook/Lab server securely* is explained in The Jupyter Notebook Docs (*https://oreil.ly/uBEeq*). There is also `JupyterHub` available, which allows the management of multiple users for a `Jupyter Notebook` server (see JupyterHub (*https://oreil.ly/-XLi5*)).

To sign up on DigitalOcean with a 10 USD starting balance in your new account, visit *http://bit.ly/do_sign_up*. This pays for two months of usage for the smallest Droplet.

## CHAPTER 3

Working with Financial Data

Clearly, data beats algorithms. Without comprehensive data, you tend to get non-comprehensive predictions.

> —Rob Thomas (2016)

In algorithmic trading, one generally has to deal with four types of data, as illustrated in Table 3-1. Although it simplifies the financial data world, distinguishing data along the pairs *historical versus real-time* and *structured versus unstructured* often proves useful in technical settings.

Table 3-1. Types of financial data (examples)

	Structured	Unstructured
Historical	End-of-day closing prices	Financial news articles
Real-time	Bid/ask prices for FX	Posts on Twitter

This book is mainly concerned with *structured data* (numerical, tabular data) of both historical and real-time types. This chapter in particular focuses on historical, structured data, like end-of-day closing values for the SAP SE stock traded at the Frankfurt Stock Exchange. However, this category also subsumes intraday data, such as 1-minute-bar data for the Apple, Inc. stock traded at the NASDAQ stock exchange. The processing of real-time, structured data is covered in Chapter 7.

An algorithmic trading project typically starts with a trading idea or hypothesis that needs to be (back)tested based on historical financial data. This is the context for this chapter, the plan for which is as follows. "Reading Financial Data From Different Sources" on page 46 uses pandas to read data from different file- and web-based sources. "Working with Open Data Sources" on page 52 introduces Quandl (*http://quandl.com*) as a popular open data source platform. "Eikon Data API" on page 55 introduces the Python wrapper for the Refinitiv Eikon Data API. Finally, "Storing

Financial Data Efficiently" on page 65 briefly shows how to store historical, structured data efficiently with pandas based on the HDF5 (*http://hdfgroup.org*) binary storage format.

The goal for this chapter is to have available financial data in a format with which the backtesting of trading ideas and hypotheses can be implemented effectively. The three major themes are the importing of data, the handling of the data, and the storage of it. This and subsequent chapters assume a Python 3.8 installation with Python packages installed as explained in detail in Chapter 2. For the time being, it is not yet relevant on which infrastructure exactly this Python environment is provided. For more details on efficient input-output operations with Python, see Hilpisch (2018, ch. 9).

Reading Financial Data From Different Sources

This section makes heavy use of the capabilities of pandas, the popular data analysis package for Python (see pandas home page (*http://pandas.pydata.org*)). pandas comprehensively supports the three main tasks this chapter is concerned with: *reading data*, *handling data*, and *storing data*. One of its strengths is the reading of data from different types of sources, as the remainder of this section illustrates.

The Data Set

In this section, we work with a fairly small data set for the Apple Inc. stock price (with symbol AAPL and Reuters Instrument Code or RIC AAPL.O) as retrieved from the Eikon Data API for April 2020.

Since such historical financial data has been stored in a CSV file on disk, pure Python can be used to read and print its content:

```
In [1]: fn = '../data/AAPL.csv'  ❶

In [2]: with open(fn, 'r') as f:  ❶
            for _ in range(5):  ❷
                print(f.readline(), end='')  ❸
        Date,HIGH,CLOSE,LOW,OPEN,COUNT,VOLUME
        2020-04-01,248.72,240.91,239.13,246.5,460606.0,44054638.0
        2020-04-02,245.15,244.93,236.9,240.34,380294.0,41483493.0
        2020-04-03,245.7,241.41,238.9741,242.8,293699.0,32470017.0
        2020-04-06,263.11,262.47,249.38,250.9,486681.0,50455071.0
```

❶ Opens the file on disk (adjust path and filename if necessary).

❷ Sets up a for loop with five iterations.

❸ Prints the first five lines in the opened CSV file.

This approach allows for simple inspection of the data. One learns that there is a header line and that the single data points per row represent `Date`, `OPEN`, `HIGH`, `LOW`, `CLOSE`, `COUNT`, and `VOLUME`, respectively. However, the data is not yet available in memory for further usage with Python.

Reading from a CSV File with Python

To work with data stored as a CSV file, the file needs to be parsed and the data needs to be stored in a Python data structure. Python has a built-in module called `csv` that supports the reading of data from a CSV file. The first approach yields a `list` object containing other `list` objects with the data from the file:

```
In [3]: import csv   ❶

In [4]: csv_reader = csv.reader(open(fn, 'r'))   ❷

In [5]: data = list(csv_reader)   ❸

In [6]: data[:5]   ❹
Out[6]: [['Date', 'HIGH', 'CLOSE', 'LOW', 'OPEN', 'COUNT', 'VOLUME'],
         ['2020-04-01',
          '248.72',
          '240.91',
          '239.13',
          '246.5',
          '460606.0',
          '44054638.0'],
         ['2020-04-02',
          '245.15',
          '244.93',
          '236.9',
          '240.34',
          '380294.0',
          '41483493.0'],
         ['2020-04-03',
          '245.7',
          '241.41',
          '238.9741',
          '242.8',
          '293699.0',
          '32470017.0'],
         ['2020-04-06',
          '263.11',
          '262.47',
          '249.38',
          '250.9',
          '486681.0',
          '50455071.0']]
```

❶ Imports the `csv` module.

❷ Instantiates a `csv.reader` iterator object.

❸ A `list` comprehension adding every single line from the CSV file as a `list` object to the resulting `list` object.

❹ Prints out the first five elements of the `list` object.

Working with such a nested `list` object—for the calculation of the average closing price, for exammple—is possible in principle but not really efficient or intuitive. Using a `csv.DictReader` iterator object instead of the standard `csv.reader` object makes such tasks a bit more manageable. Every row of data in the CSV file (apart from the header row) is then imported as a `dict` object so that single values can be accessed via the respective key:

```
In [7]: csv_reader = csv.DictReader(open(fn, 'r'))   ❶

In [8]: data = list(csv_reader)

In [9]: data[:3]
Out[9]: [{'Date': '2020-04-01',
          'HIGH': '248.72',
          'CLOSE': '240.91',
          'LOW': '239.13',
          'OPEN': '246.5',
          'COUNT': '460606.0',
          'VOLUME': '44054638.0'},
         {'Date': '2020-04-02',
          'HIGH': '245.15',
          'CLOSE': '244.93',
          'LOW': '236.9',
          'OPEN': '240.34',
          'COUNT': '380294.0',
          'VOLUME': '41483493.0'},
         {'Date': '2020-04-03',
          'HIGH': '245.7',
          'CLOSE': '241.41',
          'LOW': '238.9741',
          'OPEN': '242.8',
          'COUNT': '293699.0',
          'VOLUME': '32470017.0'}]
```

❶ Here, the `csv.DictReader` iterator object is instantiated, which reads every data row into a `dict` object, given the information in the header row.

Based on the single `dict` objects, aggregations are now somewhat easier to accomplish. However, one still cannot speak of a convenient way of calculating the mean of the Apple closing stock price when inspecting the respective Python code:

```
In [10]: sum([float(l['CLOSE']) for l in data]) / len(data)  ❶
Out[10]: 272.38619047619045
```

❶ First, a `list` object is generated via a list comprehension with all closing values; second, the sum is taken over all these values; third, the resulting sum is divided by the number of closing values.

This is one of the major reasons why `pandas` has gained such popularity in the Python community. It makes the importing of data and the handling of, for example, financial time series data sets more convenient (and also often considerably faster) than pure Python.

Reading from a CSV File with pandas

From this point on, this section uses `pandas` to work with the Apple stock price data set. The major function used is `read_csv()`, which allows for a number of customizations via different parameters (see the `read_csv()` API reference (*https://oreil.ly/IAVfO*)). `read_csv()` yields as a result of the data reading procedure a `DataFrame` object, which is the central means of storing (tabular) data with `pandas`. The `DataFrame` class has many powerful methods that are particularly helpful in financial applications (refer to the `DataFrame` API reference (*https://oreil.ly/5-sNr*)):

```
In [11]: import pandas as pd  ❶

In [12]: data = pd.read_csv(fn, index_col=0,
                            parse_dates=True)  ❷

In [13]: data.info()  ❸
         <class 'pandas.core.frame.DataFrame'>
         DatetimeIndex: 21 entries, 2020-04-01 to 2020-04-30
         Data columns (total 6 columns):
          #   Column  Non-Null Count  Dtype
         ---  ------  --------------  -----
          0   HIGH    21 non-null     float64
          1   CLOSE   21 non-null     float64
          2   LOW     21 non-null     float64
          3   OPEN    21 non-null     float64
          4   COUNT   21 non-null     float64
          5   VOLUME  21 non-null     float64
         dtypes: float64(6)
         memory usage: 1.1 KB

In [14]: data.tail()  ❹
Out[14]:                HIGH    CLOSE    LOW    OPEN    COUNT    VOLUME
         Date
```

```
2020-04-24   283.01   282.97   277.00   277.20   306176.0   31627183.0
2020-04-27   284.54   283.17   279.95   281.80   300771.0   29271893.0
2020-04-28   285.83   278.58   278.20   285.08   285384.0   28001187.0
2020-04-29   289.67   287.73   283.89   284.73   324890.0   34320204.0
2020-04-30   294.53   293.80   288.35   289.96   471129.0   45765968.0
```

❶ The pandas package is imported.

❷ This imports the data from the CSV file, indicating that the first column shall be treated as the index column and letting the entries in that column be interpreted as date-time information.

❸ This method call prints out meta information regarding the resulting DataFrame object.

❹ The data.tail() method prints out by default the five most recent data rows.

Calculating the mean of the Apple stock closing values now is only a single method call:

```
In [15]: data['CLOSE'].mean()
Out[15]: 272.38619047619056
```

Chapter 4 introduces more functionality of pandas for the handling of financial data. For details on working with pandas and the powerful DataFrame class, also refer to the official pandas Documentation page (*https://oreil.ly/5PM-O*) and to McKinney (2017).

Although the Python standard library provides capabilities to read data from CSV files, pandas in general significantly simplifies and speeds up such operations. An additional benefit is that the data analysis capabilities of pandas are immediately available since read_csv() returns a DataFrame object.

Exporting to Excel and JSON

pandas also excels at exporting data stored in DataFrame objects when this data needs to be shared in a non-Python specific format. Apart from being able to export to CSV files, pandas also allows one to do the export in the form of Excel spreadsheet files as well as JSON files, both of which are popular data exchange formats in the financial industry. Such an exporting procedure typically needs a single method call only:

```
In [16]: data.to_excel('data/aapl.xls', 'AAPL')  ❶
```

```
In [17]: data.to_json('data/aapl.json')  ❷
```

```
In [18]: ls -n data/
```

```
total 24
-rw-r--r--  1 501  20  3067 Aug 25 11:47 aapl.json
-rw-r--r--  1 501  20  5632 Aug 25 11:47 aapl.xls
```

❶ Exports the data to an Excel spreadsheet file on disk.

❷ Exports the data to a JSON file on disk.

In particular when it comes to the interaction with Excel spreadsheet files, there are more elegant ways than just doing a data dump to a new file. xlwings, for example, is a powerful Python package that allows for an efficient and intelligent interaction between Python and Excel (visit the xlwings home page (*http://xlwings.org*)).

Reading from Excel and JSON

Now that the data is also available in the form of an Excel spreadsheet file and a JSON data file, pandas can read data from these sources, as well. The approach is as straightforward as with CSV files:

```
In [19]: data_copy_1 = pd.read_excel('data/aapl.xls', 'AAPL',
                                      index_col=0)  ❶

In [20]: data_copy_1.head()  ❷
Out[20]:             HIGH    CLOSE      LOW    OPEN   COUNT    VOLUME
         Date
         2020-04-01  248.72  240.91  239.1300  246.50  460606  44054638
         2020-04-02  245.15  244.93  236.9000  240.34  380294  41483493
         2020-04-03  245.70  241.41  238.9741  242.80  293699  32470017
         2020-04-06  263.11  262.47  249.3800  250.90  486681  50455071
         2020-04-07  271.70  259.43  259.0000  270.80  467375  50721831

In [21]: data_copy_2 = pd.read_json('data/aapl.json')  ❸

In [22]: data_copy_2.head()  ❹
Out[22]:             HIGH    CLOSE      LOW    OPEN   COUNT    VOLUME
         2020-04-01  248.72  240.91  239.1300  246.50  460606  44054638
         2020-04-02  245.15  244.93  236.9000  240.34  380294  41483493
         2020-04-03  245.70  241.41  238.9741  242.80  293699  32470017
         2020-04-06  263.11  262.47  249.3800  250.90  486681  50455071
         2020-04-07  271.70  259.43  259.0000  270.80  467375  50721831

In [23]: !rm data/*
```

❶ This reads the data from the Excel spreadsheet file to a new DataFrame object.

❷ The first five rows of the first in-memory copy of the data are printed.

❸ This reads the data from the JSON file to yet another `DataFrame` object.

❹ This then prints the first five rows of the second in-memory copy of the data.

`pandas` proves useful for reading and writing financial data from and to different types of data files. Often the reading might be tricky due to nonstandard storage formats (like a ";" instead of a "," as separator), but `pandas` generally provides the right set of parameter combinations to cope with such cases. Although all examples in this section use a small data set only, one can expect high performance input-output operations from `pandas` in the most important scenarios when the data sets are much larger.

Working with Open Data Sources

To a great extent, the attractiveness of the Python ecosystem stems from the fact that almost all packages available are open source and can be used for free. Financial analytics in general and algorithmic trading in particular, however, cannot live with open source software and algorithms alone; data also plays a vital role, as the quotation at the beginning of the chapter emphasizes. The previous section uses a small data set from a commercial data source. While there have been helpful open (financial) data sources available for some years (such as the ones provided by Yahoo! Finance or Google Finance), there are not too many left at the time of this writing in 2020. One of the more obvious reasons for this trend might be the ever-changing terms of data licensing agreements.

The one notable exception for the purposes of this book is Quandl (*http:// quandl.com*), a platform that aggregates a large number of open, as well as premium (i.e., to-be-paid-for) data sources. The data is provided via a unified API for which a Python wrapper package is available.

The Python wrapper package for the Quandl data API (see the Python wrapper page on Quandl (*https://oreil.ly/xRt5x*) and the GitHub page (*https://oreil.ly/LcJEo*) of the package) is installed with `conda` through `conda install quandl`. The first example shows how to retrieve historical average prices for the BTC/USD exchange rate since the introduction of Bitcoin as a cryptocurrency. With Quandl, requests always expect a combination of the *database* and the specific *data set* desired. (In the example, `BCHAIN` and `MKPRU`.) Such information can generally be looked up on the Quandl platform. For the example, the relevant page on Quandl is BCHAIN/MKPRU (*https:// oreil.ly/APwvn*).

By default, the `quandl` package returns a `pandas` `DataFrame` object. In the example, the `Value` column is also presented in annualized fashion (that is, with year end values). Note that the number shown for 2020 is the last available value in the data set (from May 2020) and not necessarily the year end value.

While a large part of the data sets on the Quandl platform are free, some of the free data sets require an API key. Such a key is required after a certain limit of free API calls too. Every user obtains such a key by signing up for a free Quandl account on the Quandl sign up page (*https://oreil.ly/sbh9j*). Data requests requiring an API key expect the key to be provided as the parameter api_key. In the example, the API key (which is found on the account settings page) is stored as a string in the variable quandl_api_key. The concrete value for the key is read from a configuration file via the configparser module:

```
In [24]: import configparser
         config = configparser.ConfigParser()
         config.read('../pyalgo.cfg')
Out[24]: ['../pyalgo.cfg']

In [25]: import quandl as q  ❶

In [26]: data = q.get('BCHAIN/MKPRU', api_key=config['quandl']['api_key'])  ❷

In [27]: data.info()
         <class 'pandas.core.frame.DataFrame'>
         DatetimeIndex: 4254 entries, 2009-01-03 to 2020-08-26
         Data columns (total 1 columns):
          #   Column  Non-Null Count  Dtype
         ---  ------  --------------  -----
          0   Value   4254 non-null   float64
         dtypes: float64(1)
         memory usage: 66.5 KB

In [28]: data['Value'].resample('A').last()  ❸
Out[28]: Date
         2009-12-31        0.000000
         2010-12-31        0.299999
         2011-12-31        4.995000
         2012-12-31       13.590000
         2013-12-31      731.000000
         2014-12-31      317.400000
         2015-12-31      428.000000
         2016-12-31      952.150000
         2017-12-31    13215.574000
         2018-12-31     3832.921667
         2019-12-31     7385.360000
         2020-12-31    11763.930000
         Freq: A-DEC, Name: Value, dtype: float64
```

❶ Imports the Python wrapper package for Quandl.

❷ Reads historical data for the BTC/USD exchange rate.

❸ Selects the `Value` column, resamples it—from the originally *daily* values to *yearly* values—and defines the last available observation to be the relevant one.

Quandl also provides, for example, diverse data sets for single stocks, like end-of-day stock prices, stock fundamentals, or data sets related to options traded on a certain stock:

```
In [29]: data = q.get('FSE/SAP_X', start_date='2018-1-1',
                       end_date='2020-05-01',
                       api_key=config['quandl']['api_key'])
```

```
In [30]: data.info()
         <class 'pandas.core.frame.DataFrame'>
         DatetimeIndex: 579 entries, 2018-01-02 to 2020-04-30
         Data columns (total 10 columns):
          #   Column              Non-Null Count  Dtype
         ---  ------              --------------  -----
          0   Open                257 non-null    float64
          1   High                579 non-null    float64
          2   Low                 579 non-null    float64
          3   Close               579 non-null    float64
          4   Change              0 non-null      object
          5   Traded Volume       533 non-null    float64
          6   Turnover            533 non-null    float64
          7   Last Price of the Day  0 non-null   object
          8   Daily Traded Units  0 non-null      object
          9   Daily Turnover      0 non-null      object
         dtypes: float64(6), object(4)
         memory usage: 49.8+ KB
```

The API key can also be configured permanently with the Python wrapper via the following:

```
q.ApiConfig.api_key = 'YOUR_API_KEY'
```

The Quandl platform also offers premium data sets for which a subscription or fee is required. Most of these data sets offer free samples. The example retrieves option implied volatilities for the Microsoft Corp. stock. The free sample data set is quite large, with more than 4,100 rows and many columns (only a subset is shown). The last lines of code display the 30, 60, and 90 days implied volatility values for the five most recent days available:

```
In [31]: q.ApiConfig.api_key = config['quandl']['api_key']
```

```
In [32]: vol = q.get('VOL/MSFT')
```

```
In [33]: vol.iloc[:, :10].info()
         <class 'pandas.core.frame.DataFrame'>
         DatetimeIndex: 1006 entries, 2015-01-02 to 2018-12-31
         Data columns (total 10 columns):
          #   Column  Non-Null Count   Dtype
         ---  ------  --------------   -----
          0   Hv10    1006 non-null    float64
          1   Hv20    1006 non-null    float64
          2   Hv30    1006 non-null    float64
          3   Hv60    1006 non-null    float64
          4   Hv90    1006 non-null    float64
          5   Hv120   1006 non-null    float64
          6   Hv150   1006 non-null    float64
          7   Hv180   1006 non-null    float64
          8   Phv10   1006 non-null    float64
          9   Phv20   1006 non-null    float64
         dtypes: float64(10)
         memory usage: 86.5 KB

In [34]: vol[['IvMean30', 'IvMean60', 'IvMean90']].tail()
Out[34]:            IvMean30   IvMean60   IvMean90
         Date
         2018-12-24   0.4310     0.4112     0.3829
         2018-12-26   0.4059     0.3844     0.3587
         2018-12-27   0.3918     0.3879     0.3618
         2018-12-28   0.3940     0.3736     0.3482
         2018-12-31   0.3760     0.3519     0.3310
```

This concludes the overview of the Python wrapper package quandl for the Quandl data API. The Quandl platform and service is growing rapidly and proves to be a valuable source for financial data in an algorithmic trading context.

 Open source software is a trend that started many years ago. It has lowered the barriers to entry in many areas and also in algorithmic trading. A new, reinforcing trend in this regard is open data sources. In some cases, such as with Quandl, they even provide high quality data sets. It cannot be expected that open data will completely replace professional data subscriptions any time soon, but they represent a valuable means to get started with algorithmic trading in a cost efficient manner.

Eikon Data API

Open data sources are a blessing for algorithmic traders wanting to get started in the space and wanting to be able to quickly test hypotheses and ideas based on real financial data sets. Sooner or later, however, open data sets will not suffice anymore to satisfy the requirements of more ambitious traders and professionals.

Refinitiv (*http://refinitiv.com*) is one of the biggest financial data and news providers in the world. Its current desktop flagship product is Eikon (*https://oreil.ly/foYNk*), which is the equivalent to the Terminal (*https://oreil.ly/kMJl7*) by Bloomberg, the major competitor in the data services field. Figure 3-1 shows a screenshot of Eikon in the browser-based version. Eikon provides access to petabytes of data via a single access point.

Figure 3-1. Browser version of Eikon terminal

Recently, Refinitiv have streamlined their API landscape and have released a Python wrapper package, called `eikon`, for the Eikon data API, which is installed via `pip install eikon`. If you have a subscription to the Refinitiv Eikon data services, you can use the Python package to programmatically retrieve historical data, as well as streaming structured and unstructured data, from the unified API. A technical pre-requisite is that a local desktop application is running that provides a desktop API session. The latest such desktop application at the time of this writing is called Work-space (see Figure 3-2).

If you are an Eikon subscriber and have an account for the Developer Community pages (*https://oreil.ly/xowdi*), you will find an overview of the Python Eikon Scripting Library under Quick Start (*https://oreil.ly/7dnQx*).

Figure 3-2. Workspace application with desktop API services

In order to use the Eikon Data API, the Eikon `app_key` needs to be set. You get it via the App Key Generator (`APPKEY`) application in either Eikon or Workspace:

```
In [35]: import eikon as ek    ❶

In [36]: ek.set_app_key(config['eikon']['app_key'])    ❷

In [37]: help(ek)    ❸
         Help on package eikon:

         NAME
             eikon - # coding: utf-8

         PACKAGE CONTENTS
             Profile
             data_grid
             eikonError
             json_requests
             news_request
             streaming_session (package)
             symbology
             time_series
             tools

         SUBMODULES
             cache
             desktop_session
             istream_callback
```

```
                    itemstream
                    session
                    stream
                    stream_connection
                    streamingprice
                    streamingprice_callback
                    streamingprices

                VERSION
                    1.1.5

                FILE

                    /Users/yves/Python/envs/py38/lib/python3.8/site-packages/eikon/__init__
                .py
```

❶ Imports the eikon package as ek.

❷ Sets the app_key.

❸ Shows the help text for the main module.

Retrieving Historical Structured Data

The retrieval of historical financial time series data is as straightforward as with the other wrappers used before:

```
In [39]: symbols = ['AAPL.O', 'MSFT.O', 'GOOG.O']   ❶

In [40]: data = ek.get_timeseries(symbols,   ❷
                                  start_date='2020-01-01',   ❸
                                  end_date='2020-05-01',   ❹
                                  interval='daily',   ❺
                                  fields=['*'])   ❻

In [41]: data.keys()   ❼
Out[41]: MultiIndex([('AAPL.O',    'HIGH'),
                     ('AAPL.O',   'CLOSE'),
                     ('AAPL.O',     'LOW'),
                     ('AAPL.O',    'OPEN'),
                     ('AAPL.O',   'COUNT'),
                     ('AAPL.O',  'VOLUME'),
                     ('MSFT.O',    'HIGH'),
                     ('MSFT.O',   'CLOSE'),
                     ('MSFT.O',     'LOW'),
                     ('MSFT.O',    'OPEN'),
                     ('MSFT.O',   'COUNT'),
                     ('MSFT.O',  'VOLUME'),
                     ('GOOG.O',    'HIGH'),
                     ('GOOG.O',   'CLOSE'),
```

```
              ('GOOG.O',    'LOW'),
              ('GOOG.O',   'OPEN'),
              ('GOOG.O',  'COUNT'),
              ('GOOG.O', 'VOLUME')],
             )

In [42]: type(data['AAPL.O'])  ❽
Out[42]: pandas.core.frame.DataFrame

In [43]: data['AAPL.O'].info()  ❾
         <class 'pandas.core.frame.DataFrame'>
         DatetimeIndex: 84 entries, 2020-01-02 to 2020-05-01
         Data columns (total 6 columns):
          #   Column  Non-Null Count  Dtype
         ---  ------  --------------  -----
          0   HIGH    84 non-null     float64
          1   CLOSE   84 non-null     float64
          2   LOW     84 non-null     float64
          3   OPEN    84 non-null     float64
          4   COUNT   84 non-null     Int64
          5   VOLUME  84 non-null     Int64
         dtypes: Int64(2), float64(4)
         memory usage: 4.8 KB

In [44]: data['AAPL.O'].tail()  ❿
Out[44]:              HIGH   CLOSE    LOW    OPEN   COUNT    VOLUME
         Date
         2020-04-27  284.54  283.17  279.95  281.80  300771  29271893
         2020-04-28  285.83  278.58  278.20  285.08  285384  28001187
         2020-04-29  289.67  287.73  283.89  284.73  324890  34320204
         2020-04-30  294.53  293.80  288.35  289.96  471129  45765968
         2020-05-01  299.00  289.07  285.85  286.25  558319  60154175
```

❶ Defines a few symbols as a list object.

❷ The central line of code that retrieves data for the first symbol…

❸ …for the given start date and…

❹ …the given end date.

❺ The time interval is here chosen to be daily.

❻ All fields are requested.

❼ The function get_timeseries() returns a multi-index DataFrame object.

❽ The values corresponding to each level are regular DataFrame objects.

❾ This provides an overview of the data stored in the `DataFrame` object.

❿ The final five rows of data are shown.

The beauty of working with a professional data service API becomes evident when one wishes to work with multiple symbols and in particular with a different granularity of the financial data (that is, other time intervals):

```
In [45]: %%time
         data = ek.get_timeseries(symbols,   ❶
                                  start_date='2020-08-14',   ❷
                                  end_date='2020-08-15',   ❸
                                  interval='minute',   ❹
                                  fields='*')
         CPU times: user 58.2 ms, sys: 3.16 ms, total: 61.4 ms
         Wall time: 2.02 s

In [46]: print(data['GOOG.O'].loc['2020-08-14 16:00:00':
                                  '2020-08-14 16:04:00'])   ❺

                          HIGH       LOW       OPEN      CLOSE   COUNT VOLUME
         Date

         2020-08-14 16:00:00  1510.7439  1509.220  1509.940  1510.5239     48   1362
         2020-08-14 16:01:00  1511.2900  1509.980  1510.500  1511.2900     52   1002
         2020-08-14 16:02:00  1513.0000  1510.964  1510.964  1512.8600     72   1762
         2020-08-14 16:03:00  1513.6499  1512.160  1512.990  1513.2300    108   4534
         2020-08-14 16:04:00  1513.6500  1511.540  1513.418  1512.7100     40   1364

In [47]: for sym in symbols:
             print('\n' + sym + '\n', data[sym].iloc[-300:-295])   ❻

         AAPL.O
                          HIGH       LOW       OPEN     CLOSE  COUNT   VOLUME
         Date
         2020-08-14 19:01:00  457.1699  456.6300   457.14  456.83   1457   104693
         2020-08-14 19:02:00  456.9399  456.4255   456.81  456.45   1178    79740
         2020-08-14 19:03:00  456.8199  456.4402   456.45  456.67    908    68517
         2020-08-14 19:04:00  456.9800  456.6100   456.67  456.97    665    53649
         2020-08-14 19:05:00  457.1900  456.9300   456.98  457.00    679    49636

         MSFT.O
                          HIGH       LOW       OPEN     CLOSE  COUNT VOLUME
         Date

         2020-08-14 19:01:00  208.6300  208.5083  208.5500  208.5674    333   21368
         2020-08-14 19:02:00  208.5750  208.3550  208.5501  208.3600    513   37270
         2020-08-14 19:03:00  208.4923  208.3000  208.3600  208.4000    303   23903
         2020-08-14 19:04:00  208.4200  208.3301  208.3901  208.4099    222   15861
         2020-08-14 19:05:00  208.4699  208.3600  208.3920  208.4069    235    9569
```

```
GOOG.O
                          HIGH        LOW       OPEN     CLOSE   COUNT VOLUME
Date

2020-08-14 19:01:00  1510.42  1509.3288  1509.5100  1509.8550     47   1577
2020-08-14 19:02:00  1510.30  1508.8000  1509.7559  1508.8647     71   2950
2020-08-14 19:03:00  1510.21  1508.7200  1508.7200  1509.8100     33    603
2020-08-14 19:04:00  1510.21  1508.7200  1509.8800  1509.8299     41    934
2020-08-14 19:05:00  1510.21  1508.7300  1509.5500  1509.6600     30    445
```

❶ Data is retrieved for all symbols at once.

❷ The time interval…

❸ …is drastically shortened.

❹ The function call retrieves minute bars for the symbols.

❺ Prints five rows from the Google, LLC, data set.

❻ Prints three data rows from every DataFrame object.

The preceding code illustrates how convenient it is to retrieve historical financial time series data from the Eikon API with Python. By default, the function get_times eries() provides the following options for the interval parameter: tick, minute, hour, daily, weekly, monthly, quarterly, and yearly. This gives all the flexibility needed in an algorithmic trading context, particularly when combined with the resampling capabilities of pandas as shown in the following code:

```
In [48]: %%time
         data = ek.get_timeseries(symbols[0],
                          start_date='2020-08-14 15:00:00',   ❶
                          end_date='2020-08-14 15:30:00',     ❷
                          interval='tick',                    ❸
                          fields=['*'])
         CPU times: user 257 ms, sys: 17.3 ms, total: 274 ms
         Wall time: 2.31 s

In [49]: data.info()   ❹
         <class 'pandas.core.frame.DataFrame'>
         DatetimeIndex: 47346 entries, 2020-08-14 15:00:00.019000 to 2020-08-14
          15:29:59.987000
         Data columns (total 2 columns):
          #   Column  Non-Null Count  Dtype
         ---  ------  --------------  -----
          0   VALUE   47311 non-null  float64
          1   VOLUME  47346 non-null  Int64
         dtypes: Int64(1), float64(1)
         memory usage: 1.1 MB
```

```
In [50]: data.head()  ❺
Out[50]:                        VALUE   VOLUME
         Date
         2020-08-14 15:00:00.019  453.2499      60
         2020-08-14 15:00:00.036  453.2294       3
         2020-08-14 15:00:00.146  453.2100       5
         2020-08-14 15:00:00.146  453.2100     100
         2020-08-14 15:00:00.236  453.2100       2

In [51]: resampled = data.resample('30s', label='right').agg(
                     {'VALUE': 'last', 'VOLUME': 'sum'})  ❻

In [52]: resampled.tail()  ❼
Out[52]:                     VALUE   VOLUME
         Date
         2020-08-14 15:28:00  453.9000    29746
         2020-08-14 15:28:30  454.2869    86441
         2020-08-14 15:29:00  454.3900    49513
         2020-08-14 15:29:30  454.7550    98520
         2020-08-14 15:30:00  454.6200    55592
```

❶ A time interval of…

❷ …one hour is chosen (due to data retrieval limits).

❸ The interval parameter is set to tick.

❹ Close to 50,000 price ticks are retrieved for the interval.

❺ The time series data set shows highly irregular (heterogeneous) interval lengths between two ticks.

❻ The tick data is resampled to a 30 second interval length (by taking the last value and the sum, respectively)…

❼ …which is reflected in the DatetimeIndex of the new DataFrame object.

Retrieving Historical Unstructured Data

A major strength of working with the Eikon API via Python is the easy retrieval of unstructured data, which can then be parsed and analyzed with Python packages for natural language processing (NLP). Such a procedure is as simple and straightforward as for financial time series data.

The code that follows retrieves news headlines for a fixed time interval that includes Apple Inc. as a company and "Macbook" as a word. The five most recent hits are displayed as a maximum:

```
In [53]: headlines = ek.get_news_headlines(query='R:AAPL.O macbook',   ❶
                                            count=5,   ❷
                                            date_from='2020-4-1',   ❸
                                            date_to='2020-5-1')   ❹

In [54]: headlines   ❺
Out[54]:                                         versionCreated  \
         2020-04-20 21:33:37.332 2020-04-20 21:33:37.332000+00:00
         2020-04-20 10:20:23.201 2020-04-20 10:20:23.201000+00:00
         2020-04-20 02:32:27.721 2020-04-20 02:32:27.721000+00:00
         2020-04-15 12:06:58.693 2020-04-15 12:06:58.693000+00:00
         2020-04-09 21:34:08.671 2020-04-09 21:34:08.671000+00:00


                                                          text  \
         2020-04-20 21:33:37.332  Apple said to launch new AirPods, MacBook Pro ...
         2020-04-20 10:20:23.201  Apple might launch upgraded AirPods, 13-inch M...
         2020-04-20 02:32:27.721  Apple to reportedly launch new AirPods alongsi...
         2020-04-15 12:06:58.693  Apple files a patent for iPhones, MacBook indu...
         2020-04-09 21:34:08.671  Apple rolls out new software update for MacBoo...


                                                       storyId  \
         2020-04-20 21:33:37.332  urn:newsml:reuters.com:20200420:nNRAble9rq:1
         2020-04-20 10:20:23.201  urn:newsml:reuters.com:20200420:nNRAbl8eob:1
         2020-04-20 02:32:27.721  urn:newsml:reuters.com:20200420:nNRAbl4mfz:1
         2020-04-15 12:06:58.693  urn:newsml:reuters.com:20200415:nNRAbjvsix:1
         2020-04-09 21:34:08.671  urn:newsml:reuters.com:20200409:nNRAbi2nbb:1


                                  sourceCode
         2020-04-20 21:33:37.332   NS:TIMIND
         2020-04-20 10:20:23.201   NS:BUSSTA
         2020-04-20 02:32:27.721   NS:HINDUT
         2020-04-15 12:06:58.693   NS:HINDUT
         2020-04-09 21:34:08.671   NS:TIMIND

In [55]: story = headlines.iloc[0]   ❻

In [56]: story   ❼
Out[56]: versionCreated                 2020-04-20 21:33:37.332000+00:00
         text              Apple said to launch new AirPods, MacBook Pro ...
         storyId           urn:newsml:reuters.com:20200420:nNRAble9rq:1
         sourceCode                                            NS:TIMIND
         Name: 2020-04-20 21:33:37.332000, dtype: object

In [57]: news_text = ek.get_news_story(story['storyId'])   ❽

In [58]: from IPython.display import HTML   ❾
```

```
In [59]: HTML(news_text)  ❿
Out[59]: <IPython.core.display.HTML object>
```

NEW DELHI: Apple recently launched its much-awaited affordable smartphone
iPhone SE. Now it seems that the company is gearing up for another launch.
Apple is said to launch the next generation of AirPods and the all-new
13-inch MacBook Pro next month.

In February an online report revealed that the Cupertino-based tech giant
is working on AirPods Pro Lite. Now a tweet by tipster Job Posser has
revealed that Apple will soon come up with new AirPods and MacBook Pro.
Jon Posser tweeted, "New AirPods (which were supposed to be at the
March Event) is now ready to go.

Probably alongside the MacBook Pro next month." However, not many details
about the upcoming products are available right now. The company was
supposed to launch these products at the March event along with the iPhone SE.

But due to the ongoing pandemic coronavirus, the event got cancelled.
It is expected that Apple will launch the AirPods Pro Lite and the 13-inch
MacBook Pro just like the way it launched the iPhone SE. Meanwhile,
Apple has scheduled its annual developer conference WWDC to take place in June.

This year the company has decided to hold an online-only event due to
the outbreak of coronavirus. Reports suggest that this year the company
is planning to launch the all-new AirTags and a premium pair of over-ear
Bluetooth headphones at the event. Using the Apple AirTags, users will
be able to locate real-world items such as keys or suitcase in the Find My app.

The AirTags will also have offline finding capabilities that the company
introduced in the core of iOS 13. Apart from this, Apple is also said to
unveil its high-end Bluetooth headphones. It is expected that the Bluetooth
headphones will offer better sound quality and battery backup as compared
to the AirPods.

For Reprint Rights: timescontent.com

Copyright (c) 2020 BENNETT, COLEMAN & CO.LTD.

❶ The query parameter for the retrieval operation.

❷ Sets the maximum number of hits to five.

❸ Defines the interval…

❹ …for which to look for news headlines.

❺ Gives out the results object (output shortened).

❻ One particular headline is picked…

---

❼ …and the `story_id` shown.

❽ This retrieves the news text as html code.

❾ In `Jupyter Notebook`, for example, the html code…

❿ …can be rendered for better reading.

This concludes the illustration of the Python wrapper package for the Refinitiv Eikon data API.

Storing Financial Data Efficiently

In algorithmic trading, one of the most important scenarios for the management of data sets is "retrieve once, use multiple times." Or from an input-output (IO) perspective, it is "write once, read multiple times." In the first case, data might be retrieved from a web service and then used to backtest a strategy multiple times based on a temporary, in-memory copy of the data set. In the second case, tick data that is received continually is written to disk and later on again used multiple times for certain manipulations (like aggregations) in combination with a backtesting procedure.

This section assumes that the in-memory data structure to store the data is a `pandas` `DataFrame` object, no matter from which source the data is acquired (from a CSV file, a web service, etc.).

To have a somewhat meaningful data set available in terms of size, the section uses a sample financial data set generated by the use of pseudorandom numbers. "Python Scripts" on page 78 presents the Python module with a function called `generate_sam ple_data()` that accomplishes the task.

In principle, this function generates a sample financial data set in tabular form of arbitrary size (available memory, of course, sets a limit):

```
In [60]: from sample_data import generate_sample_data  ❶

In [61]: print(generate_sample_data(rows=5, cols=4))  ❷
                                   No0         No1         No2         No3
         2021-01-01 00:00:00  100.000000  100.000000  100.000000  100.000000
         2021-01-01 00:01:00  100.019641   99.950661  100.052993   99.913841
         2021-01-01 00:02:00   99.998164   99.796667  100.109971   99.955398
         2021-01-01 00:03:00  100.051537   99.660550  100.136336  100.024150
         2021-01-01 00:04:00   99.984614   99.729158  100.210888   99.976584
```

❶ Imports the function from the Python script.

❷ Prints a sample financial data set with five rows and four columns.

Storing DataFrame Objects

The storage of a pandas `DataFrame` object as a whole is made simple by the pandas `HDFStore` wrapper functionality for the HDF5 (*http://hdfgroup.org*) binary storage standard. It allows one to dump complete `DataFrame` objects in a single step to a file-based database object. To illustrate the implementation, the first step is to create a sample data set of meaningful size. Here the size of the `DataFrame` generated is about 420 MB:

```
In [62]: %time data = generate_sample_data(rows=5e6, cols=10).round(4)    ❶
         CPU times: user 3.88 s, sys: 830 ms, total: 4.71 s
         Wall time: 4.72 s

In [63]: data.info()
         <class 'pandas.core.frame.DataFrame'>
         DatetimeIndex: 5000000 entries, 2021-01-01 00:00:00 to 2030-07-05
          05:19:00
         Freq: T
         Data columns (total 10 columns):
          #   Column  Dtype
         ---  ------  -----
          0   No0     float64
          1   No1     float64
          2   No2     float64
          3   No3     float64
          4   No4     float64
          5   No5     float64
          6   No6     float64
          7   No7     float64
          8   No8     float64
          9   No9     float64
         dtypes: float64(10)
         memory usage: 419.6 MB
```

❶ A sample financial data set with 5,000,000 rows and ten columns is generated; the generation takes a couple of seconds.

The second step is to open a `HDFStore` object (that is, a HDF5 database file) on disk and to write the `DataFrame` object to it.[1] The size on disk of about 440 MB is a bit larger than for the in-memory `DataFrame` object. However, the writing speed is about five times faster than the in-memory generation of the sample data set.

---

1 Of course, multiple `DataFrame` objects could also be stored in a single `HDFStore` object.

Working in Python with binary stores like HDF5 database files usually gets you writing speeds close to the theoretical maximum of the hardware available:[2]

```
In [64]: h5 = pd.HDFStore('data/data.h5', 'w')   ❶

In [65]: %time h5['data'] = data   ❷
         CPU times: user 356 ms, sys: 472 ms, total: 828 ms
         Wall time: 1.08 s

In [66]: h5   ❸
Out[66]: <class 'pandas.io.pytables.HDFStore'>
         File path: data/data.h5

In [67]: ls -n data/data.*
         -rw-r--r--@ 1 501  20  440007240 Aug 25 11:48 data/data.h5

In [68]: h5.close()   ❹
```

❶ This opens the database file on disk for writing (and overwrites a potentially existing file with the same name).

❷ Writing the DataFrame object to disk takes less than a second.

❸ This prints out meta information for the database file.

❹ This closes the database file.

The third step is to read the data from the file-based HDFStore object. Reading also generally takes place close to the theoretical maximum speed:

```
In [69]: h5 = pd.HDFStore('data/data.h5', 'r')   ❶

In [70]: %time data_copy = h5['data']   ❷
         CPU times: user 388 ms, sys: 425 ms, total: 813 ms
         Wall time: 812 ms

In [71]: data_copy.info()
         <class 'pandas.core.frame.DataFrame'>
         DatetimeIndex: 5000000 entries, 2021-01-01 00:00:00 to 2030-07-05
          05:19:00
         Freq: T
         Data columns (total 10 columns):
          #   Column  Dtype
         ---  ------  -----
          0   No0     float64
          1   No1     float64
```

---

2 All values reported here are from the author's MacMini with Intel i7 hexa core processor (12 threads), 32 GB of random access memory (DDR4 RAM), and a 512 GB solid state drive (SSD).

```
          2    No2    float64
          3    No3    float64
          4    No4    float64
          5    No5    float64
          6    No6    float64
          7    No7    float64
          8    No8    float64
          9    No9    float64
         dtypes: float64(10)
         memory usage: 419.6 MB

In [72]: h5.close()

In [73]: rm data/data.h5
```

❶ Opens the database file for reading.

❷ Reading takes less than half of a second.

There is another, somewhat more flexible way of writing the data from a `DataFrame` object to an `HDFStore` object. To this end, one can use the `to_hdf()` method of the `DataFrame` object and set the `format` parameter to `table` (see the `to_hdf` API reference page (*https://oreil.ly/uu0_j*)). This allows the appending of new data to the `table` object on disk and also, for example, the searching over the data on disk, which is not possible with the first approach. The price to pay is slower writing and reading speeds:

```
In [74]: %time data.to_hdf('data/data.h5', 'data', format='table')   ❶
         CPU times: user 3.25 s, sys: 491 ms, total: 3.74 s
         Wall time: 3.8 s

In [75]: ls -n data/data.*
         -rw-r--r--@ 1 501  20  446911563 Aug 25 11:48 data/data.h5

In [76]: %time data_copy = pd.read_hdf('data/data.h5', 'data')   ❷
         CPU times: user 236 ms, sys: 266 ms, total: 502 ms
         Wall time: 503 ms

In [77]: data_copy.info()
         <class 'pandas.core.frame.DataFrame'>
         DatetimeIndex: 5000000 entries, 2021-01-01 00:00:00 to 2030-07-05
          05:19:00
         Freq: T
         Data columns (total 10 columns):
          #    Column  Dtype
         ---   ------  -----
          0    No0     float64
          1    No1     float64
          2    No2     float64
          3    No3     float64
          4    No4     float64
```

```
5    No5    float64
6    No6    float64
7    No7    float64
8    No8    float64
9    No9    float64
dtypes: float64(10)
memory usage: 419.6 MB
```

❶ This defines the writing format to be of type `table`. Writing becomes slower since this format type involves a bit more overhead and leads to a somewhat increased file size.

❷ Reading is also slower in this application scenario.

In practice, the advantage of this approach is that one can work with the `table_frame` object on disk like with any other `table` object of the `PyTables` package that is used by `pandas` in this context. This provides access to certain basic capabilities of the PyTables (*http://pytables.org*) package, such as appending rows to a `table` object:

```
In [78]: import tables as tb   ❶

In [79]: h5 = tb.open_file('data/data.h5', 'r')   ❷

In [80]: h5   ❸
Out[80]: File(filename=data/data.h5, title='', mode='r', root_uep='/',
             filters=Filters(complevel=0, shuffle=False, bitshuffle=False,
             fletcher32=False, least_significant_digit=None))
         / (RootGroup) ''
         /data (Group) ''
         /data/table (Table(5000000,)) ''
           description := {
           "index": Int64Col(shape=(), dflt=0, pos=0),
           "values_block_0": Float64Col(shape=(10,), dflt=0.0, pos=1)}
           byteorder := 'little'
           chunkshape := (2978,)
           autoindex := True
           colindexes := {
             "index": Index(6, medium, shuffle, zlib(1)).is_csi=False}

In [81]: h5.root.data.table[:3]   ❹
Out[81]: array([(1609459200000000000, [100.     , 100.    , 100.    , 100.    ,
             100.    , 100.    , 100.    , 100.    , 100.    , 100.    ]),
             (1609459260000000000, [100.0752, 100.1164, 100.0224, 100.0073,
             100.1142, 100.0474,  99.9329, 100.0254, 100.1009, 100.066 ]),
             (1609459320000000000, [100.1593, 100.1721, 100.0519, 100.0933,
             100.1578, 100.0301,  99.92  , 100.0965, 100.1441, 100.0717])],
             dtype=[('index', '<i8'), ('values_block_0', '<f8', (10,))])

In [82]: h5.close()   ❺

In [83]: rm data/data.h5
```

❶ Imports the `PyTables` package.

❷ Opens the database file for reading.

❸ Shows the contents of the database file.

❹ Prints the first three rows in the table.

❺ Closes the database.

Although this second approach provides *more* flexibility, it does not open the doors to the full capabilities of the `PyTables` package. Nevertheless, the two approaches introduced in this sub-section are convenient and efficient when you are working with more or less *immutable data sets that fit into memory*. Nowadays, algorithmic trading, however, has to deal in general with continuously and rapidly growing data sets like, for example, tick data with regard to stock prices or foreign exchange rates. To cope with the requirements of such a scenario, alternative approaches might prove useful.

 Using the `HDFStore` wrapper for the HDF5 binary storage standard, `pandas` is able to write and read financial data almost at the maximum speed the available hardware allows. Exports to other file-based formats, like CSV, are generally much slower alternatives.

Using TsTables

The `PyTables` package, with the import name `tables`, is a wrapper for the HDF5 binary storage library that is also used by `pandas` for its `HDFStore` implementation presented in the previous sub-section. The `TsTables` package (see the GitHub page for the package (*https://oreil.ly/VGPas*)) in turn is dedicated to the efficient handling of large financial time series data sets based on the HDF5 binary storage library. It is effectively an enhancement of the `PyTables` package and adds support for time series data to its capabilities. It implements a hierarchical storage approach that allows for a fast retrieval of data sub-sets selected by providing start and end dates and times, respectively. The major scenario supported by `TsTables` is "write once, retrieve multiple times."

The setup illustrated in this sub-section is that data is continuously collected from a web source, professional data provider, etc. and is stored interim and in-memory in a `DataFrame` object. After a while or a certain number of data points retrieved, the collected data is then stored in a `TsTables table` object in an HDF5 database.

First, here is the generation of the sample data:

```
In [84]: %%time
         data = generate_sample_data(rows=2.5e6, cols=5,
                                     freq='1s').round(4)  ❶
         CPU times: user 915 ms, sys: 191 ms, total: 1.11 s
         Wall time: 1.14 s

In [85]: data.info()
         <class 'pandas.core.frame.DataFrame'>
         DatetimeIndex: 2500000 entries, 2021-01-01 00:00:00 to 2021-01-29
          22:26:39
         Freq: S
         Data columns (total 5 columns):
          #   Column  Dtype
         ---  ------  -----
          0   No0     float64
          1   No1     float64
          2   No2     float64
          3   No3     float64
          4   No4     float64
         dtypes: float64(5)
         memory usage: 114.4 MB
```

❶ This generates a sample financial data set with 2,500,000 rows and five columns with a one second frequency; the sample data is rounded to two digits.

Second, some more imports and the creation of the TsTables table object. The major part is the definition of the desc class, which provides the description for the table object's data structure:

 Currently, TsTables only works with the old pandas version 0.19. A friendly fork, working with newer versions of pandas is available under *http://github.com/yhilpisch/tstables* which can be installed with the following:

```
pip install git+https://github.com/yhilpisch/tstables.git
```

```
In [86]: import tstables  ❶

In [87]: import tables as tb  ❷

In [88]: class desc(tb.IsDescription):
             ''' Description of TsTables table structure.
             '''
             timestamp = tb.Int64Col(pos=0)  ❸
             No0 = tb.Float64Col(pos=1)  ❹
             No1 = tb.Float64Col(pos=2)
             No2 = tb.Float64Col(pos=3)
             No3 = tb.Float64Col(pos=4)
```

```
         No4 = tb.Float64Col(pos=5)
```

In [89]: h5 = tb.open_file('data/data.h5ts', 'w') ❺

In [90]: ts = h5.create_ts('/', 'data', desc) ❻

In [91]: h5 ❼
Out[91]: File(filename=data/data.h5ts, title='', mode='w', root_uep='/',
           filters=Filters(complevel=0, shuffle=False, bitshuffle=False,
           fletcher32=False, least_significant_digit=None))
         / (RootGroup) ''
         /data (Group/Timeseries) ''
         /data/y2020 (Group) ''
         /data/y2020/m08 (Group) ''
         /data/y2020/m08/d25 (Group) ''
         /data/y2020/m08/d25/ts_data (Table(0,)) ''
           description := {
           "timestamp": Int64Col(shape=(), dflt=0, pos=0),
           "No0": Float64Col(shape=(), dflt=0.0, pos=1),
           "No1": Float64Col(shape=(), dflt=0.0, pos=2),
           "No2": Float64Col(shape=(), dflt=0.0, pos=3),
           "No3": Float64Col(shape=(), dflt=0.0, pos=4),
           "No4": Float64Col(shape=(), dflt=0.0, pos=5)}
           byteorder := 'little'
           chunkshape := (1365,)
```

❶  TsTables (installed from *https://github.com/yhilpisch/tstables*)...

❷  ...PyTables are imported.

❸  The first column of the table is a timestamp represented as an int value.

❹  All data columns contain float values.

❺  This opens a new database file for writing.

❻  The TsTables table is created at the root node, with name data and given the class-based description desc.

❼  Inspecting the database file reveals the basic principle behind the hierarchical structuring in years, months, and days.

Third is the writing of the sample data stored in a DataFrame object to the table object on disk. One of the major benefits of TsTables is the convenience with which this operation is accomplished, namely by a simple method call. Even better, that convenience here is coupled with speed. With regard to the structure in the database, TsTables chunks the data into sub-sets of a single day. In the example case where the
```

frequency is set to one second, this translates into 24 x 60 x 60 = 86,400 data rows per full day's worth of data:

```
In [92]: %time ts.append(data)  ❶
          CPU times: user 476 ms, sys: 238 ms, total: 714 ms
          Wall time: 739 ms

In [93]: # h5  ❷

File(filename=data/data.h5ts, title='', mode='w', root_uep='/',
        filters=Filters(complevel=0, shuffle=False, bitshuffle=False,
        fletcher32=False, least_significant_digit=None))
/ (RootGroup) ''
/data (Group/Timeseries) ''
/data/y2020 (Group) ''
/data/y2021 (Group) ''
/data/y2021/m01 (Group) ''
/data/y2021/m01/d01 (Group) ''
/data/y2021/m01/d01/ts_data (Table(86400,)) ''
  description := {
  "timestamp": Int64Col(shape=(), dflt=0, pos=0),
  "No0": Float64Col(shape=(), dflt=0.0, pos=1),
  "No1": Float64Col(shape=(), dflt=0.0, pos=2),
  "No2": Float64Col(shape=(), dflt=0.0, pos=3),
  "No3": Float64Col(shape=(), dflt=0.0, pos=4),
  "No4": Float64Col(shape=(), dflt=0.0, pos=5)}
  byteorder := 'little'
  chunkshape := (1365,)
/data/y2021/m01/d02 (Group) ''
/data/y2021/m01/d02/ts_data (Table(86400,)) ''
  description := {
  "timestamp": Int64Col(shape=(), dflt=0, pos=0),
  "No0": Float64Col(shape=(), dflt=0.0, pos=1),
  "No1": Float64Col(shape=(), dflt=0.0, pos=2),
  "No2": Float64Col(shape=(), dflt=0.0, pos=3),
  "No3": Float64Col(shape=(), dflt=0.0, pos=4),
  "No4": Float64Col(shape=(), dflt=0.0, pos=5)}
  byteorder := 'little'
  chunkshape := (1365,)
/data/y2021/m01/d03 (Group) ''
/data/y2021/m01/d03/ts_data (Table(86400,)) ''
  description := {
  "timestamp": Int64Col(shape=(), dflt=0, pos=0),
     ...
```

❶ This appends the DataFrame object via a simple method call.

❷ The table object shows 86,400 rows per day after the append() operation.

Reading sub-sets of the data from a TsTables table object is generally really fast since this is what it is optimized for in the first place. In this regard, TsTables supports typical algorithmic trading applications, like backtesting, pretty well. Another contributing factor is that TsTables returns the data already as a DataFrame object such that additional conversions are not necessary in general:

```
In [94]: import datetime

In [95]: start = datetime.datetime(2021, 1, 2)   ❶

In [96]: end = datetime.datetime(2021, 1, 3)   ❷

In [97]: %time subset = ts.read_range(start, end)   ❸
         CPU times: user 10.3 ms, sys: 3.63 ms, total: 14 ms
         Wall time: 12.8 ms

In [98]: start = datetime.datetime(2021, 1, 2, 12, 30, 0)

In [99]: end = datetime.datetime(2021, 1, 5, 17, 15, 30)

In [100]: %time subset = ts.read_range(start, end)
          CPU times: user 28.6 ms, sys: 18.5 ms, total: 47.1 ms
          Wall time: 46.1 ms

In [101]: subset.info()
          <class 'pandas.core.frame.DataFrame'>
          DatetimeIndex: 276331 entries, 2021-01-02 12:30:00 to 2021-01-05
           17:15:30
          Data columns (total 5 columns):
           #   Column  Non-Null Count   Dtype
          ---  ------  --------------   -----
           0   No0     276331 non-null  float64
           1   No1     276331 non-null  float64
           2   No2     276331 non-null  float64
           3   No3     276331 non-null  float64
           4   No4     276331 non-null  float64
          dtypes: float64(5)
          memory usage: 12.6 MB

In [102]: h5.close()

In [103]: rm data/*
```

❶ This defines the starting date and…

❷ …end date for the data retrieval operation.

❸ The read_range() method takes the start and end dates as input—reading here is only a matter of milliseconds.

New data that is retrieved during a day can be appended to the TsTables table object, as illustrated previously. The package is therefore a valuable addition to the capabilities of `pandas` in combination with `HDFStore` objects when it comes to the efficient storage and retrieval of (large) financial time series data sets over time.

Storing Data with SQLite3

Financial time series data can also be written directly from a `DataFrame` object to a relational database like `SQLite3`. The use of a relational database might be useful in scenarios where the SQL query language is applied to implement more sophisticated analyses. With regard to speed and also disk usage, relational databases cannot, however, compare with the other approaches that rely on binary storage formats like HDF5.

The `DataFrame` class provides the method `to_sql()` (see the `to_sql()` API reference page (*https://oreil.ly/ENhoW*)) to write data to a table in a relational database. The size on disk with 100+ MB indicates that there is quite some overhead when using relational databases:

```
In [104]: %time data = generate_sample_data(1e6, 5, '1min').round(4)   ❶
          CPU times: user 342 ms, sys: 60.5 ms, total: 402 ms
          Wall time: 405 ms

In [105]: data.info()   ❶
          <class 'pandas.core.frame.DataFrame'>
          DatetimeIndex: 1000000 entries, 2021-01-01 00:00:00 to 2022-11-26
           10:39:00
          Freq: T
          Data columns (total 5 columns):
           #   Column  Non-Null Count    Dtype
          ---  ------  --------------    -----
           0   No0     1000000 non-null  float64
           1   No1     1000000 non-null  float64
           2   No2     1000000 non-null  float64
           3   No3     1000000 non-null  float64
           4   No4     1000000 non-null  float64
          dtypes: float64(5)
          memory usage: 45.8 MB

In [106]: import sqlite3 as sq3   ❷

In [107]: con = sq3.connect('data/data.sql')   ❸

In [108]: %time data.to_sql('data', con)   ❹
          CPU times: user 4.6 s, sys: 352 ms, total: 4.95 s
          Wall time: 5.07 s

In [109]: ls -n data/data.*
          -rw-r--r--@ 1 501  20  105316352 Aug 25 11:48 data/data.sql
```

❶ The sample financial data set has 1,000,000 rows and five columns; memory usage is about 46 MB.

❷ This imports the SQLite3 module.

❸ A connection is opened to a new database file.

❹ Writing the data to the relational database takes a couple of seconds.

One strength of relational databases is the ability to implement (out-of-memory) analytics tasks based on standardized SQL statements. As an example, consider a query that selects for column No1 all those rows where the value in that row lies between 105 and 108:

```
In [110]: query = 'SELECT * FROM data WHERE No1 > 105 and No2 < 108'  ❶
```

```
In [111]: %time res = con.execute(query).fetchall()  ❷
          CPU times: user 109 ms, sys: 30.3 ms, total: 139 ms
          Wall time: 138 ms
```

```
In [112]: res[:5]  ❸
Out[112]: [('2021-01-03 19:19:00', 103.6894, 105.0117, 103.9025, 95.8619,
            93.6062),
           ('2021-01-03 19:20:00', 103.6724, 105.0654, 103.9277, 95.8915,
            93.5673),
           ('2021-01-03 19:21:00', 103.6213, 105.1132, 103.8598, 95.7606,
            93.5618),
           ('2021-01-03 19:22:00', 103.6724, 105.1896, 103.8704, 95.7302,
            93.4139),
           ('2021-01-03 19:23:00', 103.8115, 105.1152, 103.8342, 95.706,
            93.4436)]
```

```
In [113]: len(res)  ❹
Out[113]: 5035
```

```
In [114]: con.close()
```

```
In [115]: rm data/*
```

❶ The SQL query as a Python str object.

❷ The query executed to retrieve all results rows.

❸ The first five results printed.

❹ The length of the results list object.

Admittedly, such simple queries are also possible with pandas if the data set fits into memory. However, the SQL query language has proven useful and powerful for decades now and should be in the algorithmic trader's arsenal of data weapons.

 pandas also supports database connections via SQLAlchemy, a Python abstraction layer package for diverse relational databases (refer to the SQLAlchemy home page (*http://sqlalchemy.org*)). This in turn allows for the use of, for example, MySQL (*https://mysql.com*) as the relational database backend.

Conclusions

This chapter covers the handling of financial time series data. It illustrates the reading of such data from different file-based sources, like CSV files. It also shows how to retrieve financial data from web services, such as that of Quandl, for end-of-day and options data. Open financial data sources are a valuable addition to the financial landscape. Quandl is a platform integrating thousands of open data sets under the umbrella of a unified API.

Another important topic covered in this chapter is the efficient storage of complete DataFrame objects on disk, as well as of the data contained in such an in-memory object in databases. Database flavors used in this chapter include the HDF5 database standard and the light-weight relational database SQLite3. This chapter lays the foundation for Chapter 4, which addresses vectorized backtesting; Chapter 5, which covers machine learning and deep learning for market prediction; and Chapter 6, which discusses event-based backtesting of trading strategies.

References and Further Resources

You can find more information about Quandl at the following link:

- *http://quandl.org*

Information about the package used to retrieve data from that source is found here:

- Python wrapper page on Quandl (*https://www.quandl.com/tools/python*)
- GitHub page of the Quandl Python wrapper (*https://github.com/quandl/quandl-python*)

You should consult the official documentation pages for more information on the packages used in this chapter:

- pandas home page (*http://pandas.pydata.org*)
- PyTables home page (*http://pytables.org*)
- TsTables fork on GitHub (*https://github.com/yhilpisch/tstables*)
- SQLite home page (*http://sqlite.org*)

Books and articles cited in this chapter:

Hilpisch, Yves. 2018. *Python for Finance: Mastering Data-Driven Finance*. 2nd ed. Sebastopol: O'Reilly.

McKinney, Wes. 2017. *Python for Data Analysis: Data Wrangling with Pandas, NumPy, and IPython*. 2nd ed. Sebastopol: O'Reilly.

Thomas, Rob. "Bad Election Day Forecasts Deal Blow to Data Science: Prediction Models Suffered from Narrow Data, Faulty Algorithms and Human Foibles." *Wall Street Journal*, November 9, 2016.

Python Scripts

The following Python script generates sample financial time series data based on a Monte Carlo simulation for a geometric Brownian motion; for more, see Hilpisch (2018, ch. 12):

```
#
# Python Module to Generate a
# Sample Financial Data Set
#
# Python for Algorithmic Trading
# (c) Dr. Yves J. Hilpisch
# The Python Quants GmbH
```

```python
#
import numpy as np
import pandas as pd

r = 0.05  # constant short rate
sigma = 0.5  # volatility factor


def generate_sample_data(rows, cols, freq='1min'):
    '''
    Function to generate sample financial data.

    Parameters
    ==========
    rows: int
        number of rows to generate
    cols: int
        number of columns to generate
    freq: str
        frequency string for DatetimeIndex

    Returns
    =======
    df: DataFrame
        DataFrame object with the sample data
    '''
    rows = int(rows)
    cols = int(cols)
    # generate a DatetimeIndex object given the frequency
    index = pd.date_range('2021-1-1', periods=rows, freq=freq)
    # determine time delta in year fractions
    dt = (index[1] - index[0]) / pd.Timedelta(value='365D')
    # generate column names
    columns = ['No%d' % i for i in range(cols)]
    # generate sample paths for geometric Brownian motion
    raw = np.exp(np.cumsum((r - 0.5 * sigma ** 2) * dt +
                 sigma * np.sqrt(dt) *
                 np.random.standard_normal((rows, cols)), axis=0))
    # normalize the data to start at 100
    raw = raw / raw[0] * 100
    # generate the DataFrame object
    df = pd.DataFrame(raw, index=index, columns=columns)
    return df


if __name__ == '__main__':
    rows = 5  # number of rows
    columns = 3  # number of columns
    freq = 'D'  # daily frequency
    print(generate_sample_data(rows, columns, freq))
```

Mastering Vectorized Backtesting

[T]hey were silly enough to think you can look at the past to predict the future.[1]

—*The Economist*

Developing ideas and hypotheses for an algorithmic trading program is generally the more creative and sometimes even fun part in the preparation stage. Thoroughly testing them is generally the more technical and time consuming part. This chapter is about the vectorized backtesting of different algorithmic trading strategies. It covers the following types of strategies (refer also to "Trading Strategies" on page 13):

Simple moving averages (SMA) based strategies
> The basic idea of SMA usage for buy and sell signal generation is already decades old. SMAs are a major tool in the so-called technical analysis of stock prices. A signal is derived, for example, when an SMA defined on a shorter time window— say 42 days—crosses an SMA defined on a longer time window—say 252 days.

Momentum strategies
> These are strategies that are based on the hypothesis that recent performance will persist for some additional time. For example, a stock that is downward trending is assumed to do so for longer, which is why such a stock is to be shorted.

Mean-reversion strategies
> The reasoning behind mean-reversion strategies is that stock prices or prices of other financial instruments tend to revert to some mean level or to some trend level when they have deviated too much from such levels.

---

1 Source: "Does the Past Predict the Future?" *The Economist*, September 23, 2009.

The chapter proceeds as follows. "Making Use of Vectorization" on page 82 introduces vectorization as a useful technical approach to formulate and backtest trading strategies. "Strategies Based on Simple Moving Averages" on page 88 is the core of this chapter and covers vectorized backtesting of SMA-based strategies in some depth. "Strategies Based on Momentum" on page 98 introduces and backtests trading strategies based on the so-called time series momentum ("recent performance") of a stock. "Strategies Based on Mean Reversion" on page 107 finishes the chapter with coverage of mean-reversion strategies. Finally, "Data Snooping and Overfitting" on page 111 discusses the pitfalls of data snooping and overfitting in the context of the backtesting of algorithmic trading strategies.

The major goal of this chapter is to master the vectorized implementation approach, which packages like NumPy and pandas allow for, as an efficient and fast backtesting tool. To this end, the approaches presented make a number of simplifying assumptions to better focus the discussion on the major topic of vectorization.

Vectorized backtesting should be considered in the following cases:

Simple trading strategies
> The vectorized backtesting approach clearly has limits when it comes to the modeling of algorithmic trading strategies. However, many popular, simple strategies can be backtested in vectorized fashion.

Interactive strategy exploration
> Vectorized backtesting allows for an agile, interactive exploration of trading strategies and their characteristics. A few lines of code generally suffice to come up with first results, and different parameter combinations are easily tested.

Visualization as major goal
> The approach lends itself pretty well for visualizations of the used data, statistics, signals, and performance results. A few lines of Python code are generally enough to generate appealing and insightful plots.

Comprehensive backtesting programs
> Vectorized backtesting is pretty fast in general, allowing one to test a great variety of parameter combinations in a short amount of time. When speed is key, the approach should be considered.

Making Use of Vectorization

Vectorization, or *array programming*, refers to a programming style where operations on scalars (that is, integer or floating point numbers) are generalized to vectors, matrices, or even multidimensional arrays. Consider a vector of integers $v = (1, 2, 3, 4, 5)^T$ represented in Python as a list object v = [1, 2, 3, 4, 5]. Calculating the scalar product of such a vector and, say, the number 2 requires in pure

Python a for loop or something similar, such as a list comprehension, which is just different syntax for a for loop:

```
In [1]: v = [1, 2, 3, 4, 5]

In [2]: sm = [2 * i for i in v]

In [3]: sm
Out[3]: [2, 4, 6, 8, 10]
```

In principle, Python allows one to multiply a list object by an integer, but Python's data model gives back another list object in the example case containing two times the elements of the original object:

```
In [4]: 2 * v
Out[4]: [1, 2, 3, 4, 5, 1, 2, 3, 4, 5]
```

Vectorization with NumPy

The NumPy package for numerical computing (cf. NumPy home page (*http:// numpy.org*)) introduces vectorization to Python. The major class provided by NumPy is the ndarray class, which stands for *n-dimensional array*. An instance of such an object can be created, for example, on the basis of the list object v. Scalar multiplication, linear transformations, and similar operations from linear algebra then work as desired:

```
In [5]: import numpy as np   ❶

In [6]: a = np.array(v)   ❷

In [7]: a   ❸
Out[7]: array([1, 2, 3, 4, 5])

In [8]: type(a)   ❹
Out[8]: numpy.ndarray

In [9]: 2 * a   ❺
Out[9]: array([ 2,  4,  6,  8, 10])

In [10]: 0.5 * a + 2   ❻
Out[10]: array([2.5, 3. , 3.5, 4. , 4.5])
```

❶ Imports the NumPy package.

❷ Instantiates an ndarray object based on the list object.

❸ Prints out the data stored as ndarray object.

❹ Looks up the type of the object.

❺ Achieves a scalar multiplication in vectorized fashion.

❻ Achieves a linear transformation in vectorized fashion.

The transition from a one-dimensional array (a vector) to a two-dimensional array (a matrix) is natural. The same holds true for higher dimensions:

```
In [11]: a = np.arange(12).reshape((4, 3))  ❶
```

```
In [12]: a
Out[12]: array([[ 0,  1,  2],
                [ 3,  4,  5],
                [ 6,  7,  8],
                [ 9, 10, 11]])
```

```
In [13]: 2 * a
Out[13]: array([[ 0,  2,  4],
                [ 6,  8, 10],
                [12, 14, 16],
                [18, 20, 22]])
```

```
In [14]: a ** 2  ❷
Out[14]: array([[  0,   1,   4],
                [  9,  16,  25],
                [ 36,  49,  64],
                [ 81, 100, 121]])
```

❶ Creates a one-dimensional `ndarray` object and reshapes it to two dimensions.

❷ Calculates the square of every element of the object in vectorized fashion.

In addition, the `ndarray` class provides certain methods that allow vectorized operations. They often also have counterparts in the form of so-called universal functions that `NumPy` provides:

```
In [15]: a.mean()  ❶
Out[15]: 5.5
```

```
In [16]: np.mean(a)  ❷
Out[16]: 5.5
```

```
In [17]: a.mean(axis=0)  ❸
Out[17]: array([4.5, 5.5, 6.5])
```

```
In [18]: np.mean(a, axis=1)  ❹
Out[18]: array([ 1.,  4.,  7., 10.])
```

❶ Calculates the mean of all elements by a method call.

❷ Calculates the mean of all elements by a universal function.

❸ Calculates the mean along the first axis.

❹ Calculates the mean along the second axis.

As a financial example, consider the function `generate_sample_data()` in "Python Scripts" on page 78 that uses an Euler discretization to generate sample paths for a geometric Brownian motion. The implementation makes use of multiple vectorized operations that are combined to a single line of code.

See the Appendix for more details of vectorization with `NumPy`. Refer to Hilpisch (2018) for a multitude of applications of vectorization in a financial context.

 The standard instruction set and data model of Python does not generally allow for vectorized numerical operations. `NumPy` introduces powerful vectorization techniques based on the regular array class `ndarray` that lead to concise code that is close to mathematical notation in, for example, linear algebra regarding vectors and matrices.

Vectorization with pandas

The pandas package and the central `DataFrame` class make heavy use of `NumPy` and the `ndarray` class. Therefore, most of the vectorization principles seen in the `NumPy` context carry over to pandas. The mechanics are best explained again on the basis of a concrete example. To begin with, define a two-dimensional `ndarray` object first:

```
In [19]: a = np.arange(15).reshape(5, 3)
```

```
In [20]: a
Out[20]: array([[ 0,  1,  2],
                [ 3,  4,  5],
                [ 6,  7,  8],
                [ 9, 10, 11],
                [12, 13, 14]])
```

For the creation of a `DataFrame` object, generate a `list` object with column names and a `DatetimeIndex` object next, both of appropriate size given the `ndarray` object:

```
In [21]: import pandas as pd   ❶
```

```
In [22]: columns = list('abc')   ❷
```

```
In [23]: columns
Out[23]: ['a', 'b', 'c']
```

```
In [24]: index = pd.date_range('2021-7-1', periods=5, freq='B')   ❸
```

```
In [25]: index
```

```
Out[25]: DatetimeIndex(['2021-07-01', '2021-07-02', '2021-07-05',
            '2021-07-06',
                        '2021-07-07'],
                    dtype='datetime64[ns]', freq='B')

In [26]: df = pd.DataFrame(a, columns=columns, index=index)   ❹

In [27]: df
Out[27]:             a   b   c
         2021-07-01  0   1   2
         2021-07-02  3   4   5
         2021-07-05  6   7   8
         2021-07-06  9  10  11
         2021-07-07  12 13  14
```

❶ Imports the pandas package.

❷ Creates a list object out of the str object.

❸ A pandas DatetimeIndex object is created that has a "business day" frequency and goes over five periods.

❹ A DataFrame object is instantiated based on the ndarray object a with column labels and index values specified.

In principle, vectorization now works similarly to ndarray objects. One difference is that aggregation operations default to column-wise results:

```
In [28]: 2 * df   ❶
Out[28]:             a   b   c
         2021-07-01  0   2   4
         2021-07-02  6   8  10
         2021-07-05  12 14  16
         2021-07-06  18 20  22
         2021-07-07  24 26  28

In [29]: df.sum()   ❷
Out[29]: a    30
         b    35
         c    40
         dtype: int64

In [30]: np.mean(df)   ❸
Out[30]: a    6.0
         b    7.0
         c    8.0
         dtype: float64
```

❶ Calculates the scalar product for the `DataFrame` object (treated as a matrix).

❷ Calculates the sum *per column*.

❸ Calculates the mean *per column*.

Column-wise operations can be implemented by referencing the respective column names, either by the bracket notation or the dot notation:

```
In [31]: df['a'] + df['c']   ❶
Out[31]: 2021-07-01     2
         2021-07-02     8
         2021-07-05    14
         2021-07-06    20
         2021-07-07    26
         Freq: B, dtype: int64

In [32]: 0.5 * df.a + 2 * df.b - df.c   ❷
Out[32]: 2021-07-01     0.0
         2021-07-02     4.5
         2021-07-05     9.0
         2021-07-06    13.5
         2021-07-07    18.0
         Freq: B, dtype: float64
```

❶ Calculates the element-wise sum over columns a and c.

❷ Calculates a linear transform involving all three columns.

Similarly, conditions yielding Boolean results vectors and SQL-like selections based on such conditions are straightforward to implement:

```
In [33]: df['a'] > 5   ❶
Out[33]: 2021-07-01    False
         2021-07-02    False
         2021-07-05     True
         2021-07-06     True
         2021-07-07     True
         Freq: B, Name: a, dtype: bool

In [34]: df[df['a'] > 5]   ❷
Out[34]:              a    b    c
         2021-07-05   6    7    8
         2021-07-06   9   10   11
         2021-07-07  12   13   14
```

❶ Which element in column a is greater than five?

❷ Select all those rows where the element in column a is greater than five.

For a vectorized backtesting of trading strategies, comparisons between two columns or more are typical:

```
In [35]: df['c'] > df['b']   ❶
Out[35]: 2021-07-01    True
         2021-07-02    True
         2021-07-05    True
         2021-07-06    True
         2021-07-07    True
         Freq: B, dtype: bool

In [36]: 0.15 * df.a + df.b > df.c   ❷
Out[36]: 2021-07-01    False
         2021-07-02    False
         2021-07-05    False
         2021-07-06     True
         2021-07-07     True
         Freq: B, dtype: bool
```

❶ For which date is the element in column c greater than in column b?

❷ Condition comparing a linear combination of columns a and b with column c.

Vectorization with pandas is a powerful concept, in particular for the implementation of financial algorithms and the vectorized backtesting, as illustrated in the remainder of this chapter. For more on the basics of vectorization with pandas and financial examples, refer to Hilpisch (2018, ch. 5).

> While NumPy brings general vectorization approaches to the numerical computing world of Python, pandas allows vectorization over time series data. This is really helpful for the implementation of financial algorithms and the backtesting of algorithmic trading strategies. By using this approach, you can expect concise code, as well as a faster code execution, in comparison to standard Python code, making use of for loops and similar idioms to accomplish the same goal.

Strategies Based on Simple Moving Averages

Trading based on simple moving averages (SMAs) is a decades old strategy that has its origins in the technical stock analysis world. Brock et al. (1992), for example, empirically investigate such strategies in systematic fashion. They write:

> The term "technical analysis" is a general heading for a myriad of trading techniques....In this paper, we explore two of the simplest and most popular technical rules: moving average-oscillator and trading-range break (resistance and support levels). In the first method, buy and sell signals are generated by two moving averages, a long

period, and a short period....Our study reveals that technical analysis helps to predict stock changes.

Getting into the Basics

This sub-section focuses on the basics of backtesting trading strategies that make use of two SMAs. The example to follow works with end-of-day (EOD) closing data for the EUR/USD exchange rate, as provided in the *csv* file under the EOD data file (*https://oreil.ly/AzE-p*). The data in the data set is from the Refinitiv Eikon Data API and represents EOD values for the respective instruments (RICs):

```
In [37]: raw = pd.read_csv('http://hilpisch.com/pyalgo_eikon_eod_data.csv',
                           index_col=0, parse_dates=True).dropna()   ❶

In [38]: raw.info()   ❷
         <class 'pandas.core.frame.DataFrame'>
         DatetimeIndex: 2516 entries, 2010-01-04 to 2019-12-31
         Data columns (total 12 columns):
          #   Column  Non-Null Count  Dtype
         ---  ------  --------------  -----
          0   AAPL.O  2516 non-null   float64
          1   MSFT.O  2516 non-null   float64
          2   INTC.O  2516 non-null   float64
          3   AMZN.O  2516 non-null   float64
          4   GS.N    2516 non-null   float64
          5   SPY     2516 non-null   float64
          6   .SPX    2516 non-null   float64
          7   .VIX    2516 non-null   float64
          8   EUR=    2516 non-null   float64
          9   XAU=    2516 non-null   float64
          10  GDX     2516 non-null   float64
          11  GLD     2516 non-null   float64
         dtypes: float64(12)
         memory usage: 255.5 KB

In [39]: data = pd.DataFrame(raw['EUR='])   ❸

In [40]: data.rename(columns={'EUR=': 'price'}, inplace=True)   ❹

In [41]: data.info()   ❺
         <class 'pandas.core.frame.DataFrame'>
         DatetimeIndex: 2516 entries, 2010-01-04 to 2019-12-31
         Data columns (total 1 columns):
          #   Column  Non-Null Count  Dtype
         ---  ------  --------------  -----
          0   price   2516 non-null   float64
         dtypes: float64(1)
         memory usage: 39.3 KB
```

❶ Reads the data from the remotely stored CSV file.

❷ Shows the meta information for the `DataFrame` object.

❸ Transforms the `Series` object to a `DataFrame` object.

❹ Renames the only column to `price`.

❺ Shows the meta information for the new `DataFrame` object.

The calculation of SMAs is made simple by the `rolling()` method, in combination with a deferred calculation operation:

```
In [42]: data['SMA1'] = data['price'].rolling(42).mean()    ❶

In [43]: data['SMA2'] = data['price'].rolling(252).mean()   ❷

In [44]: data.tail()   ❸
Out[44]:            price      SMA1      SMA2
         Date
         2019-12-24  1.1087  1.107698  1.119630
         2019-12-26  1.1096  1.107740  1.119529
         2019-12-27  1.1175  1.107924  1.119428
         2019-12-30  1.1197  1.108131  1.119333
         2019-12-31  1.1210  1.108279  1.119231
```

❶ Creates a column with 42 days of SMA values. The first 41 values will be `NaN`.

❷ Creates a column with 252 days of SMA values. The first 251 values will be `NaN`.

❸ Prints the final five rows of the data set.

A visualization of the original time series data in combination with the SMAs best illustrates the results (see Figure 4-1):

```
In [45]: %matplotlib inline
         from pylab import mpl, plt
         plt.style.use('seaborn')
         mpl.rcParams['savefig.dpi'] = 300
         mpl.rcParams['font.family'] = 'serif'

In [46]: data.plot(title='EUR/USD | 42 & 252 days SMAs',
                    figsize=(10, 6));
```

The next step is to generate signals, or rather market positionings, based on the relationship between the two SMAs. The rule is to *go long whenever the shorter SMA is above the longer one and vice versa*. For our purposes, we indicate a long position by 1 and a short position by −1.

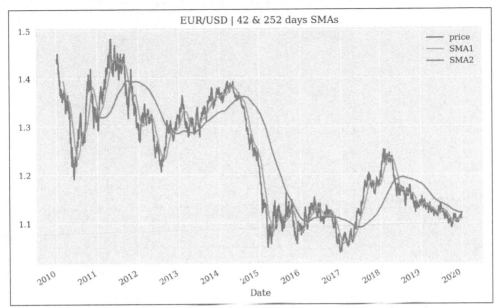

Figure 4-1. The EUR/USD exchange rate with two SMAs

Being able to directly compare two columns of the DataFrame object makes the implementation of the rule an affair of a single line of code only. The positioning over time is illustrated in Figure 4-2:

```
In [47]: data['position'] = np.where(data['SMA1'] > data['SMA2'],
                                      1, -1)  ❶

In [48]: data.dropna(inplace=True)  ❷

In [49]: data['position'].plot(ylim=[-1.1, 1.1],
                                title='Market Positioning',
                                figsize=(10, 6));  ❸
```

❶ Implements the trading rule in vectorized fashion. np.where() produces +1 for rows where the expression is True and -1 for rows where the expression is False.

❷ Deletes all rows of the data set that contain at least one NaN value.

❸ Plots the positioning over time.

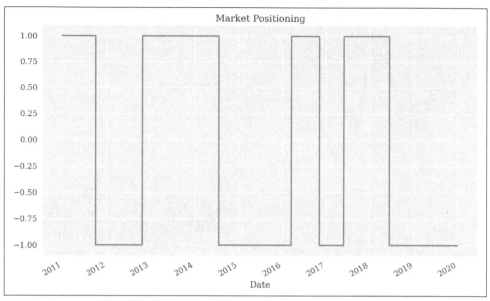

Figure 4-2. Market positioning based on the strategy with two SMAs

To calculate the performance of the strategy, calculate the log returns based on the original financial time series next. The code to do this is again rather concise due to vectorization. Figure 4-3 shows the histogram of the log returns:

```
In [50]: data['returns'] = np.log(data['price'] / data['price'].shift(1))  ❶
```

```
In [51]: data['returns'].hist(bins=35, figsize=(10, 6));  ❷
```

❶ Calculates the log returns in vectorized fashion over the price column.

❷ Plots the log returns as a histogram (frequency distribution).

To derive the strategy returns, multiply the position column—shifted by one trading day—with the returns column. Since log returns are additive, calculating the sum over the columns returns and strategy provides a first comparison of the performance of the strategy relative to the base investment itself.

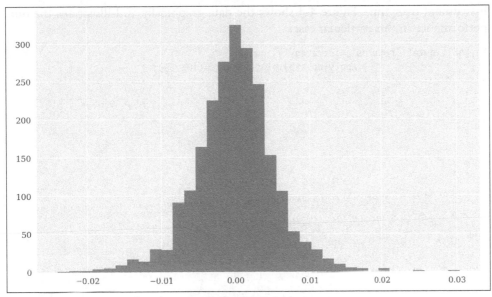

Figure 4-3. Frequency distribution of EUR/USD log returns

Comparing the returns shows that the strategy books a win over the passive benchmark investment:

```
In [52]: data['strategy'] = data['position'].shift(1) * data['returns']  ❶

In [53]: data[['returns', 'strategy']].sum()  ❷
Out[53]: returns    -0.176731
         strategy    0.253121
         dtype: float64

In [54]: data[['returns', 'strategy']].sum().apply(np.exp)  ❸
Out[54]: returns     0.838006
         strategy    1.288039
         dtype: float64
```

❶ Derives the log returns of the strategy given the positionings and market returns.

❷ Sums up the single log return values for both the stock and the strategy (for illustration only).

❸ Applies the exponential function to the sum of the log returns to calculate the *gross performance*.

Calculating the cumulative sum over time with `cumsum` and, based on this, the cumulative returns by applying the exponential function `np.exp()` gives a more comprehensive picture of how the strategy compares to the performance of the base financial instrument over time. Figure 4-4 shows the data graphically and illustrates the out-performance in this particular case:

```
In [55]: data[['returns', 'strategy']].cumsum(
                ).apply(np.exp).plot(figsize=(10, 6));
```

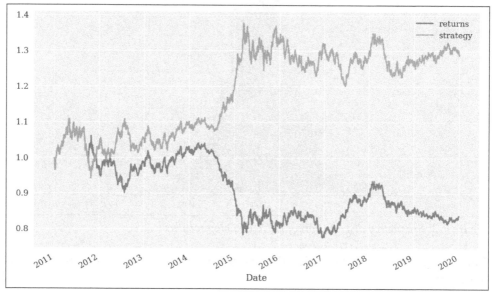

Figure 4-4. Gross performance of EUR/USD compared to the SMA-based strategy

Average, annualized risk-return statistics for both the stock and the strategy are easy to calculate:

```
In [56]: data[['returns', 'strategy']].mean() * 252    ❶
Out[56]: returns    -0.019671
         strategy    0.028174
         dtype: float64

In [57]: np.exp(data[['returns', 'strategy']].mean() * 252) - 1    ❶
Out[57]: returns    -0.019479
         strategy    0.028575
         dtype: float64

In [58]: data[['returns', 'strategy']].std() * 252 ** 0.5    ❷
Out[58]: returns    0.085414
         strategy    0.085405
         dtype: float64

In [59]: (data[['returns', 'strategy']].apply(np.exp) - 1).std() * 252 ** 0.5    ❷
Out[59]: returns    0.085405
         strategy    0.085373
         dtype: float64
```

❶ Calculates the annualized mean return in both log and regular space.

❷ Calculates the annualized standard deviation in both log and regular space.

Other risk statistics often of interest in the context of trading strategy performances are the *maximum drawdown* and the *longest drawdown period*. A helper statistic to use in this context is the cumulative maximum gross performance as calculated by the cummax() method applied to the gross performance of the strategy. Figure 4-5 shows the two time series for the SMA-based strategy:

```
In [60]: data['cumret'] = data['strategy'].cumsum().apply(np.exp)   ❶

In [61]: data['cummax'] = data['cumret'].cummax()   ❷

In [62]: data[['cumret', 'cummax']].dropna().plot(figsize=(10, 6));   ❸
```

❶ Defines a new column, cumret, with the gross performance over time.

❷ Defines yet another column with the running maximum value of the gross performance.

❸ Plots the two new columns of the DataFrame object.

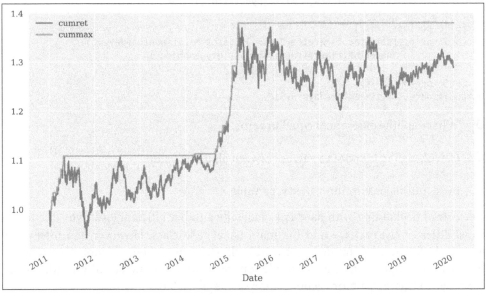

Figure 4-5. Gross performance and cumulative maximum performance of the SMA-based strategy

The maximum drawdown is then simply calculated as the maximum of the difference between the two relevant columns. The maximum drawdown in the example is about 18 percentage points:

```
In [63]: drawdown = data['cummax'] - data['cumret']   ❶

In [64]: drawdown.max()   ❷
Out[64]: 0.17779367070195917
```

❶ Calculates the element-wise difference between the two columns.

❷ Picks out the maximum value from all differences.

The determination of the longest drawdown period is a bit more involved. It requires those dates at which the gross performance equals its cumulative maximum (that is, where a new maximum is set). This information is stored in a temporary object. Then the differences in days between all such dates are calculated and the longest period is picked out. Such periods can be only one day long or more than 100 days. Here, the longest drawdown period lasts for 596 days—a pretty long period:[2]

```
In [65]: temp = drawdown[drawdown == 0]   ❶

In [66]: periods = (temp.index[1:].to_pydatetime() -
                    temp.index[:-1].to_pydatetime())   ❷

In [67]: periods[12:15]
Out[67]: array([datetime.timedelta(days=1), datetime.timedelta(days=1),
                datetime.timedelta(days=10)], dtype=object)

In [68]: periods.max()   ❸
Out[68]: datetime.timedelta(days=596)
```

❶ Where are the differences equal to zero?

❷ Calculates the timedelta values between all index values.

❸ Picks out the maximum timedelta value.

Vectorized backtesting with pandas is generally a rather efficient endeavor due to the capabilities of the package and the main DataFrame class. However, the interactive approach illustrated so far does not work well when one wishes to implement a larger backtesting program that, for example, optimizes the parameters of an SMA-based strategy. To this end, a more general approach is advisable.

---

2 For more on the datetime and timedelta objects, refer to Appendix C of Hilpisch (2018).

pandas proves to be a powerful tool for the vectorized analysis of trading strategies. Many statistics of interest, such as log returns, cumulative returns, annualized returns and volatility, maximum drawdown, and maximum drawdown period, can in general be calculated by a single line or just a few lines of code. Being able to visualize results by a simple method call is an additional benefit.

Generalizing the Approach

"SMA Backtesting Class" on page 115 presents a Python code that contains a class for the vectorized backtesting of SMA-based trading strategies. In a sense, it is a generalization of the approach introduced in the previous sub-section. It allows one to define an instance of the SMAVectorBacktester class by providing the following parameters:

- symbol: RIC (instrument data) to be used
- SMA1: for the time window in days for the *shorter* SMA
- SMA2: for the time window in days for the *longer* SMA
- start: for the start date of the data selection
- end: for the end date of the data selection

The application itself is best illustrated by an interactive session that makes use of the class. The example first replicates the backtest implemented previously based on EUR/USD exchange rate data. It then optimizes the SMA parameters for maximum gross performance. Based on the optimal parameters, it plots the resulting gross performance of the strategy compared to the base instrument over the relevant period of time:

```
In [69]: import SMAVectorBacktester as SMA   ❶

In [70]: smabt = SMA.SMAVectorBacktester('EUR=', 42, 252,
                                          '2010-1-1', '2019-12-31')   ❷

In [71]: smabt.run_strategy()   ❸
Out[71]: (1.29, 0.45)

In [72]: %%time
         smabt.optimize_parameters((30, 50, 2),
                                   (200, 300, 2))   ❹
         CPU times: user 3.76 s, sys: 15.8 ms, total: 3.78 s
         Wall time: 3.78 s

Out[72]: (array([ 48., 238.]), 1.5)

In [73]: smabt.plot_results()   ❺
```

❶   This imports the module as SMA.

---

❷ An instance of the main class is instantiated.

❸ Backtests the SMA-based strategy, given the parameters during instantiation.

❹ The `optimize_parameters()` method takes as input parameter ranges with step sizes and determines the optimal combination by a brute force approach.

❺ The `plot_results()` method plots the strategy performance compared to the benchmark instrument, given the currently stored parameter values (here from the optimization procedure).

The gross performance of the strategy with the original parametrization is 1.24 or 124%. The optimized strategy yields an absolute return of 1.44 or 144% for the parameter combination SMA1 = 48 and SMA2 = 238. Figure 4-6 shows the gross performance over time graphically, again compared to the performance of the base instrument, which represents the benchmark.

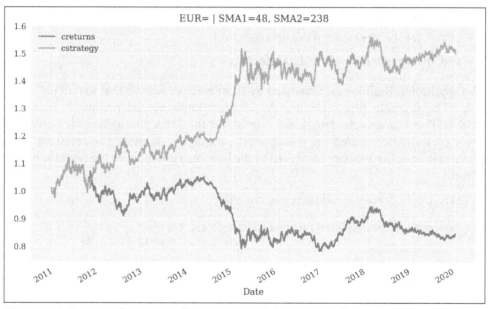

Figure 4-6. Gross performance of EUR/USD and the optimized SMA strategy

Strategies Based on Momentum

There are two basic types of momentum strategies. The first type is *cross-sectional* momentum strategies. Selecting from a larger pool of instruments, these strategies buy those instruments that have recently outperformed relative to their peers (or a benchmark) and sell those instruments that have underperformed. The basic idea is that the instruments continue to outperform and underperform, respectively—at least for a certain period of time. Jegadeesh and Titman (1993, 2001) and Chan et al. (1996) study these types of trading strategies and their potential sources of profit.

Cross-sectional momentum strategies have traditionally performed quite well. Jegadeesh and Titman (1993) write:

> This paper documents that strategies which buy stocks that have performed well in the past and sell stocks that have performed poorly in the past generate significant positive returns over 3- to 12-month holding periods.

The second type is *time series* momentum strategies. These strategies buy those instruments that have recently performed well and sell those instruments that have recently performed poorly. In this case, the benchmark is the past returns of the instrument itself. Moskowitz et al. (2012) analyze this type of momentum strategy in detail across a wide range of markets. They write:

> Rather than focus on the relative returns of securities in the cross-section, time series momentum focuses purely on a security's own past return....Our finding of time series momentum in virtually every instrument we examine seems to challenge the "random walk" hypothesis, which in its most basic form implies that knowing whether a price went up or down in the past should not be informative about whether it will go up or down in the future.

Getting into the Basics

Consider end-of-day closing prices for the gold price in USD (XAU=):

```
In [74]: data = pd.DataFrame(raw['XAU='])
```

```
In [75]: data.rename(columns={'XAU=': 'price'}, inplace=True)
```

```
In [76]: data['returns'] = np.log(data['price'] / data['price'].shift(1))
```

The most simple time series momentum strategy is to buy the stock if the last return was positive and to sell it if it was negative. With NumPy and pandas this is easy to formalize; just take the sign of the last available return as the market position. Figure 4-7 illustrates the performance of this strategy. The strategy does significantly underperform the base instrument:

```
In [77]: data['position'] = np.sign(data['returns'])   ❶
```

```
In [78]: data['strategy'] = data['position'].shift(1) * data['returns']   ❷
```

```
In [79]: data[['returns', 'strategy']].dropna().cumsum(
                ).apply(np.exp).plot(figsize=(10, 6));   ❸
```

❶ Defines a new column with the sign (that is, 1 or –1) of the relevant log return; the resulting values represent the market positionings (long or short).

❷   Calculates the strategy log returns given the market positionings.

❸   Plots and compares the strategy performance with the benchmark instrument.

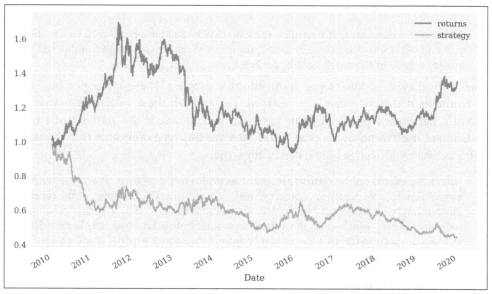

Figure 4-7. Gross performance of gold price (USD) and momentum strategy (last return only)

Using a rolling time window, the time series momentum strategy can be generalized to more than just the last return. For example, the average of the *last three returns* can be used to generate the signal for the positioning. Figure 4-8 shows that the strategy in this case does much better, both in absolute terms and relative to the base instrument:

```
In [80]: data['position'] = np.sign(data['returns'].rolling(3).mean())   ❶
```

```
In [81]: data['strategy'] = data['position'].shift(1) * data['returns']
```

```
In [82]: data[['returns', 'strategy']].dropna().cumsum(
                 ).apply(np.exp).plot(figsize=(10, 6));
```

❶   This time, the mean return over a rolling window of three days is taken.

However, the performance is quite sensitive to the time window parameter. Choosing, for example, the last two returns instead of three leads to a much worse performance, as shown in Figure 4-9.

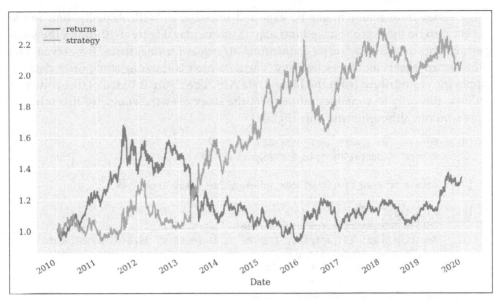

Figure 4-8. Gross performance of gold price (USD) and momentum strategy (last three returns)

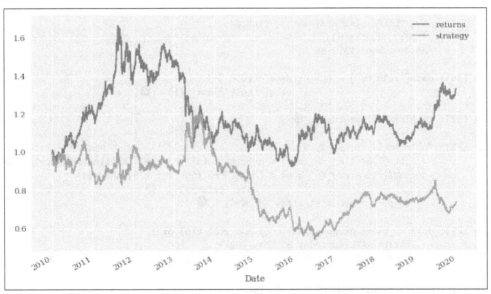

Figure 4-9. Gross performance of gold price (USD) and momentum strategy (last two returns)

Time series momentum might be expected intraday, as well. Actually, one would expect it to be more pronounced intraday than interday. Figure 4-10 shows the gross performance of five time series momentum strategies for one, three, five, seven, and nine return observations, respectively. The data used is intraday stock price data for Apple Inc., as retrieved from the Eikon Data API. The figure is based on the code that follows. Basically all strategies outperform the stock over the course of this intraday time window, although some only slightly:

```
In [83]: fn = '../data/AAPL_1min_05052020.csv'    ❶
         # fn = '../data/SPX_1min_05052020.csv'    ❶

In [84]: data = pd.read_csv(fn, index_col=0, parse_dates=True)    ❶

In [85]: data.info()    ❶
         <class 'pandas.core.frame.DataFrame'>
         DatetimeIndex: 241 entries, 2020-05-05 16:00:00 to 2020-05-05 20:00:00
         Data columns (total 6 columns):
          #   Column  Non-Null Count   Dtype
         ---  ------  --------------   -----
          0   HIGH    241 non-null     float64
          1   LOW     241 non-null     float64
          2   OPEN    241 non-null     float64
          3   CLOSE   241 non-null     float64
          4   COUNT   241 non-null     float64
          5   VOLUME  241 non-null     float64
         dtypes: float64(6)
         memory usage: 13.2 KB

In [86]: data['returns'] = np.log(data['CLOSE'] /
                                   data['CLOSE'].shift(1))    ❷

In [87]: to_plot = ['returns']    ❸

In [88]: for m in [1, 3, 5, 7, 9]:
             data['position_%d' % m] = np.sign(data['returns'].rolling(m).mean())    ❹
             data['strategy_%d' % m] = (data['position_%d' % m].shift(1) *
                                        data['returns'])    ❺
             to_plot.append('strategy_%d' % m)    ❻

In [89]: data[to_plot].dropna().cumsum().apply(np.exp).plot(
             title='AAPL intraday 05. May 2020',
             figsize=(10, 6), style=['-', '--', '--', '--', '--', '--']);    ❼
```

❶ Reads the intraday data from a CSV file.

❷ Calculates the intraday log returns.

❸ Defines a list object to select the columns to be plotted later.

❹ Derives positionings according to the momentum strategy parameter.

❺ Calculates the resulting strategy log returns.

❻ Appends the column name to the `list` object.

❼ Plots all relevant columns to compare the strategies' performances to the benchmark instrument's performance.

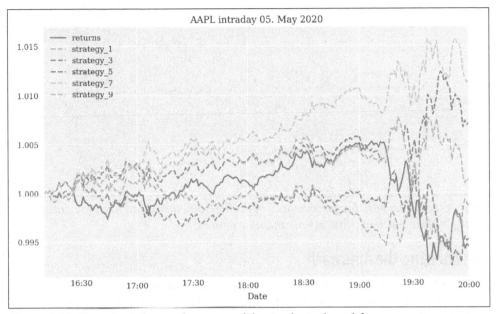

Figure 4-10. Gross intraday performance of the Apple stock and five momentum strategies (last one, three, five, seven, and nine returns)

Figure 4-11 shows the performance of the same five strategies for the S&P 500 index. Again, all five strategy configurations outperform the index and all show a positive return (before transaction costs).

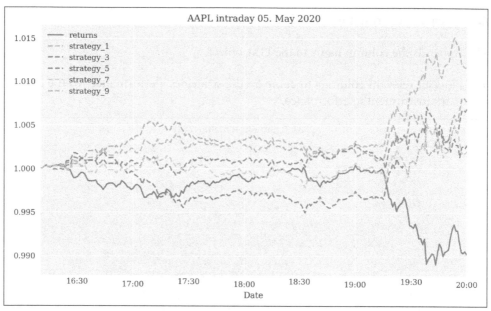

Figure 4-11. Gross intraday performance of the S&P 500 index and five momentum strategies (last one, three, five, seven, and nine returns)

Generalizing the Approach

"Momentum Backtesting Class" on page 118 presents a Python module containing the MomVectorBacktester class, which allows for a bit more standardized backtesting of momentum-based strategies. The class has the following attributes:

- symbol: RIC (instrument data) to be used
- start: for the start date of the data selection
- end: for the end date of the data selection
- amount: for the initial amount to be invested
- tc: for the proportional transaction costs per trade

Compared to the SMAVectorBacktester class, this one introduces two important generalizations: the fixed amount to be invested at the beginning of the backtesting period and proportional transaction costs to get closer to market realities cost-wise. In particular, the addition of transaction costs is important in the context of time series momentum strategies that often lead to a large number of transactions over time.

The application is as straightforward and convenient as before. The example first replicates the results from the interactive session before, but this time with an initial investment of 10,000 USD. Figure 4-12 visualizes the performance of the strategy, taking the mean of the last three returns to generate signals for the positioning. The second case covered is one with proportional transaction costs of 0.1% per trade. As Figure 4-13 illustrates, even small transaction costs deteriorate the performance significantly in this case. The driving factor in this regard is the relatively high frequency of trades that the strategy requires:

```
In [90]: import MomVectorBacktester as Mom    ❶

In [91]: mombt = Mom.MomVectorBacktester('XAU=', '2010-1-1',
                                         '2019-12-31', 10000, 0.0)   ❷

In [92]: mombt.run_strategy(momentum=3)    ❸
Out[92]: (20797.87, 7395.53)

In [93]: mombt.plot results()
In [94]: mombt = Mom.MomVectorBacktester('XAU=', '2010-1-1',
                                         '2019-12-31', 10000, 0.001)   ❹

In [95]: mombt.run_strategy(momentum=3)    ❺
Out[95]: (10749.4, -2652.93)

In [96]: mombt.plot_results()
```

❶ Imports the module as Mom

❷ Instantiates an object of the backtesting class defining the starting capital to be 10,000 USD and the proportional transaction costs to be zero.

❸ Backtests the momentum strategy based on a time window of *three days*: the strategy outperforms the benchmark passive investment.

❹ This time, proportional transaction costs of 0.1% are assumed per trade.

❺ In that case, the strategy basically loses all the outperformance.

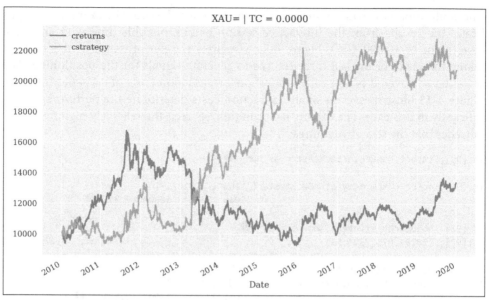

Figure 4-12. Gross performance of the gold price (USD) and the momentum strategy (last three returns, no transaction costs)

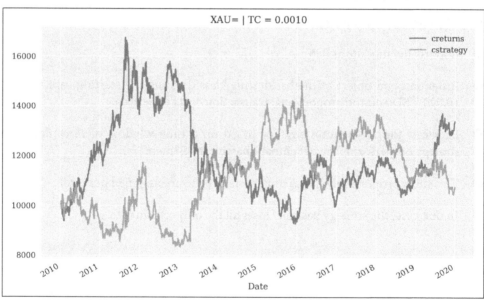

Figure 4-13. Gross performance of the gold price (USD) and the momentum strategy (last three returns, transaction costs of 0.1%)

Strategies Based on Mean Reversion

Roughly speaking, mean-reversion strategies rely on a reasoning that is the opposite of momentum strategies. If a financial instrument has performed "too well" relative to its trend, it is shorted, and vice versa. To put it differently, while (time series) momentum strategies assume a *positive correlation* between returns, mean-reversion strategies assume a *negative correlation*. Balvers et al. (2000) write:

> Mean reversion refers to a tendency of asset prices to return to a trend path.

Working with a simple moving average (SMA) as a proxy for a "trend path," a mean-reversion strategy in, say, the EUR/USD exchange rate can be backtested in a similar fashion as the backtests of the SMA- and momentum-based strategies. The idea is to define a threshold for the distance between the current stock price and the SMA, which signals a long or short position.

Getting into the Basics

The examples that follow are for two different financial instruments for which one would expect significant mean reversion since they are both based on the gold price:

- GLD is the symbol for SPDR Gold Shares, which is the largest physically backed exchange traded fund (ETF) for gold (cf. SPDR Gold Shares home page (*http://spdrgoldshares.com*)).
- GDX is the symbol for the VanEck Vectors Gold Miners ETF, which invests in equity products to track the NYSE Arca Gold Miners Index (cf. VanEck Vectors Gold Miners overview page (*https://oreil.ly/CmPBA*)).

The example starts with GDX and implements a mean-reversion strategy on the basis of an SMA of 25 days and a threshold value of 3.5 for the absolute deviation of the current price to deviate from the SMA to signal a positioning. Figure 4-14 shows the differences between the current price of GDX and the SMA, as well as the positive and negative threshold value to generate sell and buy signals, respectively:

```
In [97]: data = pd.DataFrame(raw['GDX'])

In [98]: data.rename(columns={'GDX': 'price'}, inplace=True)

In [99]: data['returns'] = np.log(data['price'] /
                                  data['price'].shift(1))

In [100]: SMA = 25  ❶

In [101]: data['SMA'] = data['price'].rolling(SMA).mean()  ❷

In [102]: threshold = 3.5  ❸
```

```
In [103]: data['distance'] = data['price'] - data['SMA']  ❹
```

```
In [104]: data['distance'].dropna().plot(figsize=(10, 6), legend=True)  ❺
          plt.axhline(threshold, color='r')
          plt.axhline(-threshold, color='r')
          plt.axhline(0, color='r');
```

❶ The SMA parameter is defined…

❷ …and SMA ("trend path") is calculated.

❸ The threshold for the signal generation is defined.

❹ The distance is calculated for every point in time.

❺ The distance values are plotted.

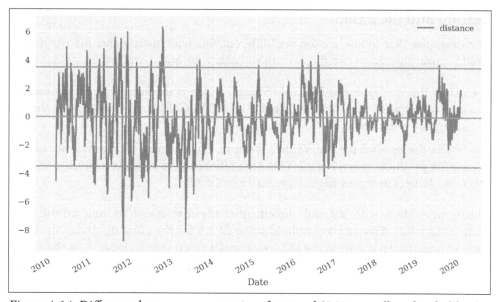

Figure 4-14. Difference between current price of GDX and SMA, as well as threshold values for generating mean-reversion signals

Based on the differences and the fixed threshold values, positionings can again be derived in vectorized fashion. Figure 4-15 shows the resulting positionings:

```
In [105]: data['position'] = np.where(data['distance'] > threshold,
                                       -1, np.nan)  ❶
```

```
In [106]: data['position'] = np.where(data['distance'] < -threshold,
                                       1, data['position'])  ❷
```

```
In [107]: data['position'] = np.where(data['distance'] *
                        data['distance'].shift(1) < 0, 0, data['position'])   ❸

In [108]: data['position'] = data['position'].ffill().fillna(0)   ❹

In [109]: data['position'].iloc[SMA:].plot(ylim=[-1.1, 1.1],
                                          figsize=(10, 6));   ❺
```

❶ If the distance value is greater than the threshold value, go short (set −1 in the new column `position`), otherwise set `NaN`.

❷ If the distance value is lower than the negative threshold value, go long (set 1), otherwise keep the column `position` unchanged.

❸ If there is a change in the sign of the distance value, go market neutral (set 0), otherwise keep the column `position` unchanged.

❹ Forward fill all `NaN` positions with the previous values; replace all remaining `NaN` values by 0.

❺ Plot the resulting positionings from the index position `SMA` on.

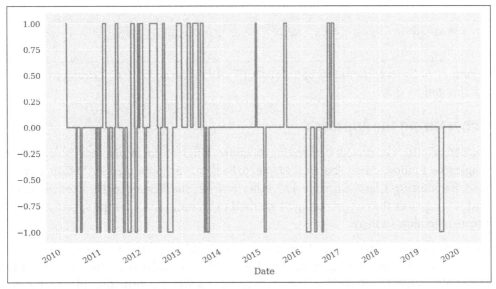

Figure 4-15. Positionings generated for GDX based on the mean-reversion strategy

The final step is to derive the strategy returns that are shown in Figure 4-16. The strategy outperforms the GDX ETF by quite a margin, although the particular parametrization leads to long periods with a neutral position (neither long or short).

These neutral positions are reflected in the flat parts of the strategy curve in Figure 4-16:

```
In [110]: data['strategy'] = data['position'].shift(1) * data['returns']
```

```
In [111]: data[['returns', 'strategy']].dropna().cumsum(
                    ).apply(np.exp).plot(figsize=(10, 6));
```

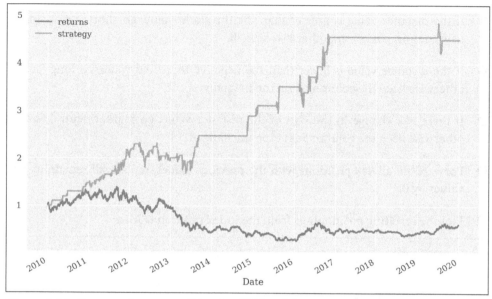

Figure 4-16. Gross performance of the GDX ETF and the mean-reversion strategy (SMA = 25, threshold = 3.5)

Generalizing the Approach

As before, the vectorized backtesting is more efficient to implement based on a respective Python class. The class `MRVectorBacktester` presented in "Mean Reversion Backtesting Class" on page 120 inherits from the `MomVectorBacktester` class and just replaces the `run_strategy()` method to accommodate for the specifics of the mean-reversion strategy.

The example now uses GLD and sets the proportional transaction costs to 0.1%. The initial amount to invest is again set to 10,000 USD. The SMA is 43 this time, and the threshold value is set to 7.5. Figure 4-17 shows the performance of the mean-reversion strategy compared to the GLD ETF:

```
In [112]: import MRVectorBacktester as MR    ❶
```

```
In [113]: mrbt = MR.MRVectorBacktester('GLD', '2010-1-1', '2019-12-31',
                                       10000, 0.001)    ❷
```

```
In [114]: mrbt.run_strategy(SMA=43, threshold=7.5)   ❸
Out[114]: (13542.15, 646.21)

In [115]: mrbt.plot_results()   ❹
```

❶ Imports the module as MR.

❷ Instantiates an object of the MRVectorBacktester class with 10,000 USD initial
   capital and 0.1% proportional transaction costs per trade; the strategy significantly outperforms the benchmark instrument in this case.

❸ Backtests the mean-reversion strategy with an SMA value of 43 and a threshold
   value of 7.5.

❹ Plots the cumulative performance of the strategy against the base instrument.

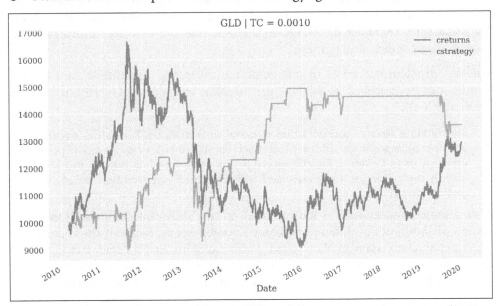

*Figure 4-17. Gross performance of the GLD ETF and the mean-reversion strategy (SMA =
43, threshold = 7.5, transaction costs of 0.1%)*

Data Snooping and Overfitting

The emphasis in this chapter, as well as in the rest of this book, is on the technological
implementation of important concepts in algorithmic trading by using Python. The
strategies, parameters, data sets, and algorithms used are sometimes arbitrarily
chosen and sometimes purposefully chosen to make a certain point. Without a doubt,
when discussing technical methods applied to finance, it is more exciting and

motivating to see examples that show "good results," even if they might not generalize on other financial instruments or time periods, for example.

The ability to show examples with good results often comes at the cost of *data snooping*. According to White (2000), data snooping can be defined as follows:

> Data snooping occurs when a given set of data is used more than once for purposes of inference or model selection.

In other words, a certain approach might be applied multiple or even many times on the same data set to arrive at satisfactory numbers and plots. This, of course, is intellectually dishonest in trading strategy research because it pretends that a trading strategy has some economic potential that might not be realistic in a real-world context. Because the focus of this book is the use of Python as a programming language for algorithmic trading, the data snooping approach might be justifiable. This is in analogy to a mathematics book which, by way of an example, solves an equation that has a unique solution that can be easily identified. In mathematics, such straightforward examples are rather the exception than the rule, but they are nevertheless frequently used for didactical purposes.

Another problem that arises in this context is *overfitting*. Overfitting in a trading context can be described as follows (see the Man Institute on Overfitting (*https://oreil.ly/uYIGs*)):

> Overfitting is when a model describes noise rather than signal. The model may have good performance on the data on which it was tested, but little or no predictive power on new data in the future. Overfitting can be described as finding patterns that aren't actually there. There is a cost associated with overfitting—an overfitted strategy will underperform in the future.

Even a simple strategy, such as the one based on two SMA values, allows for the backtesting of thousands of different parameter combinations. Some of those combinations are almost certain to show good performance results. As Bailey et al. (2015) discuss in detail, this easily leads to backtest overfitting with the people responsible for the backtesting often not even being aware of the problem. They point out:

> Recent advances in algorithmic research and high-performance computing have made it nearly trivial to test millions and billions of alternative investment strategies on a finite dataset of financial time series….[I]t is common practice to use this computational power to calibrate the parameters of an investment strategy in order to maximize its performance. But because the signal-to-noise ratio is so weak, often the result of such calibration is that parameters are chosen to profit from past noise rather than future signal. The outcome is an overfit backtest.

The problem of the validity of empirical results, in a statistical sense, is of course not constrained to strategy backtesting in a financial context.

Ioannidis (2005), referring to medical publications, emphasizes probabilistic and statistical considerations when judging the reproducibility and validity of research results:

> There is increasing concern that in modern research, false findings may be the majority or even the vast majority of published research claims. However, this should not be surprising. It can be proven that most claimed research findings are false....As has been shown previously, the probability that a research finding is indeed true depends on the prior probability of it being true (before doing the study), the statistical power of the study, and the level of statistical significance.

Against this background, if a trading strategy in this book is shown to perform well given a certain data set, combination of parameters, and maybe a specific machine learning algorithm, this neither constitutes any kind of recommendation for the particular configuration nor allows it to draw more general conclusions about the quality and performance potential of the strategy configuration at hand.

You are, of course, encouraged to use the code and examples presented in this book to explore your own algorithmic trading strategy ideas and to implement them in practice based on your own backtesting results, validations, and conclusions. After all, proper and diligent strategy research is what financial markets will compensate for, not brute-force driven data snooping and overfitting.

Conclusions

Vectorization is a powerful concept in scientific computing, as well as for financial analytics, in the context of the backtesting of algorithmic trading strategies. This chapter introduces vectorization both with NumPy and pandas and applies it to backtest three types of trading strategies: strategies based on simple moving averages, momentum, and mean reversion. The chapter admittedly makes a number of simplifying assumptions, and a rigorous backtesting of trading strategies needs to take into account more factors that determine trading success in practice, such as data issues, selection issues, avoidance of overfitting, or market microstructure elements. However, the major goal of the chapter is to focus on the concept of vectorization and what it can do in algorithmic trading from a technological and implementation point of view. With regard to all concrete examples and results presented, the problems of data snooping, overfitting, and statistical significance need to be considered.

References and Further Resources

For the basics of vectorization with NumPy and pandas, refer to these books:

McKinney, Wes. 2017. *Python for Data Analysis*. 2nd ed. Sebastopol: O'Reilly.

VanderPlas, Jake. 2016. *Python Data Science Handbook*. Sebastopol: O'Reilly.

For the use of NumPy and pandas in a financial context, refer to these books:

Hilpisch, Yves. 2015. *Derivatives Analytics with Python: Data Analysis, Models, Simulation, Calibration, and Hedging*. Wiley Finance.

―――. 2017. *Listed Volatility and Variance Derivatives: A Python-Based Guide*. Wiley Finance.

―――. 2018. *Python for Finance: Mastering Data-Driven Finance*. 2nd ed. Sebastopol: O'Reilly.

For the topics of data snooping and overfitting, refer to these papers:

Bailey, David, Jonathan Borwein, Marcos López de Prado, and Qiji Jim Zhu. 2015. "The Probability of Backtest Overfitting." *Journal of Computational Finance* 20, (4): 39-69. *https://oreil.ly/sOHlf*.

Ioannidis, John. 2005. "Why Most Published Research Findings Are False." *PLoS Medicine* 2, (8): 696-701.

White, Halbert. 2000. "A Reality Check for Data Snooping." *Econometrica* 68, (5): 1097-1126.

For more background information and empirical results about trading strategies based on simple moving averages, refer to these sources:

Brock, William, Josef Lakonishok, and Blake LeBaron. 1992. "Simple Technical Trading Rules and the Stochastic Properties of Stock Returns." *Journal of Finance* 47, (5): 1731-1764.

Droke, Clif. 2001. *Moving Averages Simplified*. Columbia: Marketplace Books.

The book by Ernest Chan covers in detail trading strategies based on momentum, as well as on mean reversion. The book is also a good source for the pitfalls of backtesting trading strategies:

Chan, Ernest. 2013. *Algorithmic Trading: Winning Strategies and Their Rationale*. Hoboken et al: John Wiley & Sons.

These research papers analyze characteristics and sources of profit for *cross-sectional momentum* strategies, the traditional approach to momentum-based trading:

Chan, Louis, Narasimhan Jegadeesh, and Josef Lakonishok. 1996. "Momentum Strategies." *Journal of Finance* 51, (5): 1681-1713.

Jegadeesh, Narasimhan, and Sheridan Titman. 1993. "Returns to Buying Winners and Selling Losers: Implications for Stock Market Efficiency." *Journal of Finance* 48, (1): 65-91.

Jegadeesh, Narasimhan, and Sheridan Titman. 2001. "Profitability of Momentum Strategies: An Evaluation of Alternative Explanations." *Journal of Finance* 56, (2): 599-720.

The paper by Moskowitz et al. provides an analysis of so-called *time series momentum* strategies:

Moskowitz, Tobias, Yao Hua Ooi, and Lasse Heje Pedersen. 2012. "Time Series Momentum." *Journal of Financial Economics* 104: 228-250.

These papers empirically analyze mean reversion in asset prices:

Balvers, Ronald, Yangru Wu, and Erik Gilliland. 2000. "Mean Reversion across National Stock Markets and Parametric Contrarian Investment Strategies." *Journal of Finance* 55, (2): 745-772.

Kim, Myung Jig, Charles Nelson, and Richard Startz. 1991. "Mean Reversion in Stock Prices? A Reappraisal of the Empirical Evidence." *Review of Economic Studies* 58: 515-528.

Spierdijk, Laura, Jacob Bikker, and Peter van den Hoek. 2012. "Mean Reversion in International Stock Markets: An Empirical Analysis of the 20th Century." *Journal of International Money and Finance* 31: 228-249.

Python Scripts

This section presents Python scripts referenced and used in this chapter.

SMA Backtesting Class

The following presents Python code with a class for the vectorized backtesting of strategies based on *simple moving averages*:

```
#
# Python Module with Class
# for Vectorized Backtesting
# of SMA-based Strategies
#
# Python for Algorithmic Trading
# (c) Dr. Yves J. Hilpisch
# The Python Quants GmbH
#
import numpy as np
import pandas as pd
from scipy.optimize import brute


class SMAVectorBacktester(object):
```

```
''' Class for the vectorized backtesting of SMA-based trading strategies.

Attributes
==========
symbol: str
    RIC symbol with which to work
SMA1: int
    time window in days for shorter SMA
SMA2: int
    time window in days for longer SMA
start: str
    start date for data retrieval
end: str
    end date for data retrieval

Methods
=======
get_data:
    retrieves and prepares the base data set
set_parameters:
    sets one or two new SMA parameters
run_strategy:
    runs the backtest for the SMA-based strategy
plot_results:
    plots the performance of the strategy compared to the symbol
update_and_run:
    updates SMA parameters and returns the (negative) absolute performance
optimize_parameters:
    implements a brute force optimization for the two SMA parameters
'''

def __init__(self, symbol, SMA1, SMA2, start, end):
    self.symbol = symbol
    self.SMA1 = SMA1
    self.SMA2 = SMA2
    self.start = start
    self.end = end
    self.results = None
    self.get_data()

def get_data(self):
    ''' Retrieves and prepares the data.
    '''
    raw = pd.read_csv('http://hilpisch.com/pyalgo_eikon_eod_data.csv',
                      index_col=0, parse_dates=True).dropna()
    raw = pd.DataFrame(raw[self.symbol])
    raw = raw.loc[self.start:self.end]
    raw.rename(columns={self.symbol: 'price'}, inplace=True)
    raw['return'] = np.log(raw / raw.shift(1))
    raw['SMA1'] = raw['price'].rolling(self.SMA1).mean()
    raw['SMA2'] = raw['price'].rolling(self.SMA2).mean()
    self.data = raw
```

```python
    def set_parameters(self, SMA1=None, SMA2=None):
        ''' Updates SMA parameters and resp. time series.
        '''
        if SMA1 is not None:
            self.SMA1 = SMA1
            self.data['SMA1'] = self.data['price'].rolling(
                self.SMA1).mean()
        if SMA2 is not None:
            self.SMA2 = SMA2
            self.data['SMA2'] = self.data['price'].rolling(self.SMA2).mean()

    def run_strategy(self):
        ''' Backtests the trading strategy.
        '''
        data = self.data.copy().dropna()
        data['position'] = np.where(data['SMA1'] > data['SMA2'], 1, -1)
        data['strategy'] = data['position'].shift(1) * data['return']
        data.dropna(inplace=True)
        data['creturns'] = data['return'].cumsum().apply(np.exp)
        data['cstrategy'] = data['strategy'].cumsum().apply(np.exp)
        self.results = data
        # gross performance of the strategy
        aperf = data['cstrategy'].iloc[-1]
        # out-/underperformance of strategy
        operf = aperf - data['creturns'].iloc[-1]
        return round(aperf, 2), round(operf, 2)

    def plot_results(self):
        ''' Plots the cumulative performance of the trading strategy
        compared to the symbol.
        '''
        if self.results is None:
            print('No results to plot yet. Run a strategy.')
        title = '%s | SMA1=%d, SMA2=%d' % (self.symbol,
                                            self.SMA1, self.SMA2)
        self.results[['creturns', 'cstrategy']].plot(title=title,
                                            figsize=(10, 6))

    def update_and_run(self, SMA):
        ''' Updates SMA parameters and returns negative absolute performance
        (for minimazation algorithm).

        Parameters
        ==========
        SMA: tuple
            SMA parameter tuple
        '''
        self.set_parameters(int(SMA[0]), int(SMA[1]))
        return -self.run_strategy()[0]

    def optimize_parameters(self, SMA1_range, SMA2_range):
```

```
    ''' Finds global maximum given the SMA parameter ranges.

    Parameters
    ==========
    SMA1_range, SMA2_range: tuple
        tuples of the form (start, end, step size)
    '''
    opt = brute(self.update_and_run, (SMA1_range, SMA2_range), finish=None)
    return opt, -self.update_and_run(opt)


if __name__ == '__main__':
    smabt = SMAVectorBacktester('EUR=', 42, 252,
                                '2010-1-1', '2020-12-31')
    print(smabt.run_strategy())
    smabt.set_parameters(SMA1=20, SMA2=100)
    print(smabt.run_strategy())
    print(smabt.optimize_parameters((30, 56, 4), (200, 300, 4)))
```

Momentum Backtesting Class

The following presents Python code with a class for the vectorized backtesting of strategies based on *time series momentum*:

```
#
# Python Module with Class
# for Vectorized Backtesting
# of Momentum-Based Strategies
#
# Python for Algorithmic Trading
# (c) Dr. Yves J. Hilpisch
# The Python Quants GmbH
#
import numpy as np
import pandas as pd


class MomVectorBacktester(object):
    ''' Class for the vectorized backtesting of
    momentum-based trading strategies.

    Attributes
    ==========
    symbol: str
        RIC (financial instrument) to work with
    start: str
        start date for data selection
    end: str
        end date for data selection
    amount: int, float
        amount to be invested at the beginning
    tc: float
```

```
        proportional transaction costs (e.g., 0.5% = 0.005) per trade

Methods
=======
get_data:
    retrieves and prepares the base data set
run_strategy:
    runs the backtest for the momentum-based strategy
plot_results:
    plots the performance of the strategy compared to the symbol
'''

def __init__(self, symbol, start, end, amount, tc):
    self.symbol = symbol
    self.start = start
    self.end = end
    self.amount = amount
    self.tc = tc
    self.results = None
    self.get_data()

def get_data(self):
    ''' Retrieves and prepares the data.
    '''
    raw = pd.read_csv('http://hilpisch.com/pyalgo_eikon_eod_data.csv',
                        index_col=0, parse_dates=True).dropna()
    raw = pd.DataFrame(raw[self.symbol])
    raw = raw.loc[self.start:self.end]
    raw.rename(columns={self.symbol: 'price'}, inplace=True)
    raw['return'] = np.log(raw / raw.shift(1))
    self.data = raw

def run_strategy(self, momentum=1):
    ''' Backtests the trading strategy.
    '''
    self.momentum = momentum
    data = self.data.copy().dropna()
    data['position'] = np.sign(data['return'].rolling(momentum).mean())
    data['strategy'] = data['position'].shift(1) * data['return']
    # determine when a trade takes place
    data.dropna(inplace=True)
    trades = data['position'].diff().fillna(0) != 0
    # subtract transaction costs from return when trade takes place
    data['strategy'][trades] -= self.tc
    data['creturns'] = self.amount * data['return'].cumsum().apply(np.exp)
    data['cstrategy'] = self.amount * \
        data['strategy'].cumsum().apply(np.exp)
    self.results = data
    # absolute performance of the strategy
    aperf = self.results['cstrategy'].iloc[-1]
    # out-/underperformance of strategy
    operf = aperf - self.results['creturns'].iloc[-1]
```

```
        return round(aperf, 2), round(operf, 2)

    def plot_results(self):
        ''' Plots the cumulative performance of the trading strategy
        compared to the symbol.
        '''
        if self.results is None:
            print('No results to plot yet. Run a strategy.')
        title = '%s | TC = %.4f' % (self.symbol, self.tc)
        self.results[['creturns', 'cstrategy']].plot(title=title,
                                                     figsize=(10, 6))


if __name__ == '__main__':
    mombt = MomVectorBacktester('XAU=', '2010-1-1', '2020-12-31',
                                10000, 0.0)
    print(mombt.run_strategy())
    print(mombt.run_strategy(momentum=2))
    mombt = MomVectorBacktester('XAU=', '2010-1-1', '2020-12-31',
                                10000, 0.001)
    print(mombt.run_strategy(momentum=2))
```

Mean Reversion Backtesting Class

The following presents Python code with a class for the vectorized backtesting of strategies based on *mean reversion:*.

```
#
# Python Module with Class
# for Vectorized Backtesting
# of Mean-Reversion Strategies
#
# Python for Algorithmic Trading
# (c) Dr. Yves J. Hilpisch
# The Python Quants GmbH
#
from MomVectorBacktester import *


class MRVectorBacktester(MomVectorBacktester):
    ''' Class for the vectorized backtesting of
    mean reversion-based trading strategies.

    Attributes
    ==========
    symbol: str
        RIC symbol with which to work
    start: str
        start date for data retrieval
    end: str
        end date for data retrieval
    amount: int, float
```

```
        amount to be invested at the beginning
    tc: float
        proportional transaction costs (e.g., 0.5% = 0.005) per trade

    Methods
    =======
    get_data:
        retrieves and prepares the base data set
    run_strategy:
        runs the backtest for the mean reversion-based strategy
    plot_results:
        plots the performance of the strategy compared to the symbol
    '''

    def run_strategy(self, SMA, threshold):
        ''' Backtests the trading strategy.
        '''
        data = self.data.copy().dropna()
        data['sma'] = data['price'].rolling(SMA).mean()
        data['distance'] = data['price'] - data['sma']
        data.dropna(inplace=True)
        # sell signals
        data['position'] = np.where(data['distance'] > threshold,
                                    -1, np.nan)
        # buy signals
        data['position'] = np.where(data['distance'] < -threshold,
                                    1, data['position'])
        # crossing of current price and SMA (zero distance)
        data['position'] = np.where(data['distance'] *
                                    data['distance'].shift(1) < 0,
                                    0, data['position'])
        data['position'] = data['position'].ffill().fillna(0)
        data['strategy'] = data['position'].shift(1) * data['return']
        # determine when a trade takes place
        trades = data['position'].diff().fillna(0) != 0
        # subtract transaction costs from return when trade takes place
        data['strategy'][trades] -= self.tc
        data['creturns'] = self.amount * \
            data['return'].cumsum().apply(np.exp)
        data['cstrategy'] = self.amount * \
            data['strategy'].cumsum().apply(np.exp)
        self.results = data
        # absolute performance of the strategy
        aperf = self.results['cstrategy'].iloc[-1]
        # out-/underperformance of strategy
        operf = aperf - self.results['creturns'].iloc[-1]
        return round(aperf, 2), round(operf, 2)


if __name__ == '__main__':
    mrbt = MRVectorBacktester('GDX', '2010-1-1', '2020-12-31',
                              10000, 0.0)
```

```
print(mrbt.run_strategy(SMA=25, threshold=5))
mrbt = MRVectorBacktester('GDX', '2010-1-1', '2020-12-31',
                          10000, 0.001)
print(mrbt.run_strategy(SMA=25, threshold=5))
mrbt = MRVectorBacktester('GLD', '2010-1-1', '2020-12-31',
                          10000, 0.001)
print(mrbt.run_strategy(SMA=42, threshold=7.5))
```

## CHAPTER 5

Predicting Market Movements with Machine Learning

Skynet begins to learn at a geometric rate. It becomes self-aware at 2:14 a.m. Eastern time, August 29th.

—The Terminator (*Terminator 2*)

Recent years have seen tremendous progress in the areas of machine learning, deep learning, and artificial intelligence. The financial industry in general and algorithmic traders around the globe in particular also try to benefit from these technological advances.

This chapter introduces techniques from statistics, like *linear regression*, and from machine learning, like *logistic regression*, to predict future price movements based on past returns. It also illustrates the use of *neural networks* to predict stock market movements. This chapter, of course, cannot replace a thorough introduction to machine learning, but it can show, from a practitioner's point of view, how to concretely apply certain techniques to the price prediction problem. For more details, refer to Hilpisch (2020).[1]

This chapter covers the following types of trading strategies:

Linear regression-based strategies
Such strategies use linear regression to extrapolate a trend or to derive a financial instrument's direction of future price movement.

---

[1] The books by Guido and Müller (2016) and VanderPlas (2016) provide practical, general introductions to machine learning with Python.

Machine learning-based strategies

In algorithmic trading it is generally enough to predict the direction of movement for a financial instrument as opposed to the absolute magnitude of that movement. With this reasoning, the prediction problem basically boils down to a *classification problem* of deciding whether there will be an upwards or downwards movement. Different machine learning algorithms have been developed to attack such classification problems. This chapter introduces logistic regression, as a typical baseline algorithm, for classification.

Deep learning-based strategies

Deep learning has been popularized by such technological giants as Facebook. Similar to machine learning algorithms, deep learning algorithms based on neural networks allow one to attack classification problems faced in financial market prediction.

The chapter is organized as follows. "Using Linear Regression for Market Movement Prediction" on page 124 introduces linear regression as a technique to predict index levels and the direction of price movements. "Using Machine Learning for Market Movement Prediction" on page 139 focuses on machine learning and introduces scikit-learn on the basis of linear regression. It mainly covers logistic regression as an alternative linear model explicitly applicable to classification problems. "Using Deep Learning for Market Movement Prediction" on page 153 introduces Keras to predict the direction of stock market movements based on neural network algorithms.

The major goal of this chapter is to provide practical approaches to predict future price movements in financial markets based on past returns. The basic assumption is that the efficient market hypothesis does not hold universally and that, similar to the reasoning behind the technical analysis of stock price charts, the history might provide some insights about the future that can be mined with statistical techniques. In other words, it is assumed that certain patterns in financial markets repeat themselves such that past observations can be leveraged to predict future price movements. More details are covered in Hilpisch (2020).

Using Linear Regression for Market Movement Prediction

Ordinary least squares (OLS) and linear regression are decades-old statistical techniques that have proven useful in many different application areas. This section uses linear regression for price prediction purposes. However, it starts with a quick review of the basics and an introduction to the basic approach.

A Quick Review of Linear Regression

Before applying linear regression, a quick review of the approach based on some randomized data might be helpful. The example code uses NumPy to first generate an ndarray object with data for the independent variable x. Based on this data, randomized data ("noisy data") for the dependent variable y is generated. NumPy provides two functions, polyfit and polyval, for a convenient implementation of OLS regression based on simple monomials. For a linear regression, the highest degree for the monomials to be used is set to 1. Figure 5-1 shows the data and the regression line:

```
In [1]: import os
        import random
        import numpy as np      ❶
        from pylab import mpl, plt      ❷
        plt.style.use('seaborn')
        mpl.rcParams['savefig.dpi'] = 300
        mpl.rcParams['font.family'] = 'serif'
        os.environ['PYTHONHASHSEED'] = '0'

In [2]: x = np.linspace(0, 10)      ❸

In [3]: def set_seeds(seed=100):
            random.seed(seed)
            np.random.seed(seed)
        set_seeds()      ❹

In [4]: y = x + np.random.standard_normal(len(x))      ❺

In [5]: reg = np.polyfit(x, y, deg=1)      ❻

In [6]: reg      ❼
Out[6]: array([0.94612934, 0.22855261])

In [7]: plt.figure(figsize=(10, 6))      ❽
        plt.plot(x, y, 'bo', label='data')      ❾
        plt.plot(x, np.polyval(reg, x), 'r', lw=2.5,
                 label='linear regression')      ❿
        plt.legend(loc=0);      ⓫
```

❶ Imports NumPy.

❷ Imports matplotlib.

❸ Generates an evenly spaced grid of floats for the x values between 0 and 10.

❹ Fixes the seed values for all relevant random number generators.

❺ Generates the randomized data for the y values.

❻ OLS regression of degree 1 (that is, linear regression) is conducted.

❼ Shows the optimal parameter values.

❽ Creates a new figure object.

❾ Plots the original data set as dots.

❿ Plots the regression line.

⓫ Creates the legend.

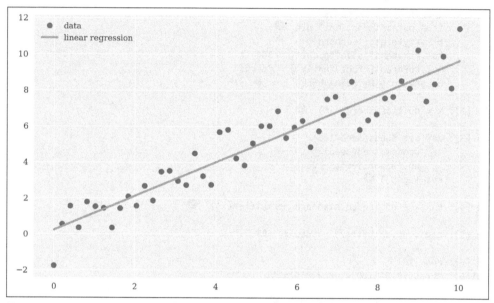

Figure 5-1. Linear regression illustrated based on randomized data

The interval for the dependent variable x is $x \in [0, 10]$. Enlarging the interval to, say, $x \in [0, 20]$ allows one to "predict" values for the dependent variable y beyond the domain of the original data set by an extrapolation given the optimal regression parameters. Figure 5-2 visualizes the extrapolation:

```
In [8]: plt.figure(figsize=(10, 6))
        plt.plot(x, y, 'bo', label='data')
        xn = np.linspace(0, 20)  ❶
        plt.plot(xn, np.polyval(reg, xn), 'r', lw=2.5,
                 label='linear regression')
        plt.legend(loc=0);
```

❶ Generates an enlarged domain for the x values.

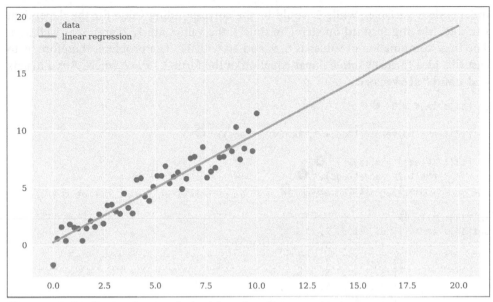

Figure 5-2. Prediction (extrapolation) based on linear regression

The Basic Idea for Price Prediction

Price prediction based on time series data has to deal with one special feature: the time-based ordering of the data. Generally, the ordering of the data is not important for the application of linear regression. In the first example in the previous section, the data on which the linear regression is implemented could have been compiled in completely different orderings, while keeping the x and y pairs constant. Independent of the ordering, the optimal regression parameters would have been the same.

However, in the context of predicting tomorrow's index level, for example, it seems to be of paramount importance to have the historic index levels in the correct order. If this is the case, one would then try to predict tomorrow's index level given the index level of today, yesterday, the day before, etc. The number of days used as input is generally called *lags*. Using today's index level and the two more from before therefore translates into *three lags*.

The next example casts this idea again into a rather simple context. The data the example uses are the numbers from 0 to 11:

```
In [9]: x = np.arange(12)

In [10]: x
Out[10]: array([ 0,  1,  2,  3,  4,  5,  6,  7,  8,  9, 10, 11])
```

Assume three lags for the regression. This implies three independent variables for the regression and one dependent one. More concretely, 0, 1, and 2 are values of the independent variables, while 3 would be the corresponding value for the dependent variable. Moving forward on step ("in time"), the values are 1, 2, and 3, as well as 4. The final combination of values is 8, 9, and 10 with 11. The problem, therefore, is to cast this idea formally into a linear equation of the form $A \cdot x = b$ where A is a matrix and x and b are vectors:

```
In [11]: lags = 3  ❶

In [12]: m = np.zeros((lags + 1, len(x) - lags))  ❷

In [13]: m[lags] = x[lags:]  ❸
            for i in range(lags):  ❹
                m[i] = x[i:i - lags]  ❺

In [14]: m.T  ❻
Out[14]: array([[ 0.,  1.,  2.,  3.],
                [ 1.,  2.,  3.,  4.],
                [ 2.,  3.,  4.,  5.],
                [ 3.,  4.,  5.,  6.],
                [ 4.,  5.,  6.,  7.],
                [ 5.,  6.,  7.,  8.],
                [ 6.,  7.,  8.,  9.],
                [ 7.,  8.,  9., 10.],
                [ 8.,  9., 10., 11.]])
```

❶ Defines the number of lags.

❷ Instantiates an `ndarray` object with the appropriate dimensions.

❸ Defines the target values (dependent variable).

❹ Iterates over the numbers from 0 to `lags` - 1.

❺ Defines the basis vectors (independent variables)

❻ Shows the transpose of the `ndarray` object m.

In the transposed `ndarray` object m, the first three columns contain the values for the three independent variables. They together form the matrix A. The fourth and final column represents the vector b. As a result, linear regression then yields the missing vector x. Since there are now more independent variables, `polyfit` and `polyval` do not work anymore. However, there is a function in the NumPy sub-package for linear algebra (`linalg`) that allows one to solve general least-squares problems: `lstsq`. Only the first element of the results array is needed since it contains the optimal regression parameters:

```
In [15]: reg = np.linalg.lstsq(m[:lags].T, m[lags], rcond=None)[0]  ❶
```

```
In [16]: reg  ❷
Out[16]: array([-0.66666667,  0.33333333,  1.33333333])

In [17]: np.dot(m[:lags].T, reg)  ❸
Out[17]: array([ 3.,  4.,  5.,  6.,  7.,  8.,  9., 10., 11.])
```

❶ Implements the linear OLS regression.

❷ Prints out the optimal parameters.

❸ The dot product yields the prediction results.

This basic idea easily carries over to real-world financial time series data.

Predicting Index Levels

The next step is to translate the basic approach to time series data for a real financial instrument, like the EUR/USD exchange rate:

```
In [18]: import pandas as pd  ❶

In [19]: raw = pd.read_csv('http://hilpisch.com/pyalgo_eikon_eod_data.csv',
                           index_col=0, parse_dates=True).dropna()  ❷

In [20]: raw.info()  ❷
         <class 'pandas.core.frame.DataFrame'>
         DatetimeIndex: 2516 entries, 2010-01-04 to 2019-12-31
         Data columns (total 12 columns):
          #   Column  Non-Null Count  Dtype
         ---  ------  --------------  -----
          0   AAPL.O  2516 non-null   float64
          1   MSFT.O  2516 non-null   float64
          2   INTC.O  2516 non-null   float64
          3   AMZN.O  2516 non-null   float64
          4   GS.N    2516 non-null   float64
          5   SPY     2516 non-null   float64
          6   .SPX    2516 non-null   float64
          7   .VIX    2516 non-null   float64
          8   EUR=    2516 non-null   float64
          9   XAU=    2516 non-null   float64
          10  GDX     2516 non-null   float64
          11  GLD     2516 non-null   float64
         dtypes: float64(12)
         memory usage: 255.5 KB

In [21]: symbol = 'EUR='

In [22]: data = pd.DataFrame(raw[symbol])  ❸

In [23]: data.rename(columns={symbol: 'price'}, inplace=True)  ❹
```

❶ Imports the pandas package.

❷ Retrieves end-of-day (EOD) data and stores it in a DataFrame object.

❸ The time series data for the specified symbol is selected from the original Data
Frame.

❹ Renames the single column to price.

Formally, the Python code from the preceding simple example hardly needs to be
changed to implement the regression-based prediction approach. Just the data object
needs to be replaced:

```
In [24]: lags = 5

In [25]: cols = []
         for lag in range(1, lags + 1):
             col = f'lag_{lag}'
             data[col] = data['price'].shift(lag)  ❶
             cols.append(col)
         data.dropna(inplace=True)

In [26]: reg = np.linalg.lstsq(data[cols], data['price'],
                               rcond=None)[0]

In [27]: reg
Out[27]: array([ 0.98635864,  0.02292172, -0.04769849,  0.05037365,
               -0.01208135])
```

❶ Takes the price column and shifts it by lag.

The optimal regression parameters illustrate what is typically called the *random walk
hypothesis*. This hypothesis states that stock prices or exchange rates, for example, follow a random walk with the consequence that the best predictor for tomorrow's price
is today's price. The optimal parameters seem to support such a hypothesis since
today's price almost completely explains the predicted price level for tomorrow. The
four other values hardly have any weight assigned.

Figure 5-3 shows the EUR/USD exchange rate and the predicted values. Due to the
sheer amount of data for the multi-year time window, the two time series are indistin-
guishable in the plot:

```
In [28]: data['prediction'] = np.dot(data[cols], reg)  ❶

In [29]: data[['price', 'prediction']].plot(figsize=(10, 6));  ❷
```

❶ Calculates the prediction values as the `dot` product.

❷ Plots the `price` and `prediction` columns.

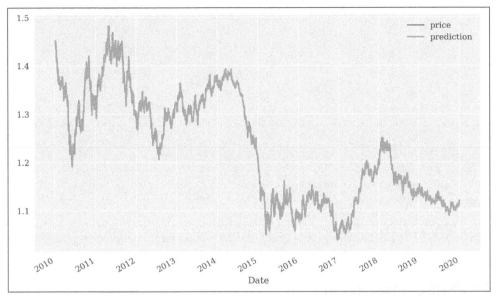

Figure 5-3. EUR/USD exchange rate and predicted values based on linear regression (five lags)

Zooming in by plotting the results for a much shorter time window allows one to better distinguish the two time series. Figure 5-4 shows the results for a three months time window. This plot illustrates that the prediction for tomorrow's rate is roughly today's rate. The prediction is more or less a shift of the original rate to the right by one trading day:

```
In [30]: data[['price', 'prediction']].loc['2019-10-1':].plot(
                 figsize=(10, 6));
```

Applying linear OLS regression to predict rates for EUR/USD based on historical rates provides support for the random walk hypothesis. The results of the numerical example show that today's rate is the best predictor for tomorrow's rate in a least-squares sense.

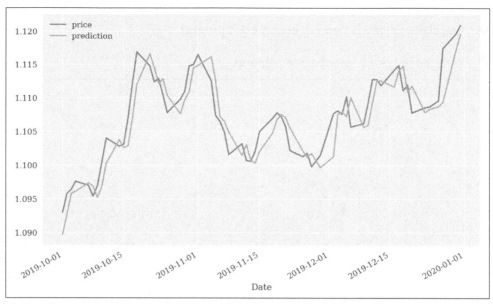

Figure 5-4. EUR/USD exchange rate and predicted values based on linear regression (five lags, three months only)

Predicting Future Returns

So far, the analysis is based on absolute rate levels. However, (log) returns might be a better choice for such statistical applications due to, for example, their characteristic of making the time series data stationary. The code to apply linear regression to the returns data is almost the same as before. This time it is not only today's return that is relevant to predict tomorrow's return, but the regression results are also completely different in nature:

```
In [31]: data['return'] = np.log(data['price'] /
                                  data['price'].shift(1))   ❶

In [32]: data.dropna(inplace=True)   ❷

In [33]: cols = []
         for lag in range(1, lags + 1):
             col = f'lag_{lag}'
             data[col] = data['return'].shift(lag)   ❸
             cols.append(col)
         data.dropna(inplace=True)

In [34]: reg = np.linalg.lstsq(data[cols], data['return'],
                               rcond=None)[0]

In [35]: reg
```

```
Out[35]: array([-0.015689  ,  0.00890227, -0.03634858,  0.01290924,
                -0.00636023])
```

❶ Calculates the log returns.

❷ Deletes all lines with NaN values.

❸ Takes the returns column for the lagged data.

Figure 5-5 shows the returns data and the prediction values. As the figure impressively illustrates, linear regression obviously cannot predict the magnitude of future returns to some significant extent:

```
In [36]: data['prediction'] = np.dot(data[cols], reg)
```

```
In [37]: data[['return', 'prediction']].iloc[lags:].plot(figsize=(10, 6));
```

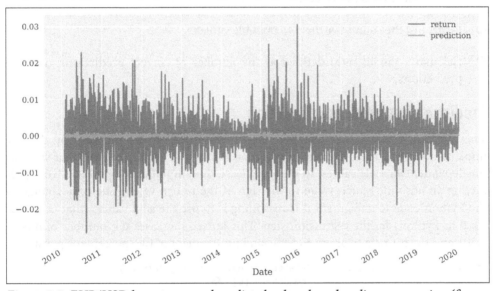

Figure 5-5. EUR/USD log returns and predicted values based on linear regression (five lags)

From a trading point of view, one might argue that it is not the magnitude of the forecasted return that is relevant, but rather whether the direction is forecasted correctly or not. To this end, a simple calculation yields an overview. Whenever the linear regression gets the direction right, meaning that the sign of the forecasted return is correct, the product of the market return and the predicted return is positive and otherwise negative.

In the example case, the prediction is 1,250 times correct and 1,242 wrong, which translates into a hit ratio of about 49.9%, or almost exactly 50%:

```
In [38]: hits = np.sign(data['return'] *
                        data['prediction']).value_counts()  ❶

In [39]: hits  ❷
Out[39]:  1.0    1250
         -1.0    1242
          0.0      13
         dtype: int64

In [40]: hits.values[0] / sum(hits)  ❸
Out[40]: 0.499001996007984
```

❶ Calculates the product of the market and predicted return, takes the sign of the results and counts the values.

❷ Prints out the counts for the two possible values.

❸ Calculates the hit ratio defined as the number of correct predictions given all predictions.

Predicting Future Market Direction

The question that arises is whether one can improve on the hit ratio by directly implementing the linear regression based on the sign of the log returns that serve as the dependent variable values. In theory at least, this simplifies the problem from predicting an absolute return value to the sign of the return value. The only change in the Python code to implement this reasoning is to use the sign values (that is, 1.0 or -1.0 in Python) for the regression step. This indeed increases the number of hits to 1,301 and the hit ratio to about 51.9%—an improvement of two percentage points:

```
In [41]: reg = np.linalg.lstsq(data[cols], np.sign(data['return']),
                               rcond=None)[0]  ❶

In [42]: reg
Out[42]: array([-5.11938725, -2.24077248, -5.13080606, -3.03753232,
                -2.14819119])

In [43]: data['prediction'] = np.sign(np.dot(data[cols], reg))  ❷

In [44]: data['prediction'].value_counts()
Out[44]:  1.0    1300
         -1.0    1205
         Name: prediction, dtype: int64

In [45]: hits = np.sign(data['return'] *
                        data['prediction']).value_counts()
```

```
In [46]: hits
Out[46]:  1.0     1301
         -1.0     1191
          0.0       13
         dtype: int64

In [47]: hits.values[0] / sum(hits)
Out[47]: 0.5193612774451097
```

❶ This directly uses the sign of the return to be predicted for the regression.

❷ Also, for the prediction step, only the sign is relevant.

Vectorized Backtesting of Regression-Based Strategy

The hit ratio alone does not tell too much about the economic potential of a trading strategy using linear regression in the way presented so far. It is well known that the ten best and worst days in the markets for a given period of time considerably influence the overall performance of investments.[2] In an ideal world, a long-short trader would try, of course, to benefit from both best and worst days by going long and short, respectively, on the basis of appropriate market timing indicators. Translated to the current context, this implies that, in addition to the hit ratio, the quality of the market timing matters. Therefore, a backtesting along the lines of the approach in Chapter 4 can give a better picture of the value of regression for prediction.

Given the data that is already available, vectorized backtesting boils down to two lines of Python code including visualization. This is due to the fact that the prediction values already reflect the market positions (long or short). Figure 5-6 shows that, in-sample, the strategy under the current assumptions outperforms the market significantly (ignoring, among other things, transaction costs):

```
In [48]: data.head()
Out[48]:              price     lag_1     lag_2     lag_3     lag_4     lag_5 \
         Date
         2010-01-20  1.4101 -0.005858 -0.008309 -0.000551  0.001103 -0.001310
         2010-01-21  1.4090 -0.013874 -0.005858 -0.008309 -0.000551  0.001103
         2010-01-22  1.4137 -0.000780 -0.013874 -0.005858 -0.008309 -0.000551
         2010-01-25  1.4150  0.003330 -0.000780 -0.013874 -0.005858 -0.008309
         2010-01-26  1.4073  0.000919  0.003330 -0.000780 -0.013874 -0.005858

                     prediction    return
         Date
         2010-01-20         1.0 -0.013874
         2010-01-21         1.0 -0.000780
```

---

2 See, for example, the discussion in The Tale of 10 Days (*https://oreil.ly/KRH78*).

```
2010-01-22        1.0  0.003330
2010-01-25        1.0  0.000919
2010-01-26        1.0 -0.005457
```

In [49]: data['strategy'] = data['prediction'] * data['return']   ❶

In [50]: data[['return', 'strategy']].sum().apply(np.exp)   ❷
Out[50]: return   0.784026
         strategy   1.654154
         dtype: float64

In [51]: data[['return', 'strategy']].dropna().cumsum(
).apply(np.exp).plot(figsize=(10, 6));   ❸

❶   Multiplies the prediction values (positionings) by the market returns.

❷   Calculates the gross performance of the base instrument and the strategy.

❸   Plots the gross performance of the base instrument and the strategy over time
    (in-sample, no transaction costs).

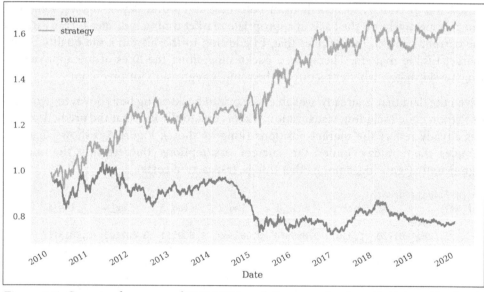

Figure 5-6. Gross performance of EUR/USD and the regression-based strategy (five lags)

The hit ratio of a prediction-based strategy is only one side of the coin when it comes to overall strategy performance. The other side is how well the strategy gets the market timing right. A strategy correctly predicting the best and worst days over a certain period of time might outperform the market even with a hit ratio below 50%. On the other hand, a strategy with a hit ratio well above 50% might still underperform the base instrument if it gets the rare, large movements wrong.

Generalizing the Approach

"Linear Regression Backtesting Class" on page 167 presents a Python module containing a class for the vectorized backtesting of the regression-based trading strategy in the spirit of Chapter 4. In addition to allowing for an arbitrary amount to invest and proportional transaction costs, it allows the *in-sample fitting* of the linear regression model and the *out-of-sample evaluation*. This means that the regression model is fitted based on one part of the data set, say for the years 2010 to 2015, and is evaluated based on another part of the data set, say for the years 2016 and 2019. For all strategies that involve an optimization or fitting step, this provides a more realistic view on the performance in practice since it helps avoid the problems arising from data snooping and the overfitting of models (see also "Data Snooping and Overfitting" on page 111).

Figure 5-7 shows that the regression-based strategy based on five lags does outperform the EUR/USD base instrument for the particular configuration also out-of-sample and before accounting for transaction costs:

```
In [52]: import LRVectorBacktester as LR  ❶

In [53]: lrbt = LR.LRVectorBacktester('EUR=', '2010-1-1', '2019-12-31',
                                      10000, 0.0)  ❷

In [54]: lrbt.run_strategy('2010-1-1', '2019-12-31',
                           '2010-1-1', '2019-12-31', lags=5)  ❸
Out[54]: (17166.53, 9442.42)

In [55]: lrbt.run_strategy('2010-1-1', '2017-12-31',
                           '2018-1-1', '2019-12-31', lags=5)  ❹
Out[55]: (10160.86, 791.87)

In [56]: lrbt.plot_results()  ❺
```

❶ Imports the module as LR.

❷ Instantiates an object of the LRVectorBacktester class.

❸ Trains and evaluates the strategy on the same data set.

➍ Uses two different data sets for the training and evaluation steps.

➎ Plots the out of sample strategy performance compared to the market.

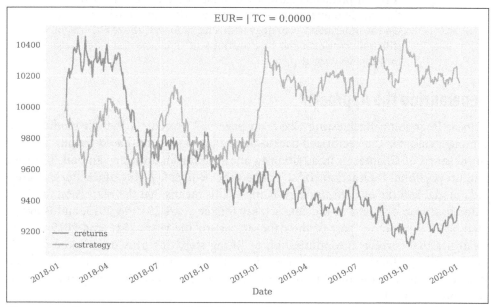

Figure 5-7. Gross performance of EUR/USD and the regression-based strategy (five lags, out-of-sample, before transaction costs)

Consider the GDX ETF. The strategy configuration chosen shows an outperformance out-of-sample and after taking transaction costs into account (see Figure 5-8):

```
In [57]: lrbt = LR.LRVectorBacktester('GDX', '2010-1-1', '2019-12-31',
                                       10000, 0.002)  ❶

In [58]: lrbt.run_strategy('2010-1-1', '2019-12-31',
                           '2010-1-1', '2019-12-31', lags=7)
Out[58]: (23642.32, 17649.69)

In [59]: lrbt.run_strategy('2010-1-1', '2014-12-31',
                           '2015-1-1', '2019-12-31', lags=7)
Out[59]: (28513.35, 14888.41)

In [60]: lrbt.plot_results()
```

❶ Changes to the time series data for GDX.

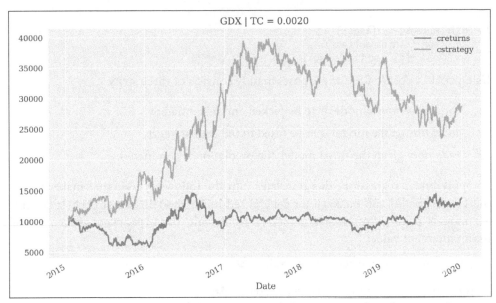

Figure 5-8. Gross performance of the GDX ETF and the regression-based strategy (seven lags, out-of-sample, after transaction costs)

Using Machine Learning for Market Movement Prediction

Nowadays, the Python ecosystem provides a number of packages in the machine learning field. The most popular of these is `scikit-learn` (see `scikit-learn` home page (*http://scikit-learn.org*)), which is also one of the best documented and maintained packages. This section first introduces the API of the package based on linear regression, replicating some of the results of the previous section. It then goes on to use logistic regression as a classification algorithm to attack the problem of predicting the future market direction.

Linear Regression with scikit-learn

To introduce the `scikit-learn` API, revisiting the basic idea behind the prediction approach presented in this chapter is fruitful. Data preparation is the same as with NumPy only:

```
In [61]: x = np.arange(12)

In [62]: x
Out[62]: array([ 0,  1,  2,  3,  4,  5,  6,  7,  8,  9, 10, 11])

In [63]: lags = 3

In [64]: m = np.zeros((lags + 1, len(x) - lags))
```

```
In [65]: m[lags] = x[lags:]
          for i in range(lags):
              m[i] = x[i:i - lags]
```

Using scikit-learn for our purposes mainly consists of three steps:

1. *Model selection*: a model is to be picked and instantiated.

2. *Model fitting*: the model is to be fitted to the data at hand.

3. *Prediction*: given the fitted model, the prediction is conducted.

To apply linear regression, this translates into the following code that makes use of the linear_model sub-package for generalized linear models (see scikit-learn linear models page (*https://oreil.ly/5XoG1*)). By default, the LinearRegression model fits an intercept value:

```
In [66]: from sklearn import linear_model   ❶

In [67]: lm = linear_model.LinearRegression()   ❷

In [68]: lm.fit(m[:lags].T, m[lags])   ❸
Out[68]: LinearRegression()

In [69]: lm.coef_   ❹
Out[69]: array([0.33333333, 0.33333333, 0.33333333])

In [70]: lm.intercept_   ❺
Out[70]: 2.0

In [71]: lm.predict(m[:lags].T)   ❻
Out[71]: array([ 3.,   4.,   5.,   6.,   7.,   8.,   9., 10.,  11.])
```

❶ Imports the generalized linear model classes.

❷ Instantiates a linear regression model.

❸ Fits the model to the data.

❹ Prints out the optimal regression parameters.

❺ Prints out the intercept values.

❻ Predicts the sought after values given the fitted model.

Setting the parameter fit_intercept to False gives the exact same regression results as with NumPy and polyfit():

```
In [72]: lm = linear_model.LinearRegression(fit_intercept=False)   ❶
```

```
In [73]: lm.fit(m[:lags].T, m[lags])
Out[73]: LinearRegression(fit_intercept=False)

In [74]: lm.coef_
Out[74]: array([-0.66666667,  0.33333333,  1.33333333])

In [75]: lm.intercept_
Out[75]: 0.0

In [76]: lm.predict(m[:lags].T)
Out[76]: array([ 3.,   4.,   5.,   6.,   7.,   8.,   9.,  10.,  11.])
```

❶ Forces a fit without intercept value.

This example already illustrates quite well how to apply scikit-learn to the prediction problem. Due to its consistent API design, the basic approach carries over to other models, as well.

A Simple Classification Problem

In a classification problem, it has to be decided to which of a limited set of categories ("classes") a new observation belongs. A classical problem studied in machine learning is the identification of handwritten digits from 0 to 9. Such an identification leads to a correct result, say 3. Or it leads to a wrong result, say 6 or 8, where all such wrong results are equally wrong. In a financial market context, predicting the price of a financial instrument can lead to a numerical result that is far off the correct one or that is quite close to it. Predicting tomorrow's market direction, there can only be a correct or a ("completely") wrong result. The latter is a *classification problem* with the set of categories limited to, for example, "up" and "down" or "+1" and "−1" or "1" and "0." By contrast, the former problem is an *estimation problem*.

A simple example for a classification problem is found on Wikipedia under Logistic Regression (*https://oreil.ly/zg8gW*). The data set relates the number of hours studied to prepare for an exam by a number of students to the success of each student in passing the exam or not. While the number of hours studied is a real number (float object), the passing of the exam is either True or False (that is, 1 or 0 in numbers). Figure 5-9 shows the data graphically:

```
In [77]: hours = np.array([0.5, 0.75, 1., 1.25, 1.5, 1.75, 1.75, 2.,
                           2.25, 2.5, 2.75, 3., 3.25, 3.5, 4., 4.25,
                           4.5, 4.75, 5., 5.5])   ❶

In [78]: success = np.array([0, 0, 0, 0, 0, 0, 1, 0, 1, 0, 1, 0, 1,
                             0, 1, 1, 1, 1, 1, 1])   ❷

In [79]: plt.figure(figsize=(10, 6))
         plt.plot(hours, success, 'ro')   ❸
         plt.ylim(-0.2, 1.2);   ❹
```

❶ The number of hours studied by the different students (sequence matters).

❷ The success of each student in passing the exam (sequence matters).

❸ Plots the data set taking hours as x values and success as y values.

❹ Adjusts the limits of the y-axis.

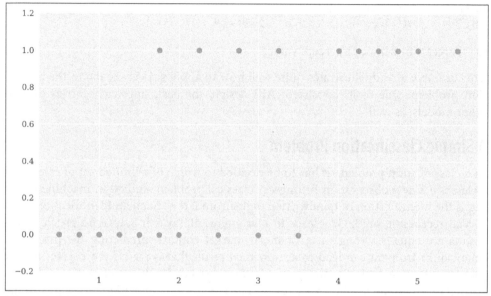

Figure 5-9. Example data for classification problem

The basic question typically raised in a such a context is: given a certain number of hours studied by a student (not in the data set), will they pass the exam or not? What answer could linear regression give? Probably not one that is satisfying, as Figure 5-10 shows. Given different numbers of hours studied, linear regression gives (prediction) values mainly between 0 and 1, as well as lower and higher. But there can only be *failure* or *success* as the outcome of taking the exam:

```
In [80]: reg = np.polyfit(hours, success, deg=1)   ❶
```

```
In [81]: plt.figure(figsize=(10, 6))
         plt.plot(hours, success, 'ro')
         plt.plot(hours, np.polyval(reg, hours), 'b')   ❷
         plt.ylim(-0.2, 1.2);
```

❶ Implements a linear regression on the data set.

❷ Plots the regression line in addition to the data set.

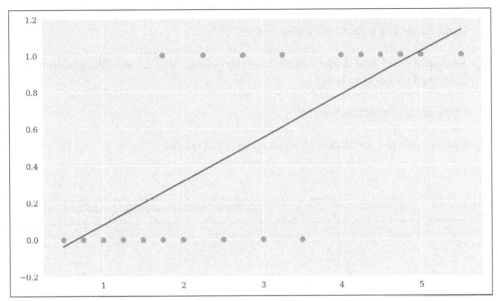

Figure 5-10. Linear regression applied to the classification problem

This is where classification algorithms, like logistic regression and support vector machines, come into play. For illustration, the application of logistic regression suffices (see James et al. (2013, ch. 4) for more background information). The respective class is also found in the linear_model sub-package. Figure 5-11 shows the result of the following Python code. This time, there is a clear cut (prediction) value for every different input value. The model predicts that students who studied for 0 to 2 hours will fail. For all values equal to or higher than 2.75 hours, the model predicts that a student passes the exam:

```
In [82]: lm = linear_model.LogisticRegression(solver='lbfgs')  ❶

In [83]: hrs = hours.reshape(1, -1).T  ❷

In [84]: lm.fit(hrs, success)  ❸
Out[84]: LogisticRegression()

In [85]: prediction = lm.predict(hrs)  ❹

In [86]: plt.figure(figsize=(10, 6))
         plt.plot(hours, success, 'ro', label='data')
         plt.plot(hours, prediction, 'b', label='prediction')
         plt.legend(loc=0)
         plt.ylim(-0.2, 1.2);
```

❶ Instantiates the logistic regression model.

❷ Reshapes the one-dimensional `ndarray` object to a two-dimensional one (required by `scikit-learn`).

❸ Implements the fitting step.

❹ Implements the prediction step given the fitted model.

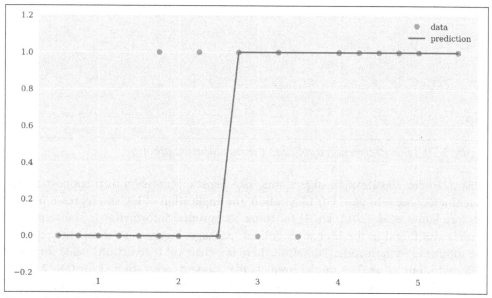

Figure 5-11. Logistic regression applied to the classification problem

However, as Figure 5-11 shows, there is no guarantee that 2.75 hours or more lead to success. It is just "more probable" to succeed from that many hours on than to fail. This probabilistic reasoning can also be analyzed and visualized based on the same model instance, as the following code illustrates. The dashed line in Figure 5-12 shows the probability for succeeding (monotonically increasing). The dash-dotted line shows the probability for failing (monotonically decreasing):

```
In [87]: prob = lm.predict_proba(hrs)  ❶

In [88]: plt.figure(figsize=(10, 6))
         plt.plot(hours, success, 'ro')
         plt.plot(hours, prediction, 'b')
         plt.plot(hours, prob.T[0], 'm--',
                 label='$p(h)$ for zero')  ❷
         plt.plot(hours, prob.T[1], 'g-.',
                 label='$p(h)$ for one')  ❸
```

```
plt.ylim(-0.2, 1.2)
plt.legend(loc=0);
```

❶ Predicts probabilities for succeeding and failing, respectively.

❷ Plots the probabilities for failing.

❸ Plots the probabilities for succeeding.

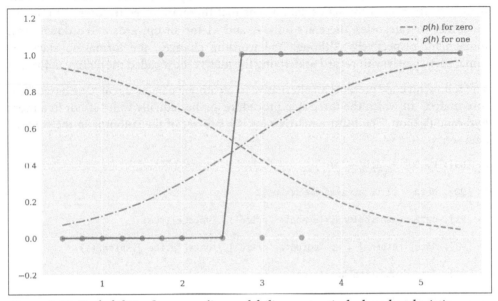

Figure 5-12. Probabilities for succeeding and failing, respectively, based on logistic regression

 scikit-learn does a good job of providing access to a great variety of machine learning models in a unified way. The examples show that the API for applying logistic regression does not differ from the one for linear regression. scikit-learn, therefore, is well suited to test a number of appropriate machine learning models in a certain application scenario without altering the Python code very much.

Equipped with the basics, the next step is to apply logistic regression to the problem of predicting market direction.

Using Logistic Regression to Predict Market Direction

In machine learning, one generally speaks of *features* instead of *independent* or *explanatory variables* as in a regression context. The simple classification example has a single feature only: the number of hours studied. In practice, one often has more than one feature that can be used for classification. Given the prediction approach introduced in this chapter, one can identify a *feature* by a *lag*. Therefore, working with three lags from the time series data means that there are three features. As possible outcomes or categories, there are only +1 and -1 for an upwards and a downwards movement, respectively. Although the wording changes, the formalism stays the same, particularly with regard to deriving the matrix, now called the *feature matrix*.

The following code presents an alternative to creating a pandas DataFrame based "feature matrix" to which the three step procedure applies equally well—if not in a more Pythonic fashion. The feature matrix now is a sub-set of the columns in the original data set:

```
In [89]: symbol = 'GLD'

In [90]: data = pd.DataFrame(raw[symbol])

In [91]: data.rename(columns={symbol: 'price'}, inplace=True)

In [92]: data['return'] = np.log(data['price'] / data['price'].shift(1))

In [93]: data.dropna(inplace=True)

In [94]: lags = 3

In [95]: cols = []  ❶
            for lag in range(1, lags + 1):
                col = 'lag_{}'.format(lag)  ❷
                data[col] = data['return'].shift(lag)  ❸
                cols.append(col)  ❹

In [96]: data.dropna(inplace=True)  ❺
```

❶ Instantiates an empty list object to collect column names.

❷ Creates a str object for the column name.

❸ Adds a new column to the DataFrame object with the respective lag data.

❹ Appends the column name to the list object.

❺ Makes sure that the data set is complete.

Logistic regression improves the hit ratio compared to linear regression by more than a percentage point to about 54.5%. Figure 5-13 shows the performance of the strategy based on logistic regression-based predictions. Although the hit ratio is higher, the performance is worse than with linear regression:

```
In [97]: from sklearn.metrics import accuracy_score

In [98]: lm = linear_model.LogisticRegression(C=1e7, solver='lbfgs',
                                               multi_class='auto',
                                               max_iter=1000)  ❶

In [99]: lm.fit(data[cols], np.sign(data['return']))  ❷
Out[99]: LogisticRegression(C=10000000.0, max_iter=1000)

In [100]: data['prediction'] = lm.predict(data[cols])  ❸

In [101]: data['prediction'].value_counts()  ❹
Out[101]:  1.0    1983
          -1.0     529
          Name: prediction, dtype: int64

In [102]: hits = np.sign(data['return'].iloc[lags:] *
                         data['prediction'].iloc[lags:]
                         ).value_counts()  ❺

In [103]: hits
Out[103]:  1.0    1338
          -1.0    1159
           0.0      12
          dtype: int64

In [104]: accuracy_score(data['prediction'],
                         np.sign(data['return']))  ❻
Out[104]: 0.5338375796178344

In [105]: data['strategy'] = data['prediction'] * data['return']  ❼

In [106]: data[['return', 'strategy']].sum().apply(np.exp)  ❼
Out[106]: return      1.289478
          strategy    2.458716
          dtype: float64

In [107]: data[['return', 'strategy']].cumsum().apply(np.exp).plot(
                                        figsize=(10, 6));  ❽
```

❶ Instantiates the model object using a C value that gives less weight to the regularization term (see the Generalized Linear Models page (*https://oreil.ly/D819h*)).

❷ Fits the model based on the sign of the returns to be predicted.

❸ Generates a new column in the DataFrame object and writes the prediction values to it.

❹ Shows the number of the resulting long and short positions, respectively.

❺ Calculates the number of correct and wrong predictions.

❻ The accuracy (hit ratio) is 53.3% in this case.

❼ However, the gross performance of the strategy…

❽ …is much higher when compared with the passive benchmark investment.

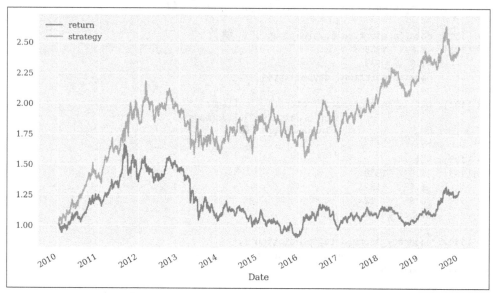

Figure 5-13. Gross performance of GLD ETF and the logistic regression-based strategy (3 lags, in-sample)

Increasing the number of lags used from three to five decreases the hit ratio but improves the gross performance of the strategy to some extent (in-sample, before transaction costs). Figure 5-14 shows the resulting performance:

```
In [108]: data = pd.DataFrame(raw[symbol])

In [109]: data.rename(columns={symbol: 'price'}, inplace=True)

In [110]: data['return'] = np.log(data['price'] / data['price'].shift(1))

In [111]: lags = 5
```

```
In [112]: cols = []
          for lag in range(1, lags + 1):
              col = 'lag_%d' % lag
              data[col] = data['price'].shift(lag)  ❶
              cols.append(col)

In [113]: data.dropna(inplace=True)

In [114]: lm.fit(data[cols], np.sign(data['return']))  ❷
Out[114]: LogisticRegression(C=10000000.0, max_iter=1000)

In [115]: data['prediction'] = lm.predict(data[cols])

In [116]: data['prediction'].value_counts()  ❸
Out[116]:  1.0    2047
          -1.0     464
          Name: prediction, dtype: int64

In [117]: hits = np.sign(data['return'].iloc[lags:] *
                         data['prediction'].iloc[lags:]
                         ).value_counts()

In [118]: hits
Out[118]:  1.0    1331
          -1.0    1163
           0.0      12
          dtype: int64

In [119]: accuracy_score(data['prediction'],
                        np.sign(data['return']))  ❹
Out[119]: 0.5312624452409399

In [120]: data['strategy'] = data['prediction'] * data['return']  ❺

In [121]: data[['return', 'strategy']].sum().apply(np.exp)  ❺
Out[121]: return      1.283110
          strategy    2.656833
          dtype: float64

In [122]: data[['return', 'strategy']].cumsum().apply(np.exp).plot(
                                          figsize=(10, 6));
```

❶ Increases the number of lags to five.

❷ Fits the model based on five lags.

❸ There are now significantly more short positions with the new parametrization.

❹ The accuracy (hit ratio) decreases to 53.1%.

❺ The cumulative performance also increases significantly.

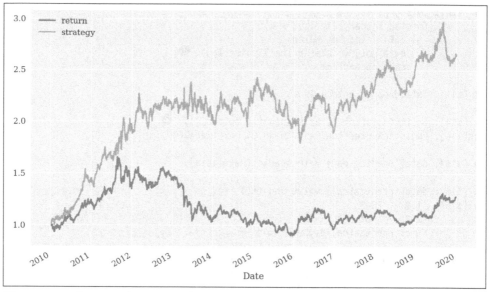

Figure 5-14. Gross performance of GLD ETF and the logistic regression-based strategy (five lags, in-sample)

 You have to be careful to not fall into the overfitting trap here. A more realistic picture is obtained by an approach that uses *training data* (= in-sample data) for the *fitting* of the model and *test data* (= out-of-sample data) for the *evaluation* of the strategy performance. This is done in the following section, when the approach is generalized again in the form of a Python class.

Generalizing the Approach

"Classification Algorithm Backtesting Class" on page 170 presents a Python module with a class for the vectorized backtesting of strategies based on linear models from scikit-learn. Although only linear and logistic regression are implemented, the number of models is easily increased. In principle, the ScikitVectorBacktester class could inherit selected methods from the LRVectorBacktester but it is presented in a self-contained fashion. This makes it easier to enhance and reuse this class for practical applications.

Based on the ScikitBacktesterClass, an out-of-sample evaluation of the logistic regression-based strategy is possible. The example uses the EUR/USD exchange rate as the base instrument.

Figure 5-15 illustrates that the strategy outperforms the base instrument during the out-of-sample period (spanning the year 2019) however, without considering transaction costs as before:

```
In [123]: import ScikitVectorBacktester as SCI

In [124]: scibt = SCI.ScikitVectorBacktester('EUR=',
                                              '2010-1-1', '2019-12-31',
                                              10000, 0.0, 'logistic')

In [125]: scibt.run_strategy('2015-1-1', '2019-12-31',
                             '2015-1-1', '2019-12-31', lags=15)
Out[125]: (12192.18, 2189.5)

In [126]: scibt.run_strategy('2016-1-1', '2018-12-31',
                             '2019-1-1', '2019-12-31', lags=15)
Out[126]: (10580.54, 729.93)

In [127]: scibt.plot_results()
```

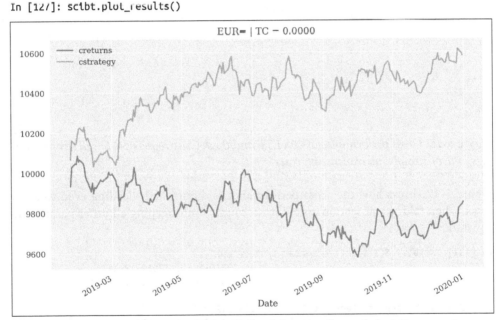

Figure 5-15. Gross performance of S&P 500 and the out-of-sample logistic regression-based strategy (15 lags, no transaction costs)

As another example, consider the same strategy applied to the GDX ETF, for which an out-of-sample outperformance (over the year 2018) is shown in Figure 5-16 (before transaction costs):

```
In [128]: scibt = SCI.ScikitVectorBacktester('GDX',
                                             '2010-1-1', '2019-12-31',
                                             10000, 0.00, 'logistic')
```

```
In [129]: scibt.run_strategy('2013-1-1', '2017-12-31',
                             '2018-1-1', '2018-12-31', lags=10)
Out[129]: (12686.81, 4032.73)

In [130]: scibt.plot_results()
```

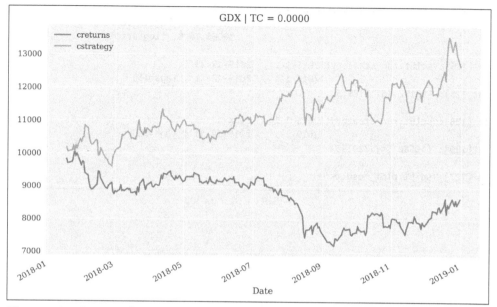

Figure 5-16. Gross performance of GDX ETF and the logistic regression-based strategy (10 lags, out-of-sample, no transaction costs)

Figure 5-17 shows how the gross performance is diminished—leading even to a net loss—when taking transaction costs into account, while keeping all other parameters constant:

```
In [131]: scibt = SCI.ScikitVectorBacktester('GDX',
                                             '2010-1-1', '2019-12-31',
                                             10000, 0.0025, 'logistic')

In [132]: scibt.run_strategy('2013-1-1', '2017-12-31',
                             '2018-1-1', '2018-12-31', lags=10)
Out[132]: (9588.48, 934.4)

In [133]: scibt.plot_results()
```

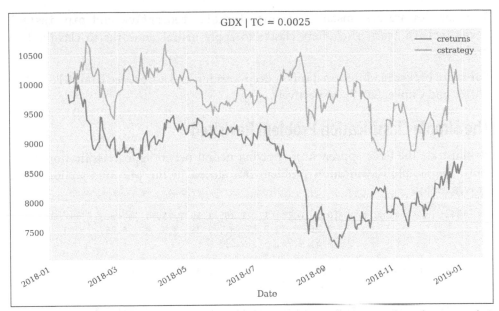

Figure 5-17. Gross performance of GDX ETF and the logistic regression-based strategy (10 lags, out-of-sample, with transaction costs)

Applying sophisticated machine learning techniques to stock market prediction often yields promising results early on. In several examples, the strategies backtested outperform the base instrument significantly in-sample. Quite often, such stellar performances are due to a mix of simplifying assumptions and also due to an overfitting of the prediction model. For example, testing the very same strategy instead of in-sample on an out-of-sample data set and adding transaction costs—as two ways of getting to a more realistic picture—often shows that the performance of the considered strategy "suddenly" trails the base instrument performance-wise or turns to a net loss.

Using Deep Learning for Market Movement Prediction

Right from the open sourcing and publication by Google, the deep learning library TensorFlow (*http://tensorflow.org*) has attracted much interest and wide-spread application. This section applies TensorFlow in the same way that the previous section applied scikit-learn to the prediction of stock market movements modeled as a classification problem. However, TensorFlow is not used directly; it is rather used via the equally popular Keras (*http://keras.io*) deep learning package. Keras can be thought of as providing a higher level abstraction to the TensorFlow package with an easier to understand and use API.

The libraries are best installed via `pip install tensorflow` and `pip install keras`. `scikit-learn` also offers classes to apply neural networks to classification problems.

For more background information on deep learning and `Keras`, see Goodfellow et al. (2016) and Chollet (2017), respectively.

The Simple Classification Problem Revisited

To illustrate the basic approach of applying neural networks to classification problems, the simple classification problem introduced in the previous section again proves useful:

```
In [134]: hours = np.array([0.5, 0.75, 1., 1.25, 1.5, 1.75, 1.75, 2.,
                            2.25, 2.5, 2.75, 3., 3.25, 3.5, 4., 4.25,
                            4.5, 4.75, 5., 5.5])

In [135]: success = np.array([0, 0, 0, 0, 0, 0, 1, 0, 1, 0, 1, 0, 1,
                              0, 1, 1, 1, 1, 1, 1])

In [136]: data = pd.DataFrame({'hours': hours, 'success': success})  ❶

In [137]: data.info()  ❷
          <class 'pandas.core.frame.DataFrame'>
          RangeIndex: 20 entries, 0 to 19
          Data columns (total 2 columns):
           #   Column   Non-Null Count  Dtype
          ---  ------   --------------  -----
           0   hours    20 non-null     float64
           1   success  20 non-null     int64
          dtypes: float64(1), int64(1)
          memory usage: 448.0 bytes
```

❶ Stores the two data sub-sets in a `DataFrame` object.

❷ Prints out the meta information for the `DataFrame` object.

With these preparations, `MLPClassifier` from `scikit-learn` can be imported and straightforwardly applied.[3] "MLP" in this context stands for *multi-layer perceptron*, which is another expression for *dense neural network*. As before, the API to apply neural networks with `scikit-learn` is basically the same:

```
In [138]: from sklearn.neural_network import MLPClassifier  ❶

In [139]: model = MLPClassifier(hidden_layer_sizes=[32],
                                max_iter=1000, random_state=100)  ❷
```

---

3 For details, see *https://oreil.ly/hOwsE*.

❶ Imports the MLPClassifier object from scikit-learn.

❷ Instantiates the MLPClassifier object.

The following code fits the model, generates the predictions, and plots the results, as shown in Figure 5-18:

```
In [140]: model.fit(data['hours'].values.reshape(-1, 1), data['success'])  ❶
Out[140]: MLPClassifier(hidden_layer_sizes=[32], max_iter=1000,
              random_state=100)

In [141]: data['prediction'] = model.predict(data['hours'].values.reshape(-1, 1))  ❷

In [142]: data.tail()
Out[142]:     hours  success  prediction
          15   4.25        1           1
          16   4.50        1           1
          17   4.75        1           1
          18   5.00        1           1
          19   5.50        1           1

In [143]: data.plot(x='hours', y=['success', 'prediction'],
                  style=['ro', 'b-'], ylim=[-.1, 1.1],
                  figsize=(10, 6));  ❸
```

❶ Fits the neural network for classification.

❷ Generates the prediction values based on the fitted model.

❸ Plots the original data and the prediction values.

This simple example shows that the application of the deep learning approach is quite similar to the approach with scikit-learn and the LogisticRegression model object. The API is basically the same; only the parameters are different.

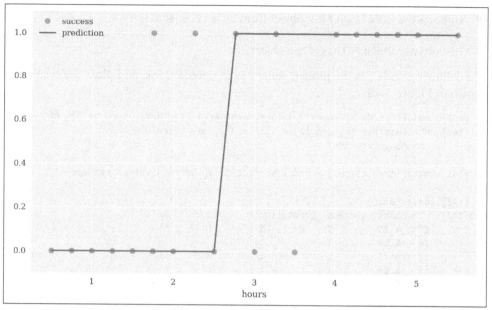

Figure 5-18. Base data and prediction results with `MLPClassifier` for the simple classi-fication example

Using Deep Neural Networks to Predict Market Direction

The next step is to apply the approach to stock market data in the form of log returns from a financial time series. First, the data needs to be retrieved and prepared:

```
In [144]: symbol = 'EUR=' ❶

In [145]: data = pd.DataFrame(raw[symbol]) ❷

In [146]: data.rename(columns={symbol: 'price'}, inplace=True) ❸

In [147]: data['return'] = np.log(data['price'] /
                                  data['price'].shift(1)) ❹

In [148]: data['direction'] = np.where(data['return'] > 0, 1, 0) ❹

In [149]: lags = 5

In [150]: cols = []
          for lag in range(1, lags + 1): ❺
              col = f'lag_{lag}'
              data[col] = data['return'].shift(lag) ❻
              cols.append(col)
          data.dropna(inplace=True) ❼
```

```
In [151]: data.round(4).tail()          ❽
Out[151]:
                price  return  direction  lag_1   lag_2    lag_3   lag_4    lag_5
   Date
   2019-12-24  1.1087  0.0001          1  0.0007 -0.0038   0.0008 -0.0034   0.0006
   2019-12-26  1.1096  0.0008          1  0.0001  0.0007  -0.0038  0.0008  -0.0034
   2019-12-27  1.1175  0.0071          1  0.0008  0.0001   0.0007 -0.0038   0.0008
   2019-12-30  1.1197  0.0020          1  0.0071  0.0008   0.0001  0.0007  -0.0038
   2019-12-31  1.1210  0.0012          1  0.0020  0.0071   0.0008  0.0001   0.0007
```

❶ Reads the data from the CSV file.

❷ Picks the single time series column of interest.

❸ Renames the only column to price.

❹ Calculates the log returns and defines the direction as a binary column.

❺ Creates the lagged data.

❻ Creates new DataFrame columns with the log returns shifted by the respective number of lags.

❼ Deletes rows containing NaN values.

❽ Prints out the final five rows indicating the "patterns" emerging in the five feature columns.

The following code uses a dense neural network (DNN) with the Keras package[4], defines training and test data sub-sets, defines the feature columns, and labels and fits the classifier. In the backend, Keras uses the TensorFlow package to accomplish the task. Figure 5-19 shows how the accuracy of the DNN classifier changes for both the training and validation data sets during training. As validation data set, 20% of the training data (without shuffling) is used:

```
In [152]: import tensorflow as tf          ❶
          from keras.models import Sequential    ❷
          from keras.layers import Dense     ❸
          from keras.optimizers import Adam, RMSprop

In [153]: optimizer = Adam(learning_rate=0.0001)

In [154]: def set_seeds(seed=100):
              random.seed(seed)
              np.random.seed(seed)
```

---

4 For details, refer to *https://keras.io/layers/core/*.

```
          tf.random.set_seed(100)

In [155]: set_seeds()
          model = Sequential()  ❹
          model.add(Dense(64, activation='relu',
                  input_shape=(lags,)))  ❺
          model.add(Dense(64, activation='relu'))  ❺
          model.add(Dense(1, activation='sigmoid'))  ❺
          model.compile(optimizer=optimizer,
                          loss='binary_crossentropy',
                          metrics=['accuracy'])  ❻

In [156]: cutoff = '2017-12-31'  ❼

In [157]: training_data = data[data.index < cutoff].copy()  ❽

In [158]: mu, std = training_data.mean(), training_data.std()  ❾

In [159]: training_data_ = (training_data - mu) / std  ❾

In [160]: test_data = data[data.index >= cutoff].copy()  ❽

In [161]: test_data_ = (test_data - mu) / std  ❾

In [162]: %%time
          model.fit(training_data[cols],
                  training_data['direction'],
                  epochs=50, verbose=False,
                  validation_split=0.2, shuffle=False)  ❿
          CPU times: user 4.86 s, sys: 989 ms, total: 5.85 s
          Wall time: 3.34 s

Out[162]: <tensorflow.python.keras.callbacks.History at 0x7f996a0a2880>

In [163]: res = pd.DataFrame(model.history.history)

In [164]: res[['accuracy', 'val_accuracy']].plot(figsize=(10, 6), style='--');
```

❶   Imports the TensorFlow package.

❷   Imports the required model object from Keras.

❸   Imports the relevant layer object from Keras.

❹   A Sequential model is instantiated.

❺   The hidden layers and the output layer are defined.

❻   Compiles the Sequential model object for classification.

⑦ Defines the cutoff date between the training and test data.

⑧ Defines the training and test data sets.

⑨ Normalizes the features data by Gaussian normalization.

⑩ Fits the model to the training data set.

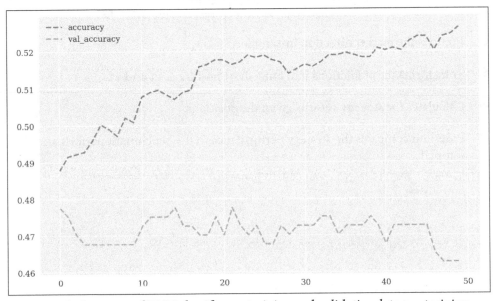

Figure 5-19. Accuracy of DNN classifier on training and validation data per training step

Equipped with the fitted classifier, the model can generate predictions on the training data set. Figure 5-20 shows the strategy gross performance compared to the base instrument (in-sample):

```
In [165]: model.evaluate(training_data_[cols], training_data['direction'])
          63/63 [==============================] - 0s 586us/step - loss: 0.7556 -
            accuracy: 0.5152

Out[165]: [0.7555528879165649, 0.5151968002319336]

In [166]: pred = np.where(model.predict(training_data_[cols]) > 0.5, 1, 0)  ❶

In [167]: pred[:30].flatten()  ❶
Out[167]: array([0, 0, 0, 0, 0, 1, 1, 1, 1, 0, 0, 0, 1, 1, 1, 0, 0, 0, 1, 1,
            0, 0, 0, 1, 0, 1, 0, 1, 0, 0])

In [168]: training_data['prediction'] = np.where(pred > 0, 1, -1)  ❷
```

```
In [169]: training_data['strategy'] = (training_data['prediction'] *
                                        training_data['return'])  ❸

In [170]: training_data[['return', 'strategy']].sum().apply(np.exp)
Out[170]: return      0.826569
          strategy    1.317303
          dtype: float64

In [171]: training_data[['return', 'strategy']].cumsum(
                        ).apply(np.exp).plot(figsize=(10, 6));  ❹
```

❶ Predicts the market direction in-sample.

❷ Transforms the predictions into long-short positions, +1 and -1.

❸ Calculates the strategy returns given the positions.

❹ Plots and compares the strategy performance to the benchmark performance (in-sample).

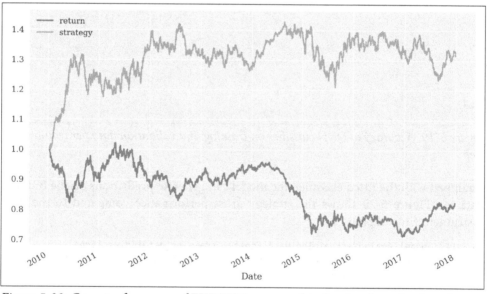

Figure 5-20. Gross performance of EUR/USD compared to the deep learning-based strategy (in-sample, no transaction costs)

The strategy seems to perform somewhat better than the base instrument on the training data set (in-sample, without transaction costs). However, the more interesting question is how it performs on the test data set (out-of-sample). After a wobbly start, the strategy also outperforms the base instrument out-of-sample, as Figure 5-21 illustrates. This is despite the fact that the accuracy of the classifier is only slightly above 50% on the test data set:

```
In [172]: model.evaluate(test_data_[cols], test_data['direction'])
          16/16 [==============================] - 0s 676us/step - loss: 0.7292 -
          accuracy: 0.5050

Out[172]: [0.7292129993438721, 0.5049701929092407]

In [173]: pred = np.where(model.predict(test_data_[cols]) > 0.5, 1, 0)

In [174]: test_data['prediction'] = np.where(pred > 0, 1, -1)

In [175]: test_data['prediction'].value_counts()
Out[175]: -1    368
           1    135
          Name: prediction, dtype: int64

In [176]: test_data['strategy'] = (test_data['prediction'] *
                                   test_data['return'])

In [177]: test_data[['return', 'strategy']].sum().apply(np.exp)
Out[177]: return      0.934478
          strategy    1.109065
          dtype: float64

In [178]: test_data[['return', 'strategy']].cumsum(
                       ).apply(np.exp).plot(figsize=(10, 6));
```

Figure 5-21. Gross performance of EUR/USD compared to the deep learning-based strategy (out-of-sample, no transaction costs)

Adding Different Types of Features

So far, the analysis mainly focuses on the log returns directly. It is, of course, possible not only to add more classes/categories but also to add other types of features to the mix, such as ones based on *momentum*, *volatility*, or *distance* measures. The code that follows derives the additional features and adds them to the data set:

```
In [179]: data['momentum'] = data['return'].rolling(5).mean().shift(1)   ❶

In [180]: data['volatility'] = data['return'].rolling(20).std().shift(1)   ❷

In [181]: data['distance'] = (data['price'] -
                        data['price'].rolling(50).mean()).shift(1)   ❸

In [182]: data.dropna(inplace=True)

In [183]: cols.extend(['momentum', 'volatility', 'distance'])

In [184]: print(data.round(4).tail())

                   price  return  direction   lag_1   lag_2   lag_3   lag_4    lag_5
          Date

          2019-12-24  1.1087  0.0001          1  0.0007 -0.0038  0.0008 -0.0034   0.0006
          2019-12-26  1.1096  0.0008          1  0.0001  0.0007 -0.0038  0.0008  -0.0034
          2019-12-27  1.1175  0.0071          1  0.0008  0.0001  0.0007 -0.0038   0.0008
          2019-12-30  1.1197  0.0020          1  0.0071  0.0008  0.0001  0.0007  -0.0038
          2019-12-31  1.1210  0.0012          1  0.0020  0.0071  0.0008  0.0001   0.0007

                      momentum  volatility  distance
          Date
          2019-12-24   -0.0010      0.0024    0.0005
          2019-12-26   -0.0011      0.0024    0.0004
          2019-12-27   -0.0003      0.0024    0.0012
          2019-12-30    0.0010      0.0028    0.0089
          2019-12-31    0.0021      0.0028    0.0110
```

❶ The momentum-based feature.

❷ The volatility-based feature.

❸ The distance-based feature.

The next steps are to redefine the training and test data sets, to normalize the features data, and to update the model to reflect the new features columns:

```
In [185]: training_data = data[data.index < cutoff].copy()

In [186]: mu, std = training_data.mean(), training_data.std()

In [187]: training_data_ = (training_data - mu) / std
```

```
In [188]: test_data = data[data.index >= cutoff].copy()

In [189]: test_data_ = (test_data - mu) / std

In [190]: set_seeds()
          model = Sequential()
          model.add(Dense(32, activation='relu',
                          input_shape=(len(cols),)))  ❶
          model.add(Dense(32, activation='relu'))
          model.add(Dense(1, activation='sigmoid'))
          model.compile(optimizer=optimizer,
                        loss='binary_crossentropy',
                        metrics=['accuracy'])
```

❶ The input_shape parameter is adjusted to reflect the new number of features.

Based on the enriched feature set, the classifier can be trained. The in-sample performance of the strategy is quite a bit better than before, as illustrated in Figure 5-22:

```
In [191]: %%time
          model.fit(training_data_[cols], training_data['direction'],
                    verbose=False, epochs=25)
          CPU times: user 2.32 s, sys: 577 ms, total: 2.9 s
          Wall time: 1.48 s

Out[191]: <tensorflow.python.keras.callbacks.History at 0x7f996d35c100>

In [192]: model.evaluate(training_data_[cols], training_data['direction'])
          62/62 [==============================] - 0s 649us/step - loss: 0.6816 -
           accuracy: 0.5646

Out[192]: [0.6816270351409912, 0.5646397471427917]

In [193]: pred = np.where(model.predict(training_data_[cols]) > 0.5, 1, 0)

In [194]: training_data['prediction'] = np.where(pred > 0, 1, -1)

In [195]: training_data['strategy'] = (training_data['prediction'] *
                                       training_data['return'])

In [196]: training_data[['return', 'strategy']].sum().apply(np.exp)
Out[196]: return      0.901074
          strategy    2.703377
          dtype: float64

In [197]: training_data[['return', 'strategy']].cumsum(
                         ).apply(np.exp).plot(figsize=(10, 6));
```

Figure 5-22. Gross performance of EUR/USD compared to the deep learning-based strategy (in-sample, additional features)

The final step is the evaluation of the classifier and the derivation of the strategy performance out-of-sample. The classifier also performs significantly better, *ceteris paribus*, when compared to the case without the additional features. As before, the start is a bit wobbly (see Figure 5-23):

```
In [198]: model.evaluate(test_data_[cols], test_data['direction'])
          16/16 [==============================] - 0s 800us/step - loss: 0.6931 -
            accuracy: 0.5507

Out[198]: [0.6931276321411133, 0.5506958365440369]

In [199]: pred = np.where(model.predict(test_data_[cols]) > 0.5, 1, 0)

In [200]: test_data['prediction'] = np.where(pred > 0, 1, -1)

In [201]: test_data['prediction'].value_counts()
Out[201]: -1    335
           1    168
          Name: prediction, dtype: int64

In [202]: test_data['strategy'] = (test_data['prediction'] *
                                   test_data['return'])

In [203]: test_data[['return', 'strategy']].sum().apply(np.exp)
Out[203]: return      0.934478
          strategy    1.144385
          dtype: float64
```

```
In [204]: test_data[['return', 'strategy']].cumsum(
                    ).apply(np.exp).plot(figsize=(10, 6));
```

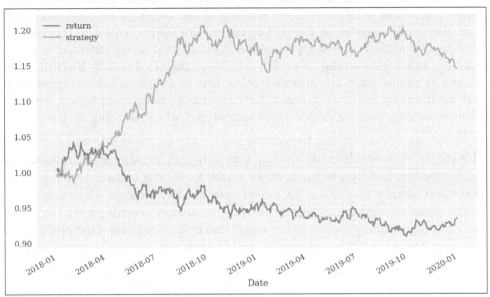

Figure 5-23. Gross performance of EUR/USD compared to the deep learning-based strategy (out-of-sample, additional features)

The Keras package, in combination with the TensorFlow package as its backend, allows one to make use of the most recent advances in deep learning, such as deep neural network (DNN) classifiers, for algorithmic trading. The application is as straightforward as applying other machine learning models with scikit-learn. The approach illustrated in this section allows for an easy enhancement with regard to the different types of features used.

As an exercise, it is worthwhile to code a Python class (in the spirit of "Linear Regression Backtesting Class" on page 167 and "Classification Algorithm Backtesting Class" on page 170) that allows for a more systematic and realistic usage of the Keras package for financial market prediction and the backtesting of respective trading strategies.

Conclusions

Predicting future market movements is the holy grail in finance. It means to find the truth. It means to overcome *efficient markets*. If one can do it with a considerable edge, then stellar investment and trading returns are the consequence. This chapter introduces statistical techniques from the fields of traditional statistics, machine learning, and deep learning to predict the future market direction based on past returns or similar financial quantities. Some first in-sample results are promising, both for linear and logistic regression. However, a more reliable impression is gained when evaluating such strategies out-of-sample and when factoring in transaction costs.

This chapter does not claim to have found the holy grail. It rather offers a glimpse on techniques that could prove useful in the search for it. The unified API of `scikit-learn` also makes it easy to replace, for example, one linear model with another one. In that sense, the `ScikitBacktesterClass` can be used as a starting point to explore more machine learning models and to apply them to financial time series prediction.

The quote at the beginning of the chapter from the *Terminator 2* movie from 1991 is rather optimistic with regard to how fast and to what extent computers might be able to learn and acquire consciousness. No matter if you believe that computers will replace human beings in most areas of life or not, or if they indeed one day become self-aware, they have proven useful to human beings as supporting devices in almost any area of life. And algorithms like those used in machine learning, deep learning, or artificial intelligence hold at least the promise to let them become better algorithmic traders in the near future. A more detailed account of these topics and considerations is found in Hilpisch (2020).

References and Further Resources

The books by Guido and Müller (2016) and VanderPlas (2016) provide practical introductions to machine learning with Python and `scikit-learn`. The book by Hilpisch (2020) focuses exclusively on the application of algorithms for machine and deep learning to the problem of identifying statistical inefficiencies and exploiting economic inefficiencies through algorithmic trading:

Guido, Sarah, and Andreas Müller. 2016. *Introduction to Machine Learning with Python: A Guide for Data Scientists*. Sebastopol: O'Reilly.

Hilpisch, Yves. 2020. *Artificial Intelligence in Finance: A Python-Based Guide*. Sebastopol: O'Reilly.

VanderPlas, Jake. 2016. *Python Data Science Handbook: Essential Tools for Working with Data*. Sebastopol: O'Reilly.

The books by Hastie et al. (2008) and James et al. (2013) provide a thorough, mathematical overview of popular machine learning techniques and algorithms:

Hastie, Trevor, Robert Tibshirani, and Jerome Friedman. 2008. *The Elements of Statistical Learning.* 2nd ed. New York: Springer.

James, Gareth, Daniela Witten, Trevor Hastie, and Robert Tibshirani. 2013. *Introduction to Statistical Learning.* New York: Springer.

For more background information on deep learning and `Keras`, refer to these books:

Chollet, Francois. 2017. *Deep Learning with Python.* Shelter Island: Manning.

Goodfellow, Ian, Yoshua Bengio, and Aaron Courville. 2016. *Deep Learning.* Cambridge: MIT Press. *http://deeplearningbook.org.*

Python Scripts

This section presents Python scripts referenced and used in this chapter.

Linear Regression Backtesting Class

The following presents Python code with a class for the vectorized backtesting of strategies based on *linear regression* used for the prediction of the direction of market movements:

```
#
# Python Module with Class
# for Vectorized Backtesting
# of Linear Regression-Based Strategies
#
# Python for Algorithmic Trading
# (c) Dr. Yves J. Hilpisch
# The Python Quants GmbH
#
import numpy as np
import pandas as pd


class LRVectorBacktester(object):
    ''' Class for the vectorized backtesting of
    linear regression-based trading strategies.

    Attributes
    ==========
    symbol: str
        TR RIC (financial instrument) to work with
    start: str
        start date for data selection
    end: str
```

```
        end date for data selection
    amount: int, float
        amount to be invested at the beginning
    tc: float
        proportional transaction costs (e.g., 0.5% = 0.005) per trade

    Methods
    =======
    get_data:
        retrieves and prepares the base data set
    select_data:
        selects a sub-set of the data
    prepare_lags:
        prepares the lagged data for the regression
    fit_model:
        implements the regression step
    run_strategy:
        runs the backtest for the regression-based strategy
    plot_results:
        plots the performance of the strategy compared to the symbol
    '''

    def __init__(self, symbol, start, end, amount, tc):
        self.symbol = symbol
        self.start = start
        self.end = end
        self.amount = amount
        self.tc = tc
        self.results = None
        self.get_data()

    def get_data(self):
        ''' Retrieves and prepares the data.
        '''
        raw = pd.read_csv('http://hilpisch.com/pyalgo_eikon_eod_data.csv',
                         index_col=0, parse_dates=True).dropna()
        raw = pd.DataFrame(raw[self.symbol])
        raw = raw.loc[self.start:self.end]
        raw.rename(columns={self.symbol: 'price'}, inplace=True)
        raw['returns'] = np.log(raw / raw.shift(1))
        self.data = raw.dropna()

    def select_data(self, start, end):
        ''' Selects sub-sets of the financial data.
        '''
        data = self.data[(self.data.index >= start) &
                        (self.data.index <= end)].copy()
        return data

    def prepare_lags(self, start, end):
        ''' Prepares the lagged data for the regression and prediction steps.
        '''
```

```python
        data = self.select_data(start, end)
        self.cols = []
        for lag in range(1, self.lags + 1):
            col = f'lag_{lag}'
            data[col] = data['returns'].shift(lag)
            self.cols.append(col)
        data.dropna(inplace=True)
        self.lagged_data = data

    def fit_model(self, start, end):
        ''' Implements the regression step.
        '''
        self.prepare_lags(start, end)
        reg = np.linalg.lstsq(self.lagged_data[self.cols],
                              np.sign(self.lagged_data['returns']),
                              rcond=None)[0]
        self.reg = reg

    def run_strategy(self, start_in, end_in, start_out, end_out, lags=3):
        ''' Backtests the trading strategy.
        '''
        self.lags = lags
        self.fit_model(start_in, end_in)
        self.results = self.select_data(start_out, end_out).iloc[lags:]
        self.prepare_lags(start_out, end_out)
        prediction = np.sign(np.dot(self.lagged_data[self.cols], self.reg))
        self.results['prediction'] = prediction
        self.results['strategy'] = self.results['prediction'] * \
                                   self.results['returns']
        # determine when a trade takes place
        trades = self.results['prediction'].diff().fillna(0) != 0
        # subtract transaction costs from return when trade takes place
        self.results['strategy'][trades] -= self.tc
        self.results['creturns'] = self.amount * \
                    self.results['returns'].cumsum().apply(np.exp)
        self.results['cstrategy'] = self.amount * \
                    self.results['strategy'].cumsum().apply(np.exp)
        # gross performance of the strategy
        aperf = self.results['cstrategy'].iloc[-1]
        # out-/underperformance of strategy
        operf = aperf - self.results['creturns'].iloc[-1]
        return round(aperf, 2), round(operf, 2)

    def plot_results(self):
        ''' Plots the cumulative performance of the trading strategy
        compared to the symbol.
        '''
        if self.results is None:
            print('No results to plot yet. Run a strategy.')
        title = '%s | TC = %.4f' % (self.symbol, self.tc)
        self.results[['creturns', 'cstrategy']].plot(title=title,
                                                     figsize=(10, 6))
```

```
if __name__ == '__main__':
    lrbt = LRVectorBacktester('.SPX', '2010-1-1', '2018-06-29', 10000, 0.0)
    print(lrbt.run_strategy('2010-1-1', '2019-12-31',
                            '2010-1-1', '2019-12-31'))
    print(lrbt.run_strategy('2010-1-1', '2015-12-31',
                            '2016-1-1', '2019-12-31'))
    lrbt = LRVectorBacktester('GDX', '2010-1-1', '2019-12-31', 10000, 0.001)
    print(lrbt.run_strategy('2010-1-1', '2019-12-31',
                            '2010-1-1', '2019-12-31', lags=5))
    print(lrbt.run_strategy('2010-1-1', '2016-12-31',
                            '2017-1-1', '2019-12-31', lags=5))
```

Classification Algorithm Backtesting Class

The following presents Python code with a class for the vectorized backtesting of strategies based on *logistic regression,* as a standard classification algorithm, used for the prediction of the direction of market movements:

```
#
# Python Module with Class
# for Vectorized Backtesting
# of Machine Learning-Based Strategies
#
# Python for Algorithmic Trading
# (c) Dr. Yves J. Hilpisch
# The Python Quants GmbH
#
import numpy as np
import pandas as pd
from sklearn import linear_model


class ScikitVectorBacktester(object):
    ''' Class for the vectorized backtesting of
    machine learning-based trading strategies.

    Attributes
    ==========
    symbol: str
        TR RIC (financial instrument) to work with
    start: str
        start date for data selection
    end: str
        end date for data selection
    amount: int, float
        amount to be invested at the beginning
    tc: float
        proportional transaction costs (e.g., 0.5% = 0.005) per trade
    model: str
        either 'regression' or 'logistic'
```

```
Methods
=======
get_data:
    retrieves and prepares the base data set
select_data:
    selects a sub-set of the data
prepare_features:
    prepares the features data for the model fitting
fit_model:
    implements the fitting step
run_strategy:
    runs the backtest for the regression-based strategy
plot_results:
    plots the performance of the strategy compared to the symbol
'''

def __init__(self, symbol, start, end, amount, tc, model):
    self.symbol = symbol
    self.start = start
    self.end = end
    self.amount = amount
    self.tc = tc
    self.results = None
    if model == 'regression':
        self.model = linear_model.LinearRegression()
    elif model == 'logistic':
        self.model = linear_model.LogisticRegression(C=1e6,
            solver='lbfgs', multi_class='ovr', max_iter=1000)
    else:
        raise ValueError('Model not known or not yet implemented.')
    self.get_data()

def get_data(self):
    ''' Retrieves and prepares the data.
    '''
    raw = pd.read_csv('http://hilpisch.com/pyalgo_eikon_eod_data.csv',
                      index_col=0, parse_dates=True).dropna()
    raw = pd.DataFrame(raw[self.symbol])
    raw = raw.loc[self.start:self.end]
    raw.rename(columns={self.symbol: 'price'}, inplace=True)
    raw['returns'] = np.log(raw / raw.shift(1))
    self.data = raw.dropna()

def select_data(self, start, end):
    ''' Selects sub-sets of the financial data.
    '''
    data = self.data[(self.data.index >= start) &
                     (self.data.index <= end)].copy()
    return data

def prepare_features(self, start, end):
```

```python
        ''' Prepares the feature columns for the regression and prediction steps.
        '''
        self.data_subset = self.select_data(start, end)
        self.feature_columns = []
        for lag in range(1, self.lags + 1):
            col = 'lag_{}'.format(lag)
            self.data_subset[col] = self.data_subset['returns'].shift(lag)
            self.feature_columns.append(col)
        self.data_subset.dropna(inplace=True)

    def fit_model(self, start, end):
        ''' Implements the fitting step.
        '''
        self.prepare_features(start, end)
        self.model.fit(self.data_subset[self.feature_columns],
                       np.sign(self.data_subset['returns']))

    def run_strategy(self, start_in, end_in, start_out, end_out, lags=3):
        ''' Backtests the trading strategy.
        '''
        self.lags = lags
        self.fit_model(start_in, end_in)
        # data = self.select_data(start_out, end_out)
        self.prepare_features(start_out, end_out)
        prediction = self.model.predict(
            self.data_subset[self.feature_columns])
        self.data_subset['prediction'] = prediction
        self.data_subset['strategy'] = (self.data_subset['prediction'] *
                                        self.data_subset['returns'])
        # determine when a trade takes place
        trades = self.data_subset['prediction'].diff().fillna(0) != 0
        # subtract transaction costs from return when trade takes place
        self.data_subset['strategy'][trades] -= self.tc
        self.data_subset['creturns'] = (self.amount *
                        self.data_subset['returns'].cumsum().apply(np.exp))
        self.data_subset['cstrategy'] = (self.amount *
                        self.data_subset['strategy'].cumsum().apply(np.exp))
        self.results = self.data_subset
        # absolute performance of the strategy
        aperf = self.results['cstrategy'].iloc[-1]
        # out-/underperformance of strategy
        operf = aperf - self.results['creturns'].iloc[-1]
        return round(aperf, 2), round(operf, 2)

    def plot_results(self):
        ''' Plots the cumulative performance of the trading strategy
        compared to the symbol.
        '''
        if self.results is None:
            print('No results to plot yet. Run a strategy.')
        title = '%s | TC = %.4f' % (self.symbol, self.tc)
        self.results[['creturns', 'cstrategy']].plot(title=title,
```

```
                                            figsize=(10, 6))


if __name__ == '__main__':
    scibt = ScikitVectorBacktester('.SPX', '2010-1-1', '2019-12-31',
                                   10000, 0.0, 'regression')
    print(scibt.run_strategy('2010-1-1', '2019-12-31',
                             '2010-1-1', '2019-12-31'))
    print(scibt.run_strategy('2010-1-1', '2016-12-31',
                             '2017-1-1', '2019-12-31'))
    scibt = ScikitVectorBacktester('.SPX', '2010-1-1', '2019-12-31',
                                   10000, 0.0, 'logistic')
    print(scibt.run_strategy('2010-1-1', '2019-12-31',
                             '2010-1-1', '2019-12-31'))
    print(scibt.run_strategy('2010-1-1', '2016-12-31',
                             '2017-1-1', '2019-12-31'))
    scibt = ScikitVectorBacktester('.SPX', '2010-1-1', '2019-12-31',
                                   10000, 0.001, 'logistic')
    print(scibt.run_strategy('2010-1-1', '2019-12-31',
                             '2010-1-1', '2019-12-31', lags=15))
    print(scibt.run_strategy('2010-1-1', '2013-12-31',
                             '2014-1-1', '2019-12-31', lags=15))
```

## CHAPTER 6

Building Classes for Event-Based Backtesting

The actual tragedies of life bear no relation to one's preconceived ideas. In the event, one is always bewildered by their simplicity, their grandeur of design, and by that element of the bizarre which seems inherent in them.

—Jean Cocteau

On the one hand, *vectorized backtesting* with NumPy and pandas is generally convenient and efficient to implement due to the concise code, and it is fast to execute due to these packages being optimized for such operations. However, the approach cannot cope with all types of trading strategies nor with all phenomena that the trading reality presents an algorithmic trader with. When it comes to vectorized backtesting, potential shortcomings of the approach are the following:

Look-ahead bias
Vectorized backtesting is based on the complete data set available and does not take into account that new data arrives incrementally.

Simplification
For example, fixed transaction costs cannot be modeled by vectorization, which is mainly based on relative returns. Also, fixed amounts per trade or the non-divisibility of single financial instruments (for example, a share of a stock) cannot be modeled properly.

Non-recursiveness
Algorithms, embodying trading strategies, might take recurse to state variables over time, like profit and loss up to a certain point in time or similar path-dependent statistics. Vectorization cannot cope with such features.

On the other hand, *event-based backtesting* allows one to address these issues by a more realistic approach to model trading realities. On a basic level, an *event* is characterized by the arrival of new data. Backtesting a trading strategy for the Apple Inc. stock based on end-of-day data, an event would be a new closing price for the Apple stock. It can also be a change in an interest rate, or the hitting of a stop loss level. Advantages of the event-based backtesting approach generally are the following:

Incremental approach
As in the trading reality, backtesting takes place on the premise that new data arrives incrementally, tick-by-tick and quote-by-quote.

Realistic modeling
One has complete freedom to model those processes that are triggered by a new and specific event.

Path dependency
It is straightforward to keep track of conditional, recursive, or otherwise path-dependent statistics, such as the maximum or minimum price seen so far, and to include them in the trading algorithm.

Reusability
Backtesting different types of trading strategies requires a similar base functionality that can be implemented and unified through object-oriented programming.

Close to trading
Certain elements of an event-based backtesting system can sometimes also be used for the automated implementation of the trading strategy.

In what follows, a new event is generally identified by a *bar*, which represents one unit of new data. For example, events can be *one-minute bars* for an intraday trading strategy or *one-day bars* for a trading strategy based on daily closing prices.

The chapter is organized as follows. "Backtesting Base Class" on page 177 presents a base class for the event-based backtesting of trading strategies. "Long-Only Backtesting Class" on page 182 and "Long-Short Backtesting Class" on page 185 make use of the base class to implement long-only and long-short backtesting classes, respectively.

The goals of this chapter are to understand event-based modeling, to create classes that allow a more realistic backtesting, and to have a foundational backtesting infrastructure available as a starting point for further enhancements and refinements.

Backtesting Base Class

When it comes to building the infrastructure—in the form of a Python class—for event-based backtesting, several requirements must be met:

Retrieving and preparing data
> The base class shall take care of the data retrieval and possibly the preparation for the backtesting itself. To keep the discussion focused, end-of-day (EOD) data as read from a CSV file is the type of data the base class shall allow for.

Helper and convenience functions
> It shall provide a couple of helper and convenience functions that make backtesting easier. Examples are functions for plotting data, printing out state variables, or returning date and price information for a given bar.

Placing orders
> The base class shall cover the placing of basic buy and sell orders. For simplicity, only market buy and sell orders are modeled.

Closing out positions
> At the end of any backtesting, any market positions need to be closed out. The base class shall take care of this final trade.

If the base class meets these requirements, respective classes to backtest strategies based on simple moving averages (SMAs), momentum, or mean reversion (see Chapter 4), as well as on machine learning-based prediction (see Chapter 5), can be built upon it. "Backtesting Base Class" on page 191 presents an implementation of such a base class called BacktestBase. The following is a walk through the single methods of this class to get an overview of its design.

With regard to the special method __main__, there are only a few noteworthy things. First, the initial amount available is stored twice, both in a private attribute _amount that is kept constant and in a regular attribute amount that represents the running balance. The default assumption is that there are no transaction costs:

```
def __init__(self, symbol, start, end, amount,
             ftc=0.0, ptc=0.0, verbose=True):
    self.symbol = symbol
    self.start = start
    self.end = end
    self.initial_amount = amount    ❶
    self.amount = amount    ❷
    self.ftc = ftc    ❸
    self.ptc = ptc    ❹
    self.units = 0    ❺
    self.position = 0    ❻
    self.trades = 0    ❼
```

```
self.verbose = verbose   ❽
self.get_data()
```

❶   Stores the initial amount in a private attribute.

❷   Sets the starting cash balance value.

❸   Defines fixed transaction costs per trade.

❹   Defines proportional transaction costs per trade.

❺   Units of the instrument (for example, number of shares) in the portfolio initially.

❻   Sets the initial position to market neutral.

❼   Sets the initial number of trades to zero.

❽   Sets `self.verbose` to `True` to get full output.

During initialization, the `get_data` method is called, which retrieves EOD data from a CSV file for the provided symbol and the given time interval. It also calculates the log returns. The Python code that follows has been used extensively in Chapters 4 and 5. Therefore, it does not need to be explained in detail here:

```python
def get_data(self):
    ''' Retrieves and prepares the data.
    '''
    raw = pd.read_csv('http://hilpisch.com/pyalgo_eikon_eod_data.csv',
                      index_col=0, parse_dates=True).dropna()
    raw = pd.DataFrame(raw[self.symbol])
    raw = raw.loc[self.start:self.end]
    raw.rename(columns={self.symbol: 'price'}, inplace=True)
    raw['return'] = np.log(raw / raw.shift(1))
    self.data = raw.dropna()
```

The `.plot_data()` method is just a simple helper method to plot the (adjusted close) values for the provided symbol:

```python
def plot_data(self, cols=None):
    ''' Plots the closing prices for symbol.
    '''
    if cols is None:
        cols = ['price']
    self.data['price'].plot(figsize=(10, 6), title=self.symbol)
```

A method that gets frequently called is `.get_date_price()`. For a given bar, it returns the date and price information:

```python
def get_date_price(self, bar):
    ''' Return date and price for bar.
```

```
'''
    date = str(self.data.index[bar])[:10]
    price = self.data.price.iloc[bar]
    return date, price
```

.print_balance() prints out the current cash balance given a certain bar,
while .print_net_wealth() does the same for the net wealth (= current balance plus
value of trading position):

```
def print_balance(self, bar):
    ''' Print out current cash balance info.
    '''
    date, price = self.get_date_price(bar)
    print(f'{date} | current balance {self.amount:.2f}')

def print_net_wealth(self, bar):
    ''' Print out current cash balance info.
    '''
    date, price = self.get_date_price(bar)
    net_wealth = self.units * price + self.amount
    print(f'{date} | current net wealth {net_wealth:.2f}')
```

Two core methods are .place_buy_order() and .place_sell_order(). They allow
the emulated buying and selling of units of a financial instrument. First is
the .place_buy_order() method, which is commented on in detail:

```
def place_buy_order(self, bar, units=None, amount=None):
    ''' Place a buy order.
    '''
    date, price = self.get_date_price(bar)        ❶
    if units is None:                             ❷
        units = int(amount / price)               ❸
    self.amount -= (units * price) * (1 + self.ptc) + self.ftc   ❹
    self.units += units                           ❺
    self.trades += 1                              ❻
    if self.verbose:                              ❼
        print(f'{date} | selling {units} units at {price:.2f}')   ❽
        self.print_balance(bar)                   ❾
        self.print_net_wealth(bar)                ❿
```

❶   The date and price information for the given bar is retrieved.

❷   If no value for units is given…

❸   …the number of units is calculated given the value for amount. (Note that one
    needs to be given.) The calculation does not include transaction costs.

❹   The current cash balance is reduced by the cash outlays for the units of the
    instrument to be bought *plus* the proportional and fixed transaction costs. Note
    that it is not checked whether there is enough liquidity available or not.

```
```

⑤ The value of `self.units` is increased by the number of units bought.

⑥ This increases the counter for the number of trades by one.

⑦ If `self.verbose` is `True`…

⑧ …print out information about trade execution…

⑨ …the current cash balance…

⑩ …and the current net wealth.

Second, the `.place_sell_order()` method, which has only two minor adjustments compared to the `.place_buy_order()` method:

```python
def place_sell_order(self, bar, units=None, amount=None):
    ''' Place a sell order.
    '''
    date, price = self.get_date_price(bar)
    if units is None:
        units = int(amount / price)
    self.amount += (units * price) * (1 - self.ptc) - self.ftc    ❶
    self.units -= units    ❷
    self.trades += 1
    if self.verbose:
        print(f'{date} | selling {units} units at {price:.2f}')
        self.print_balance(bar)
        self.print_net_wealth(bar)
```

❶ The current cash balance is increased by the proceeds of the sale *minus* transactions costs.

❷ The value of `self.units` is decreased by the number of units sold.

No matter what kind of trading strategy is backtested, the position at the end of the backtesting period needs to be closed out. The code in the `BacktestBase` class assumes that the position is not liquidated but rather accounted for with its asset value to calculate and print the performance figures:

```python
def close_out(self, bar):
    ''' Closing out a long or short position.
    '''
    date, price = self.get_date_price(bar)
    self.amount += self.units * price    ❶
    self.units = 0
    self.trades += 1
    if self.verbose:
        print(f'{date} | inventory {self.units} units at {price:.2f}')
        print('=' * 55)
```

```
        print('Final balance     [$] {:.2f}'.format(self.amount))  ❷
        perf = ((self.amount - self.initial_amount) /
                self.initial_amount * 100)
        print('Net Performance [%] {:.2f}'.format(perf))  ❸
        print('Trades Executed [#] {:.2f}'.format(self.trades))  ❸
        print('=' * 55)
```

❶ No transaction costs are subtracted at the end.

❷ The final balance consists of the current cash balance plus the value of the trading position.

❸ This calculates the net performance in percent.

The final part of the Python script is the __main__ section, which gets executed when the file is run as a script:

```
if __name__ == '__main__':
    bb = BacktestBase('AAPL.O', '2010-1-1', '2019-12-31', 10000)
    print(bb.data.info())
    print(bb.data.tail())
    bb.plot_data()
```

It instantiates an object based on the BacktestBase class. This leads automatically to the data retrieval for the symbol provided. Figure 6-1 shows the resulting plot. The following output shows the meta information for the respective DataFrame object and the five most recent data rows:

```
In [1]: %run BacktestBase.py
<class 'pandas.core.frame.DataFrame'>
DatetimeIndex: 2515 entries, 2010-01-05 to 2019-12-31
Data columns (total 2 columns):
 #   Column  Non-Null Count  Dtype
---  ------  --------------  -----
 0   price   2515 non-null   float64
 1   return  2515 non-null   float64
dtypes: float64(2)
memory usage: 58.9 KB
None
            price     return
Date
2019-12-24  284.27   0.000950
2019-12-26  289.91   0.019646
2019-12-27  289.80  -0.000380
2019-12-30  291.52   0.005918
2019-12-31  293.65   0.007280

In [2]:
```

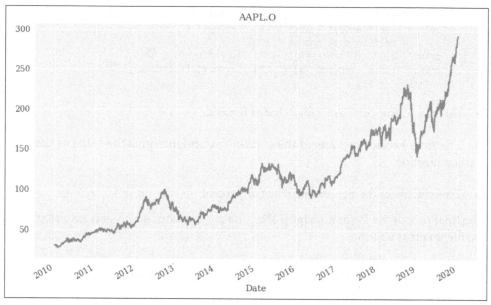

Figure 6-1. Plot of data as retrieved for `symbol` by the `BacktestBase` class

The two subsequent sections present classes to backtest long-only and long-short trading strategies. Since these classes rely on the base class presented in this section, the implementation of the backtesting routines is rather concise.

> Using object-oriented programming allows one to build a basic backtesting infrastructure in the form of a Python class. Standard functionality needed during the backtesting of different kinds of algorithmic trading strategies is made available by such a class in a non-redundant, easy-to-maintain fashion. It is also straightforward to enhance the base class to provide more features by default that might benefit a multitude of other classes built on top of it.

Long-Only Backtesting Class

Certain investor preferences or regulations might prohibit short selling as part of a trading strategy. As a consequence, a trader or portfolio manager is only allowed to enter long positions or to park capital in the form of cash or similar low risk assets, like money market accounts. "Long-Only Backtesting Class" on page 194 shows the code of a backtesting class for long-only strategies called `BacktestLongOnly`. Since it relies on and inherits from the `BacktestBase` class, the code to implement the three strategies based on SMAs, momentum, and mean reversion is rather concise.

The method `.run_mean_reversion_strategy()` implements the backtesting procedure for the mean reversion-based strategy. This method is commented on in detail, since it might be a bit trickier from an implementation standpoint. The basic insights, however, easily carry over to the methods implementing the other two strategies:

```python
def run_mean_reversion_strategy(self, SMA, threshold):
    ''' Backtesting a mean reversion-based strategy.

    Parameters
    ==========
    SMA: int
        simple moving average in days
    threshold: float
        absolute value for deviation-based signal relative to SMA
    '''
    msg = f'\n\nRunning mean reversion strategy | '
    msg += f'SMA={SMA} & thr={threshold}'
    msg += f'\nfixed costs {self.ftc} | '
    msg += f'proportional costs {self.ptc}'
    print(msg)                                           ❶
    print('=' * 55)
    self.position = 0                                    ❷
    self.trades = 0                                      ❷
    self.amount = self.initial_amount                    ❸

    self.data['SMA'] = self.data['price'].rolling(SMA).mean()  ❹

    for bar in range(SMA, len(self.data)):               ❺
        if self.position == 0:                           ❻
            if (self.data['price'].iloc[bar] <
                    self.data['SMA'].iloc[bar] - threshold):  ❼
                self.place_buy_order(bar, amount=self.amount)  ❽
                self.position = 1                        ❾
        elif self.position == 1:                         ❿
            if self.data['price'].iloc[bar] >= self.data['SMA'].iloc[bar]:  ⓫
                self.place_sell_order(bar, units=self.units)  ⓬
                self.position = 0                        ⓭
    self.close_out(bar)                                  ⓮
```

❶ At the beginning, this method prints out an overview of the major parameters for the backtesting.

❷ The position is set to market neutral, which is done here for more clarity and should be the case anyway.

❸ The current cash balance is reset to the initial amount in case another backtest run has overwritten the value.

❹ This calculates the SMA values needed for the strategy implementation.

⑤ The start value SMA ensures that there are SMA values available to start implementing and backtesting the strategy.

⑥ The condition checks whether the position is market neutral.

⑦ If the position is market neutral, it is checked whether the current price is low enough relative to the SMA to trigger a buy order and to go long.

⑧ This executes the buy order in the amount of the current cash balance.

⑨ The market position is set to long.

⑩ The condition checks whether the position is long the market.

⑪ If that is the case, it is checked whether the current price has returned to the SMA level or above.

⑫ In such a case, a sell order is placed for all units of the financial instrument.

⑬ The market position is set to neutral again.

⑭ At the end of the backtesting period, the market position gets closed out if one is open.

Executing the Python script in "Long-Only Backtesting Class" on page 194 yields backtesting results, as shown in the following. The examples illustrate the influence of fixed and proportional transaction costs. First, they eat into the performance in general. In any case, taking account of transaction costs reduces the performance. Second, they bring to light the importance of the number of trades a certain strategy triggers over time. Without transaction costs, the momentum strategy significantly outperforms the SMA-based strategy. With transaction costs, the SMA-based strategy outperforms the momentum strategy since it relies on fewer trades:

```
Running SMA strategy | SMA1=42 & SMA2=252
fixed costs 0.0 | proportional costs 0.0
=======================================================
Final balance    [$] 56204.95
Net Performance [%] 462.05
=======================================================


Running momentum strategy | 60 days
fixed costs 0.0 | proportional costs 0.0
=======================================================
Final balance    [$] 136716.52
Net Performance [%] 1267.17
=======================================================
```

```
Running mean reversion strategy | SMA=50 & thr=5
fixed costs 0.0 | proportional costs 0.0
=======================================================
Final balance    [$] 53907.99
Net Performance [%] 439.08
=======================================================


Running SMA strategy | SMA1=42 & SMA2=252
fixed costs 10.0 | proportional costs 0.01
=======================================================
Final balance    [$] 51959.62
Net Performance [%] 419.60
=======================================================


Running momentum strategy | 60 days
fixed costs 10.0 | proportional costs 0.01
=======================================================
Final balance    [$] 38074.26
Net Performance [%] 280.74
=======================================================


Running mean reversion strategy | SMA=50 & thr=5
fixed costs 10.0 | proportional costs 0.01
=======================================================
Final balance    [$] 15375.48
Net Performance [%] 53.75
=======================================================
```

Chapter 5 emphasizes that there are two sides of the performance coin: the hit ratio for the correct prediction of the market direction and the market timing (that is, when exactly the prediction is correct). The results shown here illustrate that there is even a "third side": the number of trades triggered by a strategy. A strategy that demands a higher frequency of trades has to bear higher transaction costs that easily eat up an alleged outperformance over another strategy with no or low transaction costs. Among other things, this often makes the case for low-cost passive investment strategies based, for example, on exchange-traded funds (ETFs).

Long-Short Backtesting Class

"Long-Short Backtesting Class" on page 197 presents the BacktestLongShort class, which also inherits from the BacktestBase class. In addition to implementing the respective methods for the backtesting of the different strategies, it implements two

---

additional methods to go long and short, respectively. Only the .go_long() method is commented on in detail, since the .go_short() method does exactly the same in the opposite direction:

```
def go_long(self, bar, units=None, amount=None):      ❶
    if self.position == -1:      ❷
        self.place_buy_order(bar, units=-self.units)      ❸
    if units:      ❹
        self.place_buy_order(bar, units=units)      ❺
    elif amount:      ❻
        if amount == 'all':      ❼
            amount = self.amount      ❽
        self.place_buy_order(bar, amount=amount)      ❾

def go_short(self, bar, units=None, amount=None):
    if self.position == 1:
        self.place_sell_order(bar, units=self.units)
    if units:
        self.place_sell_order(bar, units=units)
    elif amount:
        if amount == 'all':
            amount = self.amount
        self.place_sell_order(bar, amount=amount)
```

❶ In addition to bar, the methods expect either a number for the units of the traded instrument or a currency amount.

❷ In the .go_long() case, it is first checked whether there is a short position.

❸ If so, this short position gets closed first.

❹ It is then checked whether units is given…

❺ …which triggers a buy order accordingly.

❻ If amount is given, there can be two cases.

❼ First, the value is all, which translates into…

❽ …all the available cash in the current cash balance.

❾ Second, the value is a number that is then simply taken to place the respective buy order. Note that it is not checked whether there is enough liquidity or not.

To keep the implementation concise throughout, there are many simplifications in the Python classes that transfer responsibility to the user. For example, the classes do not take care of whether there is enough liquidity or not to execute a trade. This is an economic simplification since, in theory, one could assume enough or even unlimited credit for the algorithmic trader. As another example, certain methods expect that at least one of two parameters (either units or amount) is specified. There is no code that catches the case where both are not set. This is a technical simplification.

The following presents the core loop from the .run_mean_reversion_strategy() method of the BacktestLongShort class. Again, the mean-reversion strategy is picked since the implementation is a bit more involved. For instance, it is the only strategy that also leads to intermediate market neutral positions. This necessitates more checks compared to the other two strategies, as seen in "Long-Short Backtesting Class" on page 197.

```
for bar in range(SMA, len(self.data)):
    if self.position == 0:  ❶
        if (self.data['price'].iloc[bar] <
                self.data['SMA'].iloc[bar] - threshold):  ❷
            self.go_long(bar, amount=self.initial_amount)  ❸
            self.position = 1  ❹
        elif (self.data['price'].iloc[bar] >
                self.data['SMA'].iloc[bar] + threshold):  ❺
            self.go_short(bar, amount=self.initial_amount)
            self.position = -1  ❻
    elif self.position == 1:  ❼
        if self.data['price'].iloc[bar] >= self.data['SMA'].iloc[bar]:  ❽
            self.place_sell_order(bar, units=self.units)  ❾
            self.position = 0  ❿
    elif self.position == -1:  ⓫
        if self.data['price'].iloc[bar] <= self.data['SMA'].iloc[bar]:  ⓬
            self.place_buy_order(bar, units=-self.units)  ⓭
            self.position = 0  ⓮
    self.close_out(bar)
```

❶ The first top-level condition checks whether the position is market neutral.

❷ If this is true, it is then checked whether the current price is low enough relative to the SMA.

❸ In such a case, the .go_long() method is called...

❹ ...and the market position is set to long.

⑤ If the current price is high enough relative to the SMA, the `.go_short()` method is called…

⑥ …and the market position is set to short.

⑦ The second top-level condition checks for a long market position.

⑧ In such a case, it is further checked whether the current price is at or above the SMA level again.

⑨ If so, the long position gets closed out by selling all units in the portfolio.

⑩ The market position is reset to neutral.

⑪ Finally, the third top-level condition checks for a short position.

⑫ If the current price is at or below the SMA…

⑬ …a buy order for all units short is triggered to close out the short position.

⑭ The market position is then reset to neutral.

Executing the Python script in "Long-Short Backtesting Class" on page 197 yields performance results that shed further light on strategy characteristics. One might be inclined to assume that adding the flexibility to short a financial instrument yields better results. However, reality shows that this is not necessarily true. All strategies perform worse both without and after transaction costs. Some configurations even pile up net losses or even a position of debt. Although these are specific results only, they illustrate that it is risky in such a context to jump to conclusions too early and to not take into account limits for piling up debt:

```
Running SMA strategy | SMA1=42 & SMA2=252
fixed costs 0.0 | proportional costs 0.0
=======================================================
Final balance   [$] 45631.83
Net Performance [%] 356.32
=======================================================


Running momentum strategy | 60 days
fixed costs 0.0 | proportional costs 0.0
=======================================================
Final balance   [$] 105236.62
Net Performance [%] 952.37
=======================================================
```

```
Running mean reversion strategy | SMA=50 & thr=5
fixed costs 0.0 | proportional costs 0.0
===========================================================
Final balance    [$] 17279.15
Net Performance [%] 72.79
===========================================================


Running SMA strategy | SMA1=42 & SMA2=252
fixed costs 10.0 | proportional costs 0.01
===========================================================
Final balance    [$] 38369.65
Net Performance [%] 283.70
===========================================================


Running momentum strategy | 60 days
fixed costs 10.0 | proportional costs 0.01
===========================================================
Final balance    [$] 6883.45
Net Performance [%] -31.17
===========================================================


Running mean reversion strategy | SMA=50 & thr=5
fixed costs 10.0 | proportional costs 0.01
===========================================================
Final balance    [$] -5110.97
Net Performance [%] -151.11
===========================================================
```

Situations where trading might eat up all the initial equity and might even lead to a position of debt arise, for example, in the context of trading contracts-for-difference (CFDs). These are highly leveraged products for which the trader only needs to put down, say, 5% of the position value as the initial margin (when the leverage is 20). If the position value changes by, say, 10%, the trader might be required to meet a corresponding margin call. For a long position of 100,000 USD, equity of 5,000 USD is required. If the position drops to 90,000 USD, the equity is wiped out and the trader must put down 5,000 USD more to cover the losses. This assumes that no margin stop outs are in place that would close the position as soon as the remaining equity drops to 0 USD.

Conclusions

This chapter presents classes for the event-based backtesting of trading strategies. Compared to vectorized backtesting, event-based backtesting makes intentional and heavy use of loops and iterations to be able to tackle every single new event (generally, the arrival of new data) individually. This allows for a more flexible approach that can, among other things, easily cope with fixed transaction costs or more complex strategies (and variations thereof).

"Backtesting Base Class" on page 177 presents a base class with certain methods useful for the backtesting of a variety of trading strategies. "Long-Only Backtesting Class" on page 182 and "Long-Short Backtesting Class" on page 185 build on this infrastructure to implement classes that allow the backtesting of long-only and long-short trading strategies. Mainly for comparison reasons, the implementations include all three strategies formally introduced in Chapter 4. Taking the classes of this chapter as a starting point, enhancements and refinements are easily achieved.

References and Further Resources

Previous chapters introduce the basic ideas and concepts with regard to the three trading strategies covered in this chapter. This chapter for the first time makes a more systemic use of Python classes and object-oriented programming (OOP). A good introduction to OOP with Python and Python's data model is found in Ramalho (2021). A more concise introduction to OOP applied to finance is found in Hilpisch (2018, ch. 6):

Hilpisch, Yves. 2018. *Python for Finance: Mastering Data-Driven Finance*. 2nd ed. Sebastopol: O'Reilly.

Ramalho, Luciano. 2021. *Fluent Python: Clear, Concise, and Effective Programming*. 2nd ed. Sebastopol: O'Reilly.

The Python ecosystem provides a number of optional packages that allow the backtesting of algorithmic trading strategies. Four of them are the following:

- bt (*http://pmorissette.github.io/bt/*)
- Backtrader (*https://backtrader.com/*)
- PyAlgoTrade (*http://gbeced.github.io/pyalgotrade/*)
- Zipline (*https://github.com/quantopian/zipline*)

Zipline, for example, powers the popular Quantopian (*http://quantopian.com*) platform for the backtesting of algorithmic trading strategies but can also be installed and used locally.

Although these packages might allow for a more thorough backtesting of algorithmic trading strategies than the rather simple classes presented in this chapter, the main goal of this book is to empower the reader and algorithmic trader to implement Python code in a self-contained fashion. Even if standard packages are later used to do the actual backtesting, a good understanding of the different approaches and their mechanics is beneficial, if not required.

Python Scripts

This section presents Python scripts referenced and used in this chapter.

Backtesting Base Class

The following Python code contains the base class for event-based backtesting:

```
#
# Python Script with Base Class
# for Event-Based Backtesting
#
# Python for Algorithmic Trading
# (c) Dr. Yves J. Hilpisch
# The Python Quants GmbH
#
import numpy as np
import pandas as pd
from pylab import mpl, plt
plt.style.use('seaborn')
mpl.rcParams['font.family'] = 'serif'


class BacktestBase(object):
    ''' Base class for event-based backtesting of trading strategies.

    Attributes
    ==========
    symbol: str
        TR RIC (financial instrument) to be used
    start: str
        start date for data selection
    end: str
        end date for data selection
    amount: float
        amount to be invested either once or per trade
    ftc: float
        fixed transaction costs per trade (buy or sell)
    ptc: float
```

```
        proportional transaction costs per trade (buy or sell)

    Methods
    =======
    get_data:
        retrieves and prepares the base data set
    plot_data:
        plots the closing price for the symbol
    get_date_price:
        returns the date and price for the given bar
    print_balance:
        prints out the current (cash) balance
    print_net_wealth:
        prints out the current net wealth
    place_buy_order:
        places a buy order
    place_sell_order:
        places a sell order
    close_out:
        closes out a long or short position
    '''

    def __init__(self, symbol, start, end, amount,
                 ftc=0.0, ptc=0.0, verbose=True):
        self.symbol = symbol
        self.start = start
        self.end = end
        self.initial_amount = amount
        self.amount = amount
        self.ftc = ftc
        self.ptc = ptc
        self.units = 0
        self.position = 0
        self.trades = 0
        self.verbose = verbose
        self.get_data()

    def get_data(self):
        ''' Retrieves and prepares the data.
        '''
        raw = pd.read_csv('http://hilpisch.com/pyalgo_eikon_eod_data.csv',
                          index_col=0, parse_dates=True).dropna()
        raw = pd.DataFrame(raw[self.symbol])
        raw = raw.loc[self.start:self.end]
        raw.rename(columns={self.symbol: 'price'}, inplace=True)
        raw['return'] = np.log(raw / raw.shift(1))
        self.data = raw.dropna()

    def plot_data(self, cols=None):
        ''' Plots the closing prices for symbol.
        '''
        if cols is None:
```

```python
        cols = ['price']
    self.data['price'].plot(figsize=(10, 6), title=self.symbol)

def get_date_price(self, bar):
    ''' Return date and price for bar.
    '''
    date = str(self.data.index[bar])[:10]
    price = self.data.price.iloc[bar]
    return date, price

def print_balance(self, bar):
    ''' Print out current cash balance info.
    '''
    date, price = self.get_date_price(bar)
    print(f'{date} | current balance {self.amount:.2f}')

def print_net_wealth(self, bar):
    ''' Print out current cash balance info.
    '''
    date, price = self.get_date_price(bar)
    net_wealth = self.units * price + self.amount
    print(f'{date} | current net wealth {net_wealth:.2f}')

def place_buy_order(self, bar, units=None, amount=None):
    ''' Place a buy order.
    '''
    date, price = self.get_date_price(bar)
    if units is None:
        units = int(amount / price)
    self.amount -= (units * price) * (1 + self.ptc) + self.ftc
    self.units += units
    self.trades += 1
    if self.verbose:
        print(f'{date} | selling {units} units at {price:.2f}')
        self.print_balance(bar)
        self.print_net_wealth(bar)

def place_sell_order(self, bar, units=None, amount=None):
    ''' Place a sell order.
    '''
    date, price = self.get_date_price(bar)
    if units is None:
        units = int(amount / price)
    self.amount += (units * price) * (1 - self.ptc) - self.ftc
    self.units -= units
    self.trades += 1
    if self.verbose:
        print(f'{date} | selling {units} units at {price:.2f}')
        self.print_balance(bar)
        self.print_net_wealth(bar)

def close_out(self, bar):
```

```
    ''' Closing out a long or short position.
    '''
    date, price = self.get_date_price(bar)
    self.amount += self.units * price
    self.units = 0
    self.trades += 1
    if self.verbose:
        print(f'{date} | inventory {self.units} units at {price:.2f}')
        print('=' * 55)
    print('Final balance   [$] {:.2f}'.format(self.amount))
    perf = ((self.amount - self.initial_amount) /
            self.initial_amount * 100)
    print('Net Performance [%] {:.2f}'.format(perf))
    print('Trades Executed [#] {:.2f}'.format(self.trades))
    print('=' * 55)


if __name__ == '__main__':
    bb = BacktestBase('AAPL.O', '2010-1-1', '2019-12-31', 10000)
    print(bb.data.info())
    print(bb.data.tail())
    bb.plot_data()
```

Long-Only Backtesting Class

The following presents Python code with a class for the event-based backtesting of *long-only* strategies, with implementations for strategies based on *SMAs*, *momentum*, and *mean reversion*:

```
#
# Python Script with Long Only Class
# for Event-Based Backtesting
#
# Python for Algorithmic Trading
# (c) Dr. Yves J. Hilpisch
# The Python Quants GmbH
#
from BacktestBase import *


class BacktestLongOnly(BacktestBase):

    def run_sma_strategy(self, SMA1, SMA2):
        ''' Backtesting an SMA-based strategy.

        Parameters
        ==========
        SMA1, SMA2: int
            shorter and longer term simple moving average (in days)
        '''
        msg = f'\n\nRunning SMA strategy | SMA1={SMA1} & SMA2={SMA2}'
        msg += f'\nfixed costs {self.ftc} | '
```

```python
        msg += f'proportional costs {self.ptc}'
        print(msg)
        print('=' * 55)
        self.position = 0  # initial neutral position
        self.trades = 0  # no trades yet
        self.amount = self.initial_amount  # reset initial capital
        self.data['SMA1'] = self.data['price'].rolling(SMA1).mean()
        self.data['SMA2'] = self.data['price'].rolling(SMA2).mean()

        for bar in range(SMA2, len(self.data)):
            if self.position == 0:
                if self.data['SMA1'].iloc[bar] > self.data['SMA2'].iloc[bar]:
                    self.place_buy_order(bar, amount=self.amount)
                    self.position = 1  # long position
            elif self.position == 1:
                if self.data['SMA1'].iloc[bar] < self.data['SMA2'].iloc[bar]:
                    self.place_sell_order(bar, units=self.units)
                    self.position = 0  # market neutral
        self.close_out(bar)

    def run_momentum_strategy(self, momentum):
        ''' Backtesting a momentum-based strategy.

        Parameters
        ==========
        momentum: int
            number of days for mean return calculation
        '''
        msg = f'\n\nRunning momentum strategy | {momentum} days'
        msg += f'\nfixed costs {self.ftc} | '
        msg += f'proportional costs {self.ptc}'
        print(msg)
        print('=' * 55)
        self.position = 0  # initial neutral position
        self.trades = 0  # no trades yet
        self.amount = self.initial_amount  # reset initial capital
        self.data['momentum'] = self.data['return'].rolling(momentum).mean()
        for bar in range(momentum, len(self.data)):
            if self.position == 0:
                if self.data['momentum'].iloc[bar] > 0:
                    self.place_buy_order(bar, amount=self.amount)
                    self.position = 1  # long position
            elif self.position == 1:
                if self.data['momentum'].iloc[bar] < 0:
                    self.place_sell_order(bar, units=self.units)
                    self.position = 0  # market neutral
        self.close_out(bar)

    def run_mean_reversion_strategy(self, SMA, threshold):
        ''' Backtesting a mean reversion-based strategy.

        Parameters
```

```
==========
SMA: int
    simple moving average in days
threshold: float
    absolute value for deviation-based signal relative to SMA
'''
msg = f'\n\nRunning mean reversion strategy | '
msg += f'SMA={SMA} & thr={threshold}'
msg += f'\nfixed costs {self.ftc} | '
msg += f'proportional costs {self.ptc}'
print(msg)
print('=' * 55)
self.position = 0
self.trades = 0
self.amount = self.initial_amount

self.data['SMA'] = self.data['price'].rolling(SMA).mean()

for bar in range(SMA, len(self.data)):
    if self.position == 0:
        if (self.data['price'].iloc[bar] <
                self.data['SMA'].iloc[bar] - threshold):
            self.place_buy_order(bar, amount=self.amount)
            self.position = 1
    elif self.position == 1:
        if self.data['price'].iloc[bar] >= self.data['SMA'].iloc[bar]:
            self.place_sell_order(bar, units=self.units)
            self.position = 0
self.close_out(bar)


if __name__ == '__main__':
    def run_strategies():
        lobt.run_sma_strategy(42, 252)
        lobt.run_momentum_strategy(60)
        lobt.run_mean_reversion_strategy(50, 5)
    lobt = BacktestLongOnly('AAPL.O', '2010-1-1', '2019-12-31', 10000,
                            verbose=False)
    run_strategies()
    # transaction costs: 10 USD fix, 1% variable
    lobt = BacktestLongOnly('AAPL.O', '2010-1-1', '2019-12-31',
                            10000, 10.0, 0.01, False)
    run_strategies()
```

Long-Short Backtesting Class

The following Python code contains a class for the event-based backtesting of *long-short* strategies, with implementations for strategies based on *SMAs, momentum*, and *mean reversion*:

```python
#
# Python Script with Long-Short Class
# for Event-Based Backtesting
#
# Python for Algorithmic Trading
# (c) Dr. Yves J. Hilpisch
# The Python Quants GmbH
#
from BacktestBase import *


class BacktestLongShort(BacktestBase):

    def go_long(self, bar, units=None, amount=None):
        if self.position == -1:
            self.place_buy_order(bar, units=-self.units)
        if units:
            self.place_buy_order(bar, units=units)
        elif amount:
            if amount == 'all':
                amount = self.amount
            self.place_buy_order(bar, amount=amount)

    def go_short(self, bar, units=None, amount=None):
        if self.position == 1:
            self.place_sell_order(bar, units=self.units)
        if units:
            self.place_sell_order(bar, units=units)
        elif amount:
            if amount == 'all':
                amount = self.amount
            self.place_sell_order(bar, amount=amount)

    def run_sma_strategy(self, SMA1, SMA2):
        msg = f'\n\nRunning SMA strategy | SMA1={SMA1} & SMA2={SMA2}'
        msg += f'\nfixed costs {self.ftc} | '
        msg += f'proportional costs {self.ptc}'
        print(msg)
        print('=' * 55)
        self.position = 0  # initial neutral position
        self.trades = 0  # no trades yet
        self.amount = self.initial_amount  # reset initial capital
        self.data['SMA1'] = self.data['price'].rolling(SMA1).mean()
        self.data['SMA2'] = self.data['price'].rolling(SMA2).mean()
```

```
        for bar in range(SMA2, len(self.data)):
            if self.position in [0, -1]:
                if self.data['SMA1'].iloc[bar] > self.data['SMA2'].iloc[bar]:
                    self.go_long(bar, amount='all')
                    self.position = 1  # long position
            if self.position in [0, 1]:
                if self.data['SMA1'].iloc[bar] < self.data['SMA2'].iloc[bar]:
                    self.go_short(bar, amount='all')
                    self.position = -1  # short position
        self.close_out(bar)

    def run_momentum_strategy(self, momentum):
        msg = f'\n\nRunning momentum strategy | {momentum} days'
        msg += f'\nfixed costs {self.ftc} | '
        msg += f'proportional costs {self.ptc}'
        print(msg)
        print('=' * 55)
        self.position = 0  # initial neutral position
        self.trades = 0  # no trades yet
        self.amount = self.initial_amount  # reset initial capital
        self.data['momentum'] = self.data['return'].rolling(momentum).mean()
        for bar in range(momentum, len(self.data)):
            if self.position in [0, -1]:
                if self.data['momentum'].iloc[bar] > 0:
                    self.go_long(bar, amount='all')
                    self.position = 1  # long position
            if self.position in [0, 1]:
                if self.data['momentum'].iloc[bar] <= 0:
                    self.go_short(bar, amount='all')
                    self.position = -1  # short position
        self.close_out(bar)

    def run_mean_reversion_strategy(self, SMA, threshold):
        msg = f'\n\nRunning mean reversion strategy | '
        msg += f'SMA={SMA} & thr={threshold}'
        msg += f'\nfixed costs {self.ftc} | '
        msg += f'proportional costs {self.ptc}'
        print(msg)
        print('=' * 55)
        self.position = 0  # initial neutral position
        self.trades = 0  # no trades yet
        self.amount = self.initial_amount  # reset initial capital

        self.data['SMA'] = self.data['price'].rolling(SMA).mean()

        for bar in range(SMA, len(self.data)):
            if self.position == 0:
                if (self.data['price'].iloc[bar] <
                        self.data['SMA'].iloc[bar] - threshold):
                    self.go_long(bar, amount=self.initial_amount)
                    self.position = 1
                elif (self.data['price'].iloc[bar] >
```

```python
                            self.data['SMA'].iloc[bar] + threshold):
                    self.go_short(bar, amount=self.initial_amount)
                    self.position = -1
            elif self.position == 1:
                if self.data['price'].iloc[bar] >= self.data['SMA'].iloc[bar]:
                    self.place_sell_order(bar, units=self.units)
                    self.position = 0
            elif self.position == -1:
                if self.data['price'].iloc[bar] <= self.data['SMA'].iloc[bar]:
                    self.place_buy_order(bar, units=-self.units)
                    self.position = 0
        self.close_out(bar)


if __name__ == '__main__':
    def run_strategies():
        lsbt.run_sma_strategy(42, 252)
        lsbt.run_momentum_strategy(60)
        lsbt.run_mean_reversion_strategy(50, 5)
    lsbt = BacktestLongShort('EUR=', '2010-1-1', '2019-12-31', 10000,
                             verbose=False)
    run_strategies()
    # transaction costs: 10 USD fix, 1% variable
    lsbt = BacktestLongShort('AAPL.O', '2010-1-1', '2019-12-31',
                             10000, 10.0, 0.01, False)
    run_strategies()
```

## CHAPTER 7

Working with Real-Time Data and Sockets

If you want to find the secrets of the universe, think in terms of energy, frequency, and vibration.

—Nikola Tesla

Developing trading ideas and backtesting them is a rather asynchronous and non-critical process during which there are multiple steps that might or might not be repeated, during which no capital is at stake, and during which performance and speed are not the most important requirements. Turning to the markets to deploy a trading strategy changes the rules considerably. Data arrives in real time and usually in massive amounts, making a real-time processing of the data and the real-time decision making based on the streaming data a necessity. This chapter is about working with real-time data for which *sockets* are in general the technological tool of choice. In this context, here are a few words on central technical terms:

Network socket
Endpoint of a connection in a computer network, also simply *socket* for short.

Socket address
Combination of an Internet Protocol (IP) address and a port number.

Socket protocol
A protocol defining and handling the socket communication, like the Transfer Control Protocol (TCP).

Socket pair
Combination of a local and a remote socket that communicate with each other.

Socket API
The application programming interface allowing for the controlling of sockets and their communication.

This chapter focuses on the use of ZeroMQ (*http://zeromq.org*) as a lightweight, fast, and scalable socket programming library. It is available on multiple platforms with wrappers for the most popular programming languages. ZeroMQ supports different patterns for socket communication. One of those patterns is the so-called *publisher-subscriber* (PUB-SUB) pattern where a single socket publishes data and multiple sockets simultaneously retrieve the data. This is similar to a radio station that broadcasts its program that is simultaneously listened to by thousands of people via radio devices.

Given the PUB-SUB pattern, a fundamental application scenario in algorithmic trading is the retrieval of real-time financial data from an exchange, a trading platform, or a data service provider. Suppose you have developed an intraday trading idea based on the EUR/USD currency pair and have backtested it thoroughly. When deploying it, you need to be able to receive and process the price data in real-time. This fits exactly such a PUB-SUB pattern. A central instance broadcasts the new tick data as it becomes available and you, as well as probably thousands of others, receive and process it at the same time.[1]

This chapter is organized as follows. "Running a Simple Tick Data Server" on page 203 describes how to implement and run a tick data server for sample financial data. "Connecting a Simple Tick Data Client" on page 206 implements a tick data client to connect to the tick data server. "Signal Generation in Real Time" on page 208 shows how to generate trading signals in real time based on data from the tick data server. Finally, "Visualizing Streaming Data with Plotly" on page 211 introduces the Plotly (*http://plot.ly*) plotting package as an efficient way to plot streaming data in real time.

The goal of this chapter is to have a tool set and approaches available to be able to work with streaming data in the context of algorithmic trading.

The code in this chapter makes heavy use of ports over which socket communication takes place and requires the simultaneous execution of two or more scripts at the same time. It is therefore recommended to execute the codes in this chapter in different terminal instances, running different Python kernels. The execution within a single Jupyter Notebook, for instance, does not work in general. What works, however, is the execution of the tick data server script ("Running a Simple Tick Data Server" on page 203) in a terminal and the retrieval of data in a Jupyter Notebook ("Visualizing Streaming Data with Plotly" on page 211).

---

1 When speaking of *simultaneously* or *at the same time*, this is meant in a theoretical, idealized sense. In practical applications, different distances between the sending and receiving sockets, network speeds, and other factors affect the exact retrieval time per subscriber socket.

Running a Simple Tick Data Server

This section shows how to run a simple tick data server based on simulated financial instrument prices. The model used for the data generation is the geometric Brownian motion (without dividends) for which an exact Euler discretization is available, as shown in Equation 7-1. Here, S is the instrument price, r is the constant short rate, σ is the constant volatility factor, and z is a standard normal random variable. Δt is the interval between two discrete observations of the instrument price.

Equation 7-1. Euler discretization of geometric Brownian motion

$$S_t = S_{t - \Delta t} \cdot \exp\left(\left(r - \frac{\sigma^2}{2}\right)\Delta t + \sigma\sqrt{\Delta t}z\right)$$

Making use of this model, "Sample Tick Data Server" on page 218 presents a Python script that implements a tick data server using ZeroMQ and a class called Instrument Price to publish new, simulated tick data in a randomized fashion. The publishing is randomized in two ways. First, the stock price value is based on a Monte Carlo simulation. Second is the length of time interval between two publishing events it randomized. The remainder of this section explains the major parts of the script in detail.

The first part of the following script does some imports, among other things, for the Python wrapper of ZeroMQ. It also instantiates the major objects needed to open a socket of PUB type:

```
import zmq  ❶
import math
import time
import random

context = zmq.Context()  ❷
socket = context.socket(zmq.PUB)  ❸
socket.bind('tcp://0.0.0.0:5555')  ❹
```

❶ This imports the Python wrapper for the ZeroMQ library.

❷ A Context object is instantiated. It is the central object for the socket communication.

❸ The socket itself is defined based on the PUB socket type ("communication pattern").

❹ The socket gets bound to the local IP address (0.0.0.0 on Linux and Mac OS, 127.0.0.1 on Windows) and the port number 5555.

The class `InstrumentPrice` is for the simulation of instrument price values over time. As attributes, there are the major parameters for the geometric Brownian motion in addition to the instrument symbol and the time at which an instance is created. The only method `.simulate_value()` generates new values for the stock price given the time passed since it has been called the last time and a random factor:

```python
class InstrumentPrice(object):
    def __init__(self):
        self.symbol = 'SYMBOL'
        self.t = time.time()  ❶
        self.value = 100.
        self.sigma = 0.4
        self.r = 0.01

    def simulate_value(self):
        ''' Generates a new, random stock price.
        '''
        t = time.time()  ❷
        dt = (t - self.t) / (252 * 8 * 60 * 60)  ❸
        dt *= 500  ❹
        self.t = t  ❺
        self.value *= math.exp((self.r - 0.5 * self.sigma ** 2) * dt +
                               self.sigma * math.sqrt(dt) * random.gauss(0, 1))  ❻
        return self.value
```

❶ The attribute `t` stores the time of the initialization.

❷ When the `.simulate_value()` method is called, the current time is recorded.

❸ `dt` represents the time interval between the current time and the one stored in `self.t` in (trading) year fractions.

❹ To have larger instrument price movements, this line of code scales the `dt` variable (by an arbitrary factor).

❺ The attribute `t` is updated with the current time, which represents the reference point for the next call of the method.

❻ Based on an Euler scheme for the geometric Brownian motion, a new instrument price is simulated.

The main part of the script consists of the instantiation of an object of type `Instru mentPrice` and an infinite `while` loop. During the `while` loop, a new instrument price gets simulated, and a message is created, printed, and sent via the socket.

Finally, the execution pauses for a random amount of time:

```
ip = InstrumentPrice()  ❶

while True:  ❷
    msg = '{} {:.2f}'.format(ip.symbol, ip.simulate_value())  ❸
    print(msg)  ❹
    socket.send_string(msg)  ❺
    time.sleep(random.random() * 2)  ❻
```

❶ This line instantiates an `InstrumentPrice` object.

❷ An infinite `while` loop is started.

❸ The message text gets generated based on the `symbol` attribute and a newly simulated stock price value.

❹ The message `str` object is printed to the standard out.

❺ It is also sent to subscribed sockets.

❻ The execution of the loop is paused for a random amount of time (between 0 and 2 seconds), simulating the random arrival of new tick data in the markets.

Executing the script prints out messages as follows:

```
(base) pro:ch07 yves$ Python TickServer.py
SYMBOL 100.00
SYMBOL 99.65
SYMBOL 99.28
SYMBOL 99.09
SYMBOL 98.76
SYMBOL 98.83
SYMBOL 98.82
SYMBOL 98.92
SYMBOL 98.57
SYMBOL 98.81
SYMBOL 98.79
SYMBOL 98.80
```

At this point, it cannot yet be verified whether the script is also sending the same message via the socket bound to `tcp://0.0.0.0:5555` (`tcp://127.0.0.1:5555` on Windows). To this end, another socket subscribing to the publishing socket is needed to complete the socket pair.

Often, the Monte Carlo simulation of prices for financial instruments relies on homogeneous time intervals (like "one trading day"). In many cases, this is a "good enough" approximation when working with, say, end-of-day closing prices over longer horizons. In the context of intraday tick data, the random arrival of the data is an important characteristic that needs to be taken into account. The Python script for the tick data server implements the random arrival times by randomized time intervals during which it pauses the execution.

Connecting a Simple Tick Data Client

The code for the tick data server is already quite concise, with the `InstrumentPrice` simulation class representing the longest part. The code for a respective tick data client, as shown in "Tick Data Client" on page 219, is even more concise. It is only a few lines of code that instantiate the main `Context` object, connect to the publishing socket, and subscribe to the `SYMBOL` channel, which happens to be the only available channel here. In the `while` loop, the string-based message is received and printed. That makes for a rather short script.

The initial part of the following script is almost symmetrical to the tick data server script:

```
import zmq     ❶

context = zmq.Context()     ❷
socket = context.socket(zmq.SUB)     ❸
socket.connect('tcp://0.0.0.0:5555')     ❹
socket.setsockopt_string(zmq.SUBSCRIBE, 'SYMBOL')     ❺
```

❶ This imports the Python wrapper for the `ZeroMQ` library.

❷ For the client, the main object also is an instance of `zmq.Context`.

❸ From here, the code is different; the socket type is set to `SUB`.

❹ This socket connects to the respective IP address and port combination.

❺ This line of code defines the so-called channel to which the socket subscribes. Here, there is only one, but a specification is nevertheless required. In real-world applications, however, you might receive data for a multitude of different symbols via a socket connection.

The while loop boils down to the retrieval of the messages sent by the server socket and printing them out:

```
while True:  ❶
    data = socket.recv_string()  ❷
    print(data)  ❸
```

❶ This socket receives data in an infinite loop.

❷ This is the main line of code where the data (string-based message) is received.

❸ data is printed to stdout.

The output of the Python script for the socket client is exactly the same as the one from the Python script for the socket server:

```
(base) pro:ch07 yves$ Python TickClient.py
SYMBOL 100.00
SYMBOL 99.65
SYMBOL 99.28
SYMBOL 99.09
SYMBOL 98.76
SYMBOL 98.83
SYMBOL 98.82
SYMBOL 98.92
SYMBOL 98.57
SYMBOL 98.81
SYMBOL 98.79
SYMBOL 98.80
```

Retrieving data in the form of string-based messages via socket communication is only a prerequisite for the very tasks to be accomplished based on the data, like generating trading signals in real time or visualizing the data. This is what the two next sections cover.

> ZeroMQ allows the transmission of other object types, as well. For example, there is an option to send a Python object via a socket. To this end, the object is, by default, serialized and deserialized with pickle. The respective methods to accomplish this are .send_pyobj() and .recv_pyobj() (see The PyZMQ API (*https://oreil.ly/ok2kc*)). In practice, however, platforms and data providers cater to a diverse set of environments, with Python being only one out of many languages. Therefore, string-based socket communication is often used, for example, in combination with standard data formats such as JSON.

Signal Generation in Real Time

An *online algorithm* is an algorithm based on data that is received incrementally (bit by bit) over time. Such an algorithm only knows the current and previous states of relevant variables and parameters, but nothing about the future. This is a realistic setting for financial trading algorithms for which any element of (perfect) foresight is to be excluded. By contrast, an *offline algorithm* knows the complete data set from the beginning. Many algorithms in computer science fall into the category of offline algorithms, such as a sorting algorithm over a list of numbers.

To generate signals in real time on the basis of an online algorithm, data needs to be collected and processed over time. Consider, for example, a trading strategy based on the time series momentum of the last three five-second intervals (see Chapter 4). Tick data needs to be collected and then resampled, and the momentum needs to be calculated based on the resampled data set. When time passes by, a continuous, incremental updating takes place. "Momentum Online Algorithm" on page 219 presents a Python script that implements the momentum strategy, as described previously as an online algorithm. Technically, there are two major parts in addition to handling the socket communication. First are the retrieval and storage of the tick data:

```
df = pd.DataFrame()    ❶
mom = 3    ❷
min_length = mom + 1    ❸

while True:
    data = socket.recv_string()    ❹
    t = datetime.datetime.now()    ❺
    sym, value = data.split()    ❻
    df = df.append(pd.DataFrame({sym: float(value)}, index=[t]))    ❼
```

❶ Instantiates an empty pandas DataFrame to collect the tick data.

❷ Defines the number of time intervals for the momentum calculation.

❸ Specifies the (initial) minimum length for the signal generation to be triggered.

❹ The retrieval of the tick data via the socket connection.

❺ A timestamp is generated for the data retrieval.

❻ The string-based message is split into the symbol and the numerical value (still a str object here).

❼ This line of code first generates a temporary DataFrame object with the new data and then appends it to the existing DataFrame object.

Second is the resampling and processing of the data, as shown in the following Python code. This happens based on the tick data collected up to a certain point in time. During this step, log returns are calculated based on the resampled data and the momentum is derived. The sign of the momentum defines the positioning to be taken in the financial instrument:

```
dr = df.resample('5s', label='right').last()    ❶
dr['returns'] = np.log(dr / dr.shift(1))    ❷
if len(dr) > min_length:
    min_length += 1    ❸
    dr['momentum'] = np.sign(dr['returns'].rolling(mom).mean())    ❹
    print('\n' + '=' * 51)
    print('NEW SIGNAL | {}'.format(datetime.datetime.now()))
    print('=' * 51)
    print(dr.iloc[:-1].tail())    ❺
    if dr['momentum'].iloc[-2] == 1.0:    ❻
        print('\nLong market position.')
        # take some action (e.q., place buy order)
    elif dr['momentum'].iloc[-2] == -1.0:    ❼
        print('\nShort market position.')
        # take some action (e.g., place sell order)
```

❶ The tick data is resampled to a five-second interval, taking the last available tick value as the relevant one.

❷ This calculates the log returns over the five-second intervals.

❸ This increases the minimum length of the resampled DataFrame object by one.

❹ The momentum and, based on its sign, the positioning are derived given the log returns from three resampled time intervals.

❺ This prints the final five rows of the resampled DataFrame object.

❻ A momentum value of 1.0 means a long market position. In production, the first signal or a change in the signal then triggers certain actions, like placing an order with the broker. Note that the second but last value of the momentum column is used since the last value is based at this stage on incomplete data for the relevant (not yet finished) time interval. Technically, this is due to using the pan das .resample() method with the label='right' parametrization.

❼ Similarly, a momentum value of -1.0 implies a short market position and potentially certain actions that might be triggered, such as a sell order with a broker. Again, the second but last value from the momentum column is used.

When the script is executed, it takes some time, depending on the very parameters chosen, until there is enough (resampled) data available to generate the first signal.

Here is an intermediate example output of the online trading algorithm script:

```
(base) yves@pro ch07 $ python OnlineAlgorithm.py

=======================================================
NEW SIGNAL | 2020-05-23 11:33:31.233606
=======================================================
                     SYMBOL  ...  momentum
2020-05-23 11:33:15   98.65  ...       NaN
2020-05-23 11:33:20   98.53  ...       NaN
2020-05-23 11:33:25   98.83  ...       NaN
2020-05-23 11:33:30   99.33  ...       1.0

[4 rows x 3 columns]

Long market position.


=======================================================
NEW SIGNAL | 2020-05-23 11:33:36.185453
=======================================================
                     SYMBOL  ...  momentum
2020-05-23 11:33:15   98.65  ...       NaN
2020-05-23 11:33:20   98.53  ...       NaN
2020-05-23 11:33:25   98.83  ...       NaN
2020-05-23 11:33:30   99.33  ...       1.0
2020-05-23 11:33:35   97.76  ...      -1.0

[5 rows x 3 columns]

Short market position.


=======================================================
NEW SIGNAL | 2020-05-23 11:33:40.077869
=======================================================
                     SYMBOL  ...  momentum
2020-05-23 11:33:20   98.53  ...       NaN
2020-05-23 11:33:25   98.83  ...       NaN
2020-05-23 11:33:30   99.33  ...       1.0
2020-05-23 11:33:35   97.76  ...      -1.0
2020-05-23 11:33:40   98.51  ...      -1.0

[5 rows x 3 columns]

Short market position.
```

It is a good exercise to implement, based on the presented tick client script, both an SMA-based strategy and a mean-reversion strategy as an online algorithm.

Visualizing Streaming Data with Plotly

The visualization of streaming data in real time is generally a demanding task. Fortunately, there are quite a few technologies and Python packages available nowadays that significantly simplify such a task. In what follows, we will work with Plotly (*http://plot.ly*), which is both a technology and a service used to generate nice looking, interactive plots for static and streaming data. To follow along, the `plotly` package needs to be installed. Also, several Jupyter Lab extensions need to be installed when working with Jupyter Lab. The following command should be executed on the terminal:

```
conda install plotly ipywidgets
jupyter labextension install jupyterlab-plotly
jupyter labextension install @jupyter-widgets/jupyterlab-manager
jupyter labextension install plotlywidget
```

The Basics

Once the required packages and extension are installed, the generation of a streaming plot is quite efficient. The first step is the creation of a Plotly figure widget:

```
In [1]: import zmq
        from datetime import datetime
        import plotly.graph_objects as go    ❶

In [2]: symbol = 'SYMBOL'

In [3]: fig = go.FigureWidget()    ❷
        fig.add_scatter()    ❷
        fig    ❷
Out[3]: FigureWidget({
        'data': [{'type': 'scatter', 'uid':
        'e1a65f25-287d-4021-a210-c2f41f32426a'}], 'layout': {'t…
```

❶ This imports the graphical objects from `plotly`.

❷ This instantiates a Plotly figure widget within the Jupyter Notebook.

The second step is to set up the socket communication with the sample tick data server, which needs to run on the same machine in a separate Python process. The incoming data is enriched by a timestamp and collected in `list` objects. These `list` objects in turn are used to update the `data` objects of the figure widget (see Figure 7-1):

```
In [4]: context = zmq.Context()

In [5]: socket = context.socket(zmq.SUB)

In [6]: socket.connect('tcp://0.0.0.0:5555')
```

```
In [7]: socket.setsockopt_string(zmq.SUBSCRIBE, 'SYMBOL')

In [8]: times = list()   ❶
        prices = list()  ❷

In [9]: for _ in range(50):
            msg = socket.recv_string()
            t = datetime.now()   ❸
            times.append(t)   ❸
            _, price = msg.split()
            prices.append(float(price))
            fig.data[0].x = times   ❹
            fig.data[0].y = prices  ❹
```

❶ list object for the timestamps.

❷ list object for the real-time prices.

❸ Generates a timestamp and appends it.

❹ Updates the data object with the amended x (times) and y (prices) data sets.

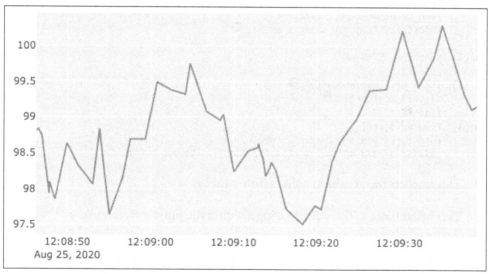

Figure 7-1. Plot of streaming price data, as retrieved in real time via socket connection

Three Real-Time Streams

A streaming plot with Plotly can have multiple graph objects. This comes in handy when, for instance, two simple moving averages (SMAs) shall be visualized in real time in addition to the price ticks. The following code instantiates again a figure widget—this time with three `scatter` objects. The tick data from the sample tick data server is collected in a `pandas` `DataFrame` object. The two SMAs are calculated after each update from the socket. The amended data sets are used to update the `data` object of the figure widget (see Figure 7-2):

```
In [10]: fig = go.FigureWidget()
         fig.add_scatter(name='SYMBOL')
         fig.add_scatter(name='SMA1', line=dict(width=1, dash='dot'),
                         mode='lines+markers')
         fig.add_scatter(name='SMA2', line=dict(width=1, dash='dash'),
                         mode='lines+markers')
         fig
Out[10]: FigureWidget({
         'data': [{'name': 'SYMBOL', 'type': 'scatter', 'uid':
         'bcf83157-f015-411b-a834-d5fd6ac509ba…

In [11]: import pandas as pd

In [12]: df = pd.DataFrame()  ❶

In [13]: for _ in range(75):
             msg = socket.recv_string()
             t = datetime.now()
             sym, price = msg.split()
             df = df.append(pd.DataFrame({sym: float(price)}, index=[t]))  ❶
             df['SMA1'] = df[sym].rolling(5).mean()  ❷
             df['SMA2'] = df[sym].rolling(10).mean()  ❷
             fig.data[0].x = df.index
             fig.data[1].x = df.index
             fig.data[2].x = df.index
             fig.data[0].y = df[sym]
             fig.data[1].y = df['SMA1']
             fig.data[2].y = df['SMA2']
```

❶ Collects the tick data in a `DataFrame` object.

❷ Adds the two SMAs in separate columns to the `DataFrame` object.

 Again, it is a good exercise to combine the plotting of streaming tick data and the two SMAs with the implementation of an online trading algorithm based on the two SMAs. In this case, resampling should be added to the implementation since such trading algorithms are hardly ever based on tick data but rather on bars of fixed length (five seconds, one minute, etc.).

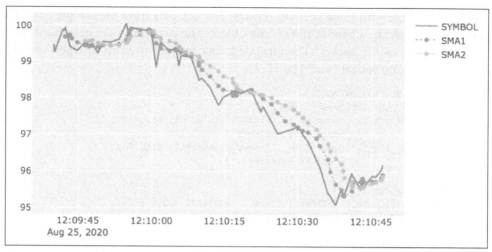

Figure 7-2. Plot of streaming price data and two SMAs calculated in real time

Three Sub-Plots for Three Streams

As with conventional Plotly plots, streaming plots based on figure widgets can also have multiple sub-plots. The example that follows creates a streaming plot with three sub-plots. The first plots the real-time tick data. The second plots the log returns data. The third plots the time series momentum based on the log returns data. Figure 7-3 shows a snapshot of the whole figure object:

```
In [14]: from plotly.subplots import make_subplots

In [15]: f = make_subplots(rows=3, cols=1, shared_xaxes=True)   ❶
         f.append_trace(go.Scatter(name='SYMBOL'), row=1, col=1)   ❷
         f.append_trace(go.Scatter(name='RETURN', line=dict(width=1, dash='dot'),
                 mode='lines+markers', marker={'symbol': 'triangle-up'}),
                 row=2, col=1)   ❸
         f.append_trace(go.Scatter(name='MOMENTUM', line=dict(width=1, dash='dash'),
                 mode='lines+markers', marker={'symbol': 'x'}), row=3, col=1)   ❹
         # f.update_layout(height=600)   ❺

In [16]: fig = go.FigureWidget(f)

In [17]: fig
Out[17]: FigureWidget({
             'data': [{'name': 'SYMBOL',
                       'type': 'scatter',
                       'uid': 'c8db0cac…

In [18]: import numpy as np

In [19]: df = pd.DataFrame()
```

```
In [20]: for _ in range(75):
             msg = socket.recv_string()
             t = datetime.now()
             sym, price = msg.split()
             df = df.append(pd.DataFrame({sym: float(price)}, index=[t]))
             df['RET'] = np.log(df[sym] / df[sym].shift(1))
             df['MOM'] = df['RET'].rolling(10).mean()
             fig.data[0].x = df.index
             fig.data[1].x = df.index
             fig.data[2].x = df.index
             fig.data[0].y = df[sym]
             fig.data[1].y = df['RET']
             fig.data[2].y = df['MOM']
```

❶ Creates three sub-plots that share the x-axis.

❷ Creates the first sub-plot for the price data.

❸ Creates the second sub-plot for the log returns data.

❹ Creates the third sub-plot for the momentum data.

❺ Adjusts the height of the figure object.

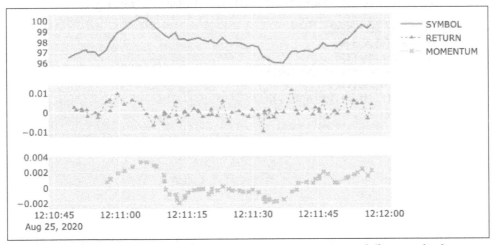

Figure 7-3. Streaming price data, log returns, and momentum in different sub-plots

Streaming Data as Bars

Not all streaming data is best visualized as a time series (Scatter object). Some streaming data is better visualized as bars with changing height. "Sample Data Server for Bar Plot" on page 220 contains a Python script that serves sample data suited for a bar-based visualization. A single data set (message) consists of eight floating point numbers. The following Python code generates a streaming bar plot (see Figure 7-4). In this context, the x data usually does not change. For the following code to work, the BarsServer.py script needs to be executed in a separate, local Python instance:

```
In [21]: socket = context.socket(zmq.SUB)

In [22]: socket.connect('tcp://0.0.0.0:5556')

In [23]: socket.setsockopt_string(zmq.SUBSCRIBE, '')

In [24]: for _ in range(5):
             msg = socket.recv_string()
             print(msg)
         60.361 53.504 67.782 64.165 35.046 94.227 20.221 54.716
         79.508 48.210 84.163 73.430 53.288 38.673 4.962 78.920
         53.316 80.139 73.733 55.549 21.015 20.556 49.090 29.630
         86.664 93.919 33.762 82.095 3.108 92.122 84.194 36.666
         37.192 85.305 48.397 36.903 81.835 98.691 61.818 87.121

In [25]: fig = go.FigureWidget()
         fig.add_bar()
         fig
Out[25]: FigureWidget({
         'data': [{'type': 'bar', 'uid':
         '51c6069f-4924-458d-a1ae-c5b5b5f3b07f'}], 'layout': {'templ…

In [26]: x = list('abcdefgh')
         fig.data[0].x = x
         for _ in range(25):
             msg = socket.recv_string()
             y = msg.split()
             y = [float(n) for n in y]
             fig.data[0].y = y
```

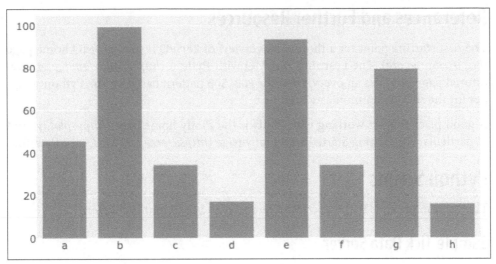

Figure 7-4. Streaming data as bars with changing height

Conclusions

Nowadays, algorithmic trading has to deal with different types of streaming (real-time) data types. The most important type in this regard is tick data for financial instruments that is, in principle, generated and published around the clock.[2] Sockets are the technological tool of choice to deal with streaming data. A powerful and at the same time easy-to-use library in this regard is ZeroMQ, which is used in this chapter to create a simple tick data server that endlessly emits sample tick data.

Different tick data clients are introduced and explained to generate trading signals in real time based on online algorithms and to visualize the incoming tick data by streaming plots using Plotly. Plotly makes streaming visualization within a Jupyter Notebook an efficient affair, allowing for, among other things, multiple streams at the same time—both in a single plot or in different sub-plots.

Based on the topics covered in this chapter and the previous ones, you are now able to work with both *historical structured data* (for example, in the context of the back-testing of trading strategies) and *real-time streaming data* (for example, in the context of generating trading signals in real time). This represents a major milestone in the endeavor to build an automated, algorithmic trading operation.

---

2 Not all markets are open 24 hours, 7 days per week, and for sure not all financial instruments are traded around the clock. However, cryptocurrency markets, for example, for Bitcoin, indeed operate around the clock, constantly creating new data that needs to be digested in real-time by players active in these markets.

References and Further Resources

The best starting point for a thorough overview of ZeroMQ is the ZeroMQ home page (*http://zeromq.org*). The Learning ZeroMQ with Python (*https://bit.ly/zmq_pub_sub*) tutorial page provides an overview of the PUB-SUB pattern based on the Python wrapper for the socket communication library.

A good place to start working with Plotly is the Plotly home page (*http://plot.ly*) and in particular the Getting Started with Plotly page (*https://oreil.ly/7ARrQ*) for Python.

Python Scripts

This section presents Python scripts referenced and used in this chapter.

Sample Tick Data Server

The following is a script that runs a sample tick data server based on ZeroMQ. It makes use of Monte Carlo simulation for the geometric Brownian motion:

```python
#
# Python Script to Simulate a
# Financial Tick Data Server
#
# Python for Algorithmic Trading
# (c) Dr. Yves J. Hilpisch
# The Python Quants GmbH
#
import zmq
import math
import time
import random

context = zmq.Context()
socket = context.socket(zmq.PUB)
socket.bind('tcp://0.0.0.0:5555')


class InstrumentPrice(object):
    def __init__(self):
        self.symbol = 'SYMBOL'
        self.t = time.time()
        self.value = 100.
        self.sigma = 0.4
        self.r = 0.01

    def simulate_value(self):
        ''' Generates a new, random stock price.
        '''
        t = time.time()
        dt = (t - self.t) / (252 * 8 * 60 * 60)
```

```
        dt *= 500
        self.t = t
        self.value *= math.exp((self.r - 0.5 * self.sigma ** 2) * dt +
                               self.sigma * math.sqrt(dt) * random.gauss(0, 1))
        return self.value


ip = InstrumentPrice()

while True:
    msg = '{} {:.2f}'.format(ip.symbol, ip.simulate_value())
    print(msg)
    socket.send_string(msg)
    time.sleep(random.random() * 2)
```

Tick Data Client

The following is a script that runs a tick data client based on ZeroMQ. It connects to the tick data server from "Sample Tick Data Server" on page 218:

```
#
# Python Script
# with Tick Data Client
#
# Python for Algorithmic Trading
# (c) Dr. Yves J. Hilpisch
# The Python Quants GmbH
#
import zmq

context = zmq.Context()
socket = context.socket(zmq.SUB)
socket.connect('tcp://0.0.0.0:5555')
socket.setsockopt_string(zmq.SUBSCRIBE, 'SYMBOL')

while True:
    data = socket.recv_string()
    print(data)
```

Momentum Online Algorithm

The following is a script that implements a trading strategy based on time series momentum as an online algorithm. It connects to the tick data server from "Sample Tick Data Server" on page 218:

```
#
# Python Script
# with Online Trading Algorithm
#
# Python for Algorithmic Trading
# (c) Dr. Yves J. Hilpisch
```

```
# The Python Quants GmbH
#
import zmq
import datetime
import numpy as np
import pandas as pd

context = zmq.Context()
socket = context.socket(zmq.SUB)
socket.connect('tcp://0.0.0.0:5555')
socket.setsockopt_string(zmq.SUBSCRIBE, 'SYMBOL')

df = pd.DataFrame()
mom = 3
min_length = mom + 1

while True:
    data = socket.recv_string()
    t = datetime.datetime.now()
    sym, value = data.split()
    df = df.append(pd.DataFrame({sym: float(value)}, index=[t]))
    dr = df.resample('5s', label='right').last()
    dr['returns'] = np.log(dr / dr.shift(1))
    if len(dr) > min_length:
        min_length += 1
        dr['momentum'] = np.sign(dr['returns'].rolling(mom).mean())
        print('\n' + '=' * 51)
        print('NEW SIGNAL | {}'.format(datetime.datetime.now()))
        print('=' * 51)
        print(dr.iloc[:-1].tail())
        if dr['momentum'].iloc[-2] == 1.0:
            print('\nLong market position.')
            # take some action (e.g., place buy order)
        elif dr['momentum'].iloc[-2] == -1.0:
            print('\nShort market position.')
            # take some action (e.g., place sell order)
```

Sample Data Server for Bar Plot

The following is a Python script that generates sample data for a streaming bar plot:

```
#
# Python Script to Serve
# Random Bars Data
#
# Python for Algorithmic Trading
# (c) Dr. Yves J. Hilpisch
# The Python Quants GmbH
#
import zmq
import math
import time
```

```
import random

context = zmq.Context()
socket = context.socket(zmq.PUB)
socket.bind('tcp://0.0.0.0:5556')

while True:
    bars = [random.random() * 100 for _ in range(8)]
    msg = ' '.join([f'{bar:.3f}' for bar in bars])
    print(msg)
    socket.send_string(msg)
    time.sleep(random.random() * 2)
```

## CHAPTER 8

CFD Trading with Oanda

Today, even small entities that trade complex instruments or are granted sufficient leverage can threaten the global financial system.

—Paul Singer

Today, it is easier than ever to get started with trading in the financial markets. There is a large number of online trading platforms (brokers) available from which an algorithmic trader can choose. The choice of a platform might be influenced by multiple factors:

Instruments

The first criterion that comes to mind is the type of instrument one is interested in to trade. For example, one might be interested in trading stocks, exchange traded funds (ETFs), bonds, currencies, commodities, options, or futures.

Strategies

Some traders are interested in long-only strategies, while others require short selling as well. Some focus on single-instrument strategies, while others focus on those involving multiple instruments at the same time.

Costs

Fixed and variable transaction costs are an important factor for many traders. They might even decide whether a certain strategy is profitable or not (see, for instance, Chapters 4 and 6).

Technology

Technology has become an important factor in the selection of trading platforms. First, there are the tools that the platforms offer to traders. Trading tools are available, in general, for desktop/notebook computers, tablets, and smart phones. Second, there are the application programming interfaces (APIs) that can be accessed programmatically by traders.

Jurisdiction

Financial trading is a heavily regulated field with different legal frameworks in place for different countries or regions. This might prohibit certain traders from using certain platforms and/or financial instruments depending on their residence.

This chapter focuses on Oanda (*http://oanda.com*), an online trading platform that is well suited to deploy automated, algorithmic trading strategies, even for retail traders. The following is a brief description of Oanda along the criteria as outlined previously:

Instruments

Oanda offers a wide range of so-called *contracts for difference* (CFD) products (see also "Contracts for Difference (CFDs)" on page 225 and "Disclaimer" on page 249). Main characteristics of CFDs are that they are leveraged (for example, 10:1 or 50:1) and traded on margin such that losses might exceed the initial capital.

Strategies

Oanda allows both to go long (buy) and to go short (sell) CFDs. Different order types are available, such as market or limit orders, with or without profit targets and/or (trailing) stop losses.

Costs

There are no fixed transaction costs associated with the trading of CFDs at Oanda. However, there is a bid-ask spread that leads to variable transaction costs when trading CFDs.

Technology

Oanda provides the trading application fxTrade (Practice), which retrieves data in real time and allows the (manual, discretionary) trading of all instruments (see Figure 8-1). There is also a browser-based trading application available (see Figure 8-2). A major strength of the platform are the RESTful and streaming APIs (see Oanda v20 API (*https://oreil.ly/_AHHI*)) via which traders can programmatically access historical and streaming data, place buy and sell orders, or retrieve account information. A Python wrapper package is available (see v20 on PyPi (*https://oreil.ly/iZuuV*)). Oanda offers free paper trading accounts that provide full access to all technological capabilities, which is really helpful in getting started on the platform. This also simplifies the transitioning from paper to live trading.

Jurisdiction

Depending on the residence of the account holder, the selection of CFDs that can be traded changes. FX-related CFDs are available basically everywhere Oanda is active. CFDs on stock indices, for instance, might not be available in certain jurisdictions.

Figure 8-1. Oanda trading application fxTrade Practice

Contracts for Difference (CFDs)

For more details on CFDs, see the Investopedia CFD page (*https://oreil.ly/wsoAz*) or the more detailed Wikipedia CFD page (*https://oreil.ly/2PnEQ*). There are CFDs available on currency pairs (for example, EUR/USD), commodities (for example, gold), stock indices (for example, S&P 500 stock index), bonds (for example, German 10 Year Bund), and more. One can think of a product range that basically allows one to implement global macro strategies. Financially speaking, CFDs are derivative products that derive their payoff based on the development of prices for other instruments. In addition, trading activity (liquidity) influences the price of CFDs. Although a CFD might be based on the S&P 500 index, it is a completely different product issued, quoted, and supported by Oanda (or a similar provider).

This brings along certain risks that traders should be aware of. A recent event that illustrates this issue is the *Swiss Franc event* that led to a number of insolvencies in the online broker space. See, for instance, the article Currency Brokers Fall Over Like Dominoes After SNB Decison on Swiss Franc (*https://oreil.ly/dx7ps*).

Figure 8-2. Oanda browser-based trading application

The chapter is organized as follows. "Setting Up an Account" on page 227 briefly discusses how to set up an account. "The Oanda API" on page 229 illustrates the necessary steps to access the API. Based on the API access, "Retrieving Historical Data" on page 230 retrieves and works with historical data for a certain CFD. "Working with Streaming Data" on page 236 introduces the streaming API of Oanda for data retrieval and visualization. "Implementing Trading Strategies in Real Time" on page 239 implements an automated, algorithmic trading strategy in real time. Finally, "Retrieving Account Information" on page 244 deals with retrieving data about the account itself, such as the current balance or recent trades. Throughout, the code makes use of a Python wrapper class called tpqoa (see GitHub repository (*https://oreil.ly/E95UV*)).

The goal of this chapter is to make use of the approaches and technologies as introduced in previous chapters to automatically trade on the Oanda platform.

Setting Up an Account

The process for setting up an account with Oanda is simple and efficient. You can choose between a real account and a free demo ("practice") account, which absolutely suffices to implement what follows (see Figures 8-3 and 8-4).

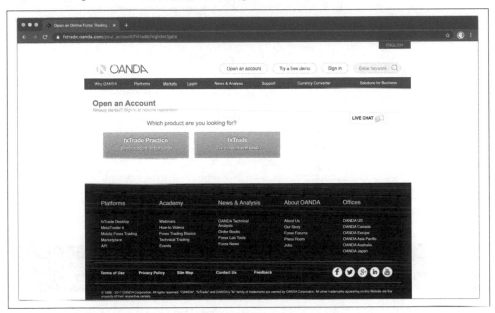

Figure 8-3. Oanda account registration (account types)

If the registration is successful and you are logged in to the account on the platform, you should see a starting page, as shown in Figure 8-5. In the middle, you will find a download link for the `fxTrade Practice for Desktop` application, which you should install. Once it is running, it looks similar to the screenshot shown in Figure 8-1.

Figure 8-4. Oanda account registration (registration form)

Figure 8-5. Oanda account starting page

The Oanda API

After registration, getting access to the APIs of Oanda is an easy affair. The major ingredients needed are the account number and the access token (API key). You will find the account number, for instance, in the area `Manage Funds`. The access token can be generated in the area `Manage API Access` (see Figure 8-6).[1]

From now on, the `configparser` (*https://oreil.ly/UaQyo*) module is used to manage account credentials. The module expects a text file—with a filename, say, of *pyalgo.cfg*—in the following format for use with an Oanda practice account:

```
[oanda]
account_id = YOUR_ACCOUNT_ID
access_token = YOUR_ACCESS_TOKEN
account_type = practice
```

Figure 8-6. Oanda API access managing page

To access the API via Python, it is recommended to use the Python wrapper package `tpqoa` (see GitHub repository (*http://github.com/yhilpisch/tpqoa*)) that in turn relies on the `v20` package from Oanda (see GitHub repository (*https://oreil.ly/F_cB2*)).

---

1 The naming of certain objects is not completely consistent in the context of the Oanda APIs. For example, *API key* and *access token* are used interchangeably. Also, *account ID* and *account number* refer to the same number.

It is installed with the following command:

```
pip install git+https://github.com/yhilpisch/tpqoa.git
```

With these prerequisites, you can connect to the API with a single line of code:

```
In [1]: import tpqoa

In [2]: api = tpqoa.tpqoa('../pyalgo.cfg')  ❶
```

❶   Adjust the path and filename if required.

This is a major milestone: being connected to the Oanda API allows for the retrieval of historical data, the programmatic placement of orders, and more.

> The upside of using the `configparser` module is that it simplifies the storage and management of account credentials. In algorithmic trading, the number of accounts needed can quickly grow. Examples are a cloud instance or server, data service provider, online trading platform, and so on.
>
> The downside is that the account information is stored in the form of plain text, which represents a considerable security risk, particularly since the information about multiple accounts is stored in a single file. When moving to production, you should therefore apply, for example, file encryption methods to keep the credentials safe.

Retrieving Historical Data

A major benefit of working with the Oanda platform is that the complete price history of all Oanda instruments is accessible via the RESTful API. In this context, *complete history* refers to the different CFDs themselves, not the underlying instruments they are defined on.

Looking Up Instruments Available for Trading

For an overview of what instruments can be traded for a given account, use the `.get_instruments()` method. It only retrieves the display names and technical instruments, names from the API. More details are available via the API, such as minimum position size:

```
In [3]: api.get_instruments()[:15]
Out[3]: [('AUD/CAD', 'AUD_CAD'),
         ('AUD/CHF', 'AUD_CHF'),
         ('AUD/HKD', 'AUD_HKD'),
         ('AUD/JPY', 'AUD_JPY'),
         ('AUD/NZD', 'AUD_NZD'),
         ('AUD/SGD', 'AUD_SGD'),
```

```
         ('AUD/USD', 'AUD_USD'),
         ('Australia 200', 'AU200_AUD'),
         ('Brent Crude Oil', 'BCO_USD'),
         ('Bund', 'DE10YB_EUR'),
         ('CAD/CHF', 'CAD_CHF'),
         ('CAD/HKD', 'CAD_HKD'),
         ('CAD/JPY', 'CAD_JPY'),
         ('CAD/SGD', 'CAD_SGD'),
         ('CHF/HKD', 'CHF_HKD')]
```

Backtesting a Momentum Strategy on Minute Bars

The example that follows uses the instrument EUR_USD based on the EUR/USD currency pair. The goal is to backtest *momentum-based strategies on one-minute bars*. The data used is for two days in May 2020. The first step is to *retrieve the raw data* from Oanda:

```
In [4]: help(api.get_history)    ❶
        Help on method get_history in module tpqoa.tpqoa:

        get_history(instrument, start, end, granularity, price, localize=True)
         method of tpqoa.tpqoa.tpqoa instance
            Retrieves historical data for instrument.

            Parameters
            ==========
            instrument: string
                valid instrument name
            start, end: datetime, str
                Python datetime or string objects for start and end
            granularity: string
                a string like 'S5', 'M1' or 'D'
            price: string
                one of 'A' (ask), 'B' (bid) or 'M' (middle)

            Returns
            =======
            data: pd.DataFrame
                pandas DataFrame object with data


In [5]: instrument = 'EUR_USD'    ❷
        start = '2020-08-10'      ❷
        end = '2020-08-12'        ❷
        granularity = 'M1'        ❷
        price = 'M'               ❷

In [6]: data = api.get_history(instrument, start, end,
                               granularity, price)    ❸

In [7]: data.info()    ❹
```

```
<class 'pandas.core.frame.DataFrame'>
DatetimeIndex: 2814 entries, 2020-08-10 00:00:00 to 2020-08-11
 23:59:00
Data columns (total 6 columns):
 #   Column    Non-Null Count  Dtype
---  ------    --------------  -----
 0   o         2814 non-null   float64
 1   h         2814 non-null   float64
 2   l         2814 non-null   float64
 3   c         2814 non-null   float64
 4   volume    2814 non-null   int64
 5   complete  2814 non-null   bool
dtypes: bool(1), float64(4), int64(1)
memory usage: 134.7 KB

In [8]: data[['c', 'volume']].head()     ❺
Out[8]:                            c  volume
        time
        2020-08-10 00:00:00  1.17822      18
        2020-08-10 00:01:00  1.17836      32
        2020-08-10 00:02:00  1.17828      25
        2020-08-10 00:03:00  1.17834      13
        2020-08-10 00:04:00  1.17847      43
```

❶ Shows the docstring (help text) for the .get_history() method.

❷ Defines the parameter values.

❸ Retrieves the raw data from the API.

❹ Shows the meta information for the retrieved data set.

❺ Shows the first five data rows for two columns.

The second step is to *implement the vectorized backtesting*. The idea is to simultaneously backtest a couple of momentum strategies. The code is straightforward and concise (see also Chapter 4).

For simplicity, the following code uses close (c) values of mid prices only:[2]

```
In [9]: import numpy as np

In [10]: data['returns'] = np.log(data['c'] / data['c'].shift(1))     ❶

In [11]: cols = []     ❷
```

---

[2] This implicitly neglects transaction costs in the form of bid-ask spreads when selling and buying units of the instrument, respectively.

```
In [12]: for momentum in [15, 30, 60, 120]:    ❸
             col = 'position_{}'.format(momentum)    ❹
             data[col] = np.sign(data['returns'].rolling(momentum).mean())    ❺
             cols.append(col)    ❻
```

❶ Calculates the log returns based on the close values of the mid prices.

❷ Instantiates an empty list object to collect column names.

❸ Defines the time interval in minute bars for the momentum strategy.

❹ Defines the name of the column to be used for storage in the DataFrame object.

❺ Adds the strategy positionings as a new column.

❻ Appends the name of the column to the list object.

The final step is the *derivation and plotting of the absolute performance* of the different momentum strategies. The plot Figure 8-7 shows the performances of the momentum-based strategies graphically and compares them to the performance of the base instrument itself:

```
In [13]: from pylab import plt
         plt.style.use('seaborn')
         import matplotlib as mpl
         mpl.rcParams['savefig.dpi'] = 300
         mpl.rcParams['font.family'] = 'serif'

In [14]: strats = ['returns']    ❶

In [15]: for col in cols:    ❷
             strat = 'strategy_{}'.format(col.split('_')[1])    ❸
             data[strat] = data[col].shift(1) * data['returns']    ❹
             strats.append(strat)    ❺

In [16]: data[strats].dropna().cumsum(
             ).apply(np.exp).plot(figsize=(10, 6));    ❻
```

❶ Defines another list object to store the column names to be plotted later on.

❷ Iterates over columns with the positionings for the different strategies.

❸ Derives the name for the new column in which the strategy performance is stored.

❹ Calculates the log returns for the different strategies and stores them as new columns.

❺ Appends the column names to the `list` object for later plotting.

❻ Plots the cumulative performances for the instrument and the strategies.

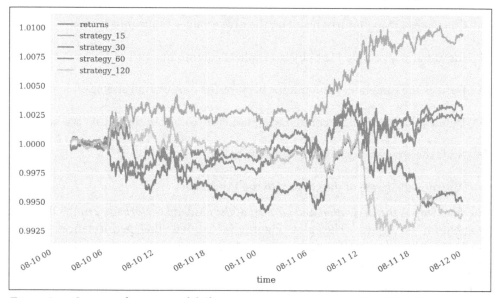

Figure 8-7. Gross performance of different momentum strategies for EUR_USD instrument (minute bars)

Factoring In Leverage and Margin

In general, when you buy a share of a stock for, say, 100 USD, the profit and loss (P&L) calculations are straightforward: if the stock price rises by 1 USD, you earn 1 USD (unrealized profit); if the stock price falls by 1 USD, you lose 1 USD (unrealized loss). If you buy 10 shares, just multiply the results by 10.

Trading CFDs on the Oanda platform involves leverage and margin. This significantly influences the P&L calculation. For an introduction to and overview of this topic refer to Oanda fxTrade Margin Rules (*https://oreil.ly/8I5Eg*). A simple example can illustrate the major aspects in this context.

Consider that a EUR-based algorithmic trader wants to trade the EUR_USD instrument on the Oanda platform and wants to get a long exposure of 10,000 EUR at an ask price of 1.1. Without leverage and margin, the trader (or Python program) would buy

10,000 units of the CFD.[3] If the price of the instrument (exchange rate) rises to 1.105 (as the midpoint rate between bid and ask prices), the absolute profit is 10,000 x 0.005 = 50 or 0.5%.

What impact do leverage and margining have? Suppose the algorithmic trader chooses a leverage ratio of 20:1, which translates into a 5% margin (= 100% / 20). This in turn implies that the trader only needs to put up a margin upfront of 10,000 EUR x 5% = 500 EUR to get the same exposure. If the price of the instrument then rises to 1.105, the absolute profit stays the same at 50 EUR, but the relative profit rises to 50 EUR / 500 EUR = 10%. The return is considerably amplified by a factor of 20; this is the benefit of leverage when things go as desired.

What happens if things go south? Assume the instrument price drops to 1.08 (as the midpoint rate between bid and ask prices), leading to a loss of 10,000 x (1.08 - 1.1) = -200 EUR. The relative loss now is -200 EUR / 500 EUR = -40%. If the account the algorithmic trader is trading with has less than 200 EUR left in equity/cash, the position needs to be closed out since the (regulatory) margin requirements cannot be met anymore. If losses eat up the margin completely, additional funds need to be allocated as margin to keep the trade alive.[4]

Figure 8-8 shows the amplifying effect on the performance of the momentum strategies for a leverage ratio of 20:1. The initial margin of 5% suffices to cover potential losses since it is not eaten up even in the worst case depicted:

```
In [17]: data[strats].dropna().cumsum().apply(
                 lambda x: x * 20).apply(np.exp).plot(figsize=(10, 6));   ➊
```

➊ Multiplies the log returns by a factor of 20 according to the leverage ratio assumed.

Leveraged trading does not only amplify potentials profits, but it also amplifies potential losses. With leveraged trading based on a 10:1 factor (10% margin), a 10% adverse move in the base instrument already wipes out the complete margin. In other words, a 10% move leads to a 100% loss. Therefore, you should make sure to fully understand all risks involved in leveraged trading. You should also make sure to apply appropriate risk measures, such as stop loss orders, that are in line with your risk profile and appetite.

---

3 Note that for some instruments, *one unit* means 1 USD, like for currency-related CFDs. For others, like for index-related CFDs (for example, DE30_EUR), *one unit* means a currency exposure at the (bid/ask) price of the CFD (for example, 11,750 EUR).

4 The simplified calculations neglect, for example, *financing costs* that might become due for leveraged trading.

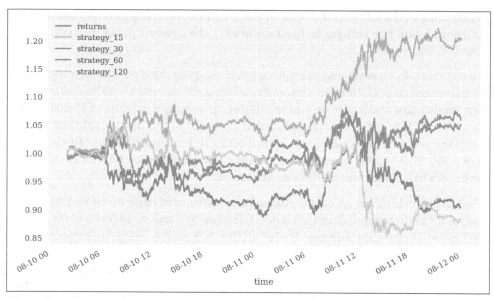

Figure 8-8. Gross performance of momentum strategies for EUR_USD instrument with 20:1 leverage (minute bars)

Working with Streaming Data

Working with streaming data is again made simple and straightforward by the Python wrapper package `tpqoa`. The package, in combination with the `v20` package, takes care of the socket communication such that the algorithmic trader only needs to decide what to do with the streaming data:

```
In [18]: instrument = 'EUR_USD'

In [19]: api.stream_data(instrument, stop=10)    ❶
         2020-08-19T14:39:13.560138152Z 1.19131 1.1915
         2020-08-19T14:39:14.088511060Z 1.19134 1.19152
         2020-08-19T14:39:14.390081879Z 1.19124 1.19145
         2020-08-19T14:39:15.105974700Z 1.19129 1.19144
         2020-08-19T14:39:15.375370451Z 1.19128 1.19144
         2020-08-19T14:39:15.501380756Z 1.1912 1.19141
         2020-08-19T14:39:15.951793928Z 1.1912 1.19138
         2020-08-19T14:39:16.354844135Z 1.19123 1.19138
         2020-08-19T14:39:16.661440356Z 1.19118 1.19133
         2020-08-19T14:39:16.912150908Z 1.19112 1.19132
```

❶   The `stop` parameter stops the streaming after a certain number of ticks retrieved.

Placing Market Orders

Similarly, it is straightforward to place market buy or sell orders with the `cre ate_order()` method:

```
In [20]: help(api.create_order)  ❶
         Help on method create_order in module tpqoa.tpqoa:

         create_order(instrument, units, price=None, sl_distance=None,
          tsl_distance=None, tp_price=None, comment=None, touch=False,
          suppress=False, ret=False) method of tpqoa.tpqoa.tpqoa instance
             Places order with Oanda.

             Parameters
             ==========
             instrument: string
                 valid instrument name
             units: int
                 number of units of instrument to be bought
                 (positive int, e.g., 'units=50')
                 or to be sold (negative int, e.g., 'units=-100')
             price: float
                 limit order price, touch order price
             sl_distance: float
                 stop loss distance price, mandatory e.g., in Germany
             tsl_distance: float
                 trailing stop loss distance
             tp_price: float
                 take profit price to be used for the trade
             comment: str
                 string
             touch: boolean
                 market_if_touched order (requires price to be set)
             suppress: boolean
                 whether to suppress print out
             ret: boolean
                 whether to return the order object
```

```
In [21]: api.create_order(instrument, 1000)  ❷


         {'id': '1721', 'time': '2020-08-19T14:39:17.062399275Z', 'userID':
         13834683, 'accountID': '101-004-13834683-001', 'batchID': '1720',
         'requestID': '24716258589170956', 'type': 'ORDER_FILL', 'orderID':
         '1720', 'instrument': 'EUR_USD', 'units': '1000.0',
         'gainQuoteHomeConversionFactor': '0.835288642787',
         'lossQuoteHomeConversionFactor': '0.843683503518', 'price': 1.19131,
         'fullVWAP': 1.19131, 'fullPrice': {'type': 'PRICE', 'bids': [{'price':
         1.1911, 'liquidity': '10000000'}], 'asks': [{'price': 1.19131,
         'liquidity': '10000000'}], 'closeoutBid': 1.1911, 'closeoutAsk':
         1.19131}, 'reason': 'MARKET_ORDER', 'pl': '0.0', 'financing': '0.0',
```

```
'commission': '0.0', 'guaranteedExecutionFee': '0.0',
'accountBalance': '98510.7986', 'tradeOpened': {'tradeID': '1721',
'units': '1000.0', 'price': 1.19131, 'guaranteedExecutionFee': '0.0',
'halfSpreadCost': '0.0881', 'initialMarginRequired': '33.3'},
'halfSpreadCost': '0.0881'}
```

In [22]: api.create_order(instrument, -1500) ❸

```
{'id': '1723', 'time': '2020-08-19T14:39:17.200434462Z', 'userID':
13834683, 'accountID': '101-004-13834683-001', 'batchID': '1722',
'requestID': '24716258589171315', 'type': 'ORDER_FILL', 'orderID':
'1722', 'instrument': 'EUR_USD', 'units': '-1500.0',
'gainQuoteHomeConversionFactor': '0.835288642787',
'lossQuoteHomeConversionFactor': '0.843683503518', 'price': 1.1911,
'fullVWAP': 1.1911, 'fullPrice': {'type': 'PRICE', 'bids': [{'price':
1.1911, 'liquidity': '10000000'}], 'asks': [{'price': 1.19131,
'liquidity': '9999000'}], 'closeoutBid': 1.1911, 'closeoutAsk':
1.19131}, 'reason': 'MARKET_ORDER', 'pl': '-0.1772', 'financing':
'0.0', 'commission': '0.0', 'guaranteedExecutionFee': '0.0',
'accountBalance': '98510.6214', 'tradeOpened': {'tradeID': '1723',
'units': '-500.0', 'price': 1.1911, 'guaranteedExecutionFee': '0.0',
'halfSpreadCost': '0.0441', 'initialMarginRequired': '16.65'},
'tradesClosed': [{'tradeID': '1721', 'units': '-1000.0', 'price':
1.1911, 'realizedPL': '-0.1772', 'financing': '0.0',
'guaranteedExecutionFee': '0.0', 'halfSpreadCost': '0.0881'}],
'halfSpreadCost': '0.1322'}
```

In [23]: api.create_order(instrument, 500) ❹

```
{'id': '1725', 'time': '2020-08-19T14:39:17.348231507Z', 'userID':
13834683, 'accountID': '101-004-13834683-001', 'batchID': '1724',
'requestID': '24716258589171775', 'type': 'ORDER_FILL', 'orderID':
'1724', 'instrument': 'EUR_USD', 'units': '500.0',
'gainQuoteHomeConversionFactor': '0.835313189428',
'lossQuoteHomeConversionFactor': '0.84370829686', 'price': 1.1913,
'fullVWAP': 1.1913, 'fullPrice': {'type': 'PRICE', 'bids': [{'price':
1.19104, 'liquidity': '9998500'}], 'asks': [{'price': 1.1913,
'liquidity': '9999000'}], 'closeoutBid': 1.19104, 'closeoutAsk':
1.1913}, 'reason': 'MARKET_ORDER', 'pl': '-0.0844', 'financing':
'0.0', 'commission': '0.0', 'guaranteedExecutionFee': '0.0',
'accountBalance': '98510.537', 'tradesClosed': [{'tradeID': '1723',
'units': '500.0', 'price': 1.1913, 'realizedPL': '-0.0844',
'financing': '0.0', 'guaranteedExecutionFee': '0.0', 'halfSpreadCost':
'0.0546'}], 'halfSpreadCost': '0.0546'}
```

❶ Shows all options for placing market, limit, and market-if-touched orders.

❷ Opens a long position via market order.

❸ Goes short after closing the long position via market order.

❹ Closes the short position via market order.

Although the Oanda API allows the placement of different order types, this chapter and the following chapter mainly focus on *market orders* to instantly go long or short whenever a new signal appears.

Implementing Trading Strategies in Real Time

This section presents a custom class that automatically trades the EUR_USD instrument on the Oanda platform based on a momentum strategy. It is called MomentumTrader and is presented in "Python Script" on page 247. The following walks through the class line by line, beginning with the ❶ method. The class itself inherits from the tpqoa class:

```
import tpqoa
import numpy as np
import pandas as pd


class MomentumTrader(tpqoa.tpqoa):
    def __init__(self, conf_file, instrument, bar_length, momentum, units,
                 *args, **kwargs):
        super(MomentumTrader, self).__init__(conf_file)
        self.position = 0  ❶
        self.instrument = instrument  ❷
        self.momentum = momentum  ❸
        self.bar_length = bar_length  ❹
        self.units = units  ❺
        self.raw_data = pd.DataFrame()  ❻
        self.min_length = self.momentum + 1  ❼
```

❶ Initial position value (market neutral).

❷ Instrument to be traded.

❸ Length of the bar for the resampling of the tick data.

❹ Number of intervals for momentum calculation.

❺ Number of units to be traded.

❻ An empty DataFrame object to be filled with tick data.

❼ The initial minimum bar length for the start of the trading itself.

The major method is the `.on_success()` method, which implements the trading logic for the momentum strategy:

```python
def on_success(self, time, bid, ask):  ❶
    ''' Takes actions when new tick data arrives. '''
    print(self.ticks, end=' ')  ❷
    self.raw_data = self.raw_data.append(pd.DataFrame(
        {'bid': bid, 'ask': ask}, index=[pd.Timestamp(time)]))  ❸
    self.data = self.raw_data.resample(
        self.bar_length, label='right').last().ffill().iloc[:-1]  ❹
    self.data['mid'] = self.data.mean(axis=1)  ❺
    self.data['returns'] = np.log(self.data['mid'] /
                                  self.data['mid'].shift(1))  ❻
    self.data['position'] = np.sign(
        self.data['returns'].rolling(self.momentum).mean())  ❼

    if len(self.data) > self.min_length:  ❽
        self.min_length += 1  ❽
        if self.data['position'].iloc[-1] == 1:  ❾
            if self.position == 0:  ❿
                self.create_order(self.instrument, self.units)  ⓫
            elif self.position == -1:  ⓬
                self.create_order(self.instrument, self.units * 2)  ⓭
            self.position = 1  ⓮
        elif self.data['position'].iloc[-1] == -1:  ⓯
            if self.position == 0:  ⓰
                self.create_order(self.instrument, -self.units)  ⓱
            elif self.position == 1:  ⓲
                self.create_order(self.instrument, -self.units * 2)  ⓳
            self.position = -1  ⓴
```

❶ This method is called whenever new tick data arrives.

❷ The number of ticks retrieved is printed.

❸ The tick data is collected and stored.

❹ The tick data is then resampled to the appropriate bar length.

❺ The mid prices are calculated…

❻ …based on which the log returns are derived.

❼ The signal (positioning) is derived based on the `momentum` parameter/attribute (via an online algorithm).

❽ When there is enough or new data, the trading logic is applied and the minimum length is increased by one every time.

⑨ Checks whether the latest positioning ("signal") is 1 (long).

⑩ If the current market position is 0 (neutral)...

⑪ ...a buy order for `self.units` is initiated.

⑫ If it is -1 (short)...

⑬ ...a buy order for 0 is initiated.

⑭ The market position `self.position` is set to +1 (long).

⑮ Checks whether the latest positioning ("signal") is -1 (short).

⑯ If the current market position is 0 (neutral)...

⑰ ...a sell order for `-self.units` is initiated.

⑱ If it is +1 (long)...

⑲ ...a sell order for 0 is initiated.

⑳ The market position `self.position` is set to -1 (short).

Based on this class, getting started with automated, algorithmic trading is just four lines of code. The Python code that follows initiates an automated trading session:

```
In [24]: import MomentumTrader as MT

In [25]: mt = MT.MomentumTrader('../pyalgo.cfg',      ❶
                        instrument=instrument,        ❷
                        bar_length='10s',             ❸
                        momentum=6,                   ❹
                        units=10000)                  ❺

In [26]: mt.stream_data(mt.instrument, stop=500)      ❻
```

❶ The configuration file with the credentials.

❷ The `instrument` parameter is specified.

❸ The `bar_length` parameter for the resampling is provided.

❹ The `momentum` parameter is defined, which is applied to the resampled data intervals.

❺ The units parameter is set, which specifies the position size for long and short positions.

❻ This starts the streaming and therewith the trading; it stops after 100 ticks.

The preceding code provides the following output:

```
1 2 3 4 5 6 7 8 9 10 11 12 13 14 15 16 17 18 19 20 21 22 23 24 25 26 27
28 29 30 31 32 33 34 35 36 37 38 39 40 41 42 43 44 45 46 47 48 49 50
51 52 53 54 55 56 57 58 59 60 61 62 63 64 65 66 67 68 69 70 71 72 73
74 75 76 77 78 79 80 81 82 83 84 85 86 87 88 89 90 91 92 93 94 95 96
97 98 99 100 101 102 103 104 105 106 107 108 109 110 111 112 113 114
115 116 117 118 119 120 121 122 123 124 125 126 127 128 129 130 131
132 133 134 135 136 137 138 139 140 141 142 143 144 145 146 147 148
149 150 151 152 153
```

```
{'id': '1727', 'time': '2020-08-19T14:40:30.443867492Z', 'userID':
13834683, 'accountID': '101-004-13834683-001', 'batchID': '1726',
'requestID': '42730657405829101', 'type': 'ORDER_FILL', 'orderID':
'1726', 'instrument': 'EUR_USD', 'units': '10000.0',
'gainQuoteHomeConversionFactor': '0.8350012403',
'lossQuoteHomeConversionFactor': '0.843393212565', 'price': 1.19168,
'fullVWAP': 1.19168, 'fullPrice': {'type': 'PRICE', 'bids': [{'price':
1.19155, 'liquidity': '10000000'}], 'asks': [{'price': 1.19168,
'liquidity': '10000000'}], 'closeoutBid': 1.19155, 'closeoutAsk':
1.19168}, 'reason': 'MARKET_ORDER', 'pl': '0.0', 'financing': '0.0',
'commission': '0.0', 'guaranteedExecutionFee': '0.0',
'accountBalance': '98510.537', 'tradeOpened': {'tradeID': '1727',
'units': '10000.0', 'price': 1.19168, 'guaranteedExecutionFee': '0.0',
'halfSpreadCost': '0.5455', 'initialMarginRequired': '333.0'},
'halfSpreadCost': '0.5455'}
```

```
154 155 156 157 158 159 160 161 162 163 164 165 166 167 168 169 170 171
172 173 174 175 176 177 178 179 180 181 182 183 184 185 186 187 188
189 190 191 192 193 194 195 196 197 198 199 200 201 202 203 204 205
206 207 208 209 210 211 212 213 214 215 216 217 218 219 220 221 222
223
```

```
{'id': '1729', 'time': '2020-08-19T14:41:11.436438078Z', 'userID':
13834683, 'accountID': '101-004-13834683-001', 'batchID': '1728',
'requestID': '42730657577912600', 'type': 'ORDER_FILL', 'orderID':
'1728', 'instrument': 'EUR_USD', 'units': '-20000.0',
'gainQuoteHomeConversionFactor': '0.83519398913',
'lossQuoteHomeConversionFactor': '0.843587898569', 'price': 1.19124,
'fullVWAP': 1.19124, 'fullPrice': {'type': 'PRICE', 'bids': [{'price':
1.19124, 'liquidity': '10000000'}], 'asks': [{'price': 1.19144,
'liquidity': '10000000'}], 'closeoutBid': 1.19124, 'closeoutAsk':
1.19144}, 'reason': 'MARKET_ORDER', 'pl': '-3.7118', 'financing':
'0.0', 'commission': '0.0', 'guaranteedExecutionFee': '0.0',
'accountBalance': '98506.8252', 'tradeOpened': {'tradeID': '1729',
'units': '-10000.0', 'price': 1.19124, 'guaranteedExecutionFee':
'0.0', 'halfSpreadCost': '0.8394', 'initialMarginRequired': '333.0'},
```

'tradesClosed': [{'tradeID': '1727', 'units': '-10000.0', 'price':
1.19124, 'realizedPL': '-3.7118', 'financing': '0.0',
'guaranteedExecutionFee': '0.0', 'halfSpreadCost': '0.8394'}],
'halfSpreadCost': '1.6788'}

224 225 226 227 228 229 230 231 232 233 234 235 236 237 238 239 240 241
242 243 244 245 246 247 248 249 250 251 252 253 254 255 256 257 258
259 260 261 262 263 264 265 266 267 268 269 270 271 272 273 274 275
276 277 278 279 280 281 282 283 284 285 286 287 288 289 290 291 292
293 294 295 296 297 298 299 300 301 302 303 304 305 306 307 308 309
310 311 312 313 314 315 316 317 318 319 320 321 322 323 324 325 326
327 328 329 330 331 332 333 334 335 336 337 338 339 340 341 342 343
344 345 346 347 348 349 350 351 352 353 354 355 356 357 358 359 360
361 362 363 364 365 366 367 368 369 370 371 372 373 374 375 376 377
378 379 380 381 382 383 384 385 386 387 388 389 390 391 392 393 394

{'id': '1731', 'time': '2020-08-19T14:42:20.525804142Z', 'userID':
13834683, 'accountID': '101-004-13834683-001', 'batchID': '1730',
'requestID': '42730657867512554', 'type': 'ORDER_FILL', 'orderID':
'1730', 'instrument': 'EUR_USD', 'units': '20000.0',
'gainQuoteHomeConversionFactor': '0.835400847964',
'lossQuoteHomeConversionFactor': '0.843796836386', 'price': 1.19111,
'fullVWAP': 1.19111, 'fullPrice': {'type': 'PRICE', 'bids': [{'price':
1.19098, 'liquidity': '10000000'}], 'asks': [{'price': 1.19111,
'liquidity': '10000000'}], 'closeoutBid': 1.19098, 'closeoutAsk':
1.19111}, 'reason': 'MARKET_ORDER', 'pl': '1.086', 'financing': '0.0',
'commission': '0.0', 'guaranteedExecutionFee': '0.0',
'accountBalance': '98507.9112', 'tradeOpened': {'tradeID': '1731',
'units': '10000.0', 'price': 1.19111, 'guaranteedExecutionFee': '0.0',
'halfSpreadCost': '0.5457', 'initialMarginRequired': '333.0'},
'tradesClosed': [{'tradeID': '1729', 'units': '10000.0', 'price':
1.19111, 'realizedPL': '1.086', 'financing': '0.0',
'guaranteedExecutionFee': '0.0', 'halfSpreadCost': '0.5457'}],
'halfSpreadCost': '1.0914'}

395 396 397 398 399 400 401 402 403 404 405 406 407 408 409 410 411 412
413 414 415 416 417 418 419 420 421 422 423 424 425 426 427 428 429
430 431 432 433 434 435 436 437 438 439 440 441 442 443 444 445 446
447 448 449 450 451 452 453 454 455 456 457 458 459 460 461 462 463
464 465 466 467 468 469 470 471 472 473 474 475 476 477 478 479 480
481 482 483 484 485 486 487 488 489 490 491 492 493 494 495 496 497
498 499 500

Finally, close out the final position:

```
In [27]: oo = mt.create_order(instrument, units=-mt.position * mt.units,
                              ret=True, suppress=True)  ❶
        oo
Out[27]: {'id': '1733',
         'time': '2020-08-19T14:43:17.107985242Z',
         'userID': 13834683,
         'accountID': '101-004-13834683-001',
         'batchID': '1732',
```

```
'requestID': '42730658106750652',
'type': 'ORDER_FILL',
'orderID': '1732',
'instrument': 'EUR_USD',
'units': '-10000.0',
'gainQuoteHomeConversionFactor': '0.835327206922',
'lossQuoteHomeConversionFactor': '0.843722455232',
'price': 1.19109,
'fullVWAP': 1.19109,
'fullPrice': {'type': 'PRICE',
 'bids': [{'price': 1.19109, 'liquidity': '10000000'}],
 'asks': [{'price': 1.19121, 'liquidity': '10000000'}],
 'closeoutBid': 1.19109,
 'closeoutAsk': 1.19121},
'reason': 'MARKET_ORDER',
'pl': '-0.1687',
'financing': '0.0',
'commission': '0.0',
'guaranteedExecutionFee': '0.0',
'accountBalance': '98507.7425',
'tradesClosed': [{'tradeID': '1731',
  'units': '-10000.0',
  'price': 1.19109,
  'realizedPL': '-0.1687',
  'financing': '0.0',
  'guaranteedExecutionFee': '0.0',
  'halfSpreadCost': '0.5037'}],
'halfSpreadCost': '0.5037'}
```

❶ Closes out the final position.

Retrieving Account Information

With regard to account information, transaction history, and the like, the Oanda RESTful API is also convenient to work with. For example, after the execution of the momentum strategy in the previous section, the algorithmic trader might want to inspect the current balance of the trading account. This is possible via the .get_account_summary() method:

```
In [28]: api.get_account_summary()
Out[28]: {'id': '101-004-13834683-001',
         'alias': 'Primary',
         'currency': 'EUR',
         'balance': '98507.7425',
         'createdByUserID': 13834683,
         'createdTime': '2020-03-19T06:08:14.363139403Z',
         'guaranteedStopLossOrderMode': 'DISABLED',
         'pl': '-1273.126',
         'resettablePL': '-1273.126',
         'resettablePLTime': '0',
         'financing': '-219.1315',
```

```
    'commission': '0.0',
    'guaranteedExecutionFees': '0.0',
    'marginRate': '0.0333',
    'openTradeCount': 1,
    'openPositionCount': 1,
    'pendingOrderCount': 0,
    'hedgingEnabled': False,
    'unrealizedPL': '929.8862',
    'NAV': '99437.6287',
    'marginUsed': '377.76',
    'marginAvailable': '99064.4945',
    'positionValue': '3777.6',
    'marginCloseoutUnrealizedPL': '935.8183',
    'marginCloseoutNAV': '99443.5608',
    'marginCloseoutMarginUsed': '377.76',
    'marginCloseoutPercent': '0.0019',
    'marginCloseoutPositionValue': '3777.6',
    'withdrawalLimit': '98507.7425',
    'marginCallMarginUsed': '377.76',
    'marginCallPercent': '0.0038',
    'lastTransactionID': '1733'}
```

Information about the last few trades is received with the `.get_transactions()` method:

```
In [29]: api.get_transactions(tid=int(oo['id']) - 2)
Out[29]: [{'id': '1732',
          'time': '2020-08-19T14:43:17.107985242Z',
          'userID': 13834683,
          'accountID': '101-004-13834683-001',
          'batchID': '1732',
          'requestID': '42730658106750652',
          'type': 'MARKET_ORDER',
          'instrument': 'EUR_USD',
          'units': '-10000.0',
          'timeInForce': 'FOK',
          'positionFill': 'DEFAULT',
          'reason': 'CLIENT_ORDER'},
         {'id': '1733',
          'time': '2020-08-19T14:43:17.107985242Z',
          'userID': 13834683,
          'accountID': '101-004-13834683-001',
          'batchID': '1732',
          'requestID': '42730658106750652',
          'type': 'ORDER_FILL',
          'orderID': '1732',
          'instrument': 'EUR_USD',
          'units': '-10000.0',
          'gainQuoteHomeConversionFactor': '0.835327206922',
          'lossQuoteHomeConversionFactor': '0.843722455232',
          'price': 1.19109,
          'fullVWAP': 1.19109,
          'fullPrice': {'type': 'PRICE',
```

```
        'bids': [{'price': 1.19109, 'liquidity': '10000000'}],
        'asks': [{'price': 1.19121, 'liquidity': '10000000'}],
        'closeoutBid': 1.19109,
        'closeoutAsk': 1.19121},
      'reason': 'MARKET_ORDER',
      'pl': '-0.1687',
      'financing': '0.0',
      'commission': '0.0',
      'guaranteedExecutionFee': '0.0',
      'accountBalance': '98507.7425',
      'tradesClosed': [{'tradeID': '1731',
        'units': '-10000.0',
        'price': 1.19109,
        'realizedPL': '-0.1687',
        'financing': '0.0',
        'guaranteedExecutionFee': '0.0',
        'halfSpreadCost': '0.5037'}],
      'halfSpreadCost': '0.5037'}]
```

For a concise overview, there is also the `.print_transactions()` method available:

```
In [30]: api.print_transactions(tid=int(oo['id']) - 18)
         1717 | 2020-08-19T14:37:00.803426931Z | EUR_USD |   -10000.0 | 0.0
         1719 | 2020-08-19T14:38:21.953399006Z | EUR_USD |    10000.0 | 6.8444
         1721 | 2020-08-19T14:39:17.062399275Z | EUR_USD |     1000.0 | 0.0
         1723 | 2020-08-19T14:39:17.200434462Z | EUR_USD |    -1500.0 | -0.1772
         1725 | 2020-08-19T14:39:17.348231507Z | EUR_USD |      500.0 | -0.0844
         1727 | 2020-08-19T14:40:30.443867492Z | EUR_USD |    10000.0 | 0.0
         1729 | 2020-08-19T14:41:11.436438078Z | EUR_USD |   -20000.0 | -3.7118
         1731 | 2020-08-19T14:42:20.525804142Z | EUR_USD |    20000.0 | 1.086
         1733 | 2020-08-19T14:43:17.107985242Z | EUR_USD |   -10000.0 | -0.1687
```

Conclusions

The Oanda platform allows for an easy and straightforward entry into the world of automated, algorithmic trading. Oanda specializes in so-called contracts for difference (CFDs). Depending on the country of residence of the trader, there is a great variety of instruments that can be traded.

A major advantage of Oanda from a technological point of view is the modern, powerful APIs that can be easily accessed via a dedicated Python wrapper package (v20). This chapter shows how to set up an account, how to connect to the APIs with Python, how to retrieve historical data (one minute bars) for backtesting purposes, how to retrieve streaming data in real time, how to automatically trade a CFD based on a momentum strategy, and how to retrieve account information and the detailed transaction history.

References and Further Resources

Visit the help and support pages of Oanda under Help and Support (*https://oreil.ly/-CMwk*) to learn more about the Oanda platform and important aspects of CFD trading.

The developer portal of Oanda Getting Started (*https://oreil.ly/oO_eV*) provides a detailed description of the APIs.

Python Script

The following Python script contains an Oanda custom streaming class that automatically trades a momentum strategy:

```python
#
# Python Script
# with Momentum Trading Class
# for Oanda v20
#
# Python for Algorithmic Trading
# (c) Dr. Yves J. Hilpisch
# The Python Quants GmbH
#
import tpqoa
import numpy as np
import pandas as pd


class MomentumTrader(tpqoa.tpqoa):
    def __init__(self, conf_file, instrument, bar_length, momentum, units,
                 *args, **kwargs):
        super(MomentumTrader, self).__init__(conf_file)
        self.position = 0
        self.instrument = instrument
        self.momentum = momentum
        self.bar_length = bar_length
        self.units = units
        self.raw_data = pd.DataFrame()
        self.min_length = self.momentum + 1

    def on_success(self, time, bid, ask):
        ''' Takes actions when new tick data arrives. '''
        print(self.ticks, end=' ')
        self.raw_data = self.raw_data.append(pd.DataFrame(
            {'bid': bid, 'ask': ask}, index=[pd.Timestamp(time)]))
        self.data = self.raw_data.resample(
            self.bar_length, label='right').last().ffill().iloc[:-1]
        self.data['mid'] = self.data.mean(axis=1)
        self.data['returns'] = np.log(self.data['mid'] /
                                      self.data['mid'].shift(1))
```

```python
        self.data['position'] = np.sign(
            self.data['returns'].rolling(self.momentum).mean())

        if len(self.data) > self.min_length:
            self.min_length += 1
            if self.data['position'].iloc[-1] == 1:
                if self.position == 0:
                    self.create_order(self.instrument, self.units)
                elif self.position == -1:
                    self.create_order(self.instrument, self.units * 2)
                self.position = 1
            elif self.data['position'].iloc[-1] == -1:
                if self.position == 0:
                    self.create_order(self.instrument, -self.units)
                elif self.position == 1:
                    self.create_order(self.instrument, -self.units * 2)
                self.position = -1


if __name__ == '__main__':
    strat = 2
    if strat == 1:
        mom = MomentumTrader('../pyalgo.cfg', 'DE30_EUR', '5s', 3, 1)
        mom.stream_data(mom.instrument, stop=100)
        mom.create_order(mom.instrument, units=-mom.position * mom.units)
    elif strat == 2:
        mom = MomentumTrader('../pyalgo.cfg', instrument='EUR_USD',
                             bar_length='5s', momentum=6, units=100000)
        mom.stream_data(mom.instrument, stop=100)
        mom.create_order(mom.instrument, units=-mom.position * mom.units)
    else:
        print('Strategy not known.')
```

## CHAPTER 9

FX Trading with FXCM

Financial institutions like to call what they do trading. Let's be honest. It's not trading; it's betting.

—Graydon Carter

This chapter introduces the trading platform from FXCM Group, LLC ("FXCM" afterwards), with its RESTful and streaming application programming interface (API) as well as the Python wrapper package fcxmpy. Similar to Oanda, it is a platform well suited for the deployment of automated, algorithmic trading strategies, even for retail traders with smaller capital positions. FXCM offers to retail and institutional traders a number of financial products that can be traded both via traditional trading applications and programmatically via their API. The focus of the products lies on currency pairs as well as contracts for difference (CFDs) on, among other things, major stock indices and commodities. In this context, also refer to "Contracts for Difference (CFDs)" on page 225 and "Disclaimer" on page 249.

Disclaimer

Trading forex/CFDs on margin carries a high level of risk and may not be suitable for all investors as you could sustain losses in excess of deposits. Leverage can work against you. The products are intended for retail and professional clients. Due to the certain restrictions imposed by the local law and regulation, German resident retail client(s) could sustain a total loss of deposited funds but are not subject to subsequent payment obligations beyond the deposited funds. Be aware of and fully understand all risks associated with the market and trading. Prior to trading any products, carefully consider your financial situation and experience level. Any opinions, news, research, analyses, prices, or other information is provided as general market commentary and does not constitute investment advice. The market commentary has not been prepared in accordance with legal requirements designed to promote the independence of investment research, and it is therefore not subject to any prohibition on dealing ahead of dissemination. Neither the trading platforms nor the author will accept liability for any loss or damage, including and without limitation to any loss of profit, which may arise directly or indirectly from use of or reliance on such information.

With regard to the platform criteria as discussed in Chapter 8, FXCM offers the following:

Instruments
FX products (for example, the trading of currency pairs), contracts for difference (CFDs) on stock indices, commodities, or rates products.

Strategies
FXCM allows for, among other things, (leveraged) long and short positions, market entry orders, and stop loss orders and take profit targets.

Costs
In addition to the bid-ask spread, a fixed fee is generally due for every trade with FXCM. Different pricing models are available.

Technology
FXCM provides the algorithmic trader with a modern RESTful API that can be accessed by, for example, the use of the Python wrapper package `fxcmpy`. Standard trading applications for desktop computers, tablets, and smartphones are also available.

Jurisdiction
FXCM is active in a number of countries globally (for instance, in the United Kingdom or Germany). Depending on the country itself, certain products might not be available/offered due to regulations and restrictions.

This chapter covers the basic functionalities of the FXCM trading API and the `fxcmpy` Python package required to implement an automated, algorithmic trading strategy programmatically. It is structured as follows. "Getting Started" on page 251 shows how to set up everything to work with the FXCM REST API for algorithmic trading. "Retrieving Data" on page 251 shows how to retrieve and work with financial data (down to the tick level). "Working with the API" on page 256 is at the core in that it illustrates typical tasks implemented using the RESTful API, such as retrieving historical and streaming data, placing orders, or looking up account information.

Getting Started

A detailed documentation of the FXCM API is found under *https://oreil.ly/Df_7e*. To install the Python wrapper package fxcmpy, execute the following on the shell:

```
pip install fxcmpy
```

The documentation of the fxcmpy package is found under *http://fxcmpy.tpq.io*.

To get started with the the FXCM trading API and the fxcmpy package, a free demo account with FXCM is sufficient. One can open such an account under FXCM Demo Account (*https://oreil.ly/v9H6z*).[1] The next step is to create a unique API token (for example, YOUR_FXCM_API_TOKEN) from within the demo account. A connection to the API is then opened, for example, via the following:

```
import fxcmpy
api = fxcmpy.fxcmpy(access_token=YOUR_FXCM_API_TOKEN, log_level='error')
```

Alternatively, you can use the configuration file as created in Chapter 8 to connect to the API. This file's content should be amended as follows:

```
[FXCM]
log_level = error
log_file = PATH_TO_AND_NAME_OF_LOG_FILE
access_token = YOUR_FXCM_API_TOKEN
```

One can then connect to the API via the following:

```
import fxcmpy
api = fxcmpy.fxcmpy(config_file='pyalgo.cfg')
```

By default, the server connects to the demo server. However, by the use of the server parameter, the connection can be made to the live trading server (if such an account exists):

```
api = fxcmpy.fxcmpy(config_file='pyalgo.cfg', server='demo')   ❶
api = fxcmpy.fxcmpy(config_file='pyalgo.cfg', server='real')   ❷
```

❶ Connects to the demo server.

❷ Connects to the live trading server.

Retrieving Data

FXCM provides access to historical market price data sets, such as tick data, in a prepackaged variant. This means that one can retrieve, for instance, compressed files from FXCM servers that contain tick data for the EUR/USD exchange rate for week

---

[1] Note that FXCM demo accounts are only offered for certain countries.

The retrieval of historical candles data from the API is explained in the subsequent section.

Retrieving Tick Data

For a number of currency pairs, FXCM provides historical tick data. The fxcmpy package makes retrieval of such tick data and working with it convenient. First, some imports:

```
In [1]: import time
        import numpy as np
        import pandas as pd
        import datetime as dt
        from pylab import mpl, plt
        plt.style.use('seaborn')
        mpl.rcParams['savefig.dpi'] = 300
        mpl.rcParams['font.family'] = 'serif'
```

Second is a look at the available symbols (currency pairs) for which tick data is available:

```
In [2]: from fxcmpy import fxcmpy_tick_data_reader as tdr
```

```
In [3]: print(tdr.get_available_symbols())
        ('AUDCAD', 'AUDCHF', 'AUDJPY', 'AUDNZD', 'CADCHF', 'EURAUD', 'EURCHF',
         'EURGBP', 'EURJPY', 'EURUSD', 'GBPCHF', 'GBPJPY', 'GBPNZD', 'GBPUSD',
         'GBPCHF', 'GBPJPY', 'GBPNZD', 'NZDCAD', 'NZDCHF', 'NZDJPY', 'NZDUSD',
         'USDCAD', 'USDCHF', 'USDJPY')
```

The following code retrieves one week's worth of tick data for a single symbol. The resulting pandas DataFrame object has more than 4.5 million data rows:

```
In [4]: start = dt.datetime(2020, 3, 25)   ❶
        stop = dt.datetime(2020, 3, 30)    ❶
```

```
In [5]: td = tdr('EURUSD', start, stop)    ❶
```

```
In [6]: td.get_raw_data().info()   ❷
        <class 'pandas.core.frame.DataFrame'>
        Index: 4504288 entries, 03/22/2020 21:12:02.256 to 03/27/2020
         20:59:00.022
        Data columns (total 2 columns):
         #    Column  Dtype
        ---   ------  -----
         0    Bid     float64
         1    Ask     float64
        dtypes: float64(2)
        memory usage: 103.1+ MB
```

```
In [7]: td.get_data().info()   ❸
        <class 'pandas.core.frame.DataFrame'>
        DatetimeIndex: 4504288 entries, 2020-03-22 21:12:02.256000 to
```

```
        2020-03-27 20:59:00.022000
        Data columns (total 2 columns):
         #   Column  Dtype
        ---  ------  -----
         0   Bid     float64
         1   Ask     float64
        dtypes: float64(2)
        memory usage: 103.1 MB

In [8]: td.get_data().head()
Out[8]:                            Bid       Ask
        2020-03-22 21:12:02.256  1.07006   1.07050
        2020-03-22 21:12:02.258  1.07002   1.07050
        2020-03-22 21:12:02.259  1.07003   1.07033
        2020-03-22 21:12:02.653  1.07003   1.07034
        2020-03-22 21:12:02.749  1.07000   1.07034
```

❶ This retrieves the data file, unpacks it, and stores the raw data in a `DataFrame` object (as an attribute to the resulting object).

❷ The `.get_raw_data()` method returns the `DataFrame` object with the raw data for which the index values are still `str` objects.

❸ The `.get_data()` method returns a `DataFrame` object for which the index has been transformed to a `DatetimeIndex`.[2]

Since the tick data is stored in a `DataFrame` object, it is straightforward to pick a sub-set of the data and to implement typical financial analytics tasks on it. Figure 9-1 shows a plot of the mid prices derived for the sub-set and a simple moving average (SMA):

```
In [9]: sub = td.get_data(start='2020-03-25 12:00:00',
                          end='2020-03-25 12:15:00')  ❶

In [10]: sub.head()
Out[10]:                            Bid      Ask
        2020-03-25 12:00:00.067  1.08109  1.0811
        2020-03-25 12:00:00.072  1.08110  1.0811
        2020-03-25 12:00:00.074  1.08109  1.0811
        2020-03-25 12:00:00.078  1.08111  1.0811
        2020-03-25 12:00:00.121  1.08112  1.0811

In [11]: sub['Mid'] = sub.mean(axis=1)  ❷

In [12]: sub['SMA'] = sub['Mid'].rolling(1000).mean()  ❸
```

---

[2] The `DatetimeIndex` conversion is time consuming, which is why there are two different methods related to tick data retrieval.

```
In [13]: sub[['Mid', 'SMA']].plot(figsize=(10, 6), lw=1.5);
```

❶ Picks a sub-set of the complete data set.

❷ Calculates the mid prices from the bid and ask prices.

❸ Derives SMA values over intervals of 1,000 ticks.

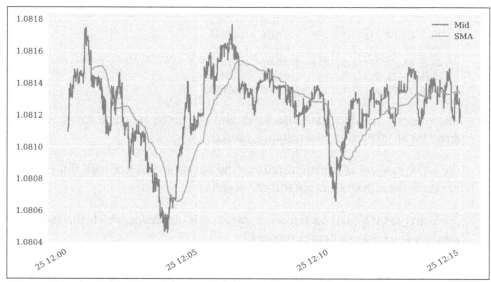

Figure 9-1. Historical mid tick prices for EUR/USD and SMA

Retrieving Candles Data

In addition, FXCM provides access to historical candles data (beyond the API). Candles data is data for certain homogeneous time intervals ("bars") with open, high, low, and close values for both bid and ask prices.

First is a look at the available symbols for which candles data is provided:

```
In [14]: from fxcmpy import fxcmpy_candles_data_reader as cdr

In [15]: print(cdr.get_available_symbols())
         ('AUDCAD', 'AUDCHF', 'AUDJPY', 'AUDNZD', 'CADCHF', 'EURAUD', 'EURCHF',
          'EURGBP', 'EURJPY', 'EURUSD', 'GBPCHF', 'GBPJPY', 'GBPNZD', 'GBPUSD',
          'GBPCHF', 'GBPJPY', 'GBPNZD', 'NZDCAD', 'NZDCHF', 'NZDJPY', 'NZDUSD',
          'USDCAD', 'USDCHF', 'USDJPY')
```

Second, the data retrieval itself. It is similar to the the tick data retrieval. The only difference is that a `period` value, or the bar length, needs to be specified (for example, `m1` for one minute, `H1` for one hour, or `D1` for one day):

```
In [16]: start = dt.datetime(2020, 4, 1)
         stop = dt.datetime(2020, 5, 1)

In [17]: period = 'H1'   ❶

In [18]: candles = cdr('EURUSD', start, stop, period)

In [19]: data = candles.get_data()

In [20]: data.info()
         <class 'pandas.core.frame.DataFrame'>
         DatetimeIndex: 600 entries, 2020-03-29 21:00:00 to 2020-05-01 20:00:00
         Data columns (total 8 columns):
          #   Column   Non-Null Count   Dtype
         ---  ------   --------------   -----
          0   BidOpen  600 non-null     float64
          1   BidHigh  600 non-null     float64
          2   BidLow   600 non-null     float64
          3   BidClose 600 non-null     float64
          4   AskOpen  600 non-null     float64
          5   AskHigh  600 non-null     float64
          6   AskLow   600 non-null     float64
          7   AskClose 600 non-null     float64
         dtypes: float64(8)
         memory usage: 42.2 KB

In [21]: data[data.columns[:4]].tail()   ❷
Out[21]:                       BidOpen  BidHigh   BidLow  BidClose
         2020-05-01 16:00:00  1.09976  1.09996  1.09850   1.09874
         2020-05-01 17:00:00  1.09874  1.09888  1.09785   1.09818
         2020-05-01 18:00:00  1.09818  1.09820  1.09757   1.09766
         2020-05-01 19:00:00  1.09766  1.09816  1.09747   1.09793
         2020-05-01 20:00:00  1.09793  1.09812  1.09730   1.09788

In [22]: data[data.columns[4:]].tail()   ❸
Out[22]:                       AskOpen  AskHigh   AskLow  AskClose
         2020-05-01 16:00:00  1.09980  1.09998  1.09853   1.09876
         2020-05-01 17:00:00  1.09876  1.09891  1.09786   1.09818
         2020-05-01 18:00:00  1.09818  1.09822  1.09758   1.09768
         2020-05-01 19:00:00  1.09768  1.09818  1.09748   1.09795
         2020-05-01 20:00:00  1.09795  1.09856  1.09733   1.09841
```

❶ Specifies the `period` value.

❷ Open, high, low, and close values for the *bid* prices.

❸ Open, high, low, and close values for the *ask* prices.

To conclude this section, the Python code that follows and calculates mid close prices, calculates two SMAs, and plots the results (see Figure 9-2):

```
In [23]: data['MidClose'] = data[['BidClose', 'AskClose']].mean(axis=1)   ❶
```

```
In [24]: data['SMA1'] = data['MidClose'].rolling(30).mean()   ❷
         data['SMA2'] = data['MidClose'].rolling(100).mean()   ❷
```

```
In [25]: data[['MidClose', 'SMA1', 'SMA2']].plot(figsize=(10, 6));
```

❶   Calculates the mid close prices from the bid and ask close prices.

❷   Calculates two SMAs: one for a shorter time interval, and one for a longer one.

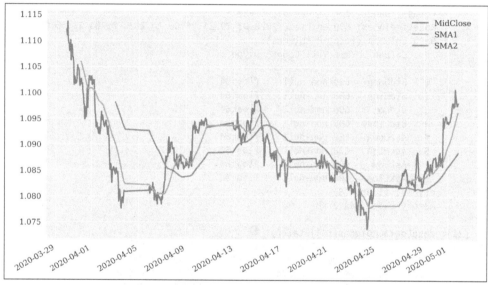

Figure 9-2. Historical hourly mid close prices for EUR/USD and two SMAs

Working with the API

While the previous sections retrieve historical tick data and candles data pre-packaged from FXCM servers, this section shows how to retrieve historical data via the API. However, a connection object to the FXCM API is needed. Therefore, first, here is the import of the `fxcmpy` package, the connection to the API (based on the unique API token), and a look at the available instruments. There might be more instruments available as compared to the pre-packaged data sets:

```
In [26]: import fxcmpy
```

```
In [27]: fxcmpy.__version__
Out[27]: '1.2.6'
```

```
In [28]: api = fxcmpy.fxcmpy(config_file='../pyalgo.cfg')  ❶

In [29]: instruments = api.get_instruments()

In [30]: print(instruments)
         ['EUR/USD', 'USD/JPY', 'GBP/USD', 'USD/CHF', 'EUR/CHF', 'AUD/USD',
          'USD/CAD', 'NZD/USD', 'EUR/GBP', 'EUR/JPY', 'GBP/JPY', 'CHF/JPY',
          'GBP/CHF', 'EUR/AUD', 'EUR/CAD', 'AUD/CAD', 'AUD/JPY', 'CAD/JPY',
          'NZD/JPY', 'GBP/CAD', 'GBP/NZD', 'GBP/AUD', 'AUD/NZD', 'USD/SEK',
          'EUR/SEK', 'EUR/NOK', 'USD/NOK', 'USD/MXN', 'AUD/CHF', 'EUR/NZD',
          'USD/ZAR', 'USD/HKD', 'ZAR/JPY', 'USD/TRY', 'EUR/TRY', 'NZD/CHF',
          'CAD/CHF', 'NZD/CAD', 'TRY/JPY', 'USD/ILS', 'USD/CNH', 'AUS200',
          'ESP35', 'FRA40', 'GER30', 'HKG33', 'JPN225', 'NAS100', 'SPX500',
          'UK100', 'US30', 'Copper', 'CHN50', 'EUSTX50', 'USDOLLAR', 'US2000',
          'USOil', 'UKOil', 'SOYF', 'NGAS', 'USOilSpot', 'UKOilSpot', 'WHEATF',
          'CORNF', 'Bund', 'XAU/USD', 'XAG/USD', 'EMBasket', 'JPYBasket',
          'BTC/USD', 'BCH/USD', 'ETH/USD', 'LTC/USD', 'XRP/USD', 'CryptoMajor',
          'EOS/USD', 'XLM/USD', 'ESPORTS', 'BIOTECH', 'CANNABIS', 'FAANG',
          'CHN.TECH', 'CHN.ECOMM', 'USEquities']
```

❶ This connects to the API; adjust the path/filename.

Retrieving Historical Data

Once connected, data retrieval for specific time intervals is accomplished via a single method call. When using the `.get_candles()` method, the parameter `period` can be one of m1, m5, m15, m30, H1, H2, H3, H4, H6, H8, D1, W1, or M1. Figure 9-3 shows one-minute bar ask close prices for the EUR/USD instrument (currency pair):

```
In [31]: candles = api.get_candles('USD/JPY', period='D1', number=10)  ❶

In [32]: candles[candles.columns[:4]]  ❶
Out[32]:                      bidopen  bidclose  bidhigh   bidlow
         date
         2020-08-07 21:00:00  105.538   105.898  106.051  105.452
         2020-08-09 21:00:00  105.871   105.846  105.871  105.844
         2020-08-10 21:00:00  105.846   105.914  106.197  105.702
         2020-08-11 21:00:00  105.914   106.466  106.679  105.870
         2020-08-12 21:00:00  106.466   106.848  107.009  106.434
         2020-08-13 21:00:00  106.848   106.893  107.044  106.560
         2020-08-14 21:00:00  106.893   106.535  107.033  106.429
         2020-08-17 21:00:00  106.559   105.960  106.648  105.937
         2020-08-18 21:00:00  105.960   105.378  106.046  105.277
         2020-08-19 21:00:00  105.378   105.528  105.599  105.097

In [33]: candles[candles.columns[4:]]  ❶
Out[33]:                      askopen  askclose  askhigh   asklow  tickqty
         date
         2020-08-07 21:00:00  105.557   105.969  106.062  105.484   253759
         2020-08-09 21:00:00  105.983   105.952  105.989  105.925       20
         2020-08-10 21:00:00  105.952   105.986  106.209  105.715   161841
```

```
            2020-08-11 21:00:00   105.986   106.541   106.689   105.929   243813
            2020-08-12 21:00:00   106.541   106.950   107.022   106.447   248989
            2020-08-13 21:00:00   106.950   106.983   107.056   106.572   214735
            2020-08-14 21:00:00   106.983   106.646   107.044   106.442   164244
            2020-08-17 21:00:00   106.680   106.047   106.711   105.948   163629
            2020-08-18 21:00:00   106.047   105.431   106.101   105.290   215574
            2020-08-19 21:00:00   105.431   105.542   105.612   105.109   151255

In [34]: start = dt.datetime(2019, 1, 1)  ❷
         end = dt.datetime(2020, 6, 1)  ❷

In [35]: candles = api.get_candles('EUR/GBP', period='D1',
                                   start=start, stop=end)  ❷

In [36]: candles.info()  ❷
         <class 'pandas.core.frame.DataFrame'>
         DatetimeIndex: 438 entries, 2019-01-02 22:00:00 to 2020-06-01 21:00:00
         Data columns (total 9 columns):
          #   Column    Non-Null Count   Dtype
         ---  ------    --------------   -----
          0   bidopen   438 non-null     float64
          1   bidclose  438 non-null     float64
          2   bidhigh   438 non-null     float64
          3   bidlow    438 non-null     float64
          4   askopen   438 non-null     float64
          5   askclose  438 non-null     float64
          6   askhigh   438 non-null     float64
          7   asklow    438 non-null     float64
          8   tickqty   438 non-null     int64
         dtypes: float64(8), int64(1)
         memory usage: 34.2 KB

In [37]: candles = api.get_candles('EUR/USD', period='m1', number=250)  ❸

In [38]: candles['askclose'].plot(figsize=(10, 6))
```

❶ Retrieves the 10 most recent end-of-day prices.

❷ Retrieves end-of-day prices for a whole year.

❸ Retrieves the most recent one-minute bar prices available.

> Historical data retrieved from the FXCM RESTful API can change
> with the pricing model of the account. In particular, the average
> bid-ask spreads can be higher or lower for different pricing models
> offered by FXCM to different groups of traders.

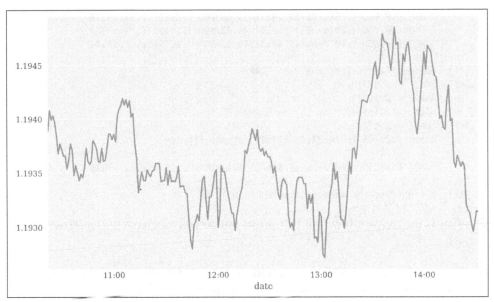

Figure 9-3. Historical ask close prices for EUR/USD (minute bars)

Retrieving Streaming Data

While *historical* data is important to, for example, backtest algorithmic trading strategies, continuous access to *real-time or streaming* data (during trading hours) is required to deploy and automate algorithmic trading strategies. Similar to the Oanda API, the FXCM API therefore also allows for the subscription to real-time data streams for all instruments. The fxcmpy wrapper package supports this functionality in that it allows one to provide user-defined functions (so called *callback functions*) to process the subscribed real-time data stream.

The following Python code presents such a simple callback function—it only prints out selected elements of the data set retrieved—and uses it to process data retrieved in real time, after a subscription for the desired instrument (here EUR/USD):

```
In [39]: def output(data, dataframe):
             print('%3d | %s | %s | %6.5f, %6.5f'
                   % (len(dataframe), data['Symbol'],
                      pd.to_datetime(int(data['Updated']), unit='ms'),
                      data['Rates'][0], data['Rates'][1]))    ❶

In [40]: api.subscribe_market_data('EUR/USD', (output,))    ❷
            2 | EUR/USD | 2020-08-19 14:32:36.204000 | 1.19319, 1.19331
            3 | EUR/USD | 2020-08-19 14:32:37.005000 | 1.19320, 1.19331
            4 | EUR/USD | 2020-08-19 14:32:37.940000 | 1.19323, 1.19333
            5 | EUR/USD | 2020-08-19 14:32:38.429000 | 1.19321, 1.19332
            6 | EUR/USD | 2020-08-19 14:32:38.915000 | 1.19323, 1.19334
            7 | EUR/USD | 2020-08-19 14:32:39.436000 | 1.19321, 1.19332
```

```
 8 | EUR/USD | 2020-08-19 14:32:39.883000 | 1.19317, 1.19328
 9 | EUR/USD | 2020-08-19 14:32:40.437000 | 1.19317, 1.19328
10 | EUR/USD | 2020-08-19 14:32:40.810000 | 1.19318, 1.19329

In [41]: api.get_last_price('EUR/USD')   ❸
Out[41]: Bid      1.19318
         Ask      1.19329
         High     1.19534
         Low      1.19217
         Name: 2020-08-19 14:32:40.810000, dtype: float64


11 | EUR/USD | 2020-08-19 14:32:41.410000 | 1.19319, 1.19329

In [42]: api.unsubscribe_market_data('EUR/USD')   ❹
```

❶ This is the callback function that prints out certain elements of the retrieved data set.

❷ Here is the subscription to a specific real-time data stream. Data is processed asynchronously as long as there is no "unsubscribe" event.

❸ During the subscription, the .get_last_price() method returns the last available data set.

❹ This unsubscribes from the real-time data stream.

Callback Functions

Callback functions are a flexible way to process real-time streaming data based on a Python function or even multiple such functions. They can be used for simple tasks, such as the printing of incoming data, or complex tasks, such as generating trading signals based on online trading algorithms.

Placing Orders

The FXCM API allows for the placement and management of all types of orders that are also available via the trading application of FXCM (such as entry orders or trailing stop loss orders).[3] However, the following code illustrates basic market buy and sell orders only since they are generally sufficient to at least get started with algorithmic trading.

---

3 See the documentation under *http://fxcmpy.tpq.io*.

The following code first verifies that there are no open positions and then opens different positions via the `.create_market_buy_order()` method:

```
In [43]: api.get_open_positions()  ❶
Out[43]: Empty DataFrame
         Columns: []
         Index: []

In [44]: order = api.create_market_buy_order('EUR/USD', 100)  ❷

In [45]: sel = ['tradeId', 'amountK', 'currency',
                'grossPL', 'isBuy']  ❸

In [46]: api.get_open_positions()[sel]  ❸
Out[46]:      tradeId  amountK currency  grossPL  isBuy
         0  169122817      100  EUR/USD -9.21945   True

In [47]: order = api.create_market_buy_order('EUR/GBP', 50)  ❹

In [48]: api.get_open_positions()[sel]
Out[48]:      tradeId  amountK currency  grossPL  isBuy
         0  169122817      100  EUR/USD -8.38125   True
         1  169122819       50  EUR/GBP -9.40900   True
```

❶ Shows the open positions for the connected (default) account.

❷ Opens a position of 100,000 in the EUR/USD currency pair.[4]

❸ Shows the open positions for selected elements only.

❹ Opens another position of 50,000 in the EUR/GBP currency pair.

While the `.create_market_buy_order()` opens or increases positions, the `.create_market_sell_order()` allows one to close or decrease positions. There are also more general methods that allow the closing out of positions, as the following code illustrates:

```
In [49]: order = api.create_market_sell_order('EUR/USD', 25)  ❶

In [50]: order = api.create_market_buy_order('EUR/GBP', 50)  ❷

In [51]: api.get_open_positions()[sel]  ❸
Out[51]:      tradeId  amountK currency  grossPL  isBuy
         0  169122817      100  EUR/USD -7.54306   True
```

---

4 Quantities are in 1,000s of the instrument for currency pairs. Also, note that different accounts might have different leverage ratios. This implies that the same position might require more or less equity (margin) depending on the relevant leverage ratio. Adjust the example quantities to lower values if necessary. See *https://oreil.ly/xUHMP*.

```
         1   169122819        50   EUR/GBP  -11.62340   True
         2   169122834        25   EUR/USD   -2.30463   False
         3   169122835        50   EUR/GBP   -9.96292   True

In [52]: api.close_all_for_symbol('EUR/GBP')  ❹

In [53]: api.get_open_positions()[sel]
Out[53]:      tradeId  amountK  currency  grossPL  isBuy
         0   169122817       100   EUR/USD  -5.02858   True
         1   169122834        25   EUR/USD  -3.14257   False

In [54]: api.close_all()  ❺

In [55]: api.get_open_positions()
Out[55]: Empty DataFrame
         Columns: []
         Index: []
```

❶ Reduces the position in the EUR/USD currency pair.

❷ Increases the position in the EUR/GBP currency pair.

❸ For EUR/GBP there are now two open long positions; contrary to the EUR/USD position, it is not netted.

❹ The .close_all_for_symbol() method closes all positions for the specified symbol.

❺ The .close_all() method closes all open positions at once.

> By default, FXCM sets up demo accounts as *hedge accounts*. This means that going long, say EUR/USD, with 10,000 and going short the same instrument with 10,000 leads to two different open positions. The default with Oanda are *net accounts* that net orders and positions for the same instrument.

Account Information

Beyond, for example, open positions, the FXCM API allows one to retrieve more general account informationm, as well. For example, one can look up the default account (if there are multiple accounts) or an overview equity and margin situation:

```
In [56]: api.get_default_account()  ❶
Out[56]: 1233279

In [57]: api.get_accounts().T  ❷
Out[57]:                             0
         t                           6
```

```
ratePrecision             0
accountId           1233279
balance             47555.2
usdMr                     0
mc                        N
mcDate
accountName        01233279
usdMr3                    0
hedging                   Y
usableMargin3       47555.2
usableMarginPerc        100
usableMargin3Perc       100
equity              47555.2
usableMargin        47555.2
bus                    1000
dayPL                653.16
grossPL                   0
```

❶ Shows the default `accountId` value.

❷ Shows for all accounts the financial situation and some parameters.

Conclusions

This chapter is about the RESTful API of FXCM for algorithmic trading and covers the following topics:

- Setting everything up for API usage
- Retrieving historical tick data
- Retrieving historical candles data
- Retrieving streaming data in real-time
- Placing market buy and sell orders
- Looking up account information

Beyond these aspects, the FXCM API and the `fxcmpy` wrapper package provide, of course, more functionality. However, the topics of this chapter are the basic building blocks needed to get started with algorithmic trading.

With Oanda and FXCM, algorithmic traders have two trading platforms (brokers) available that provide a wide-ranging spectrum of financial instruments and appropriate APIs to implement automated, algorithmic trading strategies. Some important aspects are added to the mix in Chapter 10.

References and Further Resources

The following resources cover the FXCM trading API and the Python wrapper package:

- Trading API: *https://fxcm.github.io/rest-api-docs*
- fxcmpy package: *http://fxcmpy.tpq.io*

## CHAPTER 10

Automating Trading Operations

People worry that computers will get too smart and take over the world, but the real problem is that they're too stupid and they've already taken over the world.

—Pedro Domingos

"Now what?" you might think. The trading platform that allows one to retrieve historical data and streaming data is available. It allows one to place buy and sell orders and to check the account status. A number of different methods have been introduced in this book to derive algorithmic trading strategies by predicting the direction of market price movements. You may ask, "How, after all, can this all be put together to work in automated fashion?" This cannot be answered in any generality. However, this chapter addresses a number of topics that are important in this context. The chapter assumes that a single automated, algorithmic trading strategy is to be deployed. This simplifies, for example, aspects like capital and risk management.

The chapter covers the following topics. "Capital Management" on page 266 discusses the *Kelly criterion*. Depending on the strategy characteristics and the trading capital available, the Kelly criterion helps with sizing the trades. To gain confidence in an algorithmic trading strategy, the strategy needs to be backtested thoroughly with regard to both performance and risk characteristics. "ML-Based Trading Strategy" on page 277 backtests an example strategy based on a classification algorithm from machine learning (ML), as introduced in "Trading Strategies" on page 13. To deploy the algorithmic trading strategy for automated trading, it needs to be translated into an online algorithm that works with incoming streaming data in real time. "Online Algorithm" on page 291 covers the transformation of an *offline* algorithm into an *online* algorithm.

"Infrastructure and Deployment" on page 296 then sets out to make sure that the automated, algorithmic trading strategy runs robustly and reliably in the cloud. Not all topics of relevance can be covered in detail, but *cloud deployment* seems to be the only viable option from an availability, performance, and security point of view in this context. "Logging and Monitoring" on page 297 covers logging and monitoring. Logging is important in order to be able to analyze the history and certain events during the deployment of an automated trading strategy. Monitoring via socket communication, as introduced in Chapter 7, allows one to observe events remotely in real time. The chapter concludes with "Visual Step-by-Step Overview" on page 299, which provides a visual summary of the core steps for the automated deployment of algorithmic trading strategies in the cloud.

Capital Management

A central question in algorithmic trading is how much capital to deploy to a given algorithmic trading strategy given the total available capital. The answer to this question depends on the main goal one is trying to achieve by algorithmic trading. Most individuals and financial institutions will agree that the *maximization of long-term wealth* is a good candidate objective. This is what Edward Thorp had in mind when he derived the *Kelly criterion* to investing, as described in Rotando and Thorp (1992). Simply speaking, the Kelly criterion allows for an explicit calculation of the fraction of the available capital a trader should deploy to a strategy, given its statistical return characteristics.

Kelly Criterion in Binomial Setting

The common way of introducing the theory of the Kelly criterion to investing is on the basis of a coin tossing game or, more generally, a binomial setting (only two outcomes are possible). This section follows that path. Assume a gambler is playing a coin tossing game against an infinitely rich bank or casino. Assume further that the probability for heads is some value p for which the following holds:

$$\frac{1}{2} < p < 1$$

Probability for tails is defined by the following:

$$q = 1 - p < \frac{1}{2}$$

The gambler can place bets $b > 0$ of arbitrary size, whereby the gambler wins the same amount if right and loses it all if wrong. Given the assumptions about the probabilities, the gambler would of course want to bet on heads.

Therefore, the expected value for this betting game B (that is, the random variable representing this game) in a one-shot setting is as follows:

$$E(B) = p \cdot b - q \cdot b = (p - q) \cdot b > 0$$

A risk-neutral gambler with unlimited funds would like to bet as large an amount as possible since this would maximize the expected payoff. However, trading in financial markets is not a one-shot game in general. It is a repeated game. Therefore, assume that b_i represents the amount that is bet on day i and that c_0 represents the initial capital. The capital c_1 at the end of day one depends on the betting success on that day and might be either $c_0 + b_1$ or $c_0 - b_1$. The expected value for a gamble that is repeated n times then is as follows:

$$E(B^n) = c_0 + \sum_{i=1}^{n} (p - q) \cdot b_i$$

In classical economic theory, with risk-neutral, expected utility-maximizing agents, a gambler would try to maximize the preceding expression. It is easily seen that it is maximized by betting all available funds, $b_i = c_{i-1}$, like in the one-shot scenario. However, this in turn implies that a single loss will wipe out all available funds and will lead to ruin (unless unlimited borrowing is possible). Therefore, this strategy does not lead to a maximization of long-term wealth.

While betting the maximum capital available might lead to sudden ruin, betting nothing at all avoids any kind of loss but does not benefit from the advantageous gamble either. This is where the Kelly criterion comes into play since it derives the *optimal fraction* f^* of the available capital to bet per round of betting. Assume that $n = h + t$ where h stands for the number of heads observed during n rounds of betting and where t stands for the number of tails. With these definitions, the available capital after n rounds is the following:

$$c_n = c_0 \cdot (1 + f)^h \cdot (1 - f)^t$$

In such a context, long-term wealth maximization boils down to maximizing the average geometric growth rate per bet which is given as follows:

$$r^g = \log\left(\frac{c_n}{c_0}\right)^{1/n}$$

$$= \log\left(\frac{c_0 \cdot (1+f)^h \cdot (1-f)^t}{c_0}\right)^{1/n}$$

$$= \log\left((1+f)^h \cdot (1-f)^t\right)^{1/n}$$

$$= \frac{h}{n}\log(1+f) + \frac{t}{n}\log(1-f)$$

The problem then formally is to maximize the *expected* average rate of growth by choosing f optimally. With $\mathbf{E}(h) = n \cdot p$ and $\mathbf{E}(t) = n \cdot q$, one gets:

$$\mathbf{E}(r^g) = \mathbf{E}\left(\frac{h}{n}\log(1+f) + \frac{t}{n}\log(1-f)\right)$$

$$= \mathbf{E}(p\log(1+f) + q\log(1-f))$$

$$= p\log(1+f) + q\log(1-f)$$

$$\equiv G(f)$$

One can now maximize the term by choosing the optimal fraction f^* according to the first order condition. The first derivative is given by the following:

$$G'(f) = \frac{p}{1+f} - \frac{q}{1-f}$$

$$= \frac{p - pf - q - qf}{(1+f)(1-f)}$$

$$= \frac{p - q - f}{(1+f)(1-f)}$$

From the first order condition, one gets the following:

$$G'(f) \stackrel{!}{=} 0 \Rightarrow f^* = p - q$$

If one trusts this to be the maximum (and not the minimum), this result implies that it is optimal to invest a fraction $f^* = p - q$ per round of betting. With, for example, $p = 0.55$, one has $f^* = 0.55 - 0.45 = 0.1$, or that the optimal fraction is 10%.

The following Python code formalizes these concepts and results through simulation. First, some imports and configurations:

```
In [1]: import math
        import time
        import numpy as np
        import pandas as pd
        import datetime as dt
        from pylab import plt, mpl
```

```
In [2]: np.random.seed(1000)
        plt.style.use('seaborn')
        mpl.rcParams['savefig.dpi'] = 300
        mpl.rcParams['font.family'] = 'serif'
```

The idea is to simulate, for example, 50 series with 100 coin tosses per series. The Python code for this is straightforward:

```
In [3]: p = 0.55   ❶
```

```
In [4]: f = p - (1 - p)   ❷
```

```
In [5]: f   ❷
Out[5]: 0.10000000000000009
```

```
In [6]: I = 50   ❸
```

```
In [7]: n = 100   ❹
```

❶ Fixes the probability for heads.

❷ Calculates the optimal fraction according to the Kelly criterion.

❸ The number of series to be simulated.

❹ The number of trials per series.

The major part is the Python function `run_simulation()`, which achieves the simulation according to the preceding assumptions. Figure 10-1 shows the simulation results:

```
In [8]: def run_simulation(f):
            c = np.zeros((n, I))   ❶
            c[0] = 100   ❷
            for i in range(I):   ❸
                for t in range(1, n):   ❹
                    o = np.random.binomial(1, p)   ❺
                    if o > 0:   ❻
                        c[t, i] = (1 + f) * c[t - 1, i]   ❼
                    else:   ❽
                        c[t, i] = (1 - f) * c[t - 1, i]   ❾
```

```
        return c
```

```
In [9]: c_1 = run_simulation(f)  ❿
```

```
In [10]: c_1.round(2)
Out[10]: array([[100.  , 100.  , 100.  , ..., 100.  , 100.  , 100.  ],
                [ 90.  , 110.  , 90.  , ..., 110.  , 90.  , 110.  ],
                [ 99.  , 121.  , 99.  , ..., 121.  , 81.  , 121.  ],
                ...,
                [226.35, 338.13, 413.27, ..., 123.97, 123.97, 123.97],
                [248.99, 371.94, 454.6 , ..., 136.37, 136.37, 136.37],
                [273.89, 409.14, 409.14, ..., 122.73, 150.01, 122.73]])
```

```
In [11]: plt.figure(figsize=(10, 6))
         plt.plot(c_1, 'b', lw=0.5)  ⓫
         plt.plot(c_1.mean(axis=1), 'r', lw=2.5);  ⓬
```

❶ Instantiates an ndarray object to store the simulation results.

❷ Initializes the starting capital with 100.

❸ Outer loop for the series simulations.

❹ Inner loop for the series itself.

❺ Simulates the tossing of a coin.

❻ If 1 or heads…

❼ …then add the win to the capital.

❽ If 0 or tails…

❾ …subtract the loss from the capital.

❿ This runs the simulation.

⓫ Plots all 50 series.

⓬ Plots the average over all 50 series.

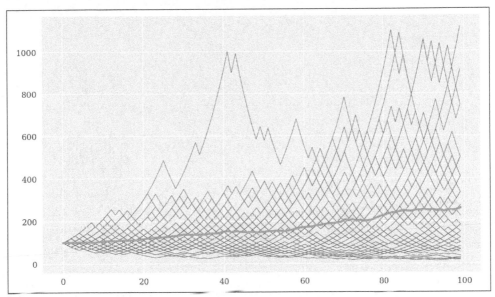

Figure 10-1. 50 simulated series with 100 trials each (red line = average)

The following code repeats the simulation for different values of f. As shown in Figure 10-2, a lower fraction leads to a lower growth rate on average. Higher values might lead both to a higher average capital at the end of the simulation ($f = 0.25$) or lead to a much lower average capital ($f = 0.5$). In both cases where the fraction f is higher, the volatility increases considerably:

```
In [12]: c_2 = run_simulation(0.05)  ❶

In [13]: c_3 = run_simulation(0.25)  ❷

In [14]: c_4 = run_simulation(0.5)  ❸

In [15]: plt.figure(figsize=(10, 6))
         plt.plot(c_1.mean(axis=1), 'r', label='$f^*=0.1$')
         plt.plot(c_2.mean(axis=1), 'b', label='$f=0.05$')
         plt.plot(c_3.mean(axis=1), 'y', label='$f=0.25$')
         plt.plot(c_4.mean(axis=1), 'm', label='$f=0.5$')
         plt.legend(loc=0);
```

❶ Simulation with $f = 0.05$.

❷ Simulation with $f = 0.25$.

❸ Simulation with $f = 0.5$.

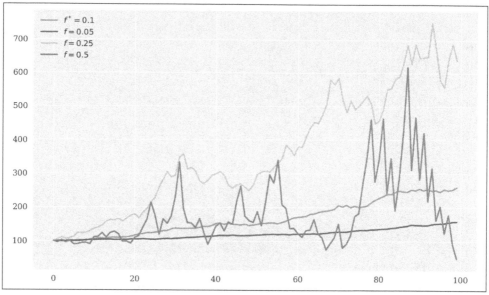

Figure 10-2. Average capital over time for different values of f

Kelly Criterion for Stocks and Indices

Assume now a stock market setting in which the relevant stock (index) can take on only two values after a period of one year from today, given its known value today. The setting is again binomial but this time a bit closer on the modeling side to stock market realities.[1] Specifically, assume the following holds true:

$$P\left(r^S = \mu + \sigma\right) = P\left(r^S = \mu - \sigma\right) = \frac{1}{2}$$

Here, $\mathbf{E}\left(r^S\right) = \mu > 0$ is the the expected return of the stock over one year, and $\sigma > 0$ is the standard deviation of returns (volatility). In a one-period setting, one gets the following for the available capital after one year (with c_0 and f defined as before):

$$c(f) = c_0 \cdot \left(1 + (1 - f) \cdot r + f \cdot r^S\right)$$

---

1 The exposition follows Hung (2010).

Here, r is the constant short rate earned on cash not invested in the stock. Maximizing the geometric growth rate means maximizing the term:

$$G(f) = \mathbf{E}\left(\log \frac{c(f)}{c_0} \right)$$

Assume now that there are n relevant trading days in the year so that for each such trading day i the following holds true:

$$P\left(r_i^S = \frac{\mu}{n} + \frac{\sigma}{\sqrt{n}}\right) = P\left(r_i^S = \frac{\mu}{n} - \frac{\sigma}{\sqrt{n}}\right) = \frac{1}{2}$$

Note that volatility scales with the square root of the number of trading days. Under these assumptions, the daily values scale up to the yearly ones from before and one gets the following:

$$c_n(f) = c_0 \cdot \prod_{i=1}^{n} \left(1 + (1 - f) \cdot \frac{r}{n} + f \cdot r_i^S\right)$$

One now has to maximize the following quantity to achieve maximum long-term wealth when investing in the stock:

$$
\begin{aligned}
G_n(f) &= \mathbf{E}\left(\log \frac{c_n(f)}{c_0} \right) \\
&= \mathbf{E}\left(\sum_{i=1}^{n} \log \left(1 + (1 - f) \cdot \frac{r}{n} + f \cdot r_i^S\right)\right) \\
&= \frac{1}{2} \sum_{i=1}^{n} \log \left(1 + (1 - f) \cdot \frac{r}{n} + f \cdot \left(\frac{\mu}{n} + \frac{\sigma}{\sqrt{n}}\right)\right) \\
&\quad + \log \left(1 + (1 - f) \cdot \frac{r}{n} + f \cdot \left(\frac{\mu}{n} - \frac{\sigma}{\sqrt{n}}\right)\right) \\
&= \frac{n}{2} \log \left(\left(1 + (1 - f) \cdot \frac{r}{n} + f \cdot \frac{\mu}{n}\right)^2 - \frac{f^2 \sigma^2}{n}\right)
\end{aligned}
$$

Using a Taylor series expansion (*https://oreil.ly/xX4tA*), one finally arrives at the following:

$$G_n(f) = r + (\mu - r) \cdot f - \frac{\sigma^2}{2} \cdot f^2 + \mathcal{O}\left(\frac{1}{\sqrt{n}}\right)$$

Or for infinitely many trading points in time (that is, for continuous trading), one arrives at the following:

$$G_\infty(f) = r + (\mu - r) \cdot f - \frac{\sigma^2}{2} \cdot f^2$$

The optimal fraction f^* then is given through the first order condition by the following expression:

$$f^* = \frac{\mu - r}{\sigma^2}$$

This represents the expected excess return of the stock over the risk-free rate divided by the variance of the returns. This expression looks similar to the Sharpe ratio but is different.

A real-world example shall illustrate the application of the preceding formula and its role in leveraging equity deployed to trading strategies. The trading strategy under consideration is simply a *passive long position in the S&P 500 index*. To this end, base data is quickly retrieved and required statistics are easily derived:

```
In [16]: raw = pd.read_csv('http://hilpisch.com/pyalgo_eikon_eod_data.csv',
                           index_col=0, parse_dates=True)

In [17]: symbol = '.SPX'

In [18]: data = pd.DataFrame(raw[symbol])

In [19]: data['return'] = np.log(data / data.shift(1))

In [20]: data.dropna(inplace=True)

In [21]: data.tail()
Out[21]:                  .SPX      return
         Date
         2019-12-23   3224.01   0.000866
         2019-12-24   3223.38  -0.000195
         2019-12-27   3240.02   0.000034
         2019-12-30   3221.29  -0.005798
         2019-12-31   3230.78   0.002942
```

The statistical properties of the S&P 500 index over the period covered suggest an optimal fraction of about 4.5 to be invested in the long position in the index. In other words, for every dollar available, 4.5 dollars shall be invested, implying a *leverage ratio* of 4.5 in accordance with the optimal Kelly fraction or, in this case, the optimal Kelly *factor*.

Everything being equal, the Kelly criterion implies a higher leverage when the expected return is higher and the volatility (variance) is lower:

```
In [22]: mu = data['return'].mean() * 252  ❶

In [23]: mu  ❶
Out[23]: 0.09992181916534204

In [24]: sigma = data['return'].std() * 252 ** 0.5  ❷

In [25]: sigma  ❷
Out[25]: 0.14761569775486563

In [26]: r = 0.0  ❸

In [27]: f = (mu - r) / sigma ** 2  ❹

In [28]: f  ❹
Out[28]: 4.585590244019818
```

❶ Calculates the annualized return.

❷ Calculates the annualized volatility.

❸ Sets the risk-free rate to 0 (for simplicity).

❹ Calculates the optimal Kelly fraction to be invested in the strategy.

The following Python code simulates the application of the Kelly criterion and the optimal leverage ratio. For simplicity and comparison reasons, the initial equity is set to 1 while the initially invested total capital is set to $1 \cdot f^*$. Depending on the performance of the capital deployed to the strategy, the total capital itself is adjusted daily according to the available equity. After a loss, the capital is reduced; after a profit, the capital is increased. The evolution of the equity position compared to the index itself is shown in Figure 10-3:

```
In [29]: equs = []

In [30]: def kelly_strategy(f):
             global equs
             equ = 'equity_{:.2f}'.format(f)
             equs.append(equ)
             cap = 'capital_{:.2f}'.format(f)
             data[equ] = 1  ❶
             data[cap] = data[equ] * f  ❷
             for i, t in enumerate(data.index[1:]):
                 t_1 = data.index[i]  ❸
                 data.loc[t, cap] = data[cap].loc[t_1] * \
                                 math.exp(data['return'].loc[t])  ❹
                 data.loc[t, equ] = data[cap].loc[t] - \
```

```
                            data[cap].loc[t_1] + \
                            data[equ].loc[t_1]   ❺
              data.loc[t, cap] = data[equ].loc[t] * f   ❻

In [31]: kelly_strategy(f * 0.5)   ❼

In [32]: kelly_strategy(f * 0.66)   ❽

In [33]: kelly_strategy(f)   ❾

In [34]: print(data[equs].tail())
                    equity_2.29  equity_3.03  equity_4.59
         Date
         2019-12-23     6.628865     9.585294    14.205748
         2019-12-24     6.625895     9.579626    14.193019
         2019-12-27     6.626410     9.580610    14.195229
         2019-12-30     6.538582     9.412991    13.818934
         2019-12-31     6.582748     9.496919    14.005618

In [35]: ax = data['return'].cumsum().apply(np.exp).plot(figsize=(10, 6))
         data[equs].plot(ax=ax, legend=True);
```

❶ Generates a new column for equity and sets the initial value to 1.

❷ Generates a new column for capital and sets the initial value to $1 \cdot f^*$.

❸ Picks the right DatetimeIndex value for the previous values.

❹ Calculates the new capital position given the return.

❺ Adjusts the equity value according to the capital position performance.

❻ Adjusts the capital position given the new equity position and the fixed leverage ratio.

❼ Simulates the Kelly criterion based strategy for half of f…

❽ …for two thirds of f…

❾ …and f itself.

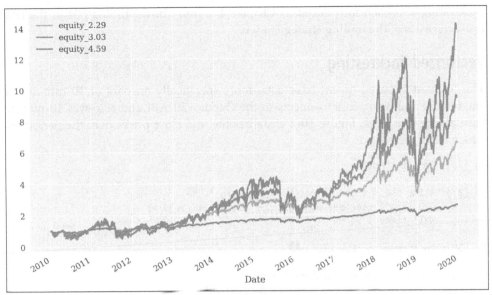

Figure 10-3. Gross performance of S&P 500 compared to equity position given different values of f

As Figure 10-3 illustrates, applying the optimal Kelly leverage leads to a rather erratic evolution of the equity position (high volatility), which is intuitively plausible, given the leverage ratio of 4.59. One would expect the volatility of the equity position to increase with increasing leverage. Therefore, practitioners often do not use "full Kelly" (4.6), but rather "half Kelly" (2.3). In the current example, this is reduced to:

$$\frac{1}{2} \cdot f^* \approx 2.3$$

Against this background, Figure 10-3 also shows the evolution of the equity position for values lower than "full Kelly." The risk indeed reduces with lower values of latex-math:[f].

ML-Based Trading Strategy

Chapter 8 introduces the Oanda trading platform, its RESTful API and the Python wrapper package tpqoa. This section combines an ML-based approach for predicting the direction of market price movements with historical data from the Oanda v20 RESTful API to backtest an algorithmic trading strategy for the EUR/USD currency pair. It uses vectorized backtesting, taking into account this time the bid-ask spread as proportional transactions costs. It also adds, compared to the plain vectorized backtesting approach introduced in Chapter 4, a more in-depth analysis of the risk characteristics of the trading strategy tested.

Vectorized Backtesting

The backtest is based on intraday data, more specifically on bars of 10 minutes in length. The following code connects to the Oanda v20 API and retrieves 10-minute bar data for one week. Figure 10-4 visualizes the mid close prices over the period for which data is retrieved:

```
In [36]: import tpqoa

In [37]: %time api = tpqoa.tpqoa('../pyalgo.cfg')  ❶
         CPU times: user 893 µs, sys: 198 µs, total: 1.09 ms
         Wall time: 1.04 ms

In [38]: instrument = 'EUR_USD'  ❶

In [39]: raw = api.get_history(instrument,
                               start='2020-06-08',
                               end='2020-06-13',
                               granularity='M10',
                               price='M')  ❶

In [40]: raw.tail()
Out[40]:                           o        h        l        c  volume  complete
         time
         2020-06-12 20:10:00  1.12572  1.12593  1.12532  1.12568     221      True
         2020-06-12 20:20:00  1.12569  1.12578  1.12532  1.12558     163      True
         2020-06-12 20:30:00  1.12560  1.12573  1.12534  1.12543     192      True
         2020-06-12 20:40:00  1.12544  1.12594  1.12528  1.12542     219      True
         2020-06-12 20:50:00  1.12544  1.12624  1.12541  1.12554     296      True

In [41]: raw.info()
         <class 'pandas.core.frame.DataFrame'>
         DatetimeIndex: 701 entries, 2020-06-08 00:00:00 to 2020-06-12 20:50:00
         Data columns (total 6 columns):
          #   Column    Non-Null Count  Dtype
         ---  ------    --------------  -----
          0   o         701 non-null    float64
          1   h         701 non-null    float64
          2   l         701 non-null    float64
          3   c         701 non-null    float64
          4   volume    701 non-null    int64
          5   complete  701 non-null    bool
         dtypes: bool(1), float64(4), int64(1)
         memory usage: 33.5 KB

In [42]: spread = 0.00012  ❷

In [43]: mean = raw['c'].mean()  ❸
```

```
In [44]: ptc = spread / mean  ❹
         ptc  ❹
Out[44]: 0.00010599557439495706

In [45]: raw['c'].plot(figsize=(10, 6), legend=True);
```

❶ Connects to the API and retrieves the data.

❷ Specifies the average bid-ask spread.

❸ Calculates the mean closing price for the data set.

❹ Calculates the average proportional transactions costs given the average spread
    and the average mid closing price.

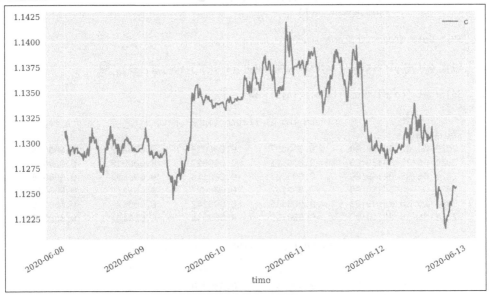

Figure 10-4. EUR/USD exchange rate (10-minute bars)

The ML-based strategy uses a number of time series features, such as the log return
and the minimum and the maximum of the closing price. In addition, the features
data is lagged. In other words, the ML algorithm shall learn from historical patterns
as embodied by the lagged features data:

```
In [46]: data = pd.DataFrame(raw['c'])

In [47]: data.columns = [instrument,]

In [48]: window = 20  ❶
         data['return'] = np.log(data / data.shift(1))  ❷
```

```
         data['vol'] = data['return'].rolling(window).std()   ❸
         data['mom'] = np.sign(data['return'].rolling(window).mean())   ❹
         data['sma'] = data[instrument].rolling(window).mean()   ❺
         data['min'] = data[instrument].rolling(window).min()   ❻
         data['max'] = data[instrument].rolling(window).max()   ❼

In [49]: data.dropna(inplace=True)

In [50]: lags = 6   ❽

In [51]: features = ['return', 'vol', 'mom', 'sma', 'min', 'max']   ❽

In [52]: cols = []
         for f in features:
             for lag in range(1, lags + 1):
                 col = f'{f}_lag_{lag}'
                 data[col] = data[f].shift(lag)   ❽
                 cols.append(col)

In [53]: data.dropna(inplace=True)

In [54]: data['direction'] = np.where(data['return'] > 0, 1, -1)   ❾

In [55]: data[cols].iloc[:lags, :lags]   ❿
Out[55]:
                       return_lag_1  return_lag_2  return_lag_3  return_lag_4 \
     time
     2020-06-08 04:20:00     0.000097      0.000018     -0.000452      0.000035
     2020-06-08 04:30:00    -0.000115      0.000097      0.000018     -0.000452
     2020-06-08 04:40:00     0.000027     -0.000115      0.000097      0.000018
     2020-06-08 04:50:00    -0.000142      0.000027     -0.000115      0.000097
     2020-06-08 05:00:00     0.000035     -0.000142      0.000027     -0.000115
     2020-06-08 05:10:00    -0.000159      0.000035     -0.000142      0.000027

                       return_lag_5  return_lag_6
     time
     2020-06-08 04:20:00     0.000000      0.000009
     2020-06-08 04:30:00     0.000035      0.000000
     2020-06-08 04:40:00    -0.000452      0.000035
     2020-06-08 04:50:00     0.000018     -0.000452
     2020-06-08 05:00:00     0.000097      0.000018
     2020-06-08 05:10:00    -0.000115      0.000097
```

❶ Specifies the window length for certain features.

❷ Calculates the log returns from the closing prices.

❸ Calculates the rolling volatility.

❹ Derives the time series momentum as the mean of the recent log returns.

❺ Calculates the simple moving average.

❻ Calculates the rolling maximum value.

❼ Calculates the rolling minimum value.

❽ Adds the lagged features data to the `DataFrame` object.

❾ Defines the labels data as the market direction (+1 or *up* and -1 or *down*).

❿ Shows a small sub-set from the resulting lagged features data.

Given the features and label data, different supervised learning algorithms could now be applied. In what follows, a so-called *AdaBoost algorithm* for classification is used from the `scikit-learn` ML package (see `AdaBoostClassifier` (*https://oreil.ly/WIANy*)). The idea of boosting in the context of classification is to use an *ensemble* of base classifiers to arrive at a superior predictor that is supposed to be less prone to overfitting (see "Data Snooping and Overfitting" on page 111). As the base classifier, a *decision tree classification algorithm* from `scikit-learn` is used (see `DecisionTree Classifier` (*https://oreil.ly/wb-wh*)).

The code trains and tests the algorithmic trading strategy based on a sequential train-test split. The accuracy scores of the model for the training and test data are both significantly above 50%. Instead of accuracy scores, one would also speak in a financial trading context of the *hit ratio* of the trading strategy (that is, the number of winning trades compared to all trades). Since the hit ratio is significantly greater than 50%, this might indicate—in the context of the Kelly criterion—a statistical edge compared to a random walk setting:

```
In [56]: from sklearn.metrics import accuracy_score
         from sklearn.tree import DecisionTreeClassifier
         from sklearn.ensemble import AdaBoostClassifier

In [57]: n_estimators=15        ❶
         random_state=100       ❶
         max_depth=2   ❶
         min_samples_leaf=15     ❶
         subsample=0.33   ❶

In [58]: dtc = DecisionTreeClassifier(random_state=random_state,
                                      max_depth=max_depth,
                                      min_samples_leaf=min_samples_leaf)   ❷

In [59]: model = AdaBoostClassifier(base_estimator=dtc,
                                    n_estimators=n_estimators,
                                    random_state=random_state)   ❸
```

```
In [60]: split = int(len(data) * 0.7)

In [61]: train = data.iloc[:split].copy()

In [62]: mu, std = train.mean(), train.std()     ❹

In [63]: train_ = (train - mu) / std     ❹

In [64]: model.fit(train_[cols], train['direction'])     ❺
Out[64]: AdaBoostClassifier(algorithm='SAMME.R',
             base_estimator=DecisionTreeClassifier(ccp_alpha=0.0,
             class_weight=None,
             criterion='gini',
             max_depth=2,
             max_features=None,
             max_leaf_nodes=None,
             min_impurity_decrease=0.0,
             min_impurity_split=None,
             min_samples_leaf=15,
             min_samples_split=2,
             min_weight_fraction_leaf=0.0,
             presort='deprecated',
             random_state=100,
             splitter='best'),
             learning_rate=1.0, n_estimators=15, random_state=100)

In [65]: accuracy_score(train['direction'], model.predict(train_[cols]))     ❻
Out[65]: 0.8050847457627118

In [66]: test = data.iloc[split:].copy()     ❼

In [67]: test_ = (test - mu) / std     ❼

In [68]: test['position'] = model.predict(test_[cols])     ❽

In [69]: accuracy_score(test['direction'], test['position'])     ❾
Out[69]: 0.5665024630541872
```

❶ Specifies major parameters for the ML algorithm (see the references for the model classes provided previously).

❷ Instantiates the base classification algorithm (decision tree).

❸ Instantiates the AdaBoost classification algorithm.

❹ Applies Gaussian normalization to the *training* features data set.

❺ Fits the model based on the training data set.

❻   Shows the accuracy of the predictions from the trained model *in-sample* (training data set).

❼   Applies Gaussian normalization to the *testing* features data set (using the parameters from the training features data set).

❽   Generates the predictions for the test data set.

❾   Shows the accuracy of the predictions from the trained model *out-of-sample* (test data set).

It is well known that the hit ratio is only one side of the coin of success in financial trading. The other side comprises, among other things, getting the important trades right, as well as the transactions costs implied by the trading strategy.[2] To this end, only a formal vectorized backtesting approach allows one to judge the quality of the trading strategy. The following code takes into account the proportional transaction costs based on the average bid-ask spread. Figure 10-5 compares the performance of the algorithmic trading strategy (without and with proportional transaction costs) to the performance of the passive benchmark investment:

```
In [70]: test['strategy'] = test['position'] * test['return']   ❶

In [71]: sum(test['position'].diff() != 0)   ❷
Out[71]: 77

In [72]: test['strategy_tc'] = np.where(test['position'].diff() != 0,
                                        test['strategy'] - ptc,   ❸
                                        test['strategy'])

In [73]: test[['return', 'strategy', 'strategy_tc']].sum(
                ).apply(np.exp)
Out[73]: return        0.990182
         strategy      1.015827
         strategy_tc   1.007570
         dtype: float64

In [74]: test[['return', 'strategy', 'strategy_tc']].cumsum(
                ).apply(np.exp).plot(figsize=(10, 6));
```

---

2 It is a stylized empirical fact that it is of paramount importance for the investment and trading performance to get the largest market movements right (that is, the biggest winner *and* loser movements). This aspect is neatly illustrated in Figure 10-5, which shows that the trading strategy gets a large downwards movement in the underlying instrument correct, leading to a larger jump for the trading strategy.

❶ Derives the log returns for the ML-based algorithmic trading strategy.

❷ Calculates the number of trades implied by the trading strategy based on changes in the position.

❸ Whenever a trade takes place, the proportional transaction costs are subtracted from the strategy's log return on that day.

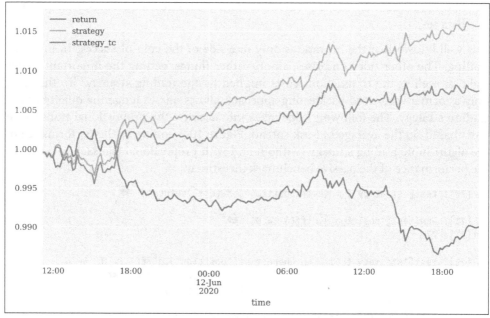

Figure 10-5. Gross performance of EUR/USD exchange rate and algorithmic trading strategy (before and after transaction costs)

 Vectorized backtesting has its limits with regard to how close to market realities strategies can be tested. For example, it does not allow one to include fixed transaction costs per trade directly. One could, as an approximation, take a multiple of the average proportional transaction costs (based on average position sizes) to account indirectly for fixed transactions costs. However, this would not be precise in general. If a higher degree of precision is required, other approaches, such as *event-based backtesting* (see Chapter 6) with explicit loops over every bar of the price data, need to be applied.

Optimal Leverage

Equipped with the trading strategy's log returns data, the mean and variance values can be calculated in order to derive the optimal leverage according to the Kelly criterion. The code that follows scales the numbers to annualized values, although this does not change the optimal leverage values according to the Kelly criterion since the mean return and the variance scale with the same factor:

```
In [75]: mean = test[['return', 'strategy_tc']].mean() * len(data) * 52    ❶
         mean
Out[75]: return       -1.705965
         strategy_tc   1.304023
         dtype: float64

In [76]: var = test[['return', 'strategy_tc']].var() * len(data) * 52    ❷
         var
Out[76]: return        0.011306
         strategy_tc   0.011370
         dtype: float64

In [77]: vol = var ** 0.5    ❸
         vol
Out[77]: return        0.106332
         strategy_tc   0.106631
         dtype: float64

In [78]: mean / var    ❹
Out[78]: return       -150.884961
         strategy_tc   114.687875
         dtype: float64

In [79]: mean / var * 0.5    ❺
Out[79]: return       -75.442481
         strategy_tc   57.343938
         dtype: float64
```

❶ Annualized mean returns.

❷ Annualized variances.

❸ Annualized volatilities.

❹ Optimal leverage according to the Kelly criterion ("full Kelly").

❺ Optimal leverage according to the Kelly criterion ("half Kelly").

Using the "half Kelly" criterion, the optimal leverage for the trading strategy is above 50. With a number of brokers, such as Oanda, and certain financial instruments, such as foreign exchange pairs and contracts for difference (CFDs), such leverage ratios

are feasible, even for retail traders. Figure 10-6 shows, in comparison, the performance of the trading strategy with transaction costs for different leverage values:

```
In [80]: to_plot = ['return', 'strategy_tc']

In [81]: for lev in [10, 20, 30, 40, 50]:
             label = 'lstrategy_tc_%d' % lev
             test[label] = test['strategy_tc'] * lev    ❶
             to_plot.append(label)

In [82]: test[to_plot].cumsum().apply(np.exp).plot(figsize=(10, 6));
```

❶ Scales the strategy returns for different leverage values.

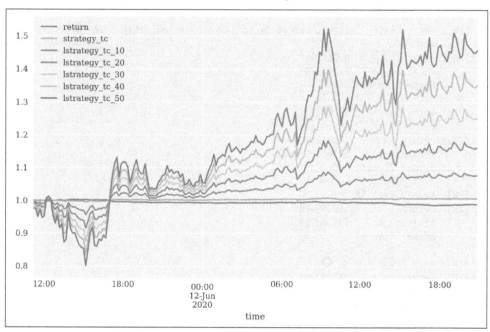

*Figure 10-6. Gross performance of the algorithmic trading strategy for different leverage
values*

Leverage increases risks associated with trading strategies significantly. Traders should read the risk disclaimers and regulations
carefully. A positive backtesting performance is also no guarantee
whatsoever for future performances. All results shown are illustra-
tive only and are meant to demonstrate the application of programming and analytics approaches. In some jurisdictions, such as in
Germany, leverage ratios are capped for retail traders based on different groups of financial instruments.

Risk Analysis

Since leverage increases the risk associated with a certain trading strategy considerably, a more in-depth risk analysis seems in order. The risk analysis that follows assumes a leverage ratio of 30. First, the maximum drawdown and the longest drawdown period shall be calculated. *Maximum drawdown* is the largest loss (dip) after a recent high. Accordingly, the *longest drawdown period* is the longest period that the trading strategy needs to get back to a recent high. The analysis assumes that the initial equity position is 3,333 EUR leading to an initial position size of 100,000 EUR for a leverage ratio of 30. It also assumes that there are no adjustments with regard to the equity over time, no matter what the performance is:

```
In [83]: equity = 3333   ❶

In [84]: risk = pd.DataFrame(test['lstrategy_tc_30'])   ❷

In [85]: risk['equity'] = risk['lstrategy_tc_30'].cumsum(
                                ).apply(np.exp) * equity   ❸

In [86]: risk['cummax'] = risk['equity'].cummax()   ❹

In [87]: risk['drawdown'] = risk['cummax'] - risk['equity']   ❺

In [88]: risk['drawdown'].max()   ❻
Out[88]: 511.38321383258017

In [89]: t_max = risk['drawdown'].idxmax()   ❼
         t_max   ❼
Out[89]: Timestamp('2020-06-12 10:30:00')
```

❶ The initial equity.

❷ The relevant log returns time series…

❸ …scaled by the initial equity.

❹ The cumulative maximum values over time.

❺ The drawdown values over time.

❻ The maximum drawdown value.

❼ The point in time when it happens.

Technically, a new high is characterized by a drawdown value of 0. The drawdown period is the time between two such highs. Figure 10-7 visualizes both the maximum drawdown and the drawdown periods:

```
In [90]: temp = risk['drawdown'][risk['drawdown'] == 0]  ❶

In [91]: periods = (temp.index[1:].to_pydatetime() -
                    temp.index[:-1].to_pydatetime())  ❷

In [92]: periods[20:30]  ❷
Out[92]: array([datetime.timedelta(seconds=600),
           datetime.timedelta(seconds=1200),
          datetime.timedelta(seconds=1200), datetime.timedelta(seconds=1200)],
            dtype=object)

In [93]: t_per = periods.max()  ❸

In [94]: t_per  ❸
Out[94]: datetime.timedelta(seconds=26400)

In [95]: t_per.seconds / 60 / 60  ❹
Out[95]: 7.333333333333333

In [96]: risk[['equity', 'cummax']].plot(figsize=(10, 6))
         plt.axvline(t_max, c='r', alpha=0.5);
```

❶ Identifies highs for which the drawdown must be 0.

❷ Calculates the `timedelta` values between all highs.

❸ The longest drawdown period in *seconds*…

❹ …transformed to *hours*.

Another important risk measure is *value-at-risk* (VaR). It is quoted as a currency amount and represents the maximum loss to be expected given both a certain time horizon and a confidence level.

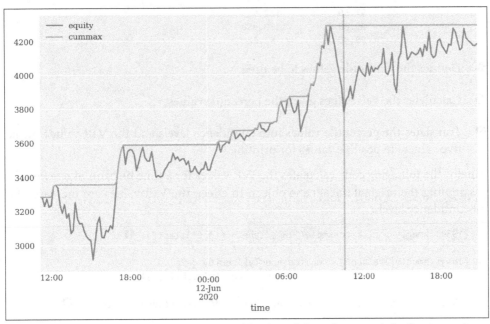

Figure 10-7. Maximum drawdown (vertical line) and drawdown periods (horizontal lines)

The following code derives VaR values based on the log returns of the equity position for the leveraged trading strategy over time for different confidence levels. The time interval is fixed to the bar length of ten minutes:

```
In [97]: import scipy.stats as scs

In [98]: percs = [0.01, 0.1, 1., 2.5, 5.0, 10.0]   ❶

In [99]: risk['return'] = np.log(risk['equity'] /
                                 risk['equity'].shift(1))

In [100]: VaR = scs.scoreatpercentile(equity * risk['return'], percs)   ❷

In [101]: def print_var():
              print('{}    {}'.format('Confidence Level', 'Value-at-Risk'))
              print(33 * '-')
              for pair in zip(percs, VaR):
                  print('{:16.2f} {:16.3f}'.format(100 - pair[0], -pair[1]))   ❸

In [102]: print_var()   ❸
          Confidence Level    Value-at-Risk
          ---------------------------------
                    99.99          162.570
                    99.90          161.348
                    99.00          132.382
```

```
                    97.50                122.913
                    95.00                100.950
                    90.00                 62.622
```

❶ Defines the percentile values to be used.

❷ Calculates the VaR values given the percentile values.

❸ Translates the percentile values into confidence levels and the VaR values (negative values) to positive values for printing.

Finally, the following code calculates the VaR values for a time horizon of *one hour* by resampling the original `DataFrame` object. In effect, the VaR values are increased for all confidence levels:

```
In [103]: hourly = risk.resample('1H', label='right').last()   ❶

In [104]: hourly['return'] = np.log(hourly['equity'] /
                                    hourly['equity'].shift(1))

In [105]: VaR = scs.scoreatpercentile(equity * hourly['return'], percs)   ❷

In [106]: print_var()
          Confidence Level    Value-at-Risk
          -------------------------------
                    99.99                252.460
                    99.90                251.744
                    99.00                244.593
                    97.50                232.674
                    95.00                125.498
                    90.00                 61.701
```

❶ Resamples the data from 10-minute to 1-hour bars.

❷ Calculates the VaR values given the percentile values.

Persisting the Model Object

Once the algorithmic trading strategy is accepted based on the backtesting, leveraging, and risk analysis results, the model object and other relevant algorithm components might be persisted for later use in deployment. It embodies now the ML-based trading strategy or the trading algorithm.

```
In [107]: import pickle

In [108]: algorithm = {'model': model, 'mu': mu, 'std': std}

In [109]: pickle.dump(algorithm, open('algorithm.pkl', 'wb'))
```

Online Algorithm

The trading algorithm tested so far is an *offline algorithm*. Such algorithms use a complete data set to solve a problem at hand. The problem has been to train an AdaBoost classification algorithm based on a decision tree as the base classifier, a number of different time series features, and directional label data. In practice, when deploying the trading algorithm in financial markets, it must consume data piece by piece as it arrives to predict the direction of the market movement for the next time interval (bar). This section makes use of the persisted model object from the previous section and embeds it into a streaming data context.

The code that transforms the *offline* trading algorithm into an *online* trading algorithm mainly addresses the following issues:

Tick data
> Tick data arrives in real time and is to be processed in real time, such as to be collected in a DataFrame object.

Resampling
> The tick data is to be resampled to the appropriate bar length given the trading algorithm. For illustration, a shorter bar length is used for resampling than for the training and backtesting.

Prediction
> The trading algorithm generates a prediction for the direction of the market movement over the relevant time interval that by nature lies in the future.

Orders
> Given the current position and the prediction ("signal") generated by the algorithm, an order is placed or the position is kept unchanged.

Chapter 8, and in particular "Working with Streaming Data" on page 236, shows how to retrieve tick data from the Oanda API in real time. The basic approach is to redefine the .on_success() method of the tpqoa.tpqoa class to implement the trading logic.

First, the persisted trading algorithm is loaded; it represents the trading logic to be followed. It consists of the trained model itself and the parameters for the normalization of the features data, which are integral parts of the algorithm:

```
In [110]: algorithm = pickle.load(open('algorithm.pkl', 'rb'))

In [111]: algorithm['model']
Out[111]: AdaBoostClassifier(algorithm='SAMME.R',
          base_estimator=DecisionTreeClassifier(ccp_alpha=0.0,
          class_weight=None,
          criterion='gini',
          max_depth=2,
```

```
                max_features=None,
                max_leaf_nodes=None,
                min_impurity_decrease=0.0,
                min_impurity_split=None,
                min_samples_leaf=15,
                min_samples_split=2,
                min_weight_fraction_leaf=0.0,
                presort='deprecated',
                random_state=100,
                splitter='best'),
                learning_rate=1.0, n_estimators=15, random_state=100)
```

In the following code, the new class `MLTrader`, which inherits from `tpqoa.tpqoa` and which, via the `.on_success()` and additional helper methods, transforms the trading algorithm into a real-time context. It is the transformation of the *offline algorithm* to a so-called *online algorithm*:

```
In [112]: class MLTrader(tpqoa.tpqoa):
              def __init__(self, config_file, algorithm):
                  super(MLTrader, self).__init__(config_file)
                  self.model = algorithm['model']       ❶
                  self.mu = algorithm['mu']             ❶
                  self.std = algorithm['std']           ❶
                  self.units = 100000                   ❷
                  self.position = 0                     ❸
                  self.bar = '5s'                       ❹
                  self.window = 2                       ❺
                  self.lags = 6                         ❻
                  self.min_length = self.lags + self.window + 1
                  self.features = ['return', 'sma', 'min', 'max', 'vol', 'mom']
                  self.raw_data = pd.DataFrame()
              def prepare_features(self):               ❼
                  self.data['return'] = np.log(self.data['mid'] /
                                               self.data['mid'].shift(1))
                  self.data['sma'] = self.data['mid'].rolling(self.window).mean()
                  self.data['min'] = self.data['mid'].rolling(self.window).min()
                  self.data['mom'] = np.sign(
                      self.data['return'].rolling(self.window).mean())
                  self.data['max'] = self.data['mid'].rolling(self.window).max()
                  self.data['vol'] = self.data['return'].rolling(
                      self.window).std()
                  self.data.dropna(inplace=True)
                  self.data[self.features] -= self.mu
                  self.data[self.features] /= self.std
                  self.cols = []
                  for f in self.features:
                      for lag in range(1, self.lags + 1):
                          col = f'{f}_lag_{lag}'
                          self.data[col] = self.data[f].shift(lag)
                          self.cols.append(col)
              def on_success(self, time, bid, ask):     ❽
                  df = pd.DataFrame({'bid': float(bid), 'ask': float(ask)},
```

```
                index=[pd.Timestamp(time).tz_localize(None)])
self.raw_data = self.raw_data.append(df)
self.data = self.raw_data.resample(self.bar,
                        label='right').last().ffill()
self.data = self.data.iloc[:-1]
if len(self.data) > self.min_length:
    self.min_length +=1
    self.data['mid'] = (self.data['bid'] +
                        self.data['ask']) / 2
    self.prepare_features()
    features = self.data[
        self.cols].iloc[-1].values.reshape(1, -1)
    signal = self.model.predict(features)[0]
    print(f'NEW SIGNAL: {signal}', end='\r')
    if self.position in [0, -1] and signal == 1:    ❾
        print('*** GOING LONG ***')
        self.create_order(self.stream_instrument,
                    units=(1 - self.position) * self.units)
        self.position = 1
    elif self.position in [0, 1] and signal == -1:    ❿
        print('*** GOING SHORT ***')
        self.create_order(self.stream_instrument,
                    units=-(1 + self.position) * self.units)
        self.position = -1
```

❶ The trained AdaBoost model object and the normalization parameters.

❷ The number of units traded.

❸ The initial, neutral position.

❹ The bar length on which the algorithm is implemented.

❺ The length of the window for selected features.

❻ The number of lags (must be in line with algorithm training).

❼ The method that generates the lagged features data.

❽ The redefined method that embodies the trading logic.

❾ Check for a long signal and long trade.

❿ Check for a short signal and short trade.

With the new class MLTrader, automated trading is made simple. A few lines of code are enough in an interactive context. The parameters are set such that the first order is placed after a short while. In reality, however, all parameters must, of course, be in line with original ones from the research and backtesting phase. They could, for example, also be persisted on disk and be read with the algorithm:

```
In [113]: mlt = MLTrader('../pyalgo.cfg', algorithm)  ❶
```

```
In [114]: mlt.stream_data(instrument, stop=500)  ❷
          print('*** CLOSING OUT ***')
          mlt.create_order(mlt.stream_instrument,
                           units=-mlt.position * mlt.units)  ❸
```

❶ Instantiates the trading object.

❷ Starts the streaming, data processing, and trading.

❸ Closes out the final open position.

The preceding code generates an output similar to the following:

```
*** GOING LONG ***


{'id': '1735', 'time': '2020-08-19T14:46:15.552233563Z', 'userID':
13834683, 'accountID': '101-004-13834683-001', 'batchID': '1734',
'requestID': '42730658849646182', 'type': 'ORDER_FILL', 'orderID':
'1734', 'instrument': 'EUR_USD', 'units': '100000.0',
'gainQuoteHomeConversionFactor': '0.835983419025',
'lossQuoteHomeConversionFactor': '0.844385262432', 'price': 1.1903,
'fullVWAP': 1.1903, 'fullPrice': {'type': 'PRICE', 'bids': [{'price':
1.19013, 'liquidity': '10000000'}], 'asks': [{'price': 1.1903,
'liquidity': '10000000'}], 'closeoutBid': 1.19013, 'closeoutAsk':
1.1903}, 'reason': 'MARKET_ORDER', 'pl': '0.0', 'financing': '0.0',
'commission': '0.0', 'guaranteedExecutionFee': '0.0',
'accountBalance': '98507.7425', 'tradeOpened': {'tradeID': '1735',
'units': '100000.0', 'price': 1.1903, 'guaranteedExecutionFee': '0.0',
'halfSpreadCost': '7.1416', 'initialMarginRequired': '3330.0'},
'halfSpreadCost': '7.1416'}

*** GOING SHORT ***


{'id': '1737', 'time': '2020-08-19T14:48:10.510726213Z', 'userID':
13834683, 'accountID': '101-004-13834683-001', 'batchID': '1736',
'requestID': '42730659332312267', 'type': 'ORDER_FILL', 'orderID':
'1736', 'instrument': 'EUR_USD', 'units': '-200000.0',
'gainQuoteHomeConversionFactor': '0.835885095595',
'lossQuoteHomeConversionFactor': '0.844285950827', 'price': 1.19029,
'fullVWAP': 1.19029, 'fullPrice': {'type': 'PRICE', 'bids': [{'price':
1.19029, 'liquidity': '10000000'}], 'asks': [{'price': 1.19042,
'liquidity': '10000000'}], 'closeoutBid': 1.19029, 'closeoutAsk':
1.19042}, 'reason': 'MARKET_ORDER', 'pl': '-0.8443', 'financing':
'0.0', 'commission': '0.0', 'guaranteedExecutionFee': '0.0',
'accountBalance': '98506.8982', 'tradeOpened': {'tradeID': '1737',
```

'units': '-100000.0', 'price': 1.19029, 'guaranteedExecutionFee':
'0.0', 'halfSpreadCost': '5.4606', 'initialMarginRequired': '3330.0'},
'tradesClosed': [{'tradeID': '1735', 'units': '-100000.0', 'price':
1.19029, 'realizedPL': '-0.8443', 'financing': '0.0',
'guaranteedExecutionFee': '0.0', 'halfSpreadCost': '5.4606'}],
'halfSpreadCost': '10.9212'}

*** GOING LONG ***

{'id': '1739', 'time': '2020-08-19T14:48:15.529680632Z', 'userID':
13834683, 'accountID': '101-004-13834683-001', 'batchID': '1738',
'requestID': '42730659353297789', 'type': 'ORDER_FILL', 'orderID':
'1738', 'instrument': 'EUR_USD', 'units': '200000.0',
'gainQuoteHomeConversionFactor': '0.835835944263',
'lossQuoteHomeConversionFactor': '0.844236305512', 'price': 1.1905,
'fullVWAP': 1.1905, 'fullPrice': {'type': 'PRICE', 'bids': [{'price':
1.19035, 'liquidity': '10000000'}], 'asks': [{'price': 1.1905,
'liquidity': '10000000'}], 'closeoutBid': 1.19035, 'closeoutAsk':
1.1905}, 'reason': 'MARKET_ORDER', 'pl': '-17.729', 'financing':
'0.0', 'commission': '0.0', 'guaranteedExecutionFee': '0.0',
'accountBalance': '98489.1692', 'tradeOpened': {'tradeID': '1739',
'units': '100000.0', 'price': 1.1905, 'guaranteedExecutionFee': '0.0',
'halfSpreadCost': '6.3003', 'initialMarginRequired': '3330.0'},
'tradesClosed': [{'tradeID': '1737', 'units': '100000.0', 'price':
1.1905, 'realizedPL': '-17.729', 'financing': '0.0',
'guaranteedExecutionFee': '0.0', 'halfSpreadCost': '6.3003'}],
'halfSpreadCost': '12.6006'}

*** CLOSING OUT ***

{'id': '1741', 'time': '2020-08-19T14:49:11.976885485Z', 'userID':
13834683, 'accountID': '101-004-13834683-001', 'batchID': '1740',
'requestID': '42730659588338204', 'type': 'ORDER_FILL', 'orderID':
'1740', 'instrument': 'EUR_USD', 'units': '-100000.0',
'gainQuoteHomeConversionFactor': '0.835730636848',
'lossQuoteHomeConversionFactor': '0.844179939731', 'price': 1.19051,
'fullVWAP': 1.19051, 'fullPrice': {'type': 'PRICE', 'bids': [{'price':
1.19051, 'liquidity': '10000000'}], 'asks': [{'price': 1.19064,
'liquidity': '10000000'}], 'closeoutBid': 1.19051, 'closeoutAsk':
1.19064}, 'reason': 'MARKET_ORDER', 'pl': '0.8357', 'financing':
'0.0', 'commission': '0.0', 'guaranteedExecutionFee': '0.0',
'accountBalance': '98490.0049', 'tradesClosed': [{'tradeID': '1739',
'units': '-100000.0', 'price': 1.19051, 'realizedPL': '0.8357',
'financing': '0.0', 'guaranteedExecutionFee': '0.0', 'halfSpreadCost':
'5.4595'}], 'halfSpreadCost': '5.4595'}

Infrastructure and Deployment

Deploying an automated algorithmic trading strategy with real funds requires an appropriate infrastructure. Among other things, the infrastructure should satisfy the following:

Reliability

> The infrastructure on which to deploy an algorithmic trading strategy should allow for high availability (for example, 99.9% or higher) and should otherwise take care of reliability (automatic backups, redundancy of drives and web connections, and so on).

Performance

> Depending on the amount of data being processed and the computational demand the algorithms generate, the infrastructure must have enough CPU cores, working memory (RAM), and storage (SSD). In addition, the web connections should be fast enough.

Security

> The operating system and the applications that run on it should be protected by strong passwords, as well as SSL encryption and hard drive encryption. The hardware should be protected from fire, water, and unauthorized physical access.

Basically, these requirements can only be fulfilled by renting an appropriate infrastructure from a professional data center or a cloud provider. Own investments in the physical infrastructure to satisfy the aforementioned requirements can in general only be justified by the bigger, or even the biggest, players in the financial markets.

From a development and testing point of view, even the smallest Droplet (cloud instance) from DigitalOcean (*http://digitalocean.com*) is enough to get started. At the time of writing, such a Droplet costs 5 USD per month and is billed by the hour, created within minutes, and destroyed within seconds.[3]

How to set up a Droplet with DigitalOcean is explained in detail in Chapter 2 (specifically in "Using Cloud Instances" on page 36), with Bash scripts that can be adjusted to reflect individual requirements regarding Python packages, for example.

---

3 Use the link *http://bit.ly/do_sign_up* to get a 10 USD bonus on DigitalOcean when signing up for a new account.

Although the development and testing of automated algorithmic trading strategies is possible from a local computer (desktop, notebook, or similar), it is not appropriate for the deployment of automated strategies trading real money. A simple loss of the web connection or a brief power outage might bring down the whole algorithm, leaving, for example, unintended open positions in the portfolio. As another example, it would cause one to miss out on real-time tick data and end up with corrupted data sets, potentially leading to wrong signals and unintended trades and positions.

Logging and Monitoring

Assume now that the automated algorithmic trading strategy is to be deployed on a remote server (virtual cloud instance or dedicated server). Further assume that all required Python packages have been installed (see "Using Cloud Instances" on page 36) and that, for instance, Jupyter Lab is running securely (see Running a notebook server (*https://oreil.ly/cnBHE*)). What else needs to be considered from the algorithmic traders' point of view if they do not want to sit all day in front of the screen being logged in to the server?

This section addresses two important topics in this regard: *logging* and *real-time monitoring*. Logging persists information and events on disk for later inspection. It is standard practice in software application development and deployment. However, here the focus might be put instead on the financial side, logging important financial data and event information for later inspection and analysis. The same holds true for real-time monitoring making use of socket communication. Via sockets, a constant real-time stream of important financial aspects can be created that can then be retrieved and processed on a local computer, even if the deployment happens in the cloud.

"Automated Trading Strategy" on page 305 presents a Python script implementing all these aspects and making use of the code from "Online Algorithm" on page 291. The script brings the code in a shape that allows, for example, the *deployment* of the algorithmic trading strategy—sbased on the persisted algorithm object—son a remote server. It adds both *logging and monitoring* capabilities based on a custom function that, among other things, makes use of ZeroMQ (see *http://zeromq.org*) for socket communication. In combination with the short script from "Strategy Monitoring" on page 308, this allows for a remote real-time monitoring of the activity on a remote server.[4]

---

4 The logging approach used here is pretty simple in the form of a simple text file. It is easy to change the logging and persisting of, say, the relevant financial data in the form of a database or appropriate binary storage formats, such as HDF5 (see Chapter 3).

When the script from "Automated Trading Strategy" on page 305 is executed, either locally or remotely, the output that is logged and sent via the socket looks as follows:

```
2020-06-15 17:04:14.298653
================================================================================
NUMBER OF TICKS: 147 | NUMBER OF BARS: 49


================================================================================
MOST RECENT DATA
                     return_lag_1  return_lag_2  ...   max_lag_5   max_lag_6
2020-06-15 15:04:06      0.026508     -0.125253  ...   -1.703276   -1.700746
2020-06-15 15:04:08     -0.049373      0.026508  ...   -1.694419   -1.703276
2020-06-15 15:04:10     -0.077828     -0.049373  ...   -1.694419   -1.694419
2020-06-15 15:04:12      0.064448     -0.077828  ...   -1.705807   -1.694419
2020-06-15 15:04:14     -0.020918      0.064448  ...   -1.710869   -1.705807

[5 rows x 36 columns]


================================================================================
features:
[[-0.02091774  0.06444794 -0.07782834 -0.04937258  0.02650799 -0.12525265
  -2.06428556 -1.96568848 -2.16288147 -2.08071843 -1.94925692 -2.19574189
   0.92939697  0.92939697 -1.07368691  0.92939697 -1.07368691 -1.07368691
  -1.41861822 -1.42605902 -1.4294412  -1.42470615 -1.4274119  -1.42470615
  -1.05508516 -1.06879043 -1.06879043 -1.0619378  -1.06741991 -1.06741991
  -1.70580717 -1.70707253 -1.71339931 -1.7108686  -1.7108686  -1.70580717]]
position: 1
signal:   1


2020-06-15 17:04:14.402154
================================================================================
*** NO TRADE PLACED ***

*** END OF CYCLE ***


2020-06-15 17:04:16.199950
================================================================================


================================================================================
*** GOING NEUTRAL ***
```

```
{'id': '979', 'time': '2020-06-15T15:04:16.1380271118Z', 'userID': 13834683,
'accountID': '101-004-13834683-001', 'batchID': '978',
'requestID': '60721506683906591', 'type': 'ORDER_FILL', 'orderID': '978',
'instrument': 'EUR_USD', 'units': '-100000.0',
'gainQuoteHomeConversionFactor': '0.882420762903',
'lossQuoteHomeConversionFactor': '0.891289313284',
'price': 1.12751, 'fullVWAP': 1.12751, 'fullPrice': {'type': 'PRICE',
'bids': [{'price': 1.12751, 'liquidity': '10000000'}],
```

```
'asks': [{'price': 1.12765, 'liquidity': '10000000'}],
'closeoutBid': 1.12751, 'closeoutAsk': 1.12765}, 'reason': 'MARKET_ORDER',
'pl': '-3.5652', 'financing': '0.0', 'commission': '0.0',
'guaranteedExecutionFee': '0.0', 'accountBalance': '99259.7485',
'tradesClosed': [{'tradeID': '975', 'units': '-100000.0',
'price': 1.12751, 'realizedPL': '-3.5652', 'financing': '0.0',
'guaranteedExecutionFee': '0.0', 'halfSpreadCost': '6.208'}],
'halfSpreadCost': '6.208'}
```
===

Running the script from "Strategy Monitoring" on page 308 locally then allows for the real-time retrieval and processing of such information. Of course, it is easy to adjust the logging and streaming data to one's own requirements.[5] Furthermore, the trading script and the whole logic can be adjusted to include such elements as stop losses or take profit targets programmatically.

 Trading currency pairs and/or CFDs is associated with a number of financial risks. Implementing an algorithmic trading strategy for such instruments automatically leads to a number of additional risks. Among them are flaws in the trading and/or execution logic, as well as technical risks including problems associated with socket communication, delayed retrieval, or even loss of tick data during the deployment. Therefore, before one deploys a trading strategy in automated fashion one should make sure that all associated market, execution, operational, technical, and other risks have been identified, evaluated, and properly addressed. The code presented in this chapter is only for technical illustration purposes.

Visual Step-by-Step Overview

This final section provides a step-by-step overview in screenshots. While the previous sections are based on the FXCM trading platform, the visual overview is based on the Oanda trading platform.

Configuring Oanda Account

The first step is to set up an account with Oanda (or any other trading platform to this end) and to set the correct leverage ratio for the account according to the Kelly criterion and as shown in Figure 10-8.

---

5 Note that the socket communication, as implemented in the two scripts, is not encrypted and is sending plain text over the web, which might represent a security risk in production.

Figure 10-8. Setting leverage on Oanda

Setting Up the Hardware

The second step is to create a DigitalOcean droplet, as shown in Figure 10-9.

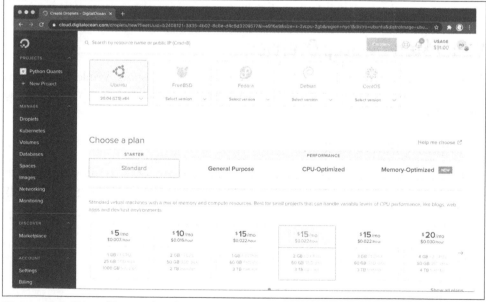

Figure 10-9. DigitalOcean droplet

Setting Up the Python Environment

The third step is to put all the software on the droplet (see Figure 10-10) in order to set up the infrastructure. When it all works fine, you can create a new Jupyter Notebook and start your interactive Python session (see Figure 10-11).

Figure 10-10. Installing Python and packages

Figure 10-11. Testing Jupyter Lab

Uploading the Code

The fourth step is to upload the Python scripts for automated trading and real-time monitoring, as shown in Figure 10-12. The configuration file with the account credentials also needs to be uploaded.

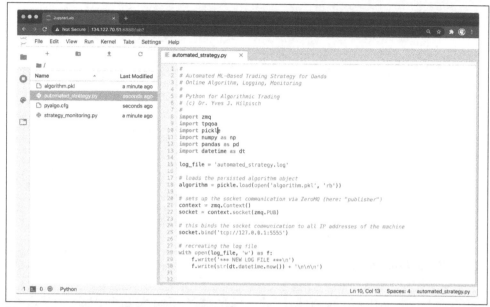

Figure 10-12. Uploading Python code files

Running the Code

The fifth step is to run the Python script for automated trading, as shown in Figure 10-13. Figure 10-14 shows a trade that the Python script has initiated.

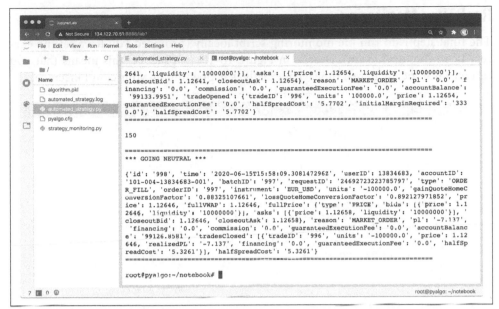

Figure 10-13. Running the Python script

Figure 10-14. A trade initiated by the Python script

Real-Time Monitoring

The final step is to run the monitoring script locally (provided you have set the correct IP in the local script), as seen in Figure 10-15. In practice, this means that you can monitor locally in real time what exactly is happening on your cloud instance.

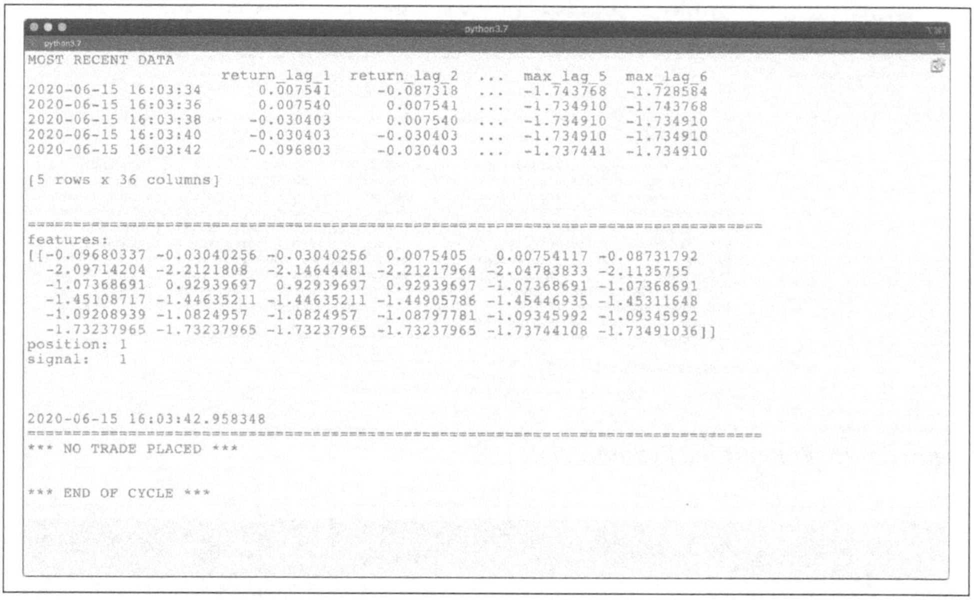

```
python3.7
python3.7
MOST RECENT DATA
                       return_lag_1  return_lag_2  ...   max_lag_5   max_lag_6
2020-06-15 16:03:34        0.007541     -0.087318  ...   -1.743768   -1.728584
2020-06-15 16:03:36        0.007540      0.007541  ...   -1.734910   -1.743768
2020-06-15 16:03:38       -0.030403      0.007540  ...   -1.734910   -1.734910
2020-06-15 16:03:40       -0.030403     -0.030403  ...   -1.734910   -1.734910
2020-06-15 16:03:42       -0.096803     -0.030403  ...   -1.737441   -1.734910

[5 rows x 36 columns]


==============================================================================
features:
[[-0.09680337 -0.03040256 -0.03040256  0.0075405   0.00754117 -0.08731792
  -2.09714204 -2.2121808  -2.14644481 -2.21217964 -2.04783833 -2.1135755
  -1.07368691  0.92939697  0.92939697  0.92939697 -1.07368691 -1.07368691
  -1.45108717 -1.44635211 -1.44635211 -1.44905786 -1.45446935 -1.45311648
  -1.09208939 -1.0824957  -1.0824957  -1.08797781 -1.09345992 -1.09345992
  -1.73237965 -1.73237965 -1.73237965 -1.73237965 -1.73744108 -1.73491036]]
position: 1
signal:  1


2020-06-15 16:03:42.958348
==============================================================================
*** NO TRADE PLACED ***

*** END OF CYCLE ***
```

Figure 10-15. Local real-time monitoring via socket

Conclusions

This chapter is about the deployment of an algorithmic trading strategy in automated fashion, based on a classification algorithm from machine learning to predict the direction of market movements. It addresses such important topics as capital management (based on the Kelly criterion), vectorized backtesting for performance and risk, the transformation of offline to online trading algorithms, an appropriate infrastructure for deployment, and logging and monitoring during deployment.

The topic of this chapter is complex and requires a broad skill set from the algorithmic trading practitioner. On the other hand, having RESTful APIs for algorithmic trading available, such as the one from Oanda, simplifies the automation task considerably since the core part boils down mainly to making use of the capabilities of the Python wrapper package tpqoa for tick data retrieval and order placement. Around this core, elements to mitigate operational and technical risks should be added as far as appropriate and possible.

References and Further Resources

Papers cited in this chapter:

Rotando, Louis, and Edward Thorp. 1992. "The Kelly Criterion and the Stock Market." *The American Mathematical Monthly* 99 (10): 922-931.

Hung, Jane. 2010. "Betting with the Kelly Criterion." *http://bit.ly/betting_with_kelly*.

Python Script

This section contains Python scripts used in this chapter.

Automated Trading Strategy

The following Python script contains the code for the automated deployment of the ML-based trading strategy, as discussed and backtested in this chapter:

```
#
# Automated ML-Based Trading Strategy for Oanda
# Online Algorithm, Logging, Monitoring
#
# Python for Algorithmic Trading
# (c) Dr. Yves J. Hilpisch
#
import zmq
import tpqoa
import pickle
import numpy as np
import pandas as pd
import datetime as dt

log_file = 'automated_strategy.log'

# loads the persisted algorithm object
algorithm = pickle.load(open('algorithm.pkl', 'rb'))

# sets up the socket communication via ZeroMQ (here: "publisher")
context = zmq.Context()
socket = context.socket(zmq.PUB)

# this binds the socket communication to all IP addresses of the machine
socket.bind('tcp://0.0.0.0:5555')

# recreating the log file
with open(log_file, 'w') as f:
    f.write('*** NEW LOG FILE ***\n')
    f.write(str(dt.datetime.now()) + '\n\n\n')
```

```python
def logger_monitor(message, time=True, sep=True):
    ''' Custom logger and monitor function.
    '''
    with open(log_file, 'a') as f:
        t = str(dt.datetime.now())
        msg = ''
        if time:
            msg += '\n' + t + '\n'
        if sep:
            msg += 80 * '=' + '\n'
        msg += message + '\n\n'
        # sends the message via the socket
        socket.send_string(msg)
        # writes the message to the log file
        f.write(msg)


class MLTrader(tpqoa.tpqoa):
    def __init__(self, config_file, algorithm):
        super(MLTrader, self).__init__(config_file)
        self.model = algorithm['model']
        self.mu = algorithm['mu']
        self.std = algorithm['std']
        self.units = 100000
        self.position = 0
        self.bar = '2s'
        self.window = 2
        self.lags = 6
        self.min_length = self.lags + self.window + 1
        self.features = ['return', 'vol', 'mom', 'sma', 'min', 'max']
        self.raw_data = pd.DataFrame()

    def prepare_features(self):
        self.data['return'] = np.log(
            self.data['mid'] / self.data['mid'].shift(1))
        self.data['vol'] = self.data['return'].rolling(self.window).std()
        self.data['mom'] = np.sign(
            self.data['return'].rolling(self.window).mean())
        self.data['sma'] = self.data['mid'].rolling(self.window).mean()
        self.data['min'] = self.data['mid'].rolling(self.window).min()
        self.data['max'] = self.data['mid'].rolling(self.window).max()
        self.data.dropna(inplace=True)
        self.data[self.features] -= self.mu
        self.data[self.features] /= self.std
        self.cols = []
        for f in self.features:
            for lag in range(1, self.lags + 1):
                col = f'{f}_lag_{lag}'
                self.data[col] = self.data[f].shift(lag)
                self.cols.append(col)

    def report_trade(self, pos, order):
```

```python
    ''' Prints, logs, and sends trade data.
    '''
    out = '\n\n' + 80 * '=' + '\n'
    out += '*** GOING {} *** \n'.format(pos) + '\n'
    out += str(order) + '\n'
    out += 80 * '=' + '\n'
    logger_monitor(out)
    print(out)

def on_success(self, time, bid, ask):
    print(self.ticks, 20 * ' ', end='\r')
    df = pd.DataFrame({'bid': float(bid), 'ask': float(ask)},
                      index=[pd.Timestamp(time).tz_localize(None)])
    self.raw_data = self.raw_data.append(df)
    self.data = self.raw_data.resample(
        self.bar, label='right').last().ffill()
    self.data = self.data.iloc[:-1]
    if len(self.data) > self.min_length:
        logger_monitor('NUMBER OF TICKS: {} | '.format(self.ticks) +
                       'NUMBER OF BARS: {}'.format(self.min_length))
        self.min_length += 1
        self.data['mid'] = (self.data['bid'] + self.data['ask']) / 2
        self.prepare_features()
        features = self.data[self.cols].iloc[-1].values.reshape(1, -1)
        signal = self.model.predict(features)[0]
        # logs and sends major financial information
        logger_monitor('MOST RECENT DATA\n' +
                       str(self.data[self.cols].tail()),
                       False)
        logger_monitor('features:\n' + str(features) + '\n' +
                       'position: ' + str(self.position) + '\n' +
                       'signal:   ' + str(signal), False)
        if self.position in [0, -1] and signal == 1:  # going long?
            order = self.create_order(self.stream_instrument,
                                      units=(1 - self.position) *
                                      self.units,
                                      suppress=True, ret=True)
            self.report_trade('LONG', order)
            self.position = 1
        elif self.position in [0, 1] and signal == -1:  # going short?
            order = self.create_order(self.stream_instrument,
                                      units=-(1 + self.position) *
                                      self.units,
                                      suppress=True, ret=True)
            self.report_trade('SHORT', order)
            self.position = -1
        else:  # no trade
            logger_monitor('*** NO TRADE PLACED ***')

        logger_monitor('*** END OF CYCLE ***\n\n', False, False)
```

```
if __name__ == '__main__':
    mlt = MLTrader('../pyalgo.cfg', algorithm)
    mlt.stream_data('EUR_USD', stop=150)
    order = mlt.create_order(mlt.stream_instrument,
                             units=-mlt.position * mlt.units,
                             suppress=True, ret=True)
    mlt.position = 0
    mlt.report_trade('NEUTRAL', order)
```

Strategy Monitoring

The following Python script contains code to remotely monitor the execution of the
Python script from "Automated Trading Strategy" on page 305.

```
#
# Automated ML-Based Trading Strategy for Oanda
# Strategy Monitoring via Socket Communication
#
# Python for Algorithmic Trading
# (c) Dr. Yves J. Hilpisch
#
import zmq

# sets up the socket communication via ZeroMQ (here: "subscriber")
context = zmq.Context()
socket = context.socket(zmq.SUB)

# adjust the IP address to reflect the remote location
socket.connect('tcp://134.122.70.51:5555')

# local IP address used for testing
# socket.connect('tcp://0.0.0.0:5555')


# configures the socket to retrieve every message
socket.setsockopt_string(zmq.SUBSCRIBE, '')

while True:
    msg = socket.recv_string()
    print(msg)
```

Python, NumPy, matplotlib, pandas

> Talk is cheap. Show me the code.
>
> —Linus Torvalds

Python has become a powerful programming language and has developed a vast ecosystem of helpful packages over the last couple of years. This appendix provides a concise overview of Python and three of the major pillars of the so-called *scientific or data science stack*:

- NumPy (see *https://numpy.org*)
- matplotlib (see *https://matplotlib.org*)
- pandas (see *https://pandas.pydata.org*)

NumPy provides performant array operations on large, homogeneous numerical data sets while pandas is primarily designed to handle tabular data, such as financial time series data, efficiently.

Such an introductory appendix—only addressing selected topics relevant to the rest of the contents of this book—cannot, of course, replace a thorough introduction to Python and the packages covered. However, if you are rather new to Python or programming in general you might get a first overview and a feeling of what Python is all about. If you are already experienced in another language typically used in quantitative finance (such as Matlab, R, C++, or VBA), you see what typical data structures, programming paradigms, and idioms in Python look like.

For a comprehensive overview of Python applied to finance see, Hilpisch (2018). Other, more general introductions to the language with a scientific and data analysis focus are VanderPlas (2017) and McKinney (2017).

Python Basics

This section introduces basic Python data types and structures, control structures, and some Python idioms.

Data Types

It is noteworthy that Python is generally a *dynamically typed system*, which means that types of objects are inferred from their contexts. Let us start with numbers:

```
In [1]: a = 3  ❶
```

```
In [2]: type(a)  ❷
Out[2]: int
```

```
In [3]: a.bit_length()  ❸
Out[3]: 2
```

```
In [4]: b = 5.  ❹
```

```
In [5]: type(b)
Out[5]: float
```

❶ Assigns the variable name a an integer value of 3.

❷ Looks up the type of a.

❸ Looks up the number of bits used to store the integer value.

❹ Assigns the variable name b a floating point value of 5.0.

Python can handle arbitrarily large integers, which is quite beneficial for number theoretical applications, for instance:

```
In [6]: c = 10 ** 100  ❶
```

```
In [7]: c
Out[7]: 10000000000000000000000000000000000000000000000000000000000000000000000
        0000000000000000000000000000000
```

```
In [8]: c.bit_length()  ❷
Out[8]: 333
```

❶ Assigns a "huge" integer value.

❷ Shows the number of bits used for the integer representation.

Arithmetic operations on these objects work as expected:

```
In [9]: 3 / 5.  ❶
Out[9]: 0.6

In [10]: a * b  ❷
Out[10]: 15.0

In [11]: a - b  ❸
Out[11]: -2.0

In [12]: b + a  ❹
Out[12]: 8.0

In [13]: a ** b  ❺
Out[13]: 243.0
```

❶ Division.

❷ Multiplication.

❸ Addition.

❹ Difference.

❺ Power.

Many commonly used mathematical functions are found in the `math` module, which is part of Python's standard library:

```
In [14]: import math  ❶

In [15]: math.log(a)  ❷
Out[15]: 1.0986122886681098

In [16]: math.exp(a)  ❸
Out[16]: 20.085536923187668

In [17]: math.sin(b)  ❹
Out[17]: -0.9589242746631385
```

❶ Imports the `math` module from the standard library.

❷ Calculates the natural logarithm.

❸ Calculates the exponential value.

❹ Calculates the sine value.

Another important basic data type is the string object (`str`):

```
In [18]: s = 'Python for Algorithmic Trading.'   ❶
```

```
In [19]: type(s)
Out[19]: str
```

```
In [20]: s.lower()   ❷
Out[20]: 'python for algorithmic trading.'
```

```
In [21]: s.upper()   ❸
Out[21]: 'PYTHON FOR ALGORITHMIC TRADING.'
```

```
In [22]: s[0:6]   ❹
Out[22]: 'Python'
```

❶ Assigns a `str` object to the variable name s.

❷ Transforms all characters to lowercase.

❸ Transforms all characters to uppercase.

❹ Selects the first six characters.

Such objects can also be combined using the + operator. The index value –1 represents the last character of a string (or last element of a sequence in general):

```
In [23]: st = s[0:6] + s[-9:-1]   ❶
```

```
In [24]: print(st)   ❷
         Python Trading
```

❶ Combines sub-sets of the `str` object to a new one.

❷ Prints out the result.

String replacements are often used to parametrize text output:

```
In [25]: repl = 'My name is %s, I am %d years old and %4.2f m tall.'   ❶
```

```
In [26]: print(repl % ('Gordon Gekko', 43, 1.78))   ❷
         My name is Gordon Gekko, I am 43 years old and 1.78 m tall.
```

```
In [27]: repl = 'My name is {:s}, I am {:d} years old and {:4.2f} m tall.'   ❸
```

```
In [28]: print(repl.format('Gordon Gekko', 43, 1.78))   ❹
         My name is Gordon Gekko, I am 43 years old and 1.78 m tall.
```

```
In [29]: name, age, height = 'Gordon Gekko', 43, 1.78   ❺
```

```
In [30]: print(f'My name is {name:s}, I am {age:d} years old and \
```

```
        {height:4.2f}m tall.')   ❻
My name is Gordon Gekko, I am 43 years old and 1.78m tall.
```

❶ Defines a string template the "old" way.

❷ Prints the template with the values replaced the "old" way.

❸ Defines a string template the "new" way.

❹ Prints the template with the values replaced the "new" way.

❺ Defines variables for later usage during replacement.

❻ Makes use of a so-called *f-string* for string replacement (introduced in Python 3.6).

Data Structures

tuple objects are light weight data structures. These are immutable collections of other objects and are constructed by objects separated by commas—with or without parentheses:

```
In [31]: t1 = (a, b, st)   ❶

In [32]: t1   ❷
Out[32]: (3, 5.0, 'Python Trading')

In [33]: type(t1)
Out[33]: tuple

In [34]: t2 = st, b, a   ❸

In [35]: t2
Out[35]: ('Python Trading', 5.0, 3)

In [36]: type(t2)
Out[36]: tuple
```

❶ Constructs a tuple object with parentheses.

❷ Prints out the str representation.

❸ Constructs a tuple object without parentheses.

Nested structures are also possible:

```
In [37]: t = (t1, t2)   ❶

In [38]: t
```

```
Out[38]: ((3, 5.0, 'Python Trading'), ('Python Trading', 5.0, 3))

In [39]: t[0][2]  ❷
Out[39]: 'Python Trading'
```

❶ Constructs a tuple object out of two others.

❷ Accesses the third element of the first object.

list objects are mutable collections of other objects and are generally constructed by providing a comma-separated collection of objects in brackets:

```
In [40]: l = [a, b, st]  ❶

In [41]: l
Out[41]: [3, 5.0, 'Python Trading']

In [42]: type(l)
Out[42]: list

In [43]: l.append(s.split()[3])  ❷

In [44]: l
Out[44]: [3, 5.0, 'Python Trading', 'Trading.']
```

❶ Generates a list object using brackets.

❷ Appends a new element (final word of s) to the list object.

Sorting is a typical operation on list objects, which can also be constructed using the list constructor (here applied to a tuple object):

```
In [45]: l = list(('Z', 'Q', 'D', 'J', 'E', 'H', '5.', 'a'))  ❶

In [46]: l
Out[46]: ['Z', 'Q', 'D', 'J', 'E', 'H', '5.', 'a']

In [47]: l.sort()  ❷

In [48]: l
Out[48]: ['5.', 'D', 'E', 'H', 'J', 'Q', 'Z', 'a']
```

❶ Creates a list object from a tuple.

❷ Sorts all elements in-place (that is, changes the object itself).

Dictionary (dict) objects are so-called key-value stores and are generally constructed with curly brackets:

```
In [49]: d = {'int_obj': a, 'float_obj': b, 'string_obj': st}  ❶
```

```
In [50]: type(d)
Out[50]: dict

In [51]: d
Out[51]: {'int_obj': 3, 'float_obj': 5.0, 'string_obj': 'Python Trading'}

In [52]: d['float_obj']  ❷
Out[52]: 5.0

In [53]: d['int_obj_long'] = 10 ** 20  ❸

In [54]: d
Out[54]: {'int_obj': 3,
          'float_obj': 5.0,
          'string_obj': 'Python Trading',
          'int_obj_long': 100000000000000000000}

In [55]: d.keys()  ❹
Out[55]: dict_keys(['int_obj', 'float_obj', 'string_obj', 'int_obj_long'])

In [56]: d.values()  ❺
Out[56]: dict_values([3, 5.0, 'Python Trading', 100000000000000000000])
```

❶ Creates a dict object using curly brackets and key-value pairs.

❷ Accesses the value given a key.

❸ Adds a new key-value pair.

❹ Selects and shows all keys.

❺ Selects and shows all values.

Control Structures

Iterations are very important operations in programming in general and financial analytics in particular. Many Python objects are iterable, which proves rather convenient in many circumstances. Consider the special iterator object range:

```
In [57]: range(5)  ❶
Out[57]: range(0, 5)

In [58]: range(3, 15, 2)  ❷
Out[58]: range(3, 15, 2)

In [59]: for i in range(5):  ❸
             print(i ** 2, end=' ')  ❹
         0 1 4 9 16
In [60]: for i in range(3, 15, 2):
             print(i, end=' ')
```

```
        3 5 7 9 11 13
In [61]: l = ['a', 'b', 'c', 'd', 'e']

In [62]: for _ in l:     ❺
             print(_)
         a
         b
         c
         d
         e

In [63]: s = 'Python Trading'

In [64]: for c in s:     ❻
             print(c + '|', end='')
         P|y|t|h|o|n| |T|r|a|d|i|n|g|
```

❶ ` object given a single parameter (end value + 1).

❷ Creates a range object with start, end, and step parameter values.

❸ Iterates over a range object and prints the squared values.

❹ Iterates over a range object using start, end, and step parameters.

❺ Iterates over a list object.

❻ Iterates over a str object.

while loops are similar to their counterparts in other languages:

```
In [65]: i = 0     ❶

In [66]: while i < 5:     ❷
             print(i ** 0.5, end=' ')     ❸
             i += 1     ❹
         0.0 1.0 1.4142135623730951 1.7320508075688772 2.0
```

❶ Sets the counter value to 0.

❷ As long as the value of i is smaller than 5...

❸ ...print the square root of i and...

❹ ...increase the value of i by 1.

Python Idioms

Python in many places relies on a number of special idioms. Let us start with a rather popular one, the *list comprehension*:

```
In [67]: lc = [i ** 2 for i in range(10)]   ❶
```

```
In [68]: lc
Out[68]: [0, 1, 4, 9, 16, 25, 36, 49, 64, 81]
```

```
In [69]: type(lc)
Out[69]: list
```

❶ Creates a new `list` object based on the *list comprehension* syntax (`for` loop in brackets).

So-called *lambda* or *anonymous functions* are useful helpers in many places:

```
In [70]: f = lambda x: math.cos(x)   ❶
```

```
In [71]: f(5)   ❷
Out[71]: 0.2836621854632263
```

```
In [72]: list(map(lambda x: math.cos(x), range(10)))   ❸
Out[72]: [1.0,
          0.5403023058681398,
          -0.4161468365471424,
          -0.9899924966004454,
          -0.6536436208636119,
          0.2836621854632263,
          0.9601702866503661,
          0.7539022543433046,
          -0.14550003380861354,
          -0.9111302618846769]
```

❶ Defines a new function `f` via the `lambda` syntax.

❷ Evaluates the function `f` for a value of 5.

❸ Maps the function `f` to all elements of the `range` object and creates a `list` object with the results, which is printed.

In general, one works with regular Python functions (as opposed to lambda functions), which are constructed as follows:

```
In [73]: def f(x):   ❶
             return math.exp(x)   ❷
```

```
In [74]: f(5)
Out[74]: 148.4131591025766
```

```
In [75]: def f(*args):   ❸
             for arg in args:   ❹
                 print(arg)   ❺
             return None   ❻

In [76]: f(l)   ❼
         ['a', 'b', 'c', 'd', 'e']
```

❶ Regular functions use the def statement for the definition.

❷ With the return statement, one defines what gets returned when the execution/evaluation is successful; multiple return statements are possible (for example, for different cases).

❸ 0 allows for multiple arguments to be passed as an iterable object (for example, list object).

❹ Iterates over the arguments.

❺ Does something with every argument: here, printing.

❻ Returns something: here, None; not necessary for a valid Python function.

❼ Passes the list object l to the function f, which interprets it as a list of arguments.

Consider the following function definition, which returns different values/strings based on an if-elif-else control structure:

```
In [77]: import random   ❶

In [78]: a = random.randint(0, 1000)   ❷

In [79]: print(f'Random number is {a}')   ❸
         Random number is 188

In [80]: def number_decide(number):
             if a < 10:   ❹
                 return "Number is single digit."
             elif 10 <= a < 100:   ❺
                 return "Number is double digit."
             else:   ❻
                 return "Number is triple digit."

In [81]: number_decide(a)   ❼
Out[81]: 'Number is triple digit.'
```

❶ Imports the `random` module to draw random numbers.

❷ Draws a random integer between 0 and 1,000.

❸ Prints the value of the drawn number.

❹ Checks for a single digit number, and if `False`...

❺ ...checks for a double digit number; if also `False`...

❻ ...the only case that remains is the triple digit case.

❼ Calls the function with the random number value `a`.

NumPy

Many operations in computational finance take place over large arrays of numerical data. `NumPy` is a Python package that allows the efficient handling of and operation on such data structures. Although quite a mighty package with a wealth of functionality, it suffices for the purposes of this book to cover the basics of `NumPy`. A neat online book that is available for free about `NumPy` is *From Python to NumPy* (*https://oreil.ly/Yxequ*). It covers many important aspects in detail that are omitted in the following sections.

Regular ndarray Object

The workhorse is the `NumPy` `ndarray` class, which provides the data structure for n-dimensional array objects. You can generate an `ndarray` object, for instance, from a `list` object:

```
In [82]: import numpy as np   ❶

In [83]: a = np.array(range(24))   ❷

In [84]: a   ❸
Out[84]: array([ 0,  1,  2,  3,  4,  5,  6,  7,  8,  9, 10, 11, 12, 13, 14,
         15, 16,
                17, 18, 19, 20, 21, 22, 23])

In [85]: b = a.reshape((4, 6))   ❹

In [86]: b   ❺
Out[86]: array([[ 0,  1,  2,  3,  4,  5],
                [ 6,  7,  8,  9, 10, 11],
                [12, 13, 14, 15, 16, 17],
                [18, 19, 20, 21, 22, 23]])
```

```
In [87]: c = a.reshape((2, 3, 4))  ❻

In [88]: c  ❼
Out[88]: array([[[ 0,  1,  2,  3],
                 [ 4,  5,  6,  7],
                 [ 8,  9, 10, 11]],

                [[12, 13, 14, 15],
                 [16, 17, 18, 19],
                 [20, 21, 22, 23]]])

In [89]: b = np.array(b, dtype=np.float)  ❽

In [90]: b  ❾
Out[90]: array([[ 0.,  1.,  2.,  3.,  4.,  5.],
                [ 6.,  7.,  8.,  9., 10., 11.],
                [12., 13., 14., 15., 16., 17.],
                [18., 19., 20., 21., 22., 23.]])
```

❶   Imports NumPy as np by convention.

❷   Instantiates an ndarray object from the range object; np.arange could also be used, for instance.

❸   Prints out the values.

❹   Reshapes the object to a two-dimensional one…

❺   …and prints out the result.

❻   Reshapes the object to a three-dimensional one…

❼   …and prints out the result.

❽   This changes the dtype of the object to np.float and…

❾   …shows the new set of (now floating point) numbers.

Many Python data structures are designed to be quite general. An example are mutable `list` objects that can be easily manipulated in many ways (adding and removing elements, storing other complex data structures, and so on). The strategy of NumPy with the regular `ndarray` object is to provide a more specialized data structure for which all elements are of the same atomic type and which in turn allows the contiguous storage in memory. This makes the `ndarray` object much better at solving problems in certain settings, such as when operating on larger, or even large, numerical data sets. In the case of NumPy, this specialization also comes along with convenience for the programmer on the one hand and often increased speed on the other hand.

Vectorized Operations

A major strength of NumPy are *vectorized operations*:

```
In [91]: 2 * b        ❶
Out[91]: array([[  0.,   2.,   4.,   6.,   8.,  10.],
                [ 12.,  14.,  16.,  18.,  20.,  22.],
                [ 24.,  26.,  28.,  30.,  32.,  34.],
                [ 36.,  38.,  40.,  42.,  44.,  46.]])

In [92]: b ** 2       ❷
Out[92]: array([[   0.,    1.,    4.,    9.,   16.,   25.],
                [  36.,   49.,   64.,   81.,  100.,  121.],
                [ 144.,  169.,  196.,  225.,  256.,  289.],
                [ 324.,  361.,  400.,  441.,  484.,  529.]])

In [93]: f = lambda x: x ** 2 - 2 * x + 0.5     ❸

In [94]: f(a)         ❹
Out[94]: array([  0.5,   -0.5,    0.5,    3.5,    8.5,   15.5,   24.5,   35.5,
          48.5,
          63.5,   80.5,   99.5,  120.5,  143.5,  168.5,  195.5,  224.5,  255.5,
         288.5,  323.5,  360.5,  399.5,  440.5,  483.5])
```

❶ Implements a scalar multiplication on the one-dimensional `ndarray` object (vector).

❷ Calculates the square of each number of b in vectorized fashion.

❸ Defines a function f via a `lambda` constructor.

❹ Applies f to the `ndarray` object a using vectorization.

In many scenarios, only a (small) part of the data stored in an `ndarray` object is of interest. NumPy supports basic and advanced slicing and other selection features:

```
In [95]: a[2:6]   ❶
Out[95]: array([2, 3, 4, 5])

In [96]: b[2, 4]   ❷
Out[96]: 16.0

In [97]: b[1:3, 2:4]   ❸
Out[97]: array([[ 8.,   9.],
                [14., 15.]])
```

❶ Selects the third to sixth elements.

❷ Selects the third row and fifth (final) row.

❸ Picks out the middle square from the b object.

Boolean Operations

Boolean operations are also supported in many places:

```
In [98]: b > 10   ❶
Out[98]: array([[False, False, False, False, False, False],
                [False, False, False, False, False,  True],
                [ True,  True,  True,  True,  True,  True],
                [ True,  True,  True,  True,  True,  True]])

In [99]: b[b > 10]   ❷
Out[99]: array([11., 12., 13., 14., 15., 16., 17., 18., 19., 20., 21., 22.,
         23.])
```

❶ Which numbers are greater than 10?

❷ Return all those numbers greater than 10.

ndarray Methods and NumPy Functions

Furthermore, `ndarray` objects have multiple (convenience) methods already built in:

```
In [100]: a.sum()   ❶
Out[100]: 276

In [101]: b.mean()   ❷
Out[101]: 11.5

In [102]: b.mean(axis=0)   ❸
Out[102]: array([ 9., 10., 11., 12., 13., 14.])
```

```
In [103]: b.mean(axis=1)   ❹
Out[103]: array([ 2.5,  8.5, 14.5, 20.5])

In [104]: c.std()   ❺
Out[104]: 6.922186552431729
```

❶   The sum of all elements.

❷   The mean of all elements.

❸   The mean along the first axis.

❹   The mean along the second axis.

❺   The standard deviation over all elements.

Similarly, there is a wealth of so-called *universal functions* that the NumPy package provides. They are universal in the sense that they can be applied in general to NumPy
ndarray objects and to standard numerical Python data types. For details, see Universal functions (ufunc) (*https://oreil.ly/Ogiah*):

```
In [105]: np.sum(a)   ❶
Out[105]: 276

In [106]: np.mean(b, axis=0)   ❷
Out[106]: array([ 9., 10., 11., 12., 13., 14.])

In [107]: np.sin(b).round(2)   ❸
Out[107]: array([[ 0.  ,  0.84,  0.91,  0.14, -0.76, -0.96],
                 [-0.28,  0.66,  0.99,  0.41, -0.54, -1.  ],
                 [-0.54,  0.42,  0.99,  0.65, -0.29, -0.96],
                 [-0.75,  0.15,  0.91,  0.84, -0.01, -0.85]])

In [108]: np.sin(4.5)   ❹
Out[108]: -0.977530117665097
```

❶   The sum of all elements.

❷   The mean along the first axis.

❸   The sine value for all elements rounded to two digits.

❹   The sine value of a Python float object.

However, you should be aware that applying NumPy universal functions to standard Python data types generally comes with a significant performance burden:

```
In [109]: %time l = [np.sin(x) for x in range(1000000)]   ❶
          CPU times: user 1.21 s, sys: 22.9 ms, total: 1.24 s
          Wall time: 1.24 s

In [110]: %time l = [math.sin(x) for x in range(1000000)]   ❷
          CPU times: user 215 ms, sys: 22.9 ms, total: 238 ms
          Wall time: 239 ms
```

❶ List comprehension using NumPy universal function on Python float objects.

❷ List comprehension using math function on Python float objects.

On the other hand, using the vectorized operations from NumPy on ndarray objects is faster than both of the preceding alternatives that result in list objects. However, the speed advantage often comes at the cost of a larger, or even huge, memory footprint:

```
In [111]: %time a = np.sin(np.arange(1000000))   ❶
          CPU times: user 20.7 ms, sys: 5.32 ms, total: 26 ms
          Wall time: 24.6 ms

In [112]: import sys   ❷

In [113]: sys.getsizeof(a)   ❸
Out[113]: 8000096

In [114]: a.nbytes   ❹
Out[114]: 8000000
```

❶ Vectorized calculation of the sine values with NumPy, which is much faster in general.

❷ Imports the sys module with many system-related functions.

❸ Shows the size of the a object in memory.

❹ Shows the number of bytes used to store the data in the a object.

 Vectorization sometimes is a very useful approach to write concise code that is often also much faster than Python code. However, be aware of the memory footprint that vectorization can have in many scenarios relevant to finance. Often, there are alternative implementations of algorithms available that are memory efficient and that, by using performance libraries such as Numba or Cython, can even be faster. See Hilpisch (2018, ch. 10).

ndarray Creation

Here, we use the ndarray object constructor np.arange(), which yields an ndarray object of integers. The following is a simple example:

```
In [115]: ai = np.arange(10)  ❶

In [116]: ai  ❷
Out[116]: array([0, 1, 2, 3, 4, 5, 6, 7, 8, 9])

In [117]: ai.dtype  ❸
Out[117]: dtype('int64')

In [118]: af = np.arange(0.5, 9.5, 0.5)  ❹

In [119]: af  ❺
Out[119]: array([0.5, 1. , 1.5, 2. , 2.5, 3. , 3.5, 4. , 4.5, 5. , 5.5, 6. ,
       6.5,
             7. , 7.5, 8. , 8.5, 9. ])

In [120]: af.dtype  ❻
Out[120]: dtype('float64')

In [121]: np.linspace(0, 10, 12)  ❼
Out[121]: array([ 0.        ,  0.90909091,  1.81818182,  2.72727273,
       3.63636364,
             4.54545455,  5.45454545,  6.36363636,  7.27272727,  8.18181818,
                9.09090909, 10.        ])
```

❶ Instantiates an ndarray object via the np.arange() constructor.

❷ Prints out the values.

❸ The resulting dtype is np.int64.

❹ Uses arange() again, but this time with start, end, and step parameters.

❺ Prints out the values.

❻ The resulting dtype is np.float64.

❼ Uses the linspace() constructor, which evenly spaces the interval between 0 and 10 in 11 intervals, giving back an ndarray object with 12 values.

Random Numbers

In financial analytics, one often needs random[1] numbers. NumPy provides many functions to sample from different distributions. Those regularly needed in quantitative finance are the standard normal distribution and the Poisson distribution. The respective functions are found in the sub-package numpy.random:

```
In [122]: np.random.standard_normal(10)    ❶
Out[122]: array([-1.06384884, -0.22662171,  1.2615483 , -0.45626608,
              -1.23231112,
              -1.51309987,  1.23938439,  0.22411366, -0.84616512, -1.09923136])

In [123]: np.random.poisson(0.5, 10)    ❷
Out[123]: array([0, 1, 1, 0, 0, 1, 0, 0, 2, 0])

In [124]: np.random.seed(1000)    ❸

In [125]: data = np.random.standard_normal((5, 100))    ❹

In [126]: data[:, :3]    ❺
Out[126]: array([[-0.8044583 ,  0.32093155, -0.02548288],
                 [-0.39031935, -0.58069634,  1.94898697],
                 [-1.11573322, -1.34477121,  0.75334374],
                 [ 0.42400699, -1.56680276,  0.76499895],
                 [-1.74866738, -0.06913021,  1.52621653]])

In [127]: data.mean()    ❻
Out[127]: -0.02714981205311327

In [128]: data.std()    ❼
Out[128]: 1.0016799134894265

In [129]: data = data - data.mean()    ❽

In [130]: data.mean()    ❾
Out[130]: 3.552713678800501e-18

In [131]: data = data / data.std()    ❿

In [132]: data.std()    ⓫
Out[132]: 1.0
```

❶ Draws ten standard normally distributed random numbers.

❷ Draws ten Poisson distributed random numbers.

❸ Fixes the seed value of the random number generator for repeatability.

---

[1] Note that computers can only generate *pseudorandom* numbers as approximations for *truly random* numbers.

❹ Generates a two-dimensional `ndarray` object with random numbers.

❺ Prints a small selection of the numbers.

❻ The mean of all values is close to 0 but not exactly 0.

❼ The standard deviation is close to 1 but not exactly 1.

❽ The first moment is corrected in vectorized fashion.

❾ The mean now is "almost equal" to 0.

❿ The second moment is corrected in vectorized fashion.

⓫ The standard deviation is now exactly 1.

matplotlib

At this point, it makes sense to introduce plotting with `matplotlib` (*http://matplot lib.org*), the plotting workhorse in the Python ecosystem. We use `matplotlib` with the settings of another library throughout, namely `seaborn` (*https://oreil.ly/SWvT6*). This results in a more modern plotting style. The following code generates Figure A-1:

```
In [133]: import matplotlib.pyplot as plt   ❶

In [134]: plt.style.use('seaborn')   ❷

In [135]: import matplotlib as mpl   ❸

In [136]: mpl.rcParams['savefig.dpi'] = 300   ❹
          mpl.rcParams['font.family'] = 'serif'   ❹
          %matplotlib inline

In [137]: data = np.random.standard_normal((5, 100))   ❺

In [138]: plt.figure(figsize=(10, 6))   ❻
          plt.plot(data.cumsum())   ❼
Out[138]: [<matplotlib.lines.Line2D at 0x7faceaaeed30>]
```

❶ Imports the main plotting library.

❷ Sets new plot style defaults.

❸ Imports the top level module.

❹ Sets the resolution to 300 DPI (for saving) and the font to `serif`.

❺ Generates an `ndarray` object with random numbers.

❻ Instantiates a new `figure` object.

❼ First calculates the cumulative sum over all elements of the `ndarray` object and then plots the result.

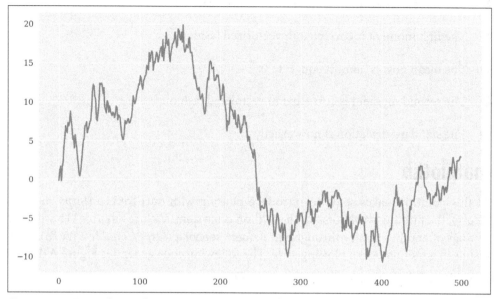

Figure A-1. Line plot with `matplotlib`

Multiple line plots in a single `figure` object are also easy to generate (see Figure A-2):

```
In [139]: plt.figure(figsize=(10, 6));   ❶
          plt.plot(data.T.cumsum(axis=0), label='line')   ❷
          plt.legend(loc=0);   ❸
          plt.xlabel('data point')   ❹
          plt.ylabel('value');   ❺
          plt.title('random series');   ❻
```

❶ Instantiates a new `figure` objects and defines the size.

❷ Plots five lines by calculating the cumulative sum along the first axis and defines a label.

❸ Puts a legend in the optimal position (`loc=0`).

❹ Adds a label to the x-axis.

⑤ Adds a label to the y-axis.

⑥ Adds a title to the figure.

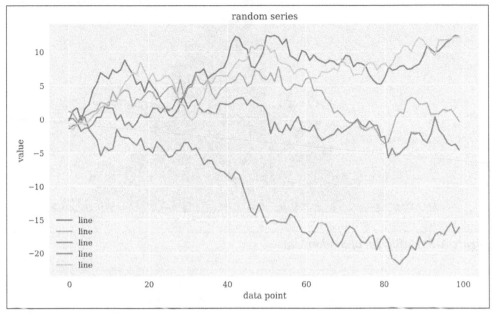

Figure A-2. Plot with multiple lines

Other important plotting types are histograms and bar charts. A histogram for all 500 values of the data object is shown as Figure A-3. In the code, the `.flatten()` method is used to generate a one-dimensional array from the two-dimensional one:

```
In [140]: plt.figure(figsize=(10, 6))
          plt.hist(data.flatten(), bins=30);  ❶
```

❶ Plots the histogram with 30 bins (data groups).

Finally, consider the bar chart presented in Figure A-4, generated by the following code:

```
In [141]: plt.figure(figsize=(10, 6))
          plt.bar(np.arange(1, 12) - 0.25,
                  data[0, :11], width=0.5);  ❶
```

❶ Plots a bar chart based on a small sub-set of the original data set.

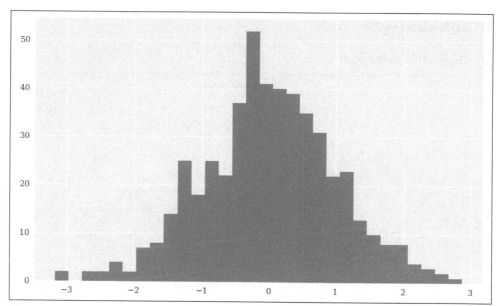

Figure A-3. Histogram of random data

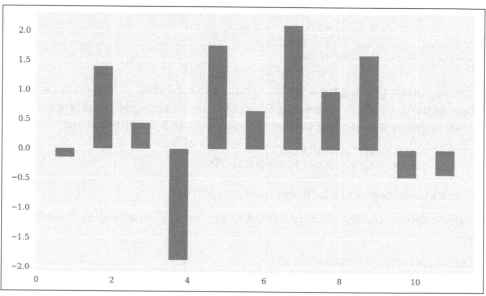

Figure A-4. Bar chart of random data

To conclude the introduction to `matplotlib`, consider the ordinary least squares (OLS) regression of the sample data displayed in Figure A-5. NumPy provides with the two functions `polyfit` and `polyval` convenience functions to implement OLS based on simple monomials, $x, x^2, x^3, \ldots, x^n$. For illustration purposes, consider linear, cubic, and ninth degree OLS regression (see Figure A-5):

```
In [142]: x = np.arange(len(data.cumsum()))  ❶

In [143]: y = 0.2 * data.cumsum() ** 2  ❷

In [144]: rg1 = np.polyfit(x, y, 1)  ❸

In [145]: rg3 = np.polyfit(x, y, 3)  ❹

In [146]: rg9 = np.polyfit(x, y, 9)  ❺

In [147]: plt.figure(figsize=(10, 6))  ❻
          plt.plot(x, y, 'r', label='data')  ❼
          plt.plot(x, np.polyval(rg1, x), 'b--', label='linear')  ❽
          plt.plot(x, np.polyval(rg3, x), 'b-.', label='cubic')  ❽
          plt.plot(x, np.polyval(rg9, x), 'b:', label='9th degree')  ❽
          plt.legend(loc=0);  ❾
```

❶ Creates an ndarray object for the x values.

❷ Defines the y values as the cumulative sum of the data object.

❸ Linear regression.

❹ Cubic regression.

❺ Ninth degree regression.

❻ The new figure object.

❼ The base data.

❽ The regression results visualized.

❾ Places a legend.

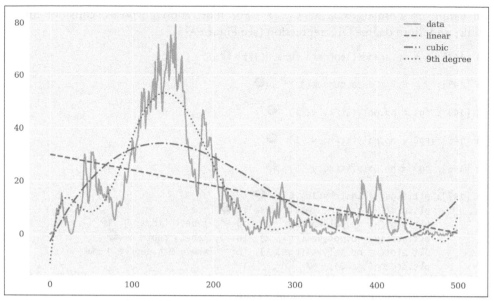

Figure A-5. Linear, cubic, and 9th degree regression

pandas

pandas is a package with which one can manage and operate on time series data and other tabular data structures efficiently. It allows implementation of even sophisticated data analytics tasks on pretty large data sets in-memory. While the focus lies on in-memory operations, there are also multiple options for out-of-memory (on-disk) operations. Although pandas provides a number of different data structures, embodied by powerful classes, the most commonly used structure is the DataFrame class, which resembles a typical table of a relational (SQL) database and is used to manage, for instance, financial time series data. This is what we focus on in this section.

DataFrame Class

In its most basic form, a DataFrame object is characterized by an index, column names, and tabular data. To make this more specific, consider the following sample data set:

```
In [148]: import pandas as pd  ❶

In [149]: np.random.seed(1000)  ❷

In [150]: raw = np.random.standard_normal((10, 3)).cumsum(axis=0)  ❸

In [151]: index = pd.date_range('2022-1-1', periods=len(raw), freq='M')  ❹
```

```
In [152]: columns = ['no1', 'no2', 'no3']   ❺

In [153]: df = pd.DataFrame(raw, index=index, columns=columns)   ❻

In [154]: df   ❼
Out[154]:                  no1        no2        no3
          2022-01-31 -0.804458   0.320932 -0.025483
          2022-02-28 -0.160134   0.020135  0.363992
          2022-03-31 -0.267572  -0.459848  0.959027
          2022-04-30 -0.732239   0.207433  0.152912
          2022-05-31 -1.928309  -0.198527 -0.029466
          2022-06-30 -1.825116  -0.336949  0.676227
          2022-07-31 -0.553321  -1.323696  0.341391
          2022-08-31 -0.652803  -0.916504  1.260779
          2022-09-30 -0.340685   0.616657  0.710605
          2022-10-31 -0.723832  -0.206284  2.310688
```

❶   Imports the pandas package.

❷   Fixes the seed value of the random number generator of NumPy.

❸   Creates an ndarray object with random numbers.

❹   Defines a DatetimeIndex object with some dates.

❺   Defines a list object containing the column names (labels).

❻   Instantiates a DataFrame object.

❼   Shows the str (HTML) representation of the new object.

DataFrame objects have built in a multitude of basic, advanced, and convenience methods, a few of which are illustrated in the Python code that follows:

```
In [155]: df.head()   ❶
Out[155]:                  no1        no2        no3
          2022-01-31 -0.804458   0.320932 -0.025483
          2022-02-28 -0.160134   0.020135  0.363992
          2022-03-31 -0.267572  -0.459848  0.959027
          2022-04-30 -0.732239   0.207433  0.152912
          2022-05-31 -1.928309  -0.198527 -0.029466

In [156]: df.tail()   ❷
Out[156]:                  no1        no2        no3
          2022-06-30 -1.825116  -0.336949  0.676227
          2022-07-31 -0.553321  -1.323696  0.341391
          2022-08-31 -0.652803  -0.916504  1.260779
          2022-09-30 -0.340685   0.616657  0.710605
          2022-10-31 -0.723832  -0.206284  2.310688
```

```
In [157]: df.index  ❸
Out[157]: DatetimeIndex(['2022-01-31', '2022-02-28', '2022-03-31',
           '2022-04-30',
           '2022-05-31', '2022-06-30', '2022-07-31', '2022-08-31',
                   '2022-09-30', '2022-10-31'],
                 dtype='datetime64[ns]', freq='M')

In [158]: df.columns  ❹
Out[158]: Index(['no1', 'no2', 'no3'], dtype='object')

In [159]: df.info()  ❺
          <class 'pandas.core.frame.DataFrame'>
          DatetimeIndex: 10 entries, 2022-01-31 to 2022-10-31
          Freq: M
          Data columns (total 3 columns):
           #   Column  Non-Null Count  Dtype
          ---  ------  --------------  -----
           0   no1     10 non-null     float64
           1   no2     10 non-null     float64
           2   no3     10 non-null     float64
          dtypes: float64(3)
          memory usage: 320.0 bytes

In [160]: df.describe()  ❻
Out[160]:               no1        no2        no3
          count  10.000000  10.000000  10.000000
          mean   -0.798847  -0.227665   0.672067
          std     0.607430   0.578071   0.712430
          min    -1.928309  -1.323696  -0.029466
          25%    -0.786404  -0.429123   0.200031
          50%    -0.688317  -0.202406   0.520109
          75%    -0.393844   0.160609   0.896922
          max    -0.160134   0.616657   2.310688
```

❶ Shows the first five data rows.

❷ Shows the last five data rows.

❸ Prints the index attribute of the object.

❹ Prints the column attribute of the object.

❺ Shows some meta data about the object.

❻ Provides selected summary statistics about the data.

While NumPy provides a specialized data structure for multi-dimensional arrays (with numerical data in general), pandas takes specialization one step further to tabular (two-dimensional) data with the DataFrame class. In particular, pandas is strong in handling financial time series data, as subsequent examples illustrate.

Numerical Operations

Numerical operations are in general as easy with DataFrame objects as with NumPy ndarray objects. They are also quite close in terms of syntax:

```
In [161]: print(df * 2)  ❶
                      no1       no2       no3
          2022-01-31 -1.608917  0.641863 -0.050966
          2022-02-28 -0.320269  0.040270  0.727983
          2022-03-31 -0.535144 -0.919696  1.918054
          2022-04-30 -1.464479  0.414866  0.305823
          2022-05-31 -3.856618 -0.397054 -0.058932
          2022-06-30 -3.650232 -0.673898  1.352453
          2022-07-31 -1.106642 -2.647393  0.682782
          2022-08-31 -1.305605 -1.833009  2.521557
          2022-09-30 -0.681369  1.233314  1.421210
          2022-10-31 -1.447664 -0.412568  4.621376

In [162]: df.std()  ❷
Out[162]: no1    0.607430
          no2    0.578071
          no3    0.712430
          dtype: float64

In [163]: df.mean()  ❸
Out[163]: no1   -0.798847
          no2   -0.227665
          no3    0.672067
          dtype: float64

In [164]: df.mean(axis=1)  ❹
Out[164]: 2022-01-31   -0.169670
          2022-02-28    0.074664
          2022-03-31    0.077202
          2022-04-30   -0.123965
          2022-05-31   -0.718767
          2022-06-30   -0.495280
          2022-07-31   -0.511875
          2022-08-31   -0.102843
          2022-09-30    0.328859
          2022-10-31    0.460191
          Freq: M, dtype: float64

In [165]: np.mean(df)  ❺
Out[165]: no1   -0.798847
```

```
          no2   -0.227665
          no3    0.672067
          dtype: float64
```

❶ Scalar (vectorized) multiplication of all elements.

❷ Calculates the column-wise standard deviation…

❸ …and mean value. With `DataFrame` objects, column-wise operations are the default.

❹ Calculates the mean value per index value (that is, row-wise).

❺ Applies a function of `NumPy` to the `DataFrame` object.

Data Selection

Pieces of data can be looked up via different mechanisms:

```
In [166]: df['no2']  ❶
Out[166]: 2022-01-31    0.320932
          2022-02-28    0.020135
          2022-03-31   -0.459848
          2022-04-30    0.207433
          2022-05-31   -0.198527
          2022-06-30   -0.336949
          2022-07-31   -1.323696
          2022-08-31   -0.916504
          2022-09-30    0.616657
          2022-10-31   -0.206284
          Freq: M, Name: no2, dtype: float64

In [167]: df.iloc[0]  ❷
Out[167]: no1   -0.804458
          no2    0.320932
          no3   -0.025483
          Name: 2022-01-31 00:00:00, dtype: float64

In [168]: df.iloc[2:4]  ❸
Out[168]:                   no1       no2       no3
          2022-03-31 -0.267572 -0.459848  0.959027
          2022-04-30 -0.732239  0.207433  0.152912

In [169]: df.iloc[2:4, 1]  ❹
Out[169]: 2022-03-31   -0.459848
          2022-04-30    0.207433
          Freq: M, Name: no2, dtype: float64

In [170]: df.no3.iloc[3:7]  ❺
Out[170]: 2022-04-30    0.152912
```

```
         2022-05-31   -0.029466
         2022-06-30    0.676227
         2022-07-31    0.341391
         Freq: M, Name: no3, dtype: float64

In [171]: df.loc['2022-3-31']  ❻
Out[171]: no1   -0.267572
          no2   -0.459848
          no3    0.959027
          Name: 2022-03-31 00:00:00, dtype: float64

In [172]: df.loc['2022-5-31', 'no3']  ❼
Out[172]: -0.02946577492329111

In [173]: df['no1'] + 3 * df['no3']  ❽
Out[173]: 2022-01-31   -0.880907
          2022-02-28    0.931841
          2022-03-31    2.609510
          2022-04-30   -0.273505
          2022-05-31    2.016706
          2022-06-30    0.203564
          2022-07-31    0.470852
          2022-08-31    3.129533
          2022-09-30    1.791130
          2022-10-31    6.208233
          Freq: M, dtype: float64
```

❶ Selects a column by name.

❷ Selects a row by index position.

❸ Selects two rows by index position.

❹ Selects two row values from one column by index positions.

❺ Uses the dot lookup syntax to select a column.

❻ Selects a row by index value.

❼ Selects a single data point by index value and column name.

❽ Implements a vectorized arithmetic operation.

Boolean Operations

Data selection based on Boolean operations is also a strength of pandas:

```
In [174]: df['no3'] > 0.5  ❶
Out[174]: 2022-01-31    False
          2022-02-28    False
```

```
         2022-03-31       True
         2022-04-30       False
         2022-05-31       False
         2022-06-30       True
         2022-07-31       False
         2022-08-31       True
         2022-09-30       True
         2022-10-31       True
         Freq: M, Name: no3, dtype: bool

In [175]: df[df['no3'] > 0.5]  ❷
Out[175]:                 no1        no2        no3
         2022-03-31 -0.267572 -0.459848   0.959027
         2022-06-30 -1.825116 -0.336949   0.676227
         2022-08-31 -0.652803 -0.916504   1.260779
         2022-09-30 -0.340685  0.616657   0.710605
         2022-10-31 -0.723832 -0.206284   2.310688

In [176]: df[(df.no3 > 0.5) & (df.no2 > -0.25)]  ❸
Out[176]:                 no1        no2        no3
         2022-09-30 -0.340685  0.616657   0.710605
         2022-10-31 -0.723832 -0.206284   2.310688

In [177]: df[df.index > '2022-5-15']  ❹
Out[177]:                 no1        no2        no3
         2022-05-31 -1.928309 -0.198527 -0.029466
         2022-06-30 -1.825116 -0.336949   0.676227
         2022-07-31 -0.553321 -1.323696   0.341391
         2022-08-31 -0.652803 -0.916504   1.260779
         2022-09-30 -0.340685  0.616657   0.710605
         2022-10-31 -0.723832 -0.206284   2.310688

In [178]: df.query('no2 > 0.1')  ❺
Out[178]:                 no1        no2        no3
         2022-01-31 -0.804458  0.320932 -0.025483
         2022-04-30 -0.732239  0.207433   0.152912
         2022-09-30 -0.340685  0.616657   0.710605

In [179]: a = -0.5  ❺

In [180]: df.query('no1 > @a')  ❺
Out[180]:                 no1        no2        no3
         2022-02-28 -0.160134  0.020135   0.363992
         2022-03-31 -0.267572 -0.459848   0.959027
         2022-09-30 -0.340685  0.616657   0.710605
```

❶ Which values in column no3 are greater than 0.5?

❷ Select all such rows for which the condition is True.

❸ Combines two conditions with the & (bitwise and) operator; | is the bitwise or operator.

❹ Selects all rows with index values greater (later) than '2020-5-15' (here, based on str object sorting).

❺ Uses the .query() method to select rows given conditions as str objects.

Plotting with pandas

pandas is well integrated with the matplotlib plotting package, which makes it convenient to plot data stored in DataFrame objects. In general, a single method call does the trick already (see Figure A-6):

```
In [181]: df.plot(figsize=(10, 6));  ❶
```

❶ Plots the data as a line plot (column-wise) and fixes the figure size.

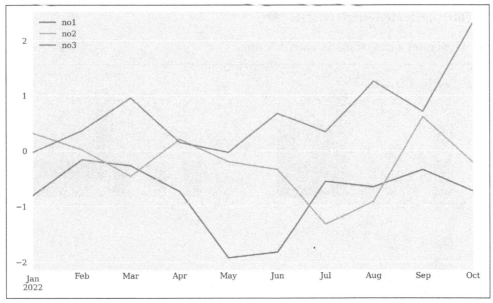

Figure A-6. Line plot with pandas

pandas takes care of the proper formatting of the index values, dates in this case. This only works for a DatetimeIndex properly. If the date-time information is available as str objects only, the DatetimeIndex() constructor can be used to transform the date-time information easily:

```
In [182]: index = ['2022-01-31', '2022-02-28', '2022-03-31', '2022-04-30',
                   '2022-05-31', '2022-06-30', '2022-07-31', '2022-08-31',
                   '2022-09-30', '2022-10-31']  ❶

In [183]: pd.DatetimeIndex(df.index)  ❷
Out[183]: DatetimeIndex(['2022-01-31', '2022-02-28', '2022-03-31',
          '2022-04-30',
          '2022-05-31', '2022-06-30', '2022-07-31', '2022-08-31',
                 '2022-09-30', '2022-10-31'],
                    dtype='datetime64[ns]', freq='M')
```

❶ Date-time index data as a `list` object of `str` objects.

❷ Generates a `DatetimeIndex` object out of the `list` object.

Histograms are also generated this way. In both cases, `pandas` takes care of the handling of the single columns and automatically generates single lines (with respective legend entries, see Figure A-6) and generates respective sub-plots with three different histograms (as in Figure A-7):

```
In [184]: df.hist(figsize=(10, 6));  ❶
```

❶ Generates a histogram for each column.

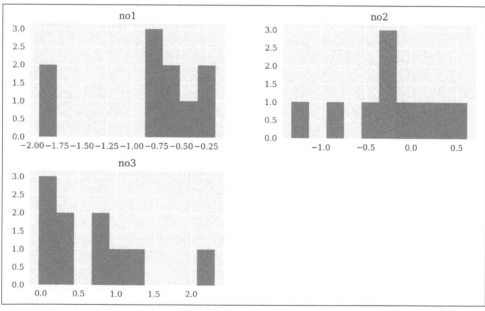

Figure A-7. Histograms with pandas

Input-Output Operations

Yet another strength of pandas is the exporting and importing of data to and from diverse data storage formats (see also Chapter 3). Consider the case of comma separated value (CSV) files:

```
In [185]: df.to_csv('data.csv')  ❶

In [186]: with open('data.csv') as f:
              for line in f.readlines():
                  print(line, end='')  ❷
          ,no1,no2,no3
          2022-01-31,-0.8044583035248052,0.3209315470898572,
          ,-0.025482880472072204
          2022-02-28,-0.16013447509799061,0.020134874302836725,0.363991673815235
          2022-03-31,-0.26757177678888727,-0.4598482010579319,0.9590271758917923
          2022-04-30,-0.7327393029842283,0.2074331059300848,0.15291156544935125
          2022-05-31,-1.9283091368170622,-0.19852705542997268,
          ,-0.029465774923291111
          2022-06-30,-1.8251162427820806,-0.33694904401573555,0.6762266000356951
          2022-07-31,-0.5533209663746153,-1.3236963728130973,0.34139114682415433
          2022-08-31,-0.6528026643843922,-0.9165042724715742,1.2607786860286034
          2022-09-30,-0.34068465431802875,0.6166567928863607,0.7106048210003031
          2022-10-31,-0.7238320652023266,-0.20628417055270565,2.310688189060956

In [187]: from_csv = pd.read_csv('data.csv',  ❸
                                 index_col=0,  ❹
                                 parse_dates=True)  ❺

In [188]: from_csv.head()  #  ❻
Out[188]:                  no1       no2       no3
          2022-01-31 -0.804458  0.320932 -0.025483
          2022-02-28 -0.160134  0.020135  0.363992
          2022-03-31 -0.267572 -0.459848  0.959027
          2022-04-30 -0.732239  0.207433  0.152912
          2022-05-31 -1.928309 -0.198527 -0.029466
```

❶ Writes the data to disk as a CSV file.

❷ Opens that file and prints the contents line by line.

❸ Reads the data stored in the CSV file into a new DataFrame object.

❹ Defines the first column to be the index column.

❺ Date-time information in the index column shall be transformed to Timestamp objects.

❻ Prints the first five rows of the new DataFrame object.

However, in general, you would store DataFrame objects on disk in more efficient binary formats like HDF5 (*http://hdfgroup.org*). pandas in this case wraps the functionality of the PyTables package (*http://pytables.org*). The constructor function to be used is HDFStore:

```
In [189]: h5 = pd.HDFStore('data.h5', 'w')  ❶

In [190]: h5['df'] = df  ❷

In [191]: h5  ❸
Out[191]: <class 'pandas.io.pytables.HDFStore'>
          File path: data.h5

In [192]: from_h5 = h5['df']  ❹

In [193]: h5.close()  ❺

In [194]: from_h5.tail()  ❻
Out[194]:                 no1        no2        no3
          2022-06-30 -1.825116 -0.336949  0.676227
          2022-07-31 -0.553321 -1.323696  0.341391
          2022-08-31 -0.652803 -0.916504  1.260779
          2022-09-30 -0.340685  0.616657  0.710605
          2022-10-31 -0.723832 -0.206284  2.310688

In [195]: !rm data.csv data.h5  ❼
```

❶ Opens an HDFStore object.

❷ Writes the DataFrame object (the data) to the HDFStore.

❸ Shows the structure/contents of the database file.

❹ Reads the data into a new DataFrame object.

❺ Closes the HDFStore object.

❻ Shows the final five rows of the new DataFrame object.

❼ Removes the CSV and HDF5 files.

Case Study

When it comes to financial data, there are useful data importing functions available in the pandas package (see also Chapter 3). The following code reads historical daily data for the S&P 500 index and the VIX volatility index from a CSV file stored on a remote server using the pd.read_csv() function:

```
In [196]: raw = pd.read_csv('http://hilpisch.com/pyalgo_eikon_eod_data.csv',
                            index_col=0, parse_dates=True).dropna()  ❶

In [197]: spx = pd.DataFrame(raw['.SPX'])  ❷

In [198]: spx.info()  ❸
          <class 'pandas.core.frame.DataFrame'>
          DatetimeIndex: 2516 entries, 2010-01-04 to 2019-12-31
          Data columns (total 1 columns):
           #   Column  Non-Null Count  Dtype
          ---  ------  --------------  -----
           0   .SPX    2516 non-null   float64
          dtypes: float64(1)
          memory usage: 39.3 KB

In [199]: vix = pd.DataFrame(raw['.VIX'])  ❹

In [200]: vix.info()  ❺
          <class 'pandas.core.frame.DataFrame'>
          DatetimeIndex: 2516 entries, 2010-01-04 to 2019-12-31
          Data columns (total 1 columns):
           #   Column  Non-Null Count  Dtype
          ---  ------  --------------  -----
           0   .VIX    2516 non-null   float64
          dtypes: float64(1)
          memory usage: 39.3 KB
```

❶ Imports the pandas package.

❷ Reads historical data for the S&P 500 stock index from a CSV file (data from Refinitiv Eikon Data API).

❸ Shows the meta information for the resulting DataFrame object.

❹ Reads historical data for the VIX volatility index.

❺ Shows the meta information for the resulting DataFrame object.

Let us combine the respective Close columns into a single DataFrame object. Multiple ways are possible to accomplish this goal:

```
In [201]: spxvix = pd.DataFrame(spx).join(vix)   ❶

In [202]: spxvix.info()
          <class 'pandas.core.frame.DataFrame'>
          DatetimeIndex: 2516 entries, 2010-01-04 to 2019-12-31
          Data columns (total 2 columns):
           #   Column  Non-Null Count  Dtype
          ---  ------  --------------  -----
           0   .SPX    2516 non-null   float64
           1   .VIX    2516 non-null   float64
          dtypes: float64(2)
          memory usage: 139.0 KB


In [203]: spxvix = pd.merge(spx, vix,
                            left_index=True,   # merge on left index
                            right_index=True,  # merge on right index
                            )   ❷

In [204]: spxvix.info()
          <class 'pandas.core.frame.DataFrame'>
          DatetimeIndex: 2516 entries, 2010-01-04 to 2019-12-31
          Data columns (total 2 columns):
           #   Column  Non-Null Count  Dtype
          ---  ------  --------------  -----
           0   .SPX    2516 non-null   float64
           1   .VIX    2516 non-null   float64
          dtypes: float64(2)
          memory usage: 139.0 KB


In [205]: spxvix = pd.DataFrame({'SPX': spx['.SPX'],
                                 'VIX': vix['.VIX']},
                                index=spx.index)   ❸

In [206]: spxvix.info()
          <class 'pandas.core.frame.DataFrame'>
          DatetimeIndex: 2516 entries, 2010-01-04 to 2019-12-31
          Data columns (total 2 columns):
           #   Column  Non-Null Count  Dtype
          ---  ------  --------------  -----
           0   SPX     2516 non-null   float64
           1   VIX     2516 non-null   float64
          dtypes: float64(2)
          memory usage: 139.0 KB
```

❶ Uses the join method to combine the relevant data sub-sets.

❷ Uses the merge function for the combination.

❸ Uses the DataFrame constructor in combination with a dict object as input.

Having available the combined data in a single object makes visual analysis straight-forward (see Figure A-8):

```
In [207]: spxvix.plot(figsize=(10, 6), subplots=True);  ❶
```

❶ Plots the two data sub-sets into separate sub-plots.

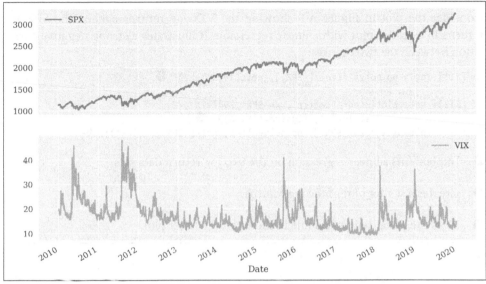

Figure A-8. Historical end-of-day closing values for the S&P 500 and VIX

pandas also allows vectorized operations on whole `DataFrame` objects. The following code calculates the log returns over the two columns of the `spxvix` object simultaneously in vectorized fashion. The `shift` method shifts the data set by the number of index values as provided (in this particular case, by one trading day):

```
In [208]: rets = np.log(spxvix / spxvix.shift(1))  ❶

In [209]: rets = rets.dropna()  ❷

In [210]: rets.head()  ❸
Out[210]:                 SPX       VIX
          Date
          2010-01-05  0.003111 -0.035038
          2010-01-06  0.000545 -0.009868
          2010-01-07  0.003993 -0.005233
          2010-01-08  0.002878 -0.050024
          2010-01-11  0.001745 -0.032514
```

❶ Calculates the log returns for the two time series in fully vectorized fashion.

❷ Drops all rows containing NaN values ("not a number").

❸ Shows the first five rows of the new DataFrame object.

Consider the plot in Figure A-9 showing the VIX log returns against the SPX log returns in a scatter plot with a linear regression. It illustrates a strong negative correlation between the two indexes:

```
In [211]: rg = np.polyfit(rets['SPX'], rets['VIX'], 1)  ❶

In [212]: rets.plot(kind='scatter', x='SPX', y='VIX',
                    style='.', figsize=(10, 6))  ❷
          plt.plot(rets['SPX'], np.polyval(rg, rets['SPX']), 'r-');  ❸
```

❶ Implements a linear regression on the two log return data sets.

❷ Creates a scatter plot of the log returns.

❸ Plots the linear regression line in the existing scatter plot.

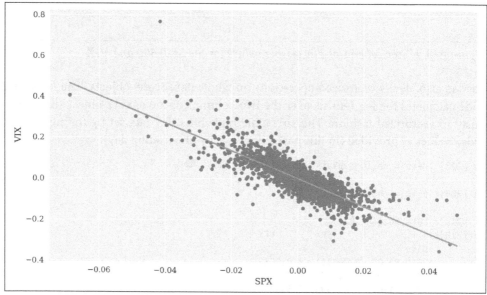

Figure A-9. Scatter plot of S&P 500 and VIX log returns with linear regression line

Having financial time series data stored in a pandas `DataFrame` object makes the calculation of typical statistics straightforward:

```
In [213]: ret = rets.mean() * 252  ❶

In [214]: ret
Out[214]: SPX    0.104995
          VIX   -0.037526
          dtype: float64

In [215]: vol = rets.std() * math.sqrt(252)  ❷

In [216]: vol
Out[216]: SPX    0.147902
          VIX    1.229086
          dtype: float64

In [217]: (ret - 0.01) / vol  ❸
Out[217]: SPX    0.642279
          VIX   -0.038667
          dtype: float64
```

❶ Calculates the annualized mean return for the two indexes.

❷ Calculates the annualized standard deviation.

❸ Calculates the Sharpe ratio for a risk-free short rate of 1%.

The maximum drawdown, which we only calculate for the S&P 500 index, is a bit more involved. For its calculation, we use the `.cummax()` method, which records the running, historical maximum of the time series up to a certain date. Consider the following code that generates the plot in Figure A-10:

```
In [218]: plt.figure(figsize=(10, 6))  ❶
          spxvix['SPX'].plot(label='S&P 500')  ❷
          spxvix['SPX'].cummax().plot(label='running maximum')  ❸
          plt.legend(loc=0);  ❹
```

❶ Instantiates a new `figure` object.

❷ Plots the historical closing values for the S&P 500 index.

❸ Calculates and plots the running maximum over time.

❹ Places a legend on the canvas.

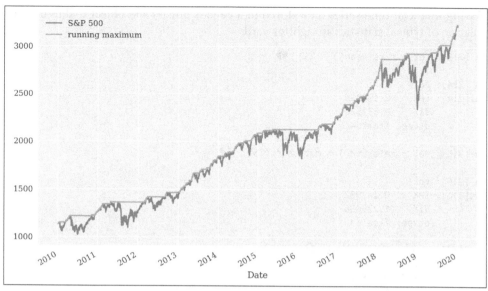

Figure A-10. Historical closing prices of S&P 500 index and running maximum

The *absolute maximum drawdown* is the largest difference between the running maximum and the current index level. In our particular case, it is about 580 index points. The *relative maximum drawdown* might sometimes be a bit more meaningful. It is here a value of about 20%:

```
In [219]: adrawdown = spxvix['SPX'].cummax() - spxvix['SPX']   ❶

In [220]: adrawdown.max()
Out[220]: 579.6500000000001

In [221]: rdrawdown = ((spxvix['SPX'].cummax() - spxvix['SPX']) /
                        spxvix['SPX'].cummax())   ❷

In [222]: rdrawdown.max()
Out[222]: 0.1977821376780688
```

❶ Derives the *absolute* maximum drawdown.

❷ Derives the *relative* maximum drawdown.

The longest drawdown period is calculated as follows. The following code selects all those data points where the drawdown is zero (where a new maximum is reached). It then calculates the difference between two consecutive index values (trading dates) for which the drawdown is zero and takes the maximum value. Given the data set we are analyzing, the longest drawdown period is 417 days:

```
In [223]: temp = adrawdown[adrawdown == 0]  ❶

In [224]: periods_spx = (temp.index[1:].to_pydatetime() -
                         temp.index[:-1].to_pydatetime())  ❷

In [225]: periods_spx[50:60]  ❸
Out[225]: array([datetime.timedelta(days=67), datetime.timedelta(days=1),
                 datetime.timedelta(days=1), datetime.timedelta(days=1),
                 datetime.timedelta(days=301), datetime.timedelta(days=3),
                 datetime.timedelta(days=1), datetime.timedelta(days=2),
                 datetime.timedelta(days=12), datetime.timedelta(days=2)],
                dtype=object)

In [226]: max(periods_spx)  ❹
Out[226]: datetime.timedelta(days=417)
```

❶ Picks out all index positions where the drawdown is 0.

❷ Calculates the `timedelta` values between all such index positions.

❸ Shows a select few of these values.

❹ Picks out the maximum value for the result.

Conclusions

This appendix provides a concise, introductory overview of selected topics relevant to use Python, NumPy, matplotlib, and pandas in the context of algorithmic trading. It cannot, of course, replace a thorough training and practical experience, but it helps those who want to get started quickly and who are willing to dive deeper into the details where necessary.

Further Resources

A valuable, free source for the topics covered in this appendix are the Scipy Lecture Notes (*http://scipy-lectures.org*) that are available in multiple electronic formats. Also freely available is the online book From Python to NumPy (*https://oreil.ly/vo54e*) by Nicolas Rougier.

Books cited in this appendix:

Hilpisch, Yves. 2018. *Python for Finance*. 2nd ed. Sebastopol: O'Reilly.

McKinney, Wes. 2017. *Python for Data Analysis*. 2nd ed. Sebastopol: O'Reilly.

VanderPlas, Jake. 2017. *Python Data Science Handbook*. Sebastopol: O'Reilly.

Index

virtual environment management, 27-30

W
while loops, 316

Z
ZeroMQ, 202

About the Author

Dr. Yves J. Hilpisch is founder and CEO of The Python Quants (*http://tpq.io*), a group focusing on the use of open source technologies for financial data science, artificial intelligence, algorithmic trading, and computational finance. He is also founder and CEO of The AI Machine (*http://aimachine.io*), a company focused on AI-powered algorithmic trading via a proprietary strategy execution platform.

In addition to this book, he is the author of the following books:

- *Artificial Intelligence in Finance* (*https://aiif.tpq.io*) (O'Reilly, 2020)
- *Python for Finance* (*https://py4fi.tpq.io*) (2nd ed., O'Reilly, 2018)
- *Derivatives Analytics with Python* (*https://dawp.tpq.io*) (Wiley, 2015)
- *Listed Volatility and Variance Derivatives* (*https://lvvd.tpq.io*) (Wiley, 2017)

Yves is an adjunct professor of computational finance and lectures on algorithmic trading at the CQF Program (*http://cqf.com*). He is also the director of the first online training programs leading to university certificates in Python for Algorithmic Trading (*http://certificate.tpq.io*) and Python for Computational Finance (*http://compfinance.tpq.io*).

Yves wrote the financial analytics library DX Analytics (*http://dx-analytics.com*) and organizes meetups, conferences, and bootcamps about Python for quantitative finance and algorithmic trading in London, Frankfurt, Berlin, Paris, and New York. He has given keynote speeches at technology conferences in the United States, Europe, and Asia.

Colophon

The animal on the cover of *Python for Algorithmic Trading* is a common barred grass snake (*Natrix helvetica*). This nonvenomous snake is found in or near fresh water in Western Europe.

The common barred grass snake, originally a member of *Natrix natrix* prior to its reclassification as a distinct species, has a grey-green body with distinctive banding along its flanks and can grow up to a meter in length. It is a prodigious swimmer and preys primarily on amphibians such as toads and frogs. Because they need to regulate their body temperatures like all reptiles, the common barred grass snake typically spends its winters underground where the temperature is more stable.

This snake's conservation status is currently of "Least Concern," and it is currently protected in Great Britain under the Wildlife and Countryside Act. Many of the animals on O'Reilly covers are endangered; all of them are important to the world.

The cover illustration is by Jose Marzan, based on a black and white engraving from *English Cyclopedia Natural History*. The cover fonts are Gilroy Semibold and Guardian Sans. The text font is Adobe Minion Pro; the heading font is Adobe Myriad Condensed; and the code font is Dalton Maag's Ubuntu Mono.

O'REILLY®

There's much more
where this came from.

Experience books, videos, live online
training courses, and more from O'Reilly
and our 200+ partners—all in one place.

Learn more at oreilly.com/online-learning

©2019 O'Reilly Media, Inc. O'Reilly is a registered trademark of O'Reilly Media, Inc. 1175

Milton Keynes UK
Ingram Content Group UK Ltd.
UKHW010922180924
448424UK00002B/8